ENCOUNTERS WITH VERDI

ENCOUNTERS WITH VERDI

Edited, Introduced and Annotated by

Marcello Conati

Translated by Richard Stokes
with a Foreword by Julian Budden

CORNELL UNIVERSITY PRESS
ITHACA
NEW YORK

© Edizioni il Formichiere srl
Via del Lauro 3, 20121 Milano

English language edition © Victor Gollancz Ltd 1984

First published in Great Britain by Victor Gollancz Ltd
under the title *Interviews and Encounters with Verdi*

First published 1984 by Cornell University Press
Second printing 1984
International Standard Book Number 0-8014-1717-1
Library of Congress Catalog Card Number 83-73736

Printed in the United States of America

The paper in this book is acid-free and meets the guidelines for permanence and durability of the Committee on Production Guidelines for Book Longevity of the Council on Library Resources.

For Virginio Marchi

TRANSLATOR'S NOTE

All translations, apart from number XL, have been made from the original French, German and Italian sources; English texts have also been reproduced from original sources.

A square bracketed ellipsis [. . .] within a quoted passage denotes an editorial omission.

My thanks to Marcello Conati and Elisa Francesca Roselli for many helpful suggestions.

RICHARD STOKES

CONTENTS

Contents

LIST OF ILLUSTRATIONS

FOREWORD

To PRESENT THE personality of an artist through the eyes of his contemporaries is undoubtedly the most vivid way of presenting him to posterity. But it should be added that not every artist of genius could stand up successfully to the test. A creative mind is not necessarily accompanied by a pleasant or even an interesting character. A man may keep his work in one compartment, his everyday life in another. His victories in the realm of art are often counterbalanced by defeats in the sphere of human relationships. Stupidity, ignorance, egocentricity – these are too often the impressions one receives from conversations with the great.

Not so with Verdi whose personality has always aroused scarcely less interest than his music. From 1842, the year of his first operatic success, until the time of his death almost sixty years later, Verdi was continually in the public eye. In Italy and abroad he stood for the spirit of the Risorgimento. Later, as the proprietor of Sant'Agata, founder of the Musicians' Rest Home and benefactor of the hospital of Villanova, he appeared as the ideal patriarch of the new Italy, just as he was its foremost composer. A man of solid culture, of which he never made a pointless display, and of strong intellectual integrity, his innate reserve lends a special interest to those opinions which he let slip in public. The fact that the interviews and conversations contained in this volume become ever more plentiful and enlightening with the passing of the years can be explained not only by his increasing fame but also by his growing willingness to communicate. Just as his music continually responded to new influences, so he himself absorbed ever more from the world about him. Commenting on the difference between the original and the revised *Simon Boccanegra* I observed, in *The Operas of Verdi*, vol. II, "The older Verdi himself, it seems, the younger his music." The same could be said of the man.

Some of the articles presented here will be familiar to the reader, but mostly only in part. All biographies of the composer include the

account by Marianna Barbieri-Nini of how Verdi, on the day of the
first performance of *Macbeth*, insisted on rehearsing the grand duet
from the first act over and over again up till the very last moment;
but they omit the preceding description of his clumsy attempts to
convey his intentions to the leader of the orchestra, Pietro Romani –
in striking contrast to his expertise as a producer as witnessed by
Ugo Pesci during rehearsals for *Otello*. But most of the eye-witness
accounts, culled as they are from a wide variety of sources, are
entirely unknown and fill important gaps in our knowledge of the
composer's thinking. It is significant, for instance, that in 1886 Verdi
regarded *Lohengrin* as the summit of Wagner's artistic achievement
(see Paul Fresnay, "Verdi in Paris") while thirteen years later he
pointed instead to the second act of *Tristan und Isolde* (see Felix
Philippi "A Meeting with Verdi"). Certainly not everyone who met
Verdi received the same impression. According to most people he
was tall, but Philippi and Blanche Roosevelt found him rather small.
To Giuseppe Giacosa and Antonio Ghislanzoni the villa of Sant'
Agata revealed an exquisite taste; while Étienne Rouillé-Destranges
was amused by the bourgeois luxury of Verdi's apartment in Genoa.
But such contradictions, stemming as they do from the inevitable
variety of human standpoints, merely serve to fill out the picture.
Every article is placed within its historical context and furnished with
detailed notes and references as well as a wealth of back-up material
which includes two virtually unknown letters written by the composer himself, one referring to *Macbeth* (revised version) the other to
Il corsaro, both of vital importance for the understanding of Verdi's
artistic ideas. By presenting this substantial collection of documents
in a scientific manner, without the biographer's usual tendency to
embroider, interpret and select according to his own preconceptions,
Marcello Conati has rendered an incalculable service to Verdi
studies, bringing before our eyes a man who less than anyone needed
to pay heed to Robert Burns' famous lines:

> O wad some Pow'r the giftie gie us
> To see oursels as others see us!

Julian Budden

INTRODUCTION

THE MAN VERDI

WITH THE QUICKENING of scholarly and general interest in the operas of Verdi, there is a growing need to learn more about the composer himself – his cultural outlook, his way of thinking – and become better acquainted with his personality, his habits and all those minute and apparently insignificant facts and anecdotes that might throw light on the temperament of an artist whose reputation increases with the passage of time. "Nothing about a great man is irrelevant," wrote Schoenberg in an early essay on Mahler. "In fact, every one of his acts is in some way revealing, and it would thus have been a great pleasure for me to watch Mahler put on his necktie, for I would assuredly have found it more interesting and instructive than observing how one of our musical big-wigs composes a 'sacred work'."[1]

But getting to know Verdi is a difficult task, difficult despite all the "documentary" biographies and the survival of a very rich – one of the most extensive in the whole history of music – but alas, also a frequently reticent and evasive body of correspondence. We have adequate information only about the external facts of the composer's life: his major achievements, the principal events of his public existence. "But whosoever attempts to penetrate the mind of the man," observes Massimo Mila, "[. . .] quickly finds himself in trouble. [. . .] It is far easier to infiltrate the military secrets of the Pentagon or the Kremlin, or to explode the silence of a Trappist monastery, than it is to reveal the soul of Verdi."[2]

Even Frank Walker has had to admit, in his exemplary biography, that "Verdi has a way of escaping his biographers. The known facts of his long and busy career have been told and retold, but the man himself remains a distant figure, still protected by his habitual reserve and mistrust . . ."[3] And Claudio Sartori has gone so far as to affirm that "Verdi does not and probably never will allow us a direct, intimate, human understanding of him. [. . .] It can almost be said that Verdi, the man Verdi, does not exist."[4] We could, however,

counter that the man Verdi exists precisely in his public inscruta-
bility, in what Sartori terms his "systematic self-effacement in order
to leave behind an oeuvre totally devoid of all personal reference".[5]

Perhaps no other great artist shunned the curiosity of his contemporaries – of his friends and close acquaintances, as well as journalists
and gazetteers – with such meticulous and constant assiduousness as
did Verdi, regardless of the enthusiasm of the masses and his
popularity at home and abroad from virtually the outset of his career.
His reserve in the face of public information was complete: he never
even deigned to refute inaccurate allegations about his character and
private life,[6] and would not allow himself to become personally
involved in the journalistic diatribes that condemned his works and
his artistic activity;[7] the artist, he thought, should create, the public
applaud or boo, the critic criticize. But no one had the right to pry
into his private life or the secrets of his artist's study. The bear would
brook no intrusion in his den. He was reserved, aloof . . . an attitude
often interpreted as boorishness, moroseness or downright arrogance.

This was the attitude of someone reared to the intellectual outlook
and ethos of a peasant society. Jealous of his own independence,
fearful of prying visitors, hating to be tied down, he devotes himself
completely to his work, resists distractions, avoids discussing it and
will still less be pressured into revealing his techniques. Every
moment of his working time is precious to him. But his rest is
equally precious, for that is when he withdraws into himself, medi-
tates, prepares himself for the seeding of a new crop or contemplates
his labour during the pauses in cultivation. There is no antithesis
between Verdi the musician and Verdi the agriculturalist. Giacosa
noted in 1889: "Verdi is reputed by many to be uncivil and disdainful. But anyone who considers the great volume of his work must
concede that he is a man who has wasted less time than most."[8] And
the life of someone who hates to waste time rarely offers anything of
interest to the curiosity of others. This much was conceded by Boito
when answering a request from a biographer: "Our Maestro has for
years now been so peacefully involved in his work and his home,
that his life is devoid of strange events or bizarre anecdotes. The only
piquant thing about it (when compared with the lives of others
among our excellent contemporaries) is that there is nothing piquant
about it to tell. This anomaly is of no use to the biographer;
nevertheless it is worthy of note, as it reveals the great simplicity of
the artist and the man."[9]

It may be excessive to affirm that "[Verdi] supervised the work of his biographers with the sole aim of suppressing, of eradicating everything that he did not wish to be known about himself".[10] But it cannot be denied that the surviving documents and letters are so very terse about the composer's private life, as to evoke the image of an obdurate and jealous self-control, operating to restrain and even mislead future biographers. Verdi's resolve to avoid publicity about himself, guard his independence and re-direct all attention away from his private life in order to focus it entirely upon his works, has had damaging consequences for an improved understanding of the man and his art. It has both stimulated the curiosity of the public in matters relating to Verdi's private life and left ample scope for the fantasy of biographers, unleashing an abundance of literature in which documented facts and romance are so indiscriminately inter-twined, as to require more books to sort them out than have been published on the composer's life to date. In addition, some of the confessions and protestations of modesty recurrent in Verdi's correspondence and anecdotes relating to him, such as *I am just a peasant from Le Roncole* or *I am just a dramatist*, have not failed to leave their mark; they have ensnared superficial and inattentive biographers, contributed to the "popular" image of Verdi as a man of innate genius, a peasant artist, a crude and uncultured composer who only climbed the ladder of cultural awareness after many laborious years, limited research to the purely dramaturgical and literary aspects of his work, and have encouraged neglect of those aspects concerning musical expression and structure.[11]

A more careful interpretation of the documents and a closer reading of the correspondence might assist in clearing up ambiguities and bringing us nearer to Verdi's personality, hitherto so elusive to scholars. But we must keep in mind that, with the exception of two recent publications,[12] no critical edition of Verdi's correspondence exists. Dispersed in books long out of print and in articles of limited accessibility, Verdi's letters are known to us only in part, through hurried, inaccurate, often incomplete transcriptions, all too often marred by glaring errors.[13] To storm the walls of the Palazzo Doria or of the villa at Sant'Agata armed only with the correspondence already known to us is too arduous an enterprise. We must circum-vent the obstacle by referring to secondary documents that might help us indirectly. Frank Walker tried this approach a few years ago with significant results that now constitute a milestone in Verdian biographical research. He sought to "depict Verdi the man through

the stories of his relationships with some of those who knew him
best, [. . .] as he was seen, at different periods of his life, by his
benefactor and father-in-law Antonio Barezzi, by his adoring pupil
Emanuele Muzio, Giuseppina Strepponi, Mariani, Teresa Stolz,
Boito and others".[14]

We would now like to try this approach once more, extending our
documentary enquiry into a sector hitherto ignored by research:
nineteenth-century periodical literature. We offer here an anthology
of eye-witness accounts from the pens of those who had the chance
to approach Verdi, to speak to him, to interview him. There are
accounts by composers (Massenet, Mascagni), by musicologists
(Destranges, Bonaventura, Tebaldini), by literati (Ghislanzoni,
Giacosa, Annie Vivanti), by artists, by occasional visitors and, above
all, by critics, chroniclers, journalists, that whole category of people
against whom the composer raised highest his wall of reserve. Some
of these accounts are already well-known (for example, the memoirs
of Barbieri Nini, which have been published several times in books
and articles about Verdi); others, the overwhelming majority,
printed in French, English, German and Italian periodicals and
publications, constitute a novelty not only for the interested layman
but also, perhaps, for the enthusiast and scholar. Our enquiry,
although we have spread the net wide, is by no means exhausted.[15]
Even more extensive and meticulous research may in the future
unearth other precious material, including some articles which we
now know to exist but which we have been unable to trace.[16] Even
so, the material gathered to date appears to contain elements of
sufficient interest and novelty to justify a publication, which is
intended as a contribution to research into the life and personality of
Verdi. The choice of texts has been based on their documentary
interest and above all on their trustworthiness, which has been
verified by repeated cross-references to the correspondence and to
other primary sources. This has occasioned the insertion of further
references[17] and numerous quotations from the correspondence –
these latter checked, wherever possible, against the autograph copy –
in the introductions and notes to the individual chapters.[18] This
verification of the material has justified the rejection of accounts that
proved largely or completely unfounded.[19]

In chronological order according to the events to which they
refer,[20] the eye-witness accounts chosen for the fifty chapters of this
collection cover a period of over fifty-five years: from May 1845
(Escudier's visit) to November 1900 (the last conversation with

Tebaldini), although the period of the composer's most intense activity, the 'galley years', are the least discussed. The accounts, rare in connection with those years (only six documents in all from 1842 to 1859, two of which, those of Barbieri Nini and Dupré, are reminiscences) increase in frequency as the composer's prestige grows abroad with his later masterpieces, from *Don Carlos* to *Falstaff*. The greater part of the testimonies deals with his years of maturity and old age – in fact, more than half of the documents concern the last fifteen years of Verdi's life. But this anthology is not intended as a biographical essay; even if it might succeed in describing incidents extending back as far as Verdi's infancy (as, for example, in the confidential reminiscences entrusted to Ghislanzoni or von Winterfeld) which are fresher or more specific than what is presently available, these incidents still fail to transcend the level of anecdote and legend, and have thus been ignored or refuted by the more conscientious researchers.[21] We would rather wish to define this work as an essay on Verdi's personality, or better still, as an attempt to draw closer to the man and the artist, than has hitherto been possible from the available information. The anthology seeks to give a more lively and immediate portrayal of the composer and to depict the man Verdi through the eyes of those who had the chance to meet him, speak with him, to paint from life his features and attitudes, and to receive some of his confidences.

Through some of these accounts (and we must bear in mind the dates and events repeatedly brought to the reader's attention in the notes to each chapter, even at the cost of constant repetition), the figure of the Maestro of Busseto frees itself from its traditional image: it moves, it takes on life, it seems to stand before us – we can almost hear it speak. Elsewhere, we have the opportunity of approaching him almost unobserved, as though meeting him by chance. Thus we find him seated on the stage of the Opéra, "his great white hands resting on his knees, motionless, like some Assyrian god [. . .] whose Atlas-like shoulders seem capable of supporting the weight of mountains". We surprise him on a street in Cremona looking into the windows of a bookshop, "his hands behind his back, and in his hands a . . . melon of vast proportions". We glimpse him at Genoa station in the depths of winter, "sprightly and cheerful", speaking animatedly with a group of people, "his overcoat slung across his shoulders". We admire him on the terrace of the Palazzo Doria, "bare-headed and upright beneath the scorching sun", showing Massenet the city and sea of Genoa stretched out beneath him with a proud and simple gesture, "evoking one of the great doges of the past". In each instant he is different, and yet everything about him is characteristic; his attitudes vary in accordance with the extreme variability of his sensitive spirit, and yet he remains constant in his strength of character, in the vigour of a personality always ready for a new challenge, for a new youth.

Youth in both body and spirit – for from his exhausting and laborious beginnings, Verdi had gradually conquered for himself an existence. An astonished Milanese hotel-keeper says to Heinrich Ehrlich of the 84-year-old man: "When Verdi walks through the streets [of Milan] with his hat cocked over his right eye, he looks like a widower in search of a wife." . . . Who would recognize in this "young" widower the "old" composer of the galley-years, the taciturn and moody artist, with his "pale face, sunken cheeks and deep-set eyes", who was introduced to Ghislanzoni in Milan, way back in 1846? Or who would recognize the composer, as Marc Monnier described him in Paris in 1855: "a slender man with a grizzled beard, a haggard face that seemed afflicted by suffering"? By 1868, Ghislanzoni had already noticed a change. He described Verdi as "strong and slender" and added that [Verdi] "may be said to have proceeded through a career of triumphs and discarded after each one part of that hard and rough exterior, which characterized him in his younger years". For one who scarcely experienced youth, who was born fully adult, whom domestic grief and the restless struggle for artistic supremacy had aged before his time, these years of maturity almost amounted to a second childhood. With remarkable consistency, his visitors depict him as young in old age, "a mixture of child and patriarch; a patriarch before his time, and a child with a grey beard" (de Lauzières); "a mixture of patriarchal dignity and childlike naïveté" (von Winterfeld); "like many men of genius, he had his childish side" (Vivanti); "a genius with the soul of a child" (Philippi).

But this patriarchal child is only the last phase of a metamorphosis begun in the remote years of his apprenticeship, of his struggles in Busseto, a metamorphosis which brings about the reconciliation of opposing passions, the contradictory emotional impulses of a man whose modesty amounted to arrogance (he liked to describe himself as "proud as Lucifer"), whose gentleness amounted to intractability (the "Busseto bear" with his "knee-jerking manner"), whose avarice amounted to munificence (he was capable of "saving pennies" and of spending "a thousand francs in a single throw"), and as jealous of his independence as he was a persecutor of his friends. The patriarchal boy is the final manifestation of a man whose character was indomitable, volatile, who could not be exhausted in the struggles for his art, whose intense activity extends almost uninterrupted through 70 years, having begun when he was thirteen[22] (in that year, 1826, Beethoven bade farewell to art with his Quartet op. 135, and Weber lay dying, having staged his *Oberon*), and only effectively ending when he was 84 (when Puccini and Strauss were already famous, Debussy's star was rising and Schoenberg was composing *Verklärte Nacht*). It was an interminable period of activity that constantly renewed itself, as society itself underwent transformation. And such transformation! Mila reminds us that "Verdi was born in an age when the sole known means of land transport was a horse-drawn coach. When he died, a network of railways linked the globe and Agnelli's Fiat corporation was already two years old. [. . .] Verdi was born into a divided Italy, a Europe intent on crushing the forces of Napoleon and the principles of liberty, equality, fraternity. At his death, Italy was in the third and last reign of its unified kingdom, and socialism was rife in Europe. Not only was Verdi's life long, not only did his creative force maintain an exceptional freshness right up to the end, but this life was lived through an age that probably has no equal for the quantity and magnitude of its transformations."[23] If dates and events are not kept constantly in mind when contemplating a phenomenon of such long duration, it is understandable that Verdi should prove elusive to biographers. So much activity cannot be reduced to a single formula, nor can the author be summarily defined.

The proverbial reserve in which Verdi enshrouded himself is not belied by a reading of these pages. On the contrary. But it does take on a new dimension: it is enlivened by an immediate and spontaneous rapport with interviewers, and is at the same time attenuated by Verdi's discretion in their presence. What is belied, on the other hand, is the no less proverbial image of Verdi as an artist without culture, or who acquired culture reluctantly, shy of educated acquaintances and withdrawn in his "stubborn spiritual isolation",[24] incapable of understanding anything new or different developing around him. Through judgements, affirmations, enquiries, confessions, sometimes new or hitherto unpublished, the testimonies in this anthology depict a man with antennae perpetually in motion, ready to catch any vibration of change in the society where he lived and worked, a man for whom culture (if we understand it not as something merely decorative, literary, superficial, but rather as a means of relating to reality and acquiring the tools to transform it) was a vital necessity, and whose unwillingness to flaunt it derived precisely from cultural savoir-faire. We have come far from describing him as "working in secret, in the manner of an incurably self-taught man"! . . .[25]

The elderly Hanslick, famous author of the controversial *Vom Musikalisch-Schönen*, an active and authoritative witness of European musical history for more than half a century, wrote of Verdi with stupefied admiration after meeting him in Rome in 1893 after *Falstaff*: "Something infinitely gentle, modest and yet distinguished radiates from this man, whom fame has not made vain, honour not arrogant and old age not cantankerous." It is an almost hallowed portrait in which we would be hard-pressed to recognize the "Salvator Rosa bandit-chief" and the "Rienzi type" described more than twenty years earlier by an American journalist . . . but nevertheless it is a true portrait, which gives us an idea of his insatiable spiritual energy which grew by degrees through the course of an interminable apprenticeship, an inexhaustible diligence and constant renewal. Above all it gives us an idea of the moral force which is so rarely found in the histories of great men, a force that overwhelms anyone who attempts to discuss him, to describe his human and artistic growth – the force of having been superior to his own glory.

MARCELLO CONATI

PARMA, JULY 1980

NOTES

1. A. SCHOENBERG: *Stil und Idee.*
2. M. MILA: *La giovinezza di Verdi*, Edizioni Rai Radiotelevisione Italiana, Turin 1974, p. 105.
3. F. WALKER: *The Man Verdi*, London 1962, J. M. Dent, p. xi.
4. C. SARTORI: "Giuseppe Verdi", in *La Musica: Enciclopedia storica*, edited by A. Basso under the direction of G. M. Gatti, Unione Tipografico-Editrice Torinese, Turin, vol. IV (1966), p. 729.
5. C. SARTORI, *op. cit.*, p. 744.
6. We must except instances in which a colleague or collaborator were involved. To the Paris periodical *Europe Artiste*, which in the March issue of 1855 had reported Scribe's alleged refusal to comply with Verdi's request for a trio in *I vespri siciliani*, when four acts of the opera were already in rehearsal, Verdi sent the following disavowal:

Allow me to report that you are ill-informed regarding my relations with Signor Scribe, with whom I neither am nor I hope ever will be in the slightest disaccord. We have peacefully and amicably agreed to make certain changes in Act 5, before I start to compose the music for it. Had it merely involved myself, I would not have incommoded you with these few lines, but since my illustrious collaborator is also involved, I consider myself bound to rectify your error.

7. Let Verdi's letter to Giovanni Ricordi of 30 September 1850 serve as an example. It refers to the first of two virulent attacks upon him by Fétis in the authoritative *Revue et Gazette Musicale de Paris*, on 13 and 19 September 1850, and translated in *Italia Musicale*, published by Lucca (cf. M. Mila: "Fétis e Verdi, ovvero Gli infortuni della critica", in *Atti del III Congresso internazionale di studi verdiani*: Milan, Piccola Scala, 12–17 June 1972, Istituto di studi verdiani, Parma 1974, pp. 312–21):

> *I have read all your letters and the articles you sent me, and I have pondered your reasons, but I shall make no reply to Fétis' article. If you wish to reply, then do so in your own name, since I do not wish to be involved.* (From an autograph letter in the property of RAI-Radiotelevisione Italiana.)

8. G. Giacosa: "Verdi in villa (Note)", See N. XXIII.
9. Arrigo Boito to Eugenio Checchi, in an undated letter of December 1886, published in E. Checchi: *Giuseppe Verdi: Il genio e le opere*, G. Barbèra, Florence 1887, pp. 106–7.
10. C. Sartori, *op. cit.*, p. 745.
11. This point was also recently made by Pierluigi Petrobelli:

> In a sense, the personality of the Busseto composer has determined the direction of research on his work and life. The image Verdi desired posterity to have of him has subconsciously, and thus perhaps more decisively than scholars have hitherto allowed, affected their writings. The stereotyping of Verdi as an uncultured "peasant", who turned a deaf ear to contemporary musical developments, interesting himself only in his own work and the principles of composition which he himself devised for it, is a cliché still subscribed to by too many people. Another hackneyed idea is that Verdi must be regarded more as a dramatist than musician. A direct consequence of this assumption is the idea that his music has only a functional character, and should be appraised only in relation to its function. (P. Petrobelli: "Osservazioni sul processo compositivo in Verdi", in *Acta Musicologica*, Basle, vol. XLIII, III–IV: July–December 1971, pp. 125–6.)

12. *Carteggio Verdi-Boito*, edited by M. Medici and M. Conati, Istituto di studi verdiani, Parma 1978; G. Marchesi: *Verdi, merli e cucú: Cronache bussetane fra il 1819 e il 1839*, with an appendix of documents collected by G. N. Vetro, Quaderno n. 1 di "Biblioteca 70", Busseto 1979.

13. And some of the letters are censored outright – for example, a letter of
    11 June 1879 to Giuseppe Piroli in which Verdi lamented the damage
    caused by the flooding of the Po, and the indifference of the govern-
    ment. Luzio transcribed a sentence of it as follows: "*And all the while the
    government contrives to raise taxes and to build railways of low priority*"
    (A. LUZIO: *Carteggi Verdiani*, vols. III and IV, Accademia Nazionale dei
    Lincei, Rome 1947; see vol. III, pp. 139–40). The autograph copy
    actually reads as follows: "*And all the while the government continues to
    raise taxes, increase armament spending, and build railways of low priority*
    [. . .]."* (Autograph: Accademia Nazionale dei Lincei, Rome.)
14. F. WALKER, *op. cit.*, p. xi.
15. I owe the locating of part of the material to the kind collaboration of
    Julian Budden, Sylviane Falcinelli, John Nadas and Franz Wallner-
    Basté, to whom I wish to express my deepest thanks.
16. For example, a portrait from life printed in *Indépendance Belge* on 3 June
    1855; an interview in *Le Gaulois* of April 1894; another interview of
    autobiographical content published in an English newspaper in August
    1899 and mentioned in the *Signale für die musikalische Welt* of Leipzig, on
    1 September 1899.
17. All the sources consulted and used in the compilation of this anthology
    are included in the Bibliography.
18. Strictly speaking, we have used not the autographs but the photostatic
    reproductions of them conserved in the photographic archives of the
    Istituto di studi verdiani in Parma. Every transcription from the
    autographs is accompanied by an indication of where the original can be
    found. In all other cases, including transcriptions from the facsimiles,
    we have indicated the bibliographic source from which the quotation
    has been drawn. In all transcriptions from autographs the original
    spelling and punctuation have been retained (but not always the para-
    graphing, by reason of the typographic composition), and the use of
    square brackets has been restricted to cases where the text was ambi-
    guous. When in doubt, we have chosen the correct orthography.
19. For example, the memoirs of Count Leopold Thurn von Valsassina,
    published by Benno Geiger in the *Deutsche Revue* in April 1902.
    (We have none the less quoted a fragment from it in the introductory
    note to chapter XII.) We have likewise rejected a report by Annetta
    Haliday-Antona ("An Afternoon with Verdi", in *The Musician*,
    Boston, X, 9: September 1905, pp. 350–1), a piece of nonsense in the
    manner of some of the worst American journalism of the age, and
    completely devoid of documentary value. It is a pastiche of rumours,
    received second or third hand or completely invented, and seasoned
    with the customary clichés: the traditional *fiasco* of wine (Valpolicella, it
    seems) and the no less traditional *macaroni* – she means spaghetti –
    which Verdi allegedly tries to teach her to eat. Only the backdrop of
    Vesuvius, complete with its cloud of smoke, is missing . . .
20. In those cases where the authors give us only a vague idea of the dates of

their encounters with Verdi, we have attempted to date them with the greatest possible precision by cross-referring to the correspondence and contemporary publications. In some cases (for example the accounts of Massenet and Mascagni), this has meant correcting the dates erroneously provided by the authors themselves.

21. But not FRANK WALKER, who has observed:

> Today the tendency is to look askance at 'anecdotal biography', distrusting every story that cannot be supported by documentary evidence. This is all to the good as long as it is not carried too far. The documents available are often insufficient to illuminate all phases of a great man's life, and where other evidence is lacking, even a legend is better than nothing. Everything depends on the number of the documents and the quality of the legends (*op. cit.*, p. 3).

22. "*Between the ages of 13 and 18 (that was the time in which I came to study counterpoint in Milan) I composed a great variety of pieces*": thus Verdi replied in the spring or summer of 1853 to a request from Isidor Cambiasi (facsimile of the autograph in the "special illustrated edition", *Nel primo centenario di Giuseppe Verdi. 1813–1913*, compiled by L. Grabinski Broglio, C. Vanbianchi, G. Adami, Milan 1913, pp. 4–5). A sinfonietta, the so-called *Capricciosa*, composed by Verdi at the age of twelve, was performed on 15 August 1868 at the opening of the Teatro Verdi in Busseto (cf. N. XI, note 9).

23. M. MILA, *op. cit.*, p. 465.

24. C. SARTORI, *op. cit.*, p. 746.

25. C. SARTORI, *op. cit.*, p. 746.

ENCOUNTERS WITH VERDI

I

A VISIT TO VERDI

1845

E. [Marie? Escudier]: "Une visite à Verdi – Un ténor en plein vent", in *La France Musicale*, Paris, VIII, 21: 25 May 1845, p. 164 (republished in *Il Pirata*, Milan, X, 100: 6 June 1845, pp. 405–6; in *Iberia Musical y Literaria*, Madrid, IV, 1845; in *Il Vaglio*, Venice, X, 32: 9 August 1845, pp. 254–5; reprinted in M. Conati: "Bibliografia verdiana. Aspetti, problemi, criteri per la sistemazione della letteratura verdiana", in *Atti del III Congresso internazionale di studi verdiani*: Milan, Piccola Scala, 12–17 June 1972, Istituto di studi verdiani, Parma, 1974, pp. 553–4).

This collection of encounters and interviews with Verdi opens with a visit to the composer during the first two weeks of May 1845 by one of the two Escudier brothers, probably Marie. We have omitted the second part ("Un ténor en plein vent" – impressions of a chance encounter in Milan with the tenor Ignazio Pasini) since it bears no relevance to the theme of this anthology.

Marie (Castelnaudary 26. 6. 1819 – Paris 7. 4. 1880) and Léon (*idem* 17. 9. 1821 – *idem* 22. 6. 1881) both began their career in journalism at a very early age, and founded the newspaper *La Patrie*. Both possessed a knowledge of music (Marie studied the violin, Léon the piano and composition) and very soon devoted most of their time to publishing and musical administration; in 1837 they founded the review *La France Musicale*, and opened a business, the Bureau Central de la Musique in Place de la Bourse, with an affiliated theatrical agency for singers and composers – Marie dealt principally with the review, Léon with the business and commercial side. From the very beginning *La France Musicale* had defended the interests of young French composers, and had above all been characterized by a markedly pro-Italian attitude, in contrast to the prestigious and pro-German *Revue et Gazette Musicale de Paris*, published by Schlesinger and supported by François-Joseph Fétis. The fortunes of the Escudier brothers soon received a strong boost from the operas of Verdi, for which from 1845 they held the copyright in France. When the two brothers fell out in 1860, Marie continued with *La France Musicale* until it closed in 1870, when he joined *Le Figaro* as a much respected correspondent on foreign affairs. Léon kept the business and the publishing house, and founded a new review, *L'Art Musical* (1860–94). With the intention of restoring the fortunes of the Théâtre Italien, which had ceased to exist when the Salle Ventadour closed in 1873, Léon, despite Verdi's calls for caution, finally embarked on his operatic enterprise and the Théâtre Italien reopened in 1876 with a performance of *Aida*, never before seen in Paris, and Verdi's *Requiem*, both conducted by the composer. Despite continual financial liabilities and enormous sums still owed to Verdi, Léon persisted in a venture which soon made him totally bankrupt: his entire property, including his publishing business, was sold at auction. This was also the end of his more than 30 years' friendship with the Italian composer.

To judge from a letter, dated 26 May 1845, from Emanuele Muzio, Verdi's pupil, to the latter's father-in-law, Antonio Barezzi –

> *Monsieur Escudier, a correspondent of "La France Musicale", has paid a visit to the Maestro, expressing the wish to own a small statue of him to place in his Paris office between Rossini and Bellini.*[1]

– one presumes that of the two Escudier brothers it was Marie, the editor of *La France Musicale*, who made this first visit to Verdi. This was not as yet a business meeting, at least it seems not to have been. But the next meeting, which took place the following October, most certainly was; and this time it was probably Léon who met Verdi, immediately after the success of *Nabucco* at the Théâtre Italien in Paris. Once again it is Muzio who provides the information in a letter to Barezzi, dated 27 October 1845:

> *As soon as Lumley had heard of the success of* Nabucco *he travelled from London with Escudier to engage the Maestro for the coming Spring. Not finding him in Milan, they went to Clusone, where he was staying* [as a guest of Clara Maffei]; *but while they travelled to Clusone, he was returning to Milan, and so they will pursue him till they track him down.*[2]

In a subsequent letter, dated November 19, Muzio informs us that

> *Escudier, when in Milan, acquired the copyright of all the Maestro's operas, beginning with* Oberto, Un giorno di regno *etc., and including all those which he will write in Italy, and he has paid 500 francs for each opera. This copyright is for France alone.*[3]

Escudier's travels in Italy during the spring of 1845 were directly connected with the launching of the "symphonic ode" in three parts to words by Auguste Colin, *Le désert* – the first important composition of the young Félicien David, a "discovery" of the Escudier brothers; the resounding success of the "ode" on 8 December 1844 at the Paris Conservatoire (Berlioz himself had spoken of it in enthusiastic terms) earned David the reputation as the founder of "musical orientalism". The first performance in Italy (part 1 only) had taken place in Florence during April 1845; the first complete performance followed in Milan at the Teatro alla Canobbiana on 20 June and aroused, as Muzio wrote the next day in a letter to Barezzi

> *fanatical enthusiasm after a perfect performance. [. . .] I adore David and his Desert! When next at Busseto I shall show it to Verdi, so that he can see and hear it.*[4]

That Verdi himself was interested in *Le désert*, which was given repeated performances during that summer in Milan, is shown by a note, without date, that he wrote to Francesco Lucca, David's Italian publisher:

> *To Signor Lucca – two of my friends Dr Tarchini and Signor Vitali wish to come and hear David's beautiful Symphonic Ode. Let me know if there is any difficulty.*[5]

Almost 50 years later, during the search for oriental dance music that might assist him in the composition of the ballet music for the first Paris performance of *Otello*, Verdi recalls David's "ode" in a letter to Ricordi, dated 26 July 1894:

> *It occurs to me that Félicien David must have written something like what I'm looking for in* Le désert: *either a* Hymn to Allah *or the* Song of the Muezzim! *Can you make enquiries, and if there is something, send me a page.*[6]

(Verdi shows an excellent memory here: both numbers appear in David's *Le désert*).

Since Escudier dates his article "13 May 1845" and states that he visited Verdi "lundi dernier", i.e. "last Monday", and since May 13 was a Tuesday, it would seem logical to deduce that his visit took

place on May 12 – but it could also have taken place on Monday
5 May, for it is difficult to understand why he did not write the more
simple "yesterday" instead of "last Monday" . . . However – when
Escudier met Verdi, almost three months had passed since the first
performance at La Scala of *Giovanna d'Arco*, the most recent opera of
the composer who had just returned from a journey to Venice,
where he had directed the staging of *I due Foscari* at the Teatro di San
Benedetto. Verdi was now busy with the composition of *Alzira*
which was to be performed at Naples' San Carlo in August, and was
planning *Attila*, which would receive its first performance in Venice
in March 1846.[7] In his article Escudier states Verdi's age to be
twenty-eight or twenty-nine; in fact he was already thirty-one, even
if at the time of his first meeting with Escudier the composer was
convinced (as he was to be for many years, until 1876) that he had
been born in 1814.[8] In describing the "utmost simplicity" of the
composer's apartment in Milan, the French journalist mentions a
small statue, modelled perhaps by Pompeo Marchesi, which Verdi
himself – as we have seen from Muzio's letter – will present to
Escudier, and also a French cartoon entitled *Le Chemin de la Posterité*.
There exists a series of three cartoons with this title, drawn by
Benjamin Rouhaud and dated 1842, 1843 and 1844.[9] The first
portrays the great figures of French literature, headed by Victor
Hugo on horseback, holding aloft a standard with the words: *Le laid
c'est le beau*; the second depicts the most famous actors of the Paris
theatres; and the third (perhaps the one Escudier saw in Verdi's
apartment?) the most celebrated singers of the age, including the
tenors Duprez and Mario, the bass Lablache, the baritone Ronconi,
and the sopranos Rosina Stoltz and Fanny Persiani. At the end of his
article Escudier mentions Verdi's friendship with the sculptor from
Como, Pompeo Marchesi, and the visit to his studio – an important
friendship from the artistic viewpoint, Marchesi (1795–1858) being
one of the major exponents of early nineteenth-century classicism.
Having finished his studies in Rome, Marchesi's first commission
was to work on the façade of Milan cathedral, where he sculpted the
statues of Saint Philip, Saint Ambrose and the prophets Ezekiel and
Amos. Appointed Professor at the Brera Academy, his fame spread
throughout Europe: he sculpted the statues of Goethe at Frankfurt,
Emperor Francis I at Graz and Vienna, Volta at Como, Emanuele
Filiberto in Turin cathedral, Cesare Beccaria, Carlo Porta and
Leopoldo Cicognara at Brera. Among his numerous works in Milan,
mention should be made of two colossal statues, Equity and Con-

cord for the Arco della Pace, the bas-reliefs and the ornamental statues on the façade of the Palazzo Saporiti and a colossal marble group in the Fatebenefratelli hospital.

A visit to Verdi

Milan, 18 May 1845

La France musicale has often spoken of Verdi. And there can be no doubt that the young composer owes the popularity which he already enjoys in France and England to the high praise that these columns have rightly bestowed on his works. Our readers already appreciate this artist's considerable talents; it will not, I think, displease them to be introduced to the man and enter with me for a moment the intimacy of his home.

I saw Verdi for the first time last Monday, at his house.

I had been given an utterly false idea of his character, imagining him to be cold, uncommunicative and always engrossed in his art. Verdi welcomed me with great affability, and with a charm that was completely French received several friends who visited him while I was there; we spoke a great deal of French music and those composers who are now writing for the Parisian theatres. He knows all the compositions that deserve to be known, and displays a keen liking for everything that comes from France. He expressed a desire to see the great score of Félicien David's *Le désert* which is soon to be performed in Milan. Having read the score avidly from beginning to end, he exclaimed: "Ah, what excellent judges the French are! I had expected to see heavy music, over-laden with notes; but instead I see a clear and straightforward instrumentation of the French school combined with the simple and poetic melodies of the Italian school. Please inform M. David that I would be delighted to express personally to him one day my admiration of his genius."

Verdi is a handsome young man of twenty-eight or twenty-nine. He has brown hair and blue eyes with an expression that is at once gentle and bright. His face lights up when he speaks; the constant mobility of his gaze reflects the diversity of his feelings; everything about him reveals a sincere heart and a sensitive soul.

I requested Verdi to play me an extract from *I Lombardi*, the *Ave Maria*,[10] which I have always considered the best number of the work. He immediately sat down at the piano and sang with touching

expression this page of music that he himself regards as one of his
finest inspirations. The works of this young and already famous
composer are much sought after in Italy and fetch the price of gold.
He is extremely wealthy but his tastes are of the utmost simplicity.
His study is sparsely furnished: four or five chairs, a grand piano, the
statuette of himself, and above the piano three garlands with golden
tassels hanging from a frame which contains, guess what? . . . a
cartoon entitled: *Le Chemin de la Postérité*.

I need few words to describe this young maestro's appearance and
character; he has a generous nature and an exceptional constitution;
he resembles Donizetti in features and stature, and Bellini in softness
of speech. Verdi is a devotee of all the arts. He took me to the famous
sculptor Marchesi, one of his close friends, and gave me a detailed
tour of his studio – the largest and richest in Europe.

E.

NOTES

1. *Giuseppe Verdi nelle lettere di Emanuele Muzio ad Antonio Barezzi* edited by L. A. GARIBALDI, F.lli Treves, Milan 1931, p. 203.
2. *G. Verdi nelle lettere di E. Muzio*, p. 227.
3. *G. Verdi nelle lettere di E. Muzio*, pp. 234–5. Escudier did not, however, acquire the French copyright of *Nabucco*, which had only just received its première at the Théâtre Italien in Paris; this had already been bought by the publisher Schoenenberger (cf. C. HOPKINSON: *A Bibliography of the Works of Giuseppe Verdi*, vol. II, Broude Brothers, New York 1978, pp. 11–13).
4. *G. Verdi nelle lettere di E. Muzio*, p. 204; see also Muzio's detailed description of this work in a letter to Barezzi on July 17 of the same year (*ibid.*, pp. 208–9).
5. Autograph: Archivio della Casa Ricordi, Milan.
6. Autograph: Archivio della Casa Ricordi, Milan.
7. See letter to F. M. Piave containing the "sketch" of *Attila* in *I Copialettere di Giuseppe Verdi*, edited by G. CESARI and A. LUZIO, Milan 1913, p. 437. This letter, dated 12 April 1844 in the *Copialettere*, belongs in fact to 1845 and is linked with another letter to Piave that Abbiati assigns to September 1845 (see F. ABBIATI: *Giuseppe Verdi*, Ricordi, Milan 1959, vol. I, p. 585), but which, on the grounds of its contents, can only refer to the period immediately after Verdi's return from Venice after the staging of *I due Foscari*, i.e. to early April 1845.
8. On 18 October 1876 Verdi writes to his friend Clara Maffei:

> *Guess what? I was actually born in 1813, and a few days ago I completed my 63rd year! My mother had always told me that I was born in 1814, and I*

naturally believed her, and have thus deceived all those people who have asked my age. A few months ago I had a look at my birth certificate, and although it was written in Latin I was able to make out that on 9 October of this month [sic] I completed my 63rd year!!!! (Autograph: Biblioteca Nazionale Braidense, Milan.)

Mary J. Matz (*"Le 'radici' dell' albero genealogico verdiano"* in *Verdi*, Bolletino dell' Istituto di studi verdiana, n. 7, pp. 810–12) considers this a "misleading, difficult and elusive" letter, and doubts Verdi's surprise and sincerity:

> He undoubtedly knew his exact age – if only because every time he left the Duchy or, after 1860, the country, he had to take with him a passport. The documents that have come down to us all bear the correct date.

Not, however, the passport issued to him in 1832 (facsimile in C. GATTI: *Verdi nelle immagini*, Garzanti, Milan 1941, p. 32); and in any case one can understand that Verdi should believe his mother more readily than a document, as long as he did not have the "birth certificate" before his eyes. Following his mother's story, who insisted that he was born on Saint Donnino's day, Verdi always celebrated his own birthday on October 9 – Saint Donnino's day – rather than on October 10, the date given by the parish register of Le Roncole and accepted since by biographers (see *Carteggio Verdi-Boito*, edited by M. MEDICI and M. CONATI, p. 501; and Matz's article, which in this case seems to bear out Verdi's version).

9. Published in *Atti del III Congresso internazionale di studi verdiani*, pp. 546–7.
10. According to the critic G. A. Biaggi, quoted by Radiciotti, this number was particularly appreciated by Rossini:

> One day a group of critics [. . .] were discussing the best religious numbers in opera. After mention had been made of the prayers from *Mosè* and *La muette de Portici*, the chorus of Christians from David's *Herculanum* etc., Rossini said "And add the *Ave Maria* from *I Lombardi*, which is as beautiful and religious as the *Pange Lingua* and the *Lauda Sion* of plainsong." And several evenings later he asked one of his guests, the celebrated Frezzolini, to sing him this piece which he accompanied *from memory!* (G. RADICIOTTI: *Gioacchino Rossini. Vita documentata, Opere ed influenza su l'arte*, vol. III, Tivoli 1929, p. 284.)

II

A PROPOS A VISIT TO VERDI

1845

[PETER LICHTENTHAL?]: "Frühlingsopern u.s.w. in Italien (Fortsetzung). Grossherzogthum Toscana [. . .]", in *Allgemeine musikalische Zeitung*, Leipzig, XLVII, 39: 24 September 1845, pp. 667–8 (republished with Italian translation in M. CONATI: "Bibliografia verdiana [. . .]", *art. cit.*, pp. 555–7).

SEVERAL ASSERTIONS MADE by Escudier in the previous chapter are challenged here. The articles from Italy which appeared between 1812 and 1846 in what was then Europe's oldest and most prestigious musical review, the *Allgemeine musikalische Zeitung* (1798–1848) founded in Leipzig by Friedrich Rochlitz, can in all probability be attributed to Peter Lichtenthal – a doctor and musician (Bratislava 1780 - Milan 1853) who moved to Milan in 1810 as censor to Lombardy-Venetia – and was author of several articles on music and medicine. He arranged concerts in his own home to promote the cause of German music, particularly that of Mozart, with whose son Carl, who was employed by the Milanese government, he was on intimate terms. Lichtenthal was also active as a composer: apart from half a dozen ballets performed at La Scala, he wrote much symphonic, sacred and chamber music. But he is chiefly known for his numerous publications, historical and theoretical in character, of which the following deserve mention: *Cenni biografici intorno al celebre maestro W. A. Mozart* (Milan 1816), *Dizionario e bibliografia della musica* in four volumes (Milan 1826; 2nd edition 1836) and an *Estetica ossia dottrina del bello e delle belle arti* (Milan 1831). I have already spoken elsewhere of the tone of these numerous articles dispatched from Italy to the Leipzig review, and of their general condemnation of the contemporary Italian musical scene.[1] It will be sufficient here to recall briefly that, despite the negative and often contemptuous criticism of the works of Verdi from *Nabucco* onwards, expressed in the columns of the *Allgemeine musikalische Zeitung*, Lichtenthal, or rather the anonymous author of these articles from Italy to the Leipzig review, had written a most flattering account of Verdi's first opera, *Oberto, Conte di San Bonifacio*, performed at La Scala, and had classified the young, unknown musician as the fourth best Italian composer still active, after Donizetti, Mercadante and Ricci, asserting that "It remains to be seen if [Verdi] will climb even higher; we hope very much that he will, since he could surpass all his colleagues."[2]

In this same issue which reported on musical events in Italy during the spring of 1845, the correspondent of the *Allgemeine musikalische Zeitung* informs his readers of the cold reception accorded to David's *Le désert* in Florence and Milan, which, as far as the reception at Milan is concerned, contrasts sharply (as we have seen) with Muzio's account and with those of contemporary Milanese newspapers, but which testifies to a hostile attitude towards the anti-German *La France Musicale* and those composers supported by the Escudiers. The author of the article sets out to refute the assertions contained in Escudier's piece quoted above, and he pens several swift but interesting sketches of famous Italian composers, including (besides Verdi) Rossini, Donizetti and Bellini. Notice in particular the sympathetic description of Donizetti, whose operas, however, were systematically disparaged by the anonymous correspondent of the Leipzig review.

[*A propos a visit to Verdi*]

Spring opera, etc. in Italy [. . .]

Florence. [. . .] The so-called Symphonic-Ode: *Le désert* by M. Félicien David has been given a cool reception, here as in Milan. M. Escudier, publisher of *La France Musicale* and copyright owner of *Le désert*, who had travelled especially to Florence and Milan to witness a glorious success, certainly arrived here too late. It is amusing to read M. Escudier's account in the afore-mentioned paper (no. 21 of 25 May 1845) of a visit he paid in Milan to M. Verdi. As copyright holder of the latter's music,[3] he naturally praises him to the skies. He then reports with great affection that Verdi is a *handsome young man* (?) of *twenty-eight or twenty-nine*;[4] who has *blue eyes with an expression that is at once gentle and bright*(?);[5] and that the *Ave Maria* from *I Lombardi*, which M. Escudier requested the composer to play, is the finest number from that opera (it is certainly the worst of *Ave Marias*). M. Escudier then proceeds: *I need few words to describe this young maestro's appearance and character: he has a generous nature*[6] (how galant!) *and an exceptional constitution*[7] (what an eye Escudier has for anatomical-physiological-psychological detail!); *he resembles Donizetti in features and stature*[8] (like a raven resembles a dove), *and Bellini in modesty of speech*[9] (neither of them possessed this virtue — Bellini was lovably conceited, Verdi is solemnly so). Would my readers care for a short description of the best-known modern Italian operatic composers? . . . Your correspondent has often enjoyed their company during the past 30 years in Italy.[10] About the characters of *Mercadante* and *Ricci* there is nothing in particular to relate. Grandfather *Rossini*: a handsome, interesting face, in his younger days a witty and jovial companion quite without pride but the king of all hoaxers. — *Donizetti*: handsome man (a faint similarity to our Spohr); his character resembles that of an honest German — pleasant and friendly, he sometimes makes witty remarks, and has no trace of pride. — *Pacini*: a somewhat small and thin man, educated, polite and modest; in society you could call him the Italian *Meyerbeer*. — *Bellini*: medium build, a handsome, somewhat pale and languishing face, blue eyes; although secretly he has a high opinion of himself, his whole personality could be termed kind. — *Verdi*: medium build, not ugly but far from handsome; earnest and self-important.

NOTES

1. M. CONATI: "Saggio di critiche e cronache verdiane dalla 'Allgemeine musikalische Zeitung' di Lipsia (1840–48)" in *Il melodramma italiano dell' Ottocento*, Studi e ricerche per Massimo Mila, Einaudi, Turin 1977, pp. 13–43.
2. M. CONATI: "L' 'Oberto conte di San Bonifacio' in due recensioni straniere poco note e in una lettera inedita di Verdi", in *Atti del I Congresso internazionale di studi verdiani*, Venezia, Fond. G. Cini, 1966", Istituto di studi verdiani, Parma 1969, pp. 83–87.
3. Officially this was not yet true, at least according to Muzio's letter of November 19, quoted in the introduction to the preceding chapter (unless Muzio by the phrase "when in Milan" intended to refer to Escudier's meeting with Verdi in May — which seems unlikely, as six months had already elapsed since then and Muzio was, as we know, always quick to inform Barezzi of the "signor Maestro's" activities; none the less, it is still possible that during the May meeting Escudier had entered into negotiations with Verdi concerning the copyright of his operas in France).
4. *Un beau jeune homme (?) de 28 à 29 ans.*
5. *Des yeux bleus d'une expression douce et vive à la fois (?)*

6. *C'est une belle nature.*
7. *Une organisation privilégiée.*
8. *Par les traits et la taille il ressemble à Donizetti.*
9. *Et par la modestie de sa parole à Bellini.* [N.B. Escudier had actually written *morbidesse* (softness) and not *modestie.*]
10. For Rossini, see J.LOSCHELDER: "Rossinis Bild und Zerrbild in der 'Allgemeinen musikalischen Zeitung' Leipzig", in *Bollettino del Centro rossiniano di studi*, Pesaro 1973, n. 1, pp. 23–42, and n. 2, pp. 23–42. For Bellini, see W. FR. KÜMMEL: "Vincenzo Bellini nello specchio dell' 'Allgemeine musikalische Zeitung' di Lipsia, 1827–1836", in *Nuova Rivista Musicale Italiana*, Rome, VII, 2: April–June 1973, pp. 185–205.

III

VERDI IN FLORENCE –
AN OPINION FROM ROSSINI

1847

GIOVANNI DUPRÉ: *Pensieri sull'arte e Ricordi autobiografici,* second edition with additions and corrections: Succ.ri Le Monnier, Florence, 1880 – chapt. II. pp. 167–74 (published also in *Gazzetta Musicale di Milano,* ed. Ricordi, XXXIV, 34: 24 August 1879, pp. 293–5, drawn from the first edition of the *Ricordi autobiografici,* Florence, 1878).

FROM POMPEO MARCHESI to Giovanni Dupré; or from one sculptor to another. Verdi's interest in contemporary sculpture is a recurrent feature in the artist's life, and more than mere occasional curiosity. The composer's letters not infrequently bear witness to his great interest in the figurative arts, especially sculpture – it is sufficient to recall his association, not only with Marchesi and Dupré, but with Lorenzo Bartolini and Jean-Pierre Dantan, and later with Vincenzo Gemito (whose bust of the composer is considered one of his masterpieces), his warm friendship with Vincenzo Luccardi, the sculptor from Friuli, and with Giulio Monteverde from Genoa in the composer's old-age.

Giovanni Dupré (Sienna 1817 – Florence 1882), at the time of this meeting with Verdi, had already established his reputation with his *Death of Abel* and *Cain* (1843), and *Giotto* for the Uffizi colonnade (1844); he had also finished his *Innocence* for the Grand Duke Nicholas of Russia and was re-modelling *Cain.* The passage quoted here was read by Verdi in the *Gazzetta Musicale di Milano* which had reproduced the article from Dupré's first edition (see introductory note to this chapter). Having read the article, the composer felt constrained to write to Giulio Ricordi, in a letter dated 26 August 1879; while protesting in an ironic vein against "Jupiter-Rossini's" pronouncement against him, made years ago in 1846, he cunningly betrays his intention of taking up his pen again, having laid it down as far as the theatre was concerned after *Aida* (1871), the opera which seemed to have concluded his career. This letter, which he was roused to write after reading the passage from Dupré's *Memoirs,* is of importance, not only because Verdi reveals for the first time in virtually unequivocal terms a project that he had cherished for "twenty years", namely to write an "opera buffa", but above all because it marks the beginning of the Maestro's final creative period, that produced the two masterpieces, *Otello* and *Falstaff*:

> *I have read in your Gazzette Dupré's account of our first meeting, and the pronouncement uttered by Jupiter-Rossini (as Meyerbeer used to call him). But listen! For twenty years I have searched for an opera buffa libretto, and now that I may have found one, you with that article put it into the public's head to hiss the opera even before it is written, thus ruining your own interests and mine. But have no fear – if by chance, by misfortune, by some disaster, despite the Great Pronouncement, my evil genius should inspire me to write this opera buffa – then, have no fear, I repeat . . . I shall ruin some other Publisher!*[1]

To the lively protests of the publisher,[2] who at that very time thought he was so close to realizing a long cherished dream, a Verdi opera to a libretto by Boito, perhaps even *Otello*, Verdi made the following reply on September 4:

> *It seems to me that there was absolutely no point in printing that extract from Dupré's book in your Gazzette, unless you wished to tell me: "Beware, signor Maestro, of ever writing an opera buffa." — — It was for this reason that I believed it my duty to say: "I shall ruin some other publisher." If you wish to ruin yourself by my writing this opera buffa, then so much the worse for the Casa Ricordi. It would always be agreeable to have a visit from you and a friend – Boito, of course.*[3] [. . .]

The authenticity of Dupré's way of introducing himself to Verdi is confirmed by a letter from Giuseppe Piroli in Florence to the composer, dated 15 July 1882:

> *I am reading a book by Dupré – Pensieri sull'arte e ricordi auto-biografici – which has enjoyed a great and deserved success. It includes a marvellous page that concerns you, and how you first met him – just as you have recounted to me on several occasions*[4]

In Dupré's account this meeting takes place soon after the Grand Duke of Tuscany's request to the sculptor for a copy of the *Death of Abel* and of the re-modelled *Cain*. It was late winter 1847; Verdi had arrived in Florence in mid-February, accompanied by Emanuele Muzio for the rehearsals of his latest opera, *Macbeth*, to a libretto by Piave, which had its première on March 14 at the Pergola. The first meeting of sculptor and composer took place between February 16 and 24, since on February 25 Muzio informs Antonio Barezzi:

> *You will already have guessed that the Maestro is being worshipped, sought and pursued by all and sundry. The most distinguished men have wished to meet him: Niccolini, Giusti, Bartolini, Dupré, etc.; even the Grand Duke has invited him to visit, and yesterday Verdi betook himself there a little unwillingly.* [5]

A propos Giuseppe Giusti, one reads in Dupré's book that Verdi, wishing to meet the Tuscan writer, had obtained a letter of introduction from Alessandro Manzoni. At that time Verdi did not yet know the author of *I promessi sposi* personally, nor had he been able to meet Giusti during the latter's stay in Milan in the summer of 1845 when he had been a frequent visitor to Manzoni's house and Clara Maffei's salon. Manzoni's letter of introduction had been obtained for the composer by Clarina herself, an intimate friend of the Lombard writer (but one should not forget the great friendship that already existed at that time between Giusti and Clarina's husband, the poet Andrea Maffei, who was also in Florence for *Macbeth*, and had re-touched the libretto a little at Verdi's request). [6] Research by Angelo Ciavarella has shown that Manzoni's autograph letter is preserved in the Autografoteca Bastogi at the Biblioteca Labronica in Leghorn; [7] as it has not been reproduced in the best-known Verdi biographies, we quote the text here:

> *Dear Geppino – Two superfluous lines: Signor Maestro Verdi desires, and here he is right, but not absolutely, to make your acquaintance. And he imagines, and here he is wrong, that he requires a letter of introduction – but my words will not be superfluous, for they will remind you of your Sandro*

Dupré recounts how, during that stay in Florence, Andrea Maffei endeavoured to persuade Verdi to write an opera to a libretto based on Byron's verse-tragedy *Cain*, which had been published in 1821; Dupré himself, who had sculpted a statue of Cain, set about illustrating the wealth of situations and contrasts that such a subject could offer to the inspiration of the composer of *Nabucco* and *Aida*, and asks himself: "If one day Verdi reads these pages, who knows?" Verdi took note of Maffei's and Dupré's suggestion, as a page from the autograph *Copialettere*, entitled "Opera subjects", bears witness. Scholars, led astray by Luzio's dating (he published a facsimile of it in isolation in the printed edition of the *Copialettere*) usually trace it back to the last months of 1843 or the first weeks of 1844; its place, however, in the autograph *Copialettere* on the verso of the last page of the second book, suggests that it probably dates back to 1849 or, at the latest, to the first months of 1850.[8] Byron's *Cain* is the fourth subject of a list which opens with three Shakespeare plays: *King Lear*, *Hamlet* and *The Tempest*; after *Cain* come *Le Roi s'amuse* (Victor Hugo), *Die Ahnfrau* (Grillparzer), *Kean* (Dumas), *Phaedra* (Euripides-Racine), *Ad oltraggio segreto segreta vendetta* (Calderón), *Attala*[9] [*sic*] (Chateaubriand) and another nine titles, including an *Arria* ("to be taken from the *Annales* of Tacitus, Book IX") and *Ruy Blas* (Victor Hugo).

The final passage of Dupré's article – concerning Scudo's review of *I vespri siciliani* and an opinion of it expressed by Rossini at a gathering which perhaps took place in the house where Rossini lived in Florence from May 1851 to April 1855 – raises doubts as to when and, hence, where the episode occurred. *I vespri siciliani* was premièred in Paris on 13 June 1855, and Scudo's review appeared in the *Revue des deux Mondes* of July 1; at that time Rossini was already in France. Afflicted by a serious form of nervous depression, he had left Florence together with his wife Olimpia Pélissier on 26 April and set out for Paris, where he arrived on May 26 after a lengthy stay at Nice; in July he visited the spa at Trouville, and at the end of September returned to Paris,[10] where he remained virtually for the rest of his life. Dupré saw Rossini again in the French capital, but this cannot have occurred before December 1858, when those famous Saturday soirées were inaugurated at Rossini's apartment in the Chaussée d'Antin,[11] which the Siennese sculptor mentions in a subsequent chapter of his *Memoirs*.[12] Dupré clearly mistakes both date and place (*I vespri siciliani*, it should be remembered, was staged again by Verdi in Paris on 18 July 1863, and reviewed again by Scudo in the *Revue des deux Mondes*) or else confuses the operas (*Il trovatore* had been produced in Paris, on 23 December 1854, before *I vespri siciliani*, but at the Théâtre Italien; and Scudo's review had appeared in the *Revue des deux Mondes* on 1 January 1855 – at which time Rossini was still in Florence).

In Verdi's correspondence the name of Dupré, apart from appearing in the letter to Ricordi quoted above, occurs again in letters to Arrivabene, dated 5 April 1865:

> [. . .] *I am delighted that Dupré has not forgotten me, and I am sure that he is still creating prodigious works which are ever more beautiful. Give him many, many regards and tell him that we shall meet here before long* [. . .];[13]

and 12 May 1865:

> [. . .] *And Dupré? Why didn't he drop in here on his way to Turin?* [. . .] *Send my regards to Dupré. I'd very much like to see the Shepherd Giotto by his daughter. A beautiful subject, lovely* [. . .];[14]

and 6 March 1868:

> [. . .] *I have a great desire to see Florence* [then capital of Italy] *with its Cavour dressed à la romana! Ah, these artists are a curious breed of creatures. Once they have established a reputation, they are afraid of themselves and become scholars. Dupré knows well that to sculpt a Cavour dressed à la romana is absurd; but it offers him the means of rendering folds and posture . . . the academics will have shouted bravo . . . the claque and publicity do the rest, and the simpletons believe them. Amen!*[15]

[*Verdi in Florence – an opinion from Rossini*]

[. . .] It was then that Giuseppe Verdi came to Florence to stage *Macbeth*. If I'm not mistaken, it was the first time that he had been in our midst. His fame had preceded him and he naturally had many enemies, but I was a champion of the works he had composed thus far: *Nabucco, I Lombardi, Ernani* and *Giovanna D'Arco*.[16] His enemies said that, as an artist, he was extremely coarse and corrupted the art of Italian bel canto, and that as a man he was quite simply a bear who, haughty and proud, disdained all social intercourse. I wanted to convince myself at once. I wrote him the following note: "Giovanni Dupré begs the most distinguished Maestro G. Verdi to honour him by a visit – at the Maestro's own convenience – to his studio, where he is putting the final touches to his marble *Cain*, which he would like to show the Maestro before dispatching it." But in order to see the extent to which he was a bear, I wished to bring him the letter in person and introduce myself as an assistant from the Professor's studio. He received me with great urbanity, read the letter and then, with an expression that was neither laughing nor serious said:

"Convey my great thanks to the Professor, and say that I shall seek him out as soon as possible, since it had anyway been my intention to make the acquaintance of a young sculptor, who . . . etc." I replied: "If, signor Maestro, it is your desire to be acquainted as soon as possible with that young sculptor, I can gratify your wishes immediately, for I am he."

He smiled agreeably and, clasping my hand, said: "Ah! Done like an artist!"

We spoke at length, and he showed me some letters of introduction that he possessed to Capponi, Giusti, Niccolini; the one to Giusti had been written by Manzoni. While he remained in Florence we saw each other almost daily, and made excursions into the surrounding countryside, for example to the Fabbrica Ginori, to Fiesole and to the Torre del Gallo. There would be four or five of us: Andrea Maffei, Manara, who then died in Rome, Giulio Patti, Verdi and I; in the evenings he allowed one or another of us to attend the rehearsals of *Macbeth*. In the mornings he and Maffei would very often come to my studio. He greatly appreciated painting and sculpture, and discussed them with rare perspicacity. He had a particular preference for Michelangelo, and I recall that at the Sacchi [*sic*] chapel below Fiesole on the old road, where there is a fine collection of works of art, he knelt for almost a quarter of an hour, admiring an altar-front, said to be the work of Michelangelo. I wanted to sculpt his portrait, but for reasons beyond our control this could not be done, and I contented myself with making a cast of his hand, which I then sculpted and presented to the Sienna Philharmonic Society that I had joined in '43 when I was in Sienna. Verdi's hand is in a writing pose: as I removed the cast, the pen remained stuck, and now serves as a little stick for my sketch of *Saint Anthony*.

He seemed pleased with my *Cain*; the almost savage fierceness excited him, and I remember how my friend Maffei endeavoured to persuade him that a libretto of great drama could be fashioned from Byron's *Cain*, which he was in the process of translating, with those situations and contrasts so dear to Verdi's nature and genius. The gentle and devout character of Abel contrasted with that of Cain, consumed with wrath and envy during their dispute because Abel's offering had pleased Heaven; Abel who embraces his brother and speaks to him of God, and Cain who scornfully rejects his gentle words and blasphemes against God; a choir of invisible angels above the earth, a chorus of demons below; Cain, blind with rage, slays his brother; then their mother, hearing Abel's cries, rushes up and finds him dead; then the father, then Abel's young wife appear – all express grief at the death of this righteous man, and horror at the killer; Cain's profound and gloomy remorse; and finally his curse. All this formed a scenario truly worthy of the dramatic and biblical genius of Giuseppe Verdi. I remember his infatuation with the theme, but then nothing came of it, and he probably had his good reasons. Perhaps nudity on the stage was a problem, but animal-hide can provide tunics and extremely picturesque cloaks. Whatever – the subject truly offered him effective and attractive situations, and he could certainly have set it to music, for Verdi in his many operas has shown that he possesses a sublimely bold genius, so suitable for that tremendous drama. He, who could find within him those great, grave melodies of *Nabucco*, the saddest songs of *Il trovatore* and *La traviata*, and the local colour and sublime harmonies of *Aida*, would certainly be capable of composing *Cain*. If one day Verdi reads these pages, who knows?

This is a suitable moment for me to digress a little and talk of the character and nature that every artist possesses, quite independent of anything else, such as education and the influence of others. [. . .] I remember (and here is the reason for this digression) that Rossini, talking to me confidentially one day about art in general, on which subject he was a sound judge, gradually began discussing music and the particular character of the composers he knew, and uttered the following words about Verdi:

"You see, Verdi is a composer whose character is melancholy and serious; his sadness reflects his true nature and is for that very reason most admirable. I esteem him greatly. But he will never write a semi-serious opera like *Linda*, and certainly not an opera buffa like *L'elisir d'amore*."

And I added: "Or *Il barbiere*."

And he replied: "But let's not talk of me."

He spoke these words 22 years ago in my Candeli studio, and Verdi has still not written a semi-serious opera or an opera buffa, nor has he, I believe, thought of doing so. And that was wise of him. The art of music and Italy await his *Cain*, for he himself has felt the will and strength to compose it.

I also recall another of Rossini's opinions of Verdi. One evening after dinner I remained with him – he always loved to talk – and we walked slowly up and down the dining-room, since he did not like changing rooms and seemed not to object to the rather unpleasant odour that lingers in a room after meals. His wife Olimpia was playing tarot with one of the regular house-guests – I mean with one of those inevitable operatic extras – who entertain old ladies in their favourite pastime of cards.

Someone would always arrive late in the evening, but he did not wish to see everyone. On that evening, if I'm not mistaken, Signora Varesi[17] arrived and Signor De Luigi, together with others whom I did not know. Then two young men appeared who, it seemed, were music teachers; no sooner had they greeted Signora Rossini than they turned to Rossini with these words: "Signor Maestro, have you read Scudo's review of Verdi's new opera, *I vespri siciliani*, that has just been staged in Paris?" – "No," replied Rossini, somewhat pensively. "A very fitting review; you must read it, in the most recent issue of the *Revue des deux Mondes*." And they began to reel off some of Scudo's criticisms with a fawning unctuousness that was indeed scarcely laudable. But Rossini interrupted them: "I find it ridiculous to criticize Verdi in such a manner and in that kind of ink. To criticize Verdi properly and effectively, you must adopt a different method and use different ink. You require two Italian composers who write better music than he; but since these Italian composers who write better music have yet to appear, you must content yourself with his music, applaud it (and he gestured with his hands) when he writes well, and admonish him fraternally when you think he could do better."

Towards the end of this speech he appeared to me rather heated and almost offended, as if he believed that they had come to give him this piece of news merely to. flatter him or seek his confirmation of Scudo's passionate criticisms.

In any case, he must have read that review, for I had seen the paper on the table before dinner. The subject was quickly changed and no more was said. [. . .]

GIOVANNI DUPRÉ

NOTES

1. Autograph: Archivio della Casa Ricordi, Milan; draft copy in *I Copialettere di Giuseppe Verdi*, pp. 308–9.

2. See Giulio Ricordi's reply, dated 28 August 1879, in *I Copialettere di Giuseppe Verdi*, pp. 309–10.
3. Wrongly dated "August 4" by Verdi; autograph: Archivio della Casa Ricordi, Milan; draft copy in *I Copialettere di Giuseppe Verdi*, p. 311.
4. A. LUZIO: *Carteggi verdiani*, vol. III, p. 157.
5. *Giuseppe Verdi nelle lettere di Emanuele Muzio*, p. 311.
6. Andrea Maffei (Molina, valle di Ledro 1798 – Milan 1885), poet, translator of Milton, Schiller, Shakespeare, Goethe, Heine. Wrote for Verdi the libretto of *I masnadieri* (London, 22 July 1847). He was separated legally from Clarina in 1846, but remained on friendly terms with her.
7. Published in facsimile in 1901 to commemorate the death of Verdi by the Coffaro family for the Dante Alighieri Society (cf. A. CIAVARELLA: "Un piccolo cimelio manzoniano: Manzoni presenta Verdi a Giusti", in *Aurea Parma*, XXXV, 4: October–December 1951, pp. 208–16, with a facsimile of Manzoni's note).
8. Facsimile published in *I Copialettere di Giuseppe Verdi*, Plate XI, between pp. 419 and 421. ABBIATI (*op. cit.*, p. 501), however, is wrong to speak of a "leaflet" included in the first book of the autograph *copialettere*.
9. And not *Attila*, as ABBIATI (*op. cit.*; p. 502) reads.
10. G. RADICIOTTI, *op. cit.*, vol. II (1928) pp. 339, 347 and 349.
11. G.RADICIOTTI, *op. cit.*, vol. II, p. 377.
12. See pp. 406–7 of the 2nd edition (1880).
13. *Verdi intimo: Carteggio di Giuseppe Verdi con il conte Opprandino Arrivabene* (1861–1886), compiled and annotated by A. ALBERTI, Mondadori, s.l. 1931, p. 48.
14. *Ibid.*, pp. 55–56.
15. *Ibid.*, p. 83.
16. These operas had already been performed in Florence before 1847, as had *I due Foscari* and *Attila*.
17. Cecilia Boccabadati, perhaps, daughter of Luigia Boccabadati, a most celebrated Rossini interpreter, and wife of the baritone Felice Varesi, who took part in the premières of *Macbeth*, *Rigoletto* and *La traviata*.
18. Paul Scudo (Venice 1806 – Blois 1864) lived and worked in Paris where he studied music and where, having for a while pursued a career as singer and clarinettist, he became a singing teacher and music critic. Like two other Italian journalists who had settled in France, Pier Agnolo Fiorentino and Enrico Montazio, Scudo was hostile to Verdi's music. From his long review of *I vespri siciliani*, which appeared in the *Revue des deux Mondes* of 1 July 1855, we print here the final paragraph which is less critical than his previous articles on the operas of Verdi:

It must be granted that the Italian composer has on this occasion made every effort to obtain that consistency of style which till now has always eluded him. In fact, *I vespri siciliani* is much better written than his previous operas: true progress has been made both in his treatment of the human voice and in instrumentation. The opera, it is true, contains a great number of familiar effects and several inevitable formulae, since these are an inherent part of the composer's way of feeling; but the melodies are less tortured and develop in such a way as to gratify the voice, the duets and ensembles are better designed, although Verdi still has much to learn in the difficult art of dramatic structure. It is in the building of finales that great composers are revealed: in *Don Giovanni*, in the second act finales of *Le nozze di Figaro*, *Il barbiere*, *Otello*, *Semiramide*, *Mosè*, and the fourth act finales of *Les Huguenots*, *Le Prophète* and *Lucia* that the creative genius is revealed with all his technical expertise which the *bel esprit* laughs at, because he does not know the secret. Verdi still falls a long way short of these models, but he is clearly proceeding in the right direction, since several numbers of *I vespri siciliani* reveal a noble ambition to raise himself to the rank of these genuine Maestri, amongst whom the Italian composer prefers Meyerbeer. [. . .] Be that as it may – Verdi, like his predecessors, has already benefited greatly from Parisian audiences, and the success of *I vespri siciliani* is indisputable.

IV

VERDI AT THE REHEARSALS FOR *MACBETH* FROM THE MEMOIRS OF MARIANNA BARBIERI NINI

1847

EUGENIO CHECCHI: *Giuseppe Verdi: Il genio e le opere*, G. Barbèra, Florence, 1887 (2nd edit., revised and improved: *ibid.* 1901; reprinted 1913; 3rd edit., with addition of final chapter: *ibid.* 1926).

THE PASSAGE QUOTED here, taken from chapter XII (pp. 64–68) of the first edition, contains eye-witness descriptions of Verdi by the soprano Marianna Barbieri Nini at the time of the rehearsals in Florence for *Macbeth*, between February and March 1847.

Barbieri Nini (Florence 1820 – Florence 1887), despite her rather unattractive appearance,[1] had already sung the heroine in the première of *I due Foscari* at the Teatro Argentina di Roma (3 November 1844). It was Verdi who wished her to replace the indisposed Sofia Loewe in *Macbeth*. She also took part in the first performance of *Il corsaro* in Trieste (25 October 1848). In her narrative she alludes to the baritone Felice Varesi (Calais 1813 – Milan 1889), who created the role of Macbeth and was one of Verdi's favourite singers, for whom he wrote the title rôle in *Rigoletto* and the part of Giorgio Germont in *La traviata*.

[*Verdi at the rehearsals for "Macbeth" from the memoirs of Marianna Barbieri Nini*]

She lives today in Florence, retired from the theatre but with her memory still fresh, the remarkable singer who made *Macbeth* such a resounding success: Barbieri Nini, it was said, had interpreted the role of Shakespeare's terrible heroine better than any greater and more renowned actress. A few weeks ago, I invited a very dear friend to rekindle in the mind of the great artist these memories, which took her back to the unforgettable days of those rehearsals and performances of *Macbeth* which shed throughout the world another ray from the divine light of this genius.

Barbieri Nini related that it was an idiosyncrasy of Verdi during rehearsals to maintain an almost complete silence. This did not signify that the Maestro was content: far from it. For as soon as a number was finished, he would signal to Romani (old Pietro Romani, the greatest orchestral director of our century, the friend of Rossini, [. . .]); Romani would draw near, and together they would go up-stage where the composer, note-book in hand, referred with his finger to those aspects of the performance which did not please him.

"Show me how you would like it played," replied Romani with great patience.

But Verdi only rarely explained how. He gestured, thumped his book, indicated rallentandi and quickening of tempi with his hand, and then, as if a lengthy and convincing explanation and colloquy had taken place, he would step back and say:

"Now you've understood: like that."

And poor Romani would have to rack his sharp brains to understand, even when he had understood nothing,[2] and explain everything to the orchestra and singers.

Between piano and orchestral sessions, there were over one hundred rehearsals for *Macbeth*. The implacable Verdi spared no thought for his artists: he tired and tormented them with the same number for hours on end, and he never moved to a different scene until they had managed to perform the piece in a manner which fell least short of his ideal. He was not much loved by the multitude, for no word of encouragement, no "bravo" of conviction ever passed his lips, not even when orchestral players and members of the chorus believed they had done everything possible to content him; and those foul-mouthed, witty Florentines, quick to take offence, gave vent to their anger by uttering epithets, one of which resembled exactly that part of the violin which is used to tighten and loosen the strings.[3]

But Pietro Romani, the leader of the orchestra, and Alamanno Biagi, the conductor, and the artists who had names as deservedly famous as Barbieri Nini and Varesi, were gradually won over by that iron will, that indomitable imagination which was never contented, and each day suggested some new interpretation which, although contradicting that of the previous day, was more perfect, artistically more telling.

[. . .] And at this point I shall willingly let Barbieri Nini speak, as she talked with increasing animation, not long ago, to my friend whom I had sent to interview her.

"During the rehearsals the Maestro took great trouble with the entire score, and I recall that every morning and evening, in the foyer or on stage (according to whether the rehearsals were with piano or orchestra) we gazed anxiously at him as soon as he appeared and tried to guess from his eyes or from the way he greeted the artists whether there was some novelty in store for us that day. If he approached me almost smiling, and uttered a phrase that resembled a compliment, I was certain that he had some innovation to spring on me during the day's rehearsal. I bowed my head in resignation, but little by little I too conceived a great passion for this *Macbeth* which was turning out so differently from everything that had been previously written and performed.

"I remember that for Verdi there were two high-points in the opera: the sleepwalking scene and my duet with the baritone.[4] You will find it difficult to understand, but the sleepwalking scene took me three months to study: for three months, morning and evening, I tried to imitate those people who talk in their sleep, who utter words (as Verdi assured me) almost without moving their lips, and keeping other parts of their face, eyes included, motionless. It was enough to drive you insane.[5]

"And the duet with the baritone which begins: *Fatal mia donna, un murmure* – you might think that I exaggerate, but it was rehearsed more than 150 times: to ensure, the Maestro said, that it was more *said* than *sung*. Now listen to this. On the evening of the dress-rehearsal, with the theatre already full, Verdi insisted that the cast wear their costumes, and when he dug his heels in, woe betide you if you contradicted! And so there we were, ready, in costume, the orchestra in the pit, the chorus on stage – when Verdi beckoned to Varesi and me, called us into the wings and asked us, as a favour, to follow him to the foyer for another piano rehearsal of that accursed duet.

" 'But Maestro,' I said, terrified, 'we are already in our Scottish costumes: how can we?'

" 'Put a cloak over them.'

"And Varesi, the baritone, exasperated at the unusual request, ventured to raise his voice a little, and said:

" 'But we've rehearsed it 150 times, for goodness' sake!'

" 'In half an hour, it'll be 151.'

"Whether one wanted to or not, one had to obey the tyrant. I still remember the threatening looks Varesi shot at him, as he headed for the foyer; clenching the hilt of his sword, he seemed about to murder Verdi, just as later he would murder Duncan. Even he complied, however, and resigned himself to his fate. The 151st rehearsal took place, while the audience clamoured impatiently in the theatre.

"And that duet – to say that it aroused enthusiasm and fanaticism would be a great understatement. It was something unbelievable, new, unheard of. Wherever I have sung *Macbeth* (and during the season at the Pergola it was every evening) the duet had to be repeated three or even four times – and once we had to give a fifth encore.

"I shall never forget how, on the evening of the first performance, before the sleepwalking scene, which is one of the last in the opera, Verdi turned to me anxiously without saying a word: it was quite clear that the success, already great, would for him only be complete after that scene. And so I made the sign of the cross (a custom maintained even today on stage during difficult moments) and I made my entrance. The newspapers of the time will tell you if I interpreted rightly the dramatic and musical thought of the great maestro in that sleepwalking scene.[6] This much I do know: the storm of applause had scarcely died down when I returned to my dressing-room, greatly moved, trembling and exhausted. The door was thrown open (I was already half undressed) and Verdi entered, waving his hands and moving his lips, as if wishing to make a great speech; he failed, however, to utter a single word. I smiled and wept and said nothing either; but as I looked at the Maestro, I noticed that he too had red eyes. We clasped hands tightly, whereupon he rushed out without a word. That violent scene of emotion more than compensated for the many months of hard work and constant agitation."

EUGENIO CHECCHI

NOTES

1. "Small and fat, poorly proportioned with a vast head twice the usual size, she had a face hardly likely to arouse sympathy at first sight." Thus wrote G. Gabardi in his obituary in the *Gazzetta Musicale di Milano* (cf. *Barbieri Nini* in the *Enciclopedia dello Spettacolo*, Le Maschere, Rome, vol. I, 1954).
2. A statement which contrasts with Verdi's esteem for Romani, as revealed in his letters; see in particular a letter addressed to him from Venice on 28 March 1845, including several suggestions on the

interpretation of *Giovanna d'Arco*, which Romani was at that time rehearsing for the first performance at the Pergola (autograph: The Treccani degli Alfieri collection, Milan; photostat copy in the archives of the Istituto di studi verdiani, Parma).

3. *Un bischero* = violin peg, simpleton, ninny (Translator's note).

4. On November 1848 Verdi writes from Paris to Cammarono, who was preparing *Macbeth* for the San Carlo opera at Naples:

> *Point out that the two most important numbers in the opera are the duet between Lady Macbeth and her husband, and the sleepwalking scene. If these do not succeed, the opera will fail. And these two numbers must not be sung: they must be acted, declaimed with a hollow, veiled voice – else the effect will be nil.*

5. On 11 March 1865 Verdi writes to Escudier on the eve of the first performance of the revised version of *Macbeth* at the Théâtre Lyrique in Paris:

> *And now for the sleepwalking scene – the most important scene of the opera. Anyone who has seen Ristori knows that it must be performed with a minimum of gesture, or rather with one single gesture: that of erasing a blood-stain she imagines to be on her hand. Each movement must be slow, and each step should be invisible: her feet must steal over the ground, as if she were a statue or a ghost. Her eyes should be glazed, her appearance corpse-like; she is on the point of death and will die immediately after. Ristori emitted a rattle – a death rattle. This should not and cannot be done in music; just as there should be no cough in the last act of* La traviata, *and no laughter in the* scherzo od e follia *in* Un ballo in maschera. *In the sleepwalking scene a lament from the cor anglais is an excellent substitute for a death-rattle, and more poetic. The scene needs to be sung with the utmost simplicity and a* hollow voice *(she is dying), but the voice should on no account sound as though it came from the stomach. There are a few moments where the voice may open out, but these must be the briefest of flashes and are marked in the score. In short: to achieve the effect and terror that this number must arouse,* "a corpse-like appearance, a minimum of gesture, slow movements, a hollow voice", *expression etc. etc. are indispensable* (autograph: Folger Library, Washington).

6. In fact the sleepwalking scene was amongst the most warmly applauded numbers of the première and contributed substantially to the outcome of the evening which, after the success of the first two acts, seemed to be jeopardized by the cold reception of the third and part of the fourth (cf. M. CONATI: "Aspetti della messinscena del *Macbeth* di Verdi", in *Il melodramma romantico in Italia*, Atti del Convegno Internazionale di Studio organizzato dalla Fondazione G. Cini, to be published shortly; see also *Macbeth's Sourcebook*, ed. by D. Rosen, Norton, New York, to be published shortly).

V

GIUSEPPE VERDI

1855

MARC MONNIER: "Giuseppe Verdi", in *Bibliothèque Universelle de Genève*, IV series, vol. XXXII, June 1856, pp. 209–24 (partially reproduced in *La France Musicale*, Paris, XX, 45: 9 November 1856, p. 357–60; cf. also "Il Maestro Verdi", summary of Monnier's article, in *Gazzetta dei Teatri*, Milan, XIX, 44: 15 August 1856, p. 176).

VERDI'S FRIENDSHIP WITH Marc Monnier has on the whole escaped the notice of Verdi scholars – but not Luzio,[1] who even recalls the enquiry conducted by Monnier into brigandage in Naples and the South of Italy at the end of the 1850s, and quotes (referring to Perinello's volume)[2] the *Bibliothèque Universelle* article, although he did not have access to it. Monnier's name appears in the Verdi–De Sanctis correspondence, following the complex events connected with *Un ballo in maschera* (the performance of which had been prohibited by the Bourbon censors), which resulted in the opera being withdrawn and Verdi returning to Sant'Agata. In a long letter, dated 31 May 1858, Cesarino De Sanctis reminds Verdi of his sad departure from Naples on board the steamer *Pompei*, as he passed in front of all the friends who had gathered at the port to bid farewell to the composer: Baron Genovese, the cartoonist Melchiorre Delfico, the poet Emmanuele Bardare and others; some accompanied Verdi on to the ship, others, including Monnier, who "read on shore the *addio*" by the poet Nicola Sole,[3] remained on dry land. On 17 June 1858 Verdi, at Sant'Agata, instructs Cesarino to greet his Neapolitan friends, Monnier included.[4] A year later, on 15 October 1859 (the previous summer Verdi and Giuseppina had travelled clandestinely to Collonges in Savoy, not far from Geneva, to contract their religious marriage, and had paid a flying visit to Paris), it is Giuseppina who charges De Sanctis to convey their greetings to Monnier:

> *Remember us to your family and to all our friends. And I must, or rather it gives me pleasure to mention Marc Monnier, whom we saw in Paris.*

*Send him our warmest greetings, if he is in Naples. Apart from his talent
and vivacity, there is an honesty and politeness about him that pleases me
greatly.* [5]

If the name of Marc Monnier is virtually unheard of by Verdi
scholars, it is well-known to scholars of the Italian Risorgimento. Among the foreign witnesses of the political unification of
Italy, "he was one of the few to seek an explanation to the
extraordinary events in the quality of recent Italian cultural achievement, and in the politics and morality of those forces involved in
unification". [6]

Born in Florence in 1829 of a French father and Swiss mother, he
studied there, became a teacher at the Istituto Superiore and travelled
widely through the Italian States, France and Switzerland; in 1864 he
took up a teaching post in Geneva and died there in 1885. He pursued
a lively campaign in the cause of Italian unification, and openly
supported Cavour's solution. The article on Verdi and the subsequent one on Leopardi, which also appeared in the Geneva magazine
in 1856, are his first important contributions to the dissemination of
modern Italian culture in Europe. An active witness of the second
war of independence and the exploits of Garibaldi's Thousand, he
had already published in 1860 in Paris *L'Italie est-elle la terre des morts?*,
his most famous book and an impassioned defence of modern Italy.
In 1861 appeared *Garibaldi: Histoire de la conquête des deux Siciles*, in
1862 a study of *Le royaume de Naples en 1861*, and *Histoire du
brigandage dans l'Italie méridionale*, another important volume, and in
1863 *La camorra: mystères de Naples* – all published in Paris. [7]

From his long article on Verdi (a sort of biographical profile) we
reproduce the final section, containing the impressions of his two
meetings with the composer in Paris in 1855. Monnier mentions
Verdi's illness in Venice during the winter of 1846 while he was
composing *Attila* – an illness which caused grave concern for the
composer's life. [8] He also mentions Pier-Agnolo Fiorentino (Naples
1808 – Paris 1864), critic and journalist, whose articles on music for
Le Constitutionnel he usually signed with his own name, while using a
pseudonym "A. De Rovray" to sign those he published simultaneously in another important Parisian review, *Le Moniteur
Universel*. Barbiera wrote of him: "He never penned eulogies unless
he was well-paid, in advance." [9] And the tenor Gilbert Duprez recounts
in his *Souvenirs d'un chanteur* the following episode about Fiorentino
at a performance of *Jérusalem* in Paris on 26 November 1847:

This opera, the last of my theatrical career and the first appearance of Verdi himself on the French stage, unleashed a bitter war, waged on me in every possible form and under every possible pretext by M. Fiorentino, a music critic of two important news-papers in the capital. M. Fiorentino did not like Verdi, whom he had always criticized unjustly and unrestrainedly; at one of the rehearsals of *Jérusalem*, however, he took it upon himself to address the Maestro and shake his hand. The future composer of *Aida*, whose dominant characteristic has always been pride, refrained from replying and turned his back. Fiorentino wreaked his revenge: the opera, the composer, the principal singers were abused in all his articles. Fortunately for us, the audience was of a different mind and our success was only interrupted by the February revolution.[10]

The première of *I vespri siciliani* took place at the Opéra (L'Académie Impériale de Musique) on the evening of 13 June 1855: the two encounters with Monnier therefore occurred in the second half of that year. Verdi and Giuseppina had moved to Paris by the second half of October 1853 and remained there, apart from short holidays at Mandres and Enghien-les-Bains, till midway through December 1855 – in effect for more than two years. It was the composer's longest stay in the French capital.

Giuseppe Verdi

[. . .] Is there any point in stating that Verdi was an artist in his actions as well as his creative works? The answer must be yes, for it is never unprofitable to reveal a great soul. Verdi, the musician, is also capable of love – and his friends adore him. His librettist Piave tended him during his long illness with more than mere fraternal devotion. Verdi is as modest as he is proud – these two great virtues go together, as do vanity and servility, their opposing vices. Do you recall La Bruyère's courtiers who agree to be submissive in one quarter in order to wield power elsewhere? Or those characters described by Voltaire, who

> Vont en poste à Versailles essuyer des mépris
> Qu'ils reviennent soudain rendre en poste à Paris.[11]

But Verdi is neither pretentious nor obsequious. He never goes out of his way to win a friend or brush aside an enemy: he makes this abundantly clear in a letter.[12] The Neapolitan Pier-Agnolo Fiorentino, wishing to make a quip at the expense of the composer of *Il trovatore*, once declared: "Even Meyerbeer comes to me of his own accord to recommend his works, but Verdi had not deigned to address me a single word."

If therefore, our Maestro is an Officer of the Legion of Honour and a Knight of Saints Maurice and Lazare, he owes it to his talent and never parades his knighthood. When I went to pay him my respects in Paris after a performance of *I vespri siciliani*, I found him in a modest room at the Hôtel Violet, well-known to commercial travellers. I saw a tall, slender man with a grizzled beard, a haggard face that seemed afflicted by suffering and work, a dark or nut-brown complexion, clear wandering, blue eyes, lips that never smiled and a demeanour at once nonchalant and resolute. He spoke to me, in a North Italian accent, of drama and poetry for more than an hour in his room, and for another half hour at the door, as if I were a celebrity and he a nonentity. I left full of thoughts.

I saw him again one evening at the Théâtre Italien, at a performance of *Otello* [Rossini's] during the interval, but not in the centre of the foyer where celebrities are wont to stand, surrounded by a galaxy of admirers who in turn are flanked by their own satellites; instead he stood to one side, engrossed in his own thoughts. I spoke to him of Rossini, he replied by discussing Shakespeare. He never misses a performance of *Il barbiere* or similar masterpieces.

Should some readers be disconcerted by the little room at the Hôtel Violet, I should inform them that, on the death of Cammarono, Verdi gave the librettist's widow 400 ducats (more than 1600 francs), to settle her husband's debts.

MARC MONNIER

NOTES

1. A. Luzio: *Carteggi Verdiani*, vols. 1 and 2, Reale Accademia d'Italia, Rome 1935; see vol. 1, pp. VIII and 48.
2. C. Perinello: "Giuseppe Verdi", *Harmonie*, Berlin 1900, p. 112.
3. A. Luzio, *op. cit.*, vol. 1, p. 46.
4. A. Luzio, *op. cit.*, vol. 1, p. 48.
5. Autograph: Accademia Nazionale dei Lincei, Rome.
6. F. Venturi: "L'Italia fuori d'Italia", in *Storia d'Italia*, Einaudi, vol. 3, Turin 1973, p. 1421.
7. S. Baridon: *Marc Monnier e l'Italia*, Paravia, Turin 1942.

8. *I shall never forget the care you lavished on me with more than merely fraternal love at the time of my illness* Verdi had written to Piave on 27 August 1846 (autograph: Biblioteca dei Concordi, Rovigo; published by J. ZENNARI in *La Cultura Musicale*, Bologna, II, 1923, pp. 83–86). Verdi's illness was so serious that the *Allgemeine musikalische Zeitung* announced his death . . . (see M. CONATI, *Saggio di Cronache* [. . .], cit. pp. 36–7).

9. R. BARBIERA: *Ideali e caratteri dell' Ottocento*, Garzanti, Milan 1940, p. 288.

10. G. DUPREZ: *Souvenirs d'un chanteur*, Calmann Lévy, Paris 1880, p. 175.

11. A pun is intended here. "Aller en poste" has two meanings: "to take up one's duty as a courtier . . . to be seen by the King" and "to travel by the cheapest possible method of transport".

12. From Mandres on 26 May 1854, Verdi had written to his friend De Sanctis:

> *Have no fear! I shall take things as they come here [in France] and very calmly. I know the country and am aware of what might happen, but I shall not lift a finger either to procure a friend or to rid myself of an enemy. I have never done so, not even when I needed employment or money; do you imagine I could do so now!!* (The Roman type is ours; autograph: Accademia Nazionale dei Lincei, Rome.)

Monnier clearly knew this letter that De Sanctis must have shown him.

VI

MAESTRO VERDI
AND THE IMPRESARIO JACOVACCI

1859

GIUSEPPE CENCETTI: "Il maestro Verdi e l'impresario Jacovacci", in *Omnibus*, Naples, March 1859; republished in "Teatri Arti e Letteratura", Bologna, XXXVII, vol. 71, n. 1788: 7 April 1859, pp. 25–26.

IT IS THE eve of Verdi's departure from Rome: 11 March 1859.[1] On February 17 at the Teatro di Apollo there had been a most successful première of *Un ballo in maschera*, which the Neapolitan censors had refused to accept in the version entitled *Una vendetta in domino*; but the astute impresario Vincenzo Jacovacci, steering a clever course between the papal censorship and the composer's demands, managed to bring *Un ballo* to Rome. And now the performances, despite difficulties caused by the indisposition of first the baritone Leone Giraldoni and then the tenor Gaetano Fraschini, were being received with increasing enthusiasm.

We are in the composer's apartment, "a most ugly house" in Via di Campo Marzio 2, rented for him by his friend Vincenzo Luccardi.[2] Besides Giuseppe Cencetti, the author of the article, Verdi and his wife's guests at the farewell dinner-party included Emilio Angelini, Vincenzo Luccardi and Vincenzo Jacovacci. Cencetti was what we would today call a producer at theatres in Rome and also a journalist. Emilio Angelini (Tivoli 1804 – Rome 1879), highly esteemed by Verdi, was first violinist and conductor at the Teatro di Apollo from 1840 to 1867. The sculptor Vincenzo Luccardi (Gemona 1811 – Genazzano, Rome 1876), settled in Rome in 1832 and was the composer's dearest and most loyal friend in that city, where he first met him in 1844, at the time of *I due Foscari*; Verdi often turned to him for information about singers and news about the arts, and used him as an intermediary in his most delicate dealings with Jacovacci. He is the "dear madman" of so many Verdi letters: "Dear Madman, twice madman" of 8 November 1845; "My dear Madman, or rather King of all madmen" of 5 April 1847; "My adorable Madman!

Permit me to use these words without offending you, because you are indeed a little mad! Ah, ah, ah . . ." of 22 December 1853. . . .

And so to Vincenzo Jacovacci (Rome 1810 – Rome 1881), the greatly admired "Sor Cencio", one of the most important impresarios of the past century. His father had steered him towards philosophy, but he broke off his studies to devote himself to commerce; he then speculated in the theatre business, competed against the awe-inspiring and powerful Lanari, and managed in a few years to become impresario at the Apollo. He also made his mark at the Argentina for several years and at the prestigious Senigallia Fair; and before he died he also supervised the opening of the Teatro Costanzi, today the Teatro dell' Opera. But his name is most closely connected with the history of the Apollo, Rome's greatest theatre of the nineteenth century. He had seven children "who all died a premature death, except one girl, the little Giuseppina who at her baptism had been held by the wife of the celebrated Verdi", as Francesco Regli informs us in his *Dizionario biografico*, published a year after the present article. Regli continues:

> The chief qualities that made Vincenzo Jacovacci the perfect impresario were almost incomparable energy and speed, combined with a profound speculative spirit which had been refined, as it were, by long experience. His theatrical business supplied all the equipment which was traditionally let out on contract, such as lighting, stage-machinery, wardrobe, and he supervised each department. With indescribable care and precision he carried out everything himself, so that he was everywhere at once and seemed to divide and multiply himself – in short to be several persons in one. [. . .] Few could predict the future like Vincenzo Jacovacci, and he could improvise like none other.[3]

As De Angelis makes clear, however, he was greedy for money

> with which he was in no way inclined to part, and although he wished to provide for good performances, these could only be commensurate with the very limited assets at his disposal. Exceptional concessions were only granted by the Pope, and Jacovacci – flatterer and courtier – resorted to a great variety of expedients to obtain them. One of the most common was to arrange for twenty or so ballerinas to sing hymns of praises to the Pontiff as he crossed Sant' Angelo bridge in his carriage. The

Pope, who was not insensible to these displays, would smile and bless the beautiful girls, and the following day "Sor Cencio's" request for a special subsidy of ten thousand crowns was accepted.

Moreover he was "very fond of indulging his particular taste for dances. A true Roman, he would have wanted them all based on events in Roman history [. . .]".[4] If, as Cametti affirms, Jacovacci had a special predilection for grand choreographic performances, "he had a veritable passion for the operas of Giuseppe Verdi which was shared by the Roman press and public, who defended the Maestro with sincere conviction in the first years of his career from the attacks and snipings of the Neapolitan press."[5]

Verdi liked this unusual impresario, although he later complained of his stinginess. Four days before the meeting related in this article, on March 7, the composer had written to Cesarino De Sanctis about a possible partnership between the impresarios Jacovacci and Vincenzo Torelli of Naples:

This Torelli–Jacovacci business could be excellent, if everything is spelt out in black and white. These two do not lack talent or vision. Jacovacci is sharp, diligent, and if he were less stingy would be a fine impresario.[6]

And several years later, on 13 September 1872, he writes to Torelli:

[. . .] I've been familiar for some time now with Jacovacci's habitual "I have the finest company in the world". It is nothing but an empty phrase, I tell you. When Il trovatore *was produced (and again Jacovacci uttered his phrase), I could only obtain two good singers, the poorest of choruses, a bad orchestra, and most shabby sets and costumes. When* Un ballo *was produced (again he uttered his habitual phrase), only the men were good, the rest resembled the cast for* Il trovatore. *In spite of the success, I simply had to tell him after the third performance: "Look, you brute of an impresario, if I had had a fine company, think what success we would have had!" And do you know what he replied? "Come, come, what more do you want! The theatre is packed each evening. Next year I shall find good women – in that way the opera will be new again to the audience. One half this year: the other half later! . . ." You can well understand that this shopkeeper's reply could not satisfy an artist.*[7]

In Cencetti's article a phrase of Verdi's recurs like an incessant

Verdi at the time of his meeting with Escudier
(lithograph after a drawing by Balestra)

Verdi's hand sculpted in marble by Giovanni Dupré

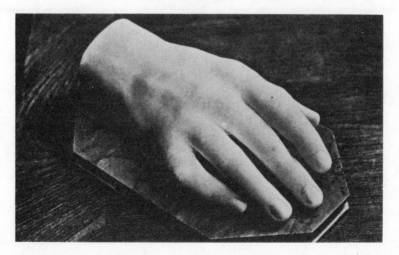

The soprano Marianna Barbieri Nini, the first Lady Macbeth

Below left: The baritone Felice Varesi, the first Macbeth
Below right: The poet Andrea Maffei, a friend of Verdi
and librettist of *I masnadieri*

Verdi photographed in Paris by Disderi (*c.* 1855–57)

Léon
Escudier

The impresario
Vincenzo Jacovacci

Verdi at the time of *Un ballo in maschera*

Verdi in Madrid for the production of *La forza del destino* (1863), a few months before the episode with the orchestra of the Paris Opéra

The writer and journalist Antonio Ghislanzoni, one-time baritone, author of the verse libretto of *Aida*, portrayed in his last years

Verdi photographed in Paris by Nadar

Adelina Patti lays a blessing on Verdi

refrain: *but I no longer compose.* It is the reply Verdi makes to Jacovacci's offers. It is also an explicit statement, more serious than the mere anecdote which the author would like it to be. This statement of the composer's marks the end of a long period of activity, now known as his "galley years": sixteen years, from *Nabucco* to *Un ballo in maschera*, during which time Verdi had been continually bound to new contracts and constantly worried by having to honour them. On 12 May 1858, having returned from Naples where the censors had failed to accept *Un ballo in maschera*, the composer wrote to his friend Clarina Maffei from Sant' Agata:

> *Here I am, and after the turmoil of Naples this profound tranquillity is ever dearer to me. It is impossible to find an uglier place than this, but on the other hand it is impossible for me to find a place where I could live with greater freedom; and then there is this silence which gives time for reflection, and it is so wonderful never to see official dress of any description! . . . From* Nabucco *on I have never enjoyed an hour of peace. Sixteen years in the galley!*[8]

And so the Verdi who here faces Jacovacci is a Verdi finally free from every sort of obligation, who has no intention whatever of committing himself to any in the future, and who at least for the moment believes that he has reached the end of his career. He will compose again, but no longer at the rate of an opera per year. And in practice he will compose only for abroad: *La forza del destino* for Petersburg, *Don Carlos* for Paris, *Aida* for Cairo. Three operas in all, excluding the new version of *Macbeth*. After *Aida* Verdi will indeed consider his operatic career closed. And yet . . .

Maestro Verdi and the impresario Jacovacci

The morning before the day fixed for his departure from Rome, Verdi graciously invited to dinner the impresario Vincenzo Jacovacci, who gladly appeared at the appointed hour at Verdi's house, believing perhaps that such a show of kindness augured well for the future of his theatrical plans. The only people Jacovacci found present at the illustrious Maestro's farewell banquet were, apart from the latter's dear spouse, the conductor Emilio Angelini, that fine sculptor Vincenzo Lucardi [sic] (an intimate friend of Verdi's) and the undersigned producer. We spent part of the dinner very happily discussing the dearth of good singing-actors, the difficulty of finding libretti with impact and dramatic situations, despite the abundance of fine poets in Italy. Contrary to his custom Jacovacci did not speak and contributed only monosyllabically to the discussion; he seemed to be quite engrossed in the victuals when suddenly he put down his fork and stared with his crystal eyes at his distinguished host who sat opposite, and exclaimed: *Maestro, I shall send you as many blank contracts as you need to form a good company of singers and you shall engage the artists you prefer for any new opera you compose.* This unexpected apostrophe was followed by a prolonged exclamation of *splendid,* which issued simultaneously from the lips of the three other guests and was soon repeated by Verdi himself, who added: *The scheme is splendid and does you honour, but . . . but I no longer compose. – But Maestro,* came Jacovacci's unflustered reply, *these are cruel words for the audiences of our theatres who so yearn for and applaud your music. – I am most grateful to them, but I no longer compose. – But Maestro, this is a terrible thing for us poor impresarios who won't know which way to turn to . . . – Make money,* the other guests interrupted in chorus. *– I am sorry,* replied Verdi, *but I no longer compose. – Take care that I don't have this barbaric decision of yours printed in the press,* added the impresario, casting me a meaningful glance. *– Go ahead, Cencetti,* replied the Maestro, who had noticed Jacovacci's glance: *but I no longer compose. – This is most distressing! . . .* Jacovacci murmured and sighed; but he soon recovered his good humour and was not the least witty of the small gathering, so that the dinner ended as happily as it had begun. Taking leave of the illustrious composer, Jacovacci shook his hand with warmth and respect, saying: *I wish you a long and happy life, and I shall pray that the balmy air of Busseto's fields might soothe your mind, relieving it of a melancholy which, if not prejudicial to your fame (since that is now immortal) is inflicting serious damage on opera-houses and . . . – There is no point in proceeding, since I . . . – No longer compose! I've understood perfectly! Yet since*

> Wise men change
> their thoughts when changing house

I beg you to remember the need for my project. ★ *– And with these words*

★ Others have already suggested this project to Verdi: his reply has always been the same – *I no longer compose.* Whereupon he was answered that the artist bears within him an indomitable will to work, to create, to progress, and that the ardent soul of a genius, though at times depressed, cannot vegetate for long. – (*L' O[mnibus]*) the zealous impresario, bowing deeply, walked to the door. As he brushed past me, I whispered in his ear: *Don't lose heart, true genius is inexhaustible and cannot resist the call of inspiration. − I know, I know,* Jacovacci grinned, *when I speak, there's always a reason!* And rubbing his hands like a satisfied man, he took his leave of the celebrated Maestro.

GIUSEPPE CENCETTI

NOTES

1. Verdi left Rome on Saturday 12 March 1859, as his letter of March 7 to Cesarino De Sanctis makes clear (in A. LUZIO, *op. cit.*, vol. 1, p. 55).
2. On February 4 Giuseppina Verdi had written to De Sanctis:

   For your information, we are living in Via di Campo Marzio n.2. *The house is very nasty, but as Luccardi has booked it for the whole Carnival we've had to stay here* (in A. LUZIO, *op. cit.*, vol. 1, p. 52).
3. F. REGLI: *Dizionario biografico dei piú celebri Poeti ed Artisti Melodrammatici* [. . .] *che fiorirono in Italia dal 1800 al 1860*, Enrico Dalmazzo, Turin 1860, pp. 265−6.
4. A. DE ANGELIS: *La musica a Roma nel secolo XIX*, 2nd ed., G. Bardi, Rome 1944, pp. 142 and 163.
5. A. CAMETTI: *Il teatro di Tordinona poi di Apollo*, Tivoli 1918, vol. I, pp. 251−2.
6. A. LUZIO, *op. cit.*, vol. I, pp. 55−56.
7. Autograph: Biblioteca Lucchesi-Palli, Naples.
8. Autograph: Biblioteca Nazionale Braidense, Milan.

VII

THE ORCHESTRA OF THE OPÉRA

1863

LÉON ESCUDIER: "L'orchestre d l'Opéra", in *L'Art Musical*, Paris III, 30: 23 July 1863, pp. 271–2.

PIERRE DIETSCH (Dijon 1808 – Paris 1865), the protagonist of this episode narrated by Escudier (of which Caponi gives a slightly different version in his notes to Pougin's biography of Verdi),[1] was singer, organist, double-bass player, composer, chorus-master at the Opéra on the recommendation of Rossini and then conductor in 1860. It can safely be said that he owed his posthumous fame to two skirmishes with two giants of the calibre of Wagner and Verdi. A previous incident with Wagner had occurred in 1843 when Dietsch had composed for the Opéra *Le Vaisseau fantôme ou Le Maudit des mers* to a text on the same theme that Wagner had submitted to Pillet, Director of the Opéra, for a future opera. On this occasion Pillet paid off Wagner by giving him, from his own pocket, five gold napoleons. A second incident, which caused a greater stir than the first, occurred when Dietsch conducted the famous Paris première of *Tannhäuser* (13 March 1861) after the Opéra had not allowed Wagner to conduct the rehearsals and the first performances himself. Dietsch's conducting, according to contemporary accounts, was disastrous: "his poor technique and lack of commitment provoked continual incidents".[2] Gounod recounts:

> I saw Wagner writhe like a raging lion in the Director's box at the Opéra during the performance of *Tannhäuser*, ready to leap at any moment into the orchestra and seize the bâton from the conductor who was performing the opera in a manner quite contrary to the composer's intentions.[3]

According to von Bülow, who lavishes insults and bitter criticism on Dietsch, Wagner had described him as an "orchestral castrato".[4]

Two years later, during rehearsals for the revival of *I vespri siciliani* (16 July 1863, a Thursday, two days before the first performance)

Dietsch had the misfortune of confronting Verdi, a much more formidable opponent for the incompetent conductor . . . After the incident between the Italian composer and the orchestra, described by Escudier in his article, Dietsch was officially dismissed. He was replaced by Georges Hainl, destined to conduct the première of *Don Carlos* in 1867. The incident created a great stir in the European press; Dietsch was defended, at least initially, in France and Germany, where journalists blamed the proud and arrogant character of the Italian composer;[5] but then the good results achieved by Hainl and the improvement in the playing and discipline of the Opéra's orchestra under his bâton confirmed Dietsch's ineptitude. Verdi did not forget the incident quickly – indeed two years later he refused to go to Paris to stage the new version of *Macbeth* at the Théâtre Lyrique; his ill-feeling towards the "grande boutique" as he called the Opéra, and the general ambience of Parisian theatres, lasted a long time. On 19 June 1865, in reply to an offer that he should compose a work for the Opéra (which he finally accepted, *Don Carlos* being the work in question) he wrote to Léon Escudier: "Is this some joke?! Write for the Opéra!!! Do you think I detect no danger in such an undertaking after all that happened two years ago at the rehearsals of *Les vêpres?*"[6]

The orchestra of the Opéra

What has just happened at the Opéra is perhaps unique in the history of this theatre. For three and a half months M. Verdi conducted the rehearsals of his work with admirable enthusiasm and calm. The artists, the sub-conductors, the management, all those who were in a position to see with what goodwill and devotion he instructed his singers, pay great tribute to his noble character and dignity. But the orchestra of the Opéra, or rather one part of the orchestra, contrived without provocation to insult the Maestro. Last Thursday Verdi had deemed it necessary to have a run-through of the opera; hitherto there had only been two orchestral rehearsals which to us, incidentally, seems far from excessive. During the first number the Maestro thought he noticed a little ill-will among the strings; very politely he remarked on this, but they took no notice. They then exaggerated the nuances that Verdi had called for to such an extent that the players' intention could no longer be in doubt. The Maestro approached one of these gentlemen and remarked, without the slightest bitterness, that he could not understand what had caused the orchestra's ill-will. The reply was very odd:

"This rehearsal is a waste of time; we could have done without it."

"But," Verdi added, "if I asked for it, it was because I thought it was necessary."

"Each of us, you see," said the artist in question, "has other business to attend to."

"Ah! You have other business to attend to! I thought," replied the Maestro, "that your business was here; it seems that I was mistaken. . . ."

Whereupon Verdi summoned the conductor, M. Dietsch, and expressed his amazement at the behaviour of his musicians. "After such a demonstration, which I consider most unseemly, I have nothing else to do here. I shall leave." Verdi then picked up his hat and left. He has never since reappeared at the Opéra. He attended neither the dress-rehearsal nor the first performance of Les vêpres siciliennes.

Such are the facts.

On several occasions since the appointment of M. Perrin,[7] there have been acts of insubordination among the orchestra of the Opéra. If what has just happened remains unpunished, it will be impossible in future to have a conductor. In the interest of composers and audience alike, strong action must be taken – let us hope that there will be no delay.

LÉON ESCUDIER

P.S. These lines had already been written when it was announced to us that, following the decision of His Excellency the Minister of State and of the Emperor's Household, M. Dietsch has been retired and replaced by an artist of proven talent, M. Georges Hainl, conductor of the Théâtre de Lyon.

M. Georges Hainl will assume his duties as conductor at the Opéra from tomorrow; he will conduct the third performance of Les vêpres siciliennes. We believe that this appointment will be greatly welcomed by both artists and public.

LÉON ESCUDIER

NOTES

1. A. POUGIN: Giuseppe Verdi: Vita aneddotica, with notes and additions by Folchetto [Jacopo Caponi], Ricordi, Milan 1881, p. 82, note 2.

2. E. HARASZTI, under *Dietsch* in *Enciclopedia dello Spettacolo*.
3. *Autobiographie de Charles Gounod* [. . .] (not strictly speaking an autobiography, but a collection of articles), London [1875], p. 101.
4. E. HARASTZI, *art. cit.*
5. Cf. for example, *Revue et Gazette Musicale de Paris*, XXX, 30: 26 July 1863, pp. 237–8, and *Niederrheinische Musik-Zeitung*, Cologne, XI, 32: 8 August 1863, p. 256. This latter magazine, however, in an article on the Paris Opéra that appeared soon after, confirmed the extent to which the Paris theatre neglected its rehearsals – so that Verdi's loathing seems justified.
6. Autograph: Bibliothèque de l'Opéra, Paris.
7. Emile Perrin, Director of the Paris Opéra.

VIII

AN EVENING AT VERDI'S

1866

RALPH: "Une soirée chez Verdi", in *L'Art Musical*, Paris, VII, 12: 22 February 1866, pp. 92–93.

THIS IS NOT an interview nor, properly speaking, an eye-witness account of Verdi's personality. It describes an event that is rather out of keeping with the character of the "bear of Busseto"; the article gives a succinct account of an evening in which part of Paris's colourful cultural society during the Second Empire met at Verdi's house – one of those soirées which Verdi was wont to avoid, but which on this occasion he accepted willingly, imbuing it, however, with a style all his own. The party, at which only a few intimate friends were present, was given in honour of the sculptor Dantan. The cause of the occasion was the unveiling of a bust of Verdi, sculpted by Jean-Pierre Dantan (Paris 1800 – Bade 1869), called Dantan *le jeune* to distinguish him from his brother Antoine-Laurent who was also a sculptor and two years older. The surprise of the evening, however, was supplied by one of Dantan's caricatures, perhaps the best of the many he had made of Verdi. Alberti describes Dantan as "a most clever Parisian", who was on the friendliest terms with the composer Pierre Zimmermann (1785–1853), another Parisian, whose pupils numbered Thomas, Bizet and Franck,

> in whose house composers, singers and musicians of all types and countries would often meet. Dantan began to model several of them with great wit, illustrating his caricatures with epigrammatic verses written on the base. Little by little he managed to assemble a most comic collection which he showed to enthusiasts at his little palace in 41 rue Blanche, and which he gradually tried to complete.[1]

Dantan's sculpted bust of Verdi was installed in the foyer of the Opéra after the first performance of *Don Carlos*.[2]

The date is 14 February 1866. Verdi had been in Paris since the beginning of December 1865; having moved house three times, he settled into an apartment at the end of the year on the Champs-Elysées (no. 67) with his wife Giuseppina. He frequented the theatres, heard Wagner's music for the first time, visited Rossini (after which Giuseppina noted in her diary: "Madame Rossini plus désagréable que d'habitude"). Rossini in turn sent Verdi a note, dated December 27, to accompany a letter from Beauchêne, the secretary of the Conservatoire. It bore the following address: "A M. Verdi/ Célèbre Compositeur de Musique/ Pianiste de la 5me. Classe!!!/ Paris"; and it was signed: "Rossini/ Ex Compositeur de Musique/ Pianiste de la 4me. Classe"[3] – a note which has excited many a biographer's imagination.

How did Verdi come to be in Paris? He himself gives the reason in a letter to Arrivabene, dated 31 December 1865:

[. . .] *I roam throughout Paris, examining attentively the new quarter which is truly beautiful. So many boulevards, so many Avenues, so many gardens etc. etc. A pity that the sun does not shine more frequently! I have been to the Opéra four times!!! I have visited once or twice all the opera houses and was bored in every one.* L'Africaine [whose première had taken place on 28 April 1865, about a year before its composer's death] *is certainly not Meyerbeer's best opera. I have also heard the overture to Wagner's* Tannhäuser. *He is mad!!! You know that I came here to stage* La forza del destino *as soon as possible and then to write a new opera for the end of '66. But there was too much to do with* La forza *and I was unable to complete so much work in the space of a year. We have agreed to give the new opera first:* Don Carlos, *taken from Schiller. Méry is to be the librettist. When everything has been arranged satisfactorily with the poet, I shall return to S. Agata to work in peace and shall be here again at the end of August or the beginning of July.* [. . .][4]

Three days before he had written to Clara Maffei:

I have been here for a month or more, as you know, and I have really not had time to be bored. My activity has been, and remains, considerable. Imagine: I have changed house three times; I have been to the Opéra four times; and I have visited all the opera-houses once or twice . . . to hear Theresa!! *And I have even attended a popular concert to hear a Wagner overture. And so I know a little of everything, and yet know nothing at all.* [. . .] *We shall work on* Don Carlos: *the librettist will*

be Méry. We shall follow Schiller closely and add just enough to create a
spettacolo. By jove! Les machines *of the* Opéra *must be put to some*
use! . . .[5]

François-Joseph Méry (Marseille 1797 – Paris 1866)[6] – who is
already sick in Ralph's article with the illness that in a few months
was to lead him to the grave – was journalist, poet, librettist,
novelist, dramatist; "a polygraph, less famous but as prolific as his
contemporaries A. Dumas and E. Sue", as François Lesure describes
him in the *Enciclopedia dello Spettacolo*, where he quotes a phrase of
Barbey d'Aurevilly: "This versatile soul has always possessed the
facility of genius, even in those days when his genius was in
abeyance". He travelled in Italy which, in homage to its artistic
genius, he defined as "God's Conservatoire", founded several liberal
journals in Marseille and launched satirical attacks on the Restoration
and the July Monarchy. He was a fervent admirer of Rossini and
translated the libretto of *Semiramide*. Amongst his libretti, those
written for David and E. Reyer are particularly worthy of mention.
In drawing up the libretto of *Don Carlos* he had summoned as
collaborator Camille du Locle, who was to finish the work.[7] At that
time Méry was living in Nice where Verdi, a month after the
evening in honour of Dantan, had stopped off on his return to Italy
to visit Méry, as we read in *La France Musicale* (XXX, 12: 25 March
1866, p. 90):

Word reaches us from Nice that Maestro Verdi, accompanied by
his publisher, arrived on Sunday in this town, coming straight
from Paris [. . .] Verdi visited his collaborator Méry, who is at
present unwell in Nice, but whose health happily causes his
numerous friends no serious anxiety.

There now follows the account of that evening in Verdi's house on
14 February 1866, from the pen of a journalist of the *Art Musical*, the
periodical founded in December 1860 by Léon Escudier, Verdi's
publisher in France.

An evening at Verdi's

All the papers have spoken of an intimate little gathering that took
place last Wednesday at Verdi's house in the Champs-Elysées. Those

readers of *L'Art Musical* who will not have read the other papers – they are not forced to – will allow me to describe in a few lines the purpose of this gathering at the home of the Maestro who dreads parties and receptions above all things, infinitely preferring to converse quietly and amicably with a small group of close friends, without being constrained to go to bed at an hour when genuine workers rise.

A fortnight ago the editor of *L'Art Musical* announced this piece of news in a paragraph which rivalled in brevity a telegram:

"The celebrated sculptor Dantan has just completed his bust of Verdi."

Connoisseurs, art-critics and admirers of Verdi pricked up their ears. Some there were who went to knock at the door of the charming Folie-Dantan in rue Blanche and asked to see the serious work of this sculptor who has two strings to his bow, i.e. two instruments in his hand: the boaster for caricatures and the chisel for works of art in marble.

Several days later the quality papers were discussing the bust of Verdi.

La Patrie, for example, reported that

The bust that Dantan has just completed, though only life-size, appears larger than life-size – and a single glance will tell you that it portrays the composer of *Il trovatore*. The resemblance is striking: the enormous, pensive forehead that would have delighted Gall; the strongly accentuated arches over his eyes, the broken, interrupted lines between his eyebrows, furrowed by study, work, struggle and strength of will; the strong nose with prominent nostrils, the bushy beard, the hair arranged or rather thrown back in unsymmetrical locks; and his gaze, which might seem vague and lost, but which is in fact dreaming, when not softened by kindness and animated by inspiration. The very image of Verdi to be seen in the foyer of every Italian theatre . . .

It is perhaps the only work of Dantan which is not popular – at least not yet. It could not be popular today, since it has hardly left the hands of its creator. Tomorrow it will be (*M. de Thémines.*)[8]

The morrow has arrived. The first hour of its popularity sounded in Verdi's own drawing-room where, on Wednesday, the Maestro had assembled a small number of friends, for the most part artists: Mlle Adelina Patti,[9] M. Strakosch,[10] Signor and Signora Fraschini,[11]

Signor and Signora Delle-Sedie,[12] Ronconi[13] and his daughter,
Signora and Signorina Tamberlich and Signor Tamberlich, brother
of the famous tenor,[14] Signora Esther Sezzi, M. du Locle, Méry's
co-librettist for *Don Carlos* that Verdi is at present composing;
M. and Mme. Léon Escudier, M. de Lauzières (M. de Thémines),[15]
the critic from *La Patrie*, and finally Mme Dantan and M. Dantan,
the hero of the party – for it was to unveil the statue and fête the
sculptor that everyone had been assembled at the Maestro's.

Only Méry was absent from this delightful gathering, and he was
clearly much missed. The poet paid the price for his own oratory: he
is immured and muffled up in his own room, since that famous
evening in the Valentino hall when he defended M. Hannibal, a
citizen of Carthage who, according to Maestro Frédéric Thomas,
had never been to Rome. That's what comes of dealing with people
who do not go to Rome!

But Méry was able to dominate the whole evening by his very
absence: the bust was displayed on the mantelpiece of the drawing-
room and M. Léon Escudier requested a moment of silence, very
easy to obtain, and read a letter from the poet. Méry sometimes
writes his letters in prose . . . when he has a cold. The letter
explained the reason for his absence and was accompanied by a piece
of verse that is now familiar to everyone [. . .].

It was Léon Escudier who read these beautiful verses[16] to the
applause of his audience. [. . .]

But a new surprise awaited us. Dantan unveiled one of his wittiest
caricatures. It portrayed Verdi, the composer of *La forza del destino*,
as half man and half lion, composing at the piano. However exaggerated the lines on his face might be, the resemblance is striking . . .
May Verdi pardon me! The composer's hair ends in a lion's mane
which envelops his torso with its luxuriance; the lion's tail, twisted
like a snake, strikes the piano keys with its tip. A powerful composition! . . .

Opera scores are strewn around the piano. On one of them is
written: "*Il trouve à tort*", a free rendering of the Italian title of Verdi's
masterpiece [*Il trovatore*] that Dantan wrote in ironic contrast to the
inscription on the plinth which states that "*trouver*" est son
"triomphe".[17]

Here is the witty quatrain engraved on the plinth:

> Il a des fiers lions la griffe et la crinière;
> *Trouver* est son triomphe, à ce maître hardi;

Il suit à travers *champs* un chemin sans ornière,
L'art fleurira toujours tant qu'il aura *Verdi*.

I leave you to imagine the enthusiasm and laughter that broke out.
[. . .] You probably imagine that with artists such as Adelina
Patti, Fraschini, Ronconi, Delle-Sedie and Strakosch – not to mention Verdi himself, who is the obvious accompanist in his own home
– we performed music? But no! The Maestro did not give his
consent. We should have had the good taste to choose his own
music, but he does not like performances of his music in his own
home. We wreak our revenge by playing it everywhere else.

I thus witnessed, for the first time in my life, a most strange
situation: great artists determined to sing, and the master of the
house preventing them.

Quite the contrary to standard practice![18]

RALPH

NOTES

1. *Verdi intimo*, p. 68 (note).
2. A. POUGIN, *op. cit.*, p. 94. But Pougin is wrong to assign Dantan's statue to the year 1867 (see p. 95) instead of 1866.
3. G. CARRARA VERDI: "Le lettere di Rossini a Verdi", in *Biblioteca 70*, Busseto, III, 1973, p. 15.
4. *Verdi intimo*, p. 61.
5. Autograph: Biblioteca Nazionale Braidense, Milan.
6. And not 1865, as stated in some dictionaries of music and in the *Enciclopedia dello Spettacolo*.
7. Camille Du Locle (Orange 1832 – Capri 1903), son-in-law of Emile Perrin, Director of the Opéra, and himself secretary of the great Parisian theatre, where in 1869 he was appointed assistant director. From 1870 to 1876 he was Director of the Opéra-Comique and commissioned, amongst other works, Bizet's *Carmen*. He wrote his first libretto in 1856 for an operetta by J. Duprato; apart from *Don Carlos* (on which he collaborated with Méry) his most important libretti include *Sigurd* and *Salammbô* for Ernest Reyer. He translated into French the libretto of *Simon Boccanegra* and the first two acts of *Otello*. His name is above all connected with *Aida*. He was the driving force behind the campaign which finally led to the choice of Verdi, from a list of composers which included Gounod and Wagner, to compose a new opera to be performed in Cairo on a subject suggested by Auguste Mariette. At Sant'Agata with Verdi in June 1870 he fashioned in less than a week (and not in three weeks, as several biographers maintain; cf. G. CARRARA VERDI: "Preliminari di *Aida*", in *Biblioteca 70*, Busseto,

II, 1971, p. 14) a scenario with prose dialogue from Mariette's synopsis. He then complained when he saw his own name disappear from the definitive wording of the libretto, of which he considered himself the author. Ursula Günther "Zur Entstehung von Verdi's *Aida*", in *Studi Musicali*, II, I, 1973, pp. 15–71) inclines to support Du Locle. But notwithstanding the latter's indisputable merit in conducting the entire operation between Verdi and the Egyptians, the fact remains that the true author of the libretto of *Aida* is Verdi himself, with Ghislanzoni virtually confining himself to the versification (cf. A. LUZIO: *Carteggi verdiani*, cit., vol. III in the chapter "Come fu composta l'*Aida*", pp. 5–27). Moreover, Verdi is most explicit in a letter to Giulio Ricordi, dated 25 June 1870:

> [. . .] *Du Locle came here at once, I expounded the terms, we studied the synopsis together and made the modifications we deemed necessary. Du Locle left with the terms and the modifications in order to submit them to the powerful and unknown author. I studied the synopsis once more and I made, and am still making, further changes. – We must now think of the libretto, or rather of versifying it, for all we need now are the verses. Can Ghislanzoni do this work for me, and would he wish to? . . . Explain to him clearly that it is not a question of producing an original work, but merely to put this into verse* [. . .] (autograph: Archivio della Casa Ricordi, Milan).

Twenty days later, on July 15, Verdi informs Du Locle:

> [. . .] *Giulio Ricordi was here with the poet who will versify Aida. We agreed on everything and I hope to receive Act I soon, so that I can start work. We have made some alterations to the Act III duet between Aida and Radames* [. . .] (autograph: Bibliothèque de l'Opéra, Paris).

8. The other name of the Neapolitan journalist of French origin, Achille de Lauzières, quoted in a later chapter.
9. Adelina Patti (Madrid 1843 – Brecknock, Wales, 1919), the most popular and sought-after singer of the age. Verdi respected her more than any other singer, Malibran included. On 5 November 1877 (not October, as the autograph letter erroneously states), Verdi writes to Giulio Ricordi following the triumph of *La traviata* at La Scala on November 3:

> *A success, then . . . a great success . . . It was bound to be! You heard her ten years ago, and now you exclaim: 'How she has changed'. But you are mistaken! Patti was then the same as she is now: a perfect blend of singer and actress . . . a born artist in every sense of the word. When I heard her for the first time (she was 18) in London* [in 1862], *I was astounded not only by her marvellous performance but by several coups de scène which revealed a great actress. I recall her chaste and modest bearing when in La sonnambula*

she lay on the soldier's bed, and how in Don Giovanni *she left the libertine's room, defiled. I recall a certain gesture of hers during Don Bartolo's aria in* Il barbiere, *and most of all I recall her in the recitative which precedes the quartet in* Rigoletto, *when her father points out her lover in the tavern and says "And you still love him?", and she replies "I love him". Words cannot express the sublime effect of these words, when sung by her. – She was capable of such things, and more, over ten years ago. But at that time there were many who did not agree. [. . .] When you see Patti, give her fond greetings from my wife and me. I shall not send her the customary congratulations, because it really seems to me that, for Patti, it would be the most pointless thing in the world. And anyway, she knows, and knows very well, that I did not wait for her Milan success, but that from the very first time I heard her in London (she was almost a girl), I considered her a remarkable singer and actress, something exceptional in our art. [. . .]*
(autograph: Archivio della Casa Ricordi, Milan).

10. Maurice Strakosch (Gross-Scelowitz, Moravia, 1825 – Paris 1887), pianist, singer, singing-teacher, composer and impresario; he was Patti's brother-in-law, having married her sister Amalia, who was also a singer. He arranged Adelina's début, when she was still a girl, at New York, presenting her as a child prodigy; he then presided over her studies, persuading her to retire from the stage for several years to concentrate on fully developing her voice, and managed her in the early years of her career. In 1868, after Adelina's marriage to the Marquis of Caux, he had no further dealings with her.

11. The tenor Gaetano Fraschini (Pavia 1816 – Naples 1887), perhaps the most Verdian tenor of the nineteenth century. He sang in the first performance of *Alzira*, *Il corsaro*, *Stiffelio* and *Un ballo in maschera*; under Verdi's guidance he also sang in *Simon Boccanegra* at Naples in 1858 and *La forza del destino* at Madrid in 1863.

On 28 October 1863, after the success of *La traviata* at the Théâtre Italien, with Fraschini singing alongside the baritone Delle Sedie, Verdi wrote to Escudier:

I take enormous pleasure in Fraschini's success, as if it were my own personal triumph or something even greater, for I love and esteem Fraschini greatly (autograph: Bibliothèque de l'Opéra, Paris).

12. The baritone Enrico Delle Sedie (Leghorn 1822 – Garenne-Colombes, Paris, 1907), one of the mainstays in those years of the Théâtre Italien, where in October 1861 he had appeared in *Un ballo in maschera* on Verdi's recommendation, who in the letter to Escudier quoted above, wrote after a performance of *La traviata* in October 1863:

And Delle Sedie? He gets better and better! Will that now convince Signor Bagier [Director of the Théâtre Italien] *that my recommendations can be trusted?*

Having studied singing and drama, he fought at Curtatone when the '48 uprisings broke out, and was imprisoned. He then renewed his singing studies and made his début in 1851 at Chianciano in *Nabucco*. Because his voice was relatively small, his career was neither rapid nor brilliant; but he gradually made his mark through his subtle interpretations, tasteful singing, clean phrasing and excellent acting. He enjoyed an international career, but it was especially in Paris during the sixties that he held sway. It was there, too, that he won himself the reputation as one of the greatest singing teachers of the second half of the century. His *Estetica del canto e dell' arte melodrammatica*, published in three languages (Milan – Paris 1885), constitutes the most important treatise on singing in the nineteenth century since Manuel Garcia junior. Delle Sedie married the singer Magherita Tizzoni who, amongst her other roles, played Fenena alongside Strepponi in *Nabucco* at Verona in January 1884, with Verdi present.

13. The baritone Giorgio Ronconi (Milan 1810 – Madrid 1890) was another singer whom Verdi greatly esteemed. He sang in the première of *Nabucco* at La Scala in 1842, and also appeared in the same opera in Vienna (1843) with Verdi conducting, and Paris (1845). He took part in the first Paris performance of *Ernani* (1845), the first London performance of *I due Foscari* (1847) and the first Petersburg performances of *Rigoletto* (1853). His final appearance at the Théâtre Italien was in 1862, though he was still singing at Covent Garden.

14. Achille Tamberlick, younger brother (and not son, as Gatti and Abbiati state; cf. G. MARTIN: "Lettere inedite: Contributo alla storia della *Forza del destino*", in *Verdi*, Bollettino dell' Istituto di studi verdiani, Parma, n. 5, pp. 1088–1102) of the Italian tenor Enrico Tamberlick (Rome 1802 – Paris 1889), who sang in the first performance of *La forza del destino* at Petersburg in 1862, and was one of the most celebrated dramatic tenors of the nineteenth century.

15. Achille de Lauzières, born in Naples in 1800, descendant of the Marquis of Lauzières de Thémines, died in Paris in March 1875; he was a librettist, who collaborated with Gaetano Braga, Pacini, Winter *et al*; journalist, music critic of *La Patrie*, contributor to the *Art Musical*, and he translated into Italian several important libretti, including Verdi's *Don Carlos*, *Dinorah*, *Faust* and *Marta*.

16. Printed in A. POUGIN: *Verdi: Histoire anecdotique de sa vie et de ses oeuvres*, Calmann Lévy, Paris, 1886, pp. 213–4.

17. The caricature is reproduced in numerous books on Verdi, including C. GATTI: *Verdi nelle immagini*, p. 159.

18. Two days after this evening, on February 16, Verdi wrote to Arrivabene:

> *Have no fear . . . I am alive! A fact of which I am well aware, since I feel the tedium of all the c . . . who inundate Paris, scourging poor humanity. It makes no difference whether one is in the Champs-Elysées three miles from*

the centre, or in the Hôtel de Bade *in the very middle of the* Boulevard des Italiens. *But the most remarkable thing is, that among so much bustle, you find when you go to bed at night that the 24 hours of day have passed and you have accomplished nothing! It will be a long time before my collaborators complete their libretto and I return to Sant' Agata to compose in peace. You will read in the newspapers, especially if you receive the minor papers such as* l'Evénement, Le petit Journal, *that I held a party in honour of Dantan who sculpted a bust of me. Strictly speaking it was not a party, for I issued no invitations; but some close friends visited me the other evening to view this bust. They wanted to make music, but I did not permit it, because I wished to avoid publicity – which I managed to do as successfully as I had found peace and quiet in the Champs-Elysées! We could certainly have made excellent music with Patti, Fraschini, Delle-Sedie, Ronconi etc. etc. The bust, everyone says, is truly fine, but Dantan surprised me with the caricature, which I find even finer. It depicts a seated lion with its devil's tail between its legs, playing the piano with one paw, while writing operas etc. with the other . . . I do go on so! And so thanks and amen.* [. . .] (Verdi intimo, pp. 68–69).

IX

A VISIT TO VERDI

1867

CHARLES SANTLEY: *Student and Singer: Reminiscences*, London, 1892, p. 248.

CHARLES SANTLEY (Liverpool 1834 – London 1922) was one of the most brilliant baritones of the second half of the nineteenth century, and certainly one of the greatest English singers of all time. He came to Milan to perfect his technique in 1855 and made his début at Pavia in *La traviata*. For the greater part of his career he sang in England where he excelled both in opera and oratorio; but he also sang at La Scala (a single performance of *Il trovatore* in January 1866, followed in February by several performances of Nicolai's *Il templario*), in Paris, Barcelona (where he made his début in *Rigoletto*) and America. Rodolfo Celletti in the *Enciclopedia dello spettacolo* speaks of his full mellow voice, vibrant and sweet in timbre, his refined style, clear, spirited diction, elegant presence and inspired expressiveness. His operatic repertoire ranged from the operas of Verdi to those of Gounod, from *Don Giovanni* to *Les Huguenots*, from Thomas' *Hamlet* to Wagner's *Der fliegende Holländer*. He took part in the first London performance of *Faust* (Gounod composed for him Valentine's aria "Avant de quitter ces lieux", which then remained in the definitive version of the opera), *Mireille*, also by Gounod, Cherubini's *Medea* and the first version (1862) of *La forza del destino* which was given in London on 22 June 1867, under the baton of Luigi Arditi, with the soprano Therese Titiens, the mezzo Zelia Trebelli and the tenor Pietro Mongini.

And it is to the rehearsals in London of *La forza del destino* that Santley refers on page 248 of his volume of memoirs, quoted here. He assigns this episode to the period when Verdi was "very busy at the Opéra with the revival of *Les vêpres siciliennes*"; this must be an error, since that revival took place in July 1863 (see N. VII), whereas *La forza del destino* was given in London four years later. Santley obviously confused *Les vêpres siciliennes* (heard by him in 1885 in Paris while travelling in Italy) with *Don Carlos*, whose exhausting and interminable rehearsals lasted from August 1866 to early March 1867 (see N. X). It is very likely that the meeting with Verdi took place between February and March of that year during the final rehearsals of *Don Carlos*, when Verdi was under the greatest strain from launching his new opera. The tension in those weeks at the Opéra was such that the composer would have been unable to turn his attention to other matters; one can therefore understand the cool reception accorded the fine English singer.

[*A visit to Verdi*]

I was in Paris for a few days before the opening of our season. At Arditi's[1] request I called on Verdi to ask him if he would point out to me any particular effects he wished brought out in my part.[2] He received me very coldly, and said as he had gone through the opera with Arditi, he did not see any reason why he should go through it with me. I was a little astonished at his brusque manner, and excused myself the best way I could, and was retiring, when he called me back and told me if I liked to call again on another day, appointing it himself and the hour, he would consider about what he could do. I returned on the day, when he informed me he was very busy at the opera with the revival of *Les vêpres siciliennes*,[3] and had no piano in his rooms, so he could not assist me in any way. I told him not to disturb himself, and that I was quite satisfied with having had the honour of making his acquaintance, on which he bowed me out. I confess I was a little hurt, as I presented myself and made my request very modestly.

CHARLES SANTLEY

NOTES

1. Luigi Arditi (Crescentino, Vercelli 1822 – Hove, Brighton 1903), violinist, conductor and composer. He started his career as conductor with his friend Bottesini at Havana and in the USA, and finally settled in London where, in 1858, he was appointed conductor at Her Majesty's Theatre. He acquired European fame during the sixties; from 1870 he conducted annually at Vienna, and also visited Petersburg and Madrid. But it was in London where he chiefly worked. His repertoire eventually included even Wagner. He was a close friend of Rossini, but also of Gounod, Verdi and Wagner (who called him "one of us", for the way he promoted his music in England).

2. Don Carlo in *La forza del destino* which was about to be staged in London.

3. In fact Verdi was busy with rehearsals for the première of *Don Carlos* at the Opéra.

X

A REHEARSAL OF *DON CARLOS* – VERDI

1867

JULES CLARETIE: "Une répétition de *Don Carlos* – Verdi", in *Le Figaro*, Paris, XIV, 94: 17 February 1867, pp. 1–2 (reproduced in *Gazzetta Musicale di Milano*, XXII, 8: 24 February 1867, pp. 57–60; in *Scena Illustrata*, Florence, XXXVI, 271 (special Verdi number): 15 November 1900, p. 4; in M. BASSO: "Giuseppe Verdi: La sua vita, le sue opere, la sua morte. Storia populare", G. Corsi & C., Milan, 1901, pp. 110–15; in *Les Annales politiques et littéraires*, Paris, XXXI/1581: 12 October 1913, p. 326; in *Musica d'Oggi*, Milan, XVII, 1: January 1935, pp. 12–14; in the special issue *Per il cinquantesimo anniversario della morte di Giuseppe Verdi*, Teatro di S. Carlo, Naples, 1950, pp. 81–5, in a free translation).

ALMOST EXACTLY A year after the party held in honour of Dantan we find Verdi once again in Paris, but this time on the stage of the *grande boutique*. We find him described in the eye-witness account of a journalist from *Le Figaro*, who had crept stealthily into the Opéra and hidden in the darkness of a box. Having heard the third act of a dress rehearsal of Verdi's new opera, he runs immediately to the offices of the newspaper and dashes down his article. This was already the fourth run-through (but four more will follow before the long-awaited première . . .):[1] the date, February 17, coincides with the date mentioned in *Le Relevé des Répétitions de Don Carlos*, which in turn is noted in *Le journal de la régie*.[2] A year has passed and *Don Carlos* seems to be finished. Seems to be . . . but is not yet; a few days later the composer again cuts the weighty score for the umpteenth time: an entire chorus in the first scene of Act 3. And other cuts, requiring other modifications, follow.[3] An enormous labour, "enough to kill a bull"; a labour that had started in mid-August, when the composer had begun to attend rehearsals.[4] Verdi is now seated on stage, motionless like "some Assyrian God", "musing", "listening with all his soul" . . . after all the work, the toil and, especially, the rehearsals, vacillations, cuts and amendments! On 28 September 1866 he had written, still confident but not excessively so, to Arrivabene:

You will understand that I am immersed in the rehearsals for Don Carlos. We are making progress but, as always at the Opéra, at a snail's pace. For the rest, all goes smoothly. We were hoping to open in mid-December, but I doubt whether we shall.[5]

And on 10 December 1867, again to Arrivabene, he writes:

I would have written to you earlier, but I have been inundated by so many notes which tumble on to the score of Don Carlos that you would have been in danger of receiving a letter full of notes worth even less than my words. Now that even the instrumentation is finished and the danger of my writing you notes instead of words has passed, I can tell you that the opera is completely finished, except for the dance-music. The rehearsals are proceeding smoothly, the stage rehearsals have begun and I hope that the first performance will take place not later than mid-January. You see what a lousy place this Opéra is. Things go on interminably![6]

As for Giuseppina Verdi, she writes on 7 December 1866 to her friend Mauro Corticelli, Adelaide Ristori's agent:

Don Carlos, if it pleases God and the tortoises of the Opéra, will receive its première at the end of January! Good gracious! How a composer is punished for his sins by having a work staged in that theatre with its machinery of marble and lead![7]

On January 15 fatal news arrives from Busseto: the composer's 82-year-old father, Carlo, has passed away. Verdi drowns his grief in the exasperating rehearsals of *Don Carlos*, and on February 8 he writes to Arrivabene:

Ah, how I should have loved to close that poor man's eyes – it would have been a comfort to both him and me. Now I long for the moment when I can return home to see how the two poor creatures who survived him are faring: an old woman of 83 and a little girl of 7 [Filomena Verdi who was rebaptized Maria, adopted by Verdi and became his heiress]. *Imagine! They are in the hands of two servants who are now, it can be said, masters of the house! . . . The première, I hope, will be on the 22nd, and I would then depart on the evening of the 23rd or 24th.*[8]

But the 24th will be the day of the sixth full dress-rehearsal. In short, the opera will not be premièred until March 11, after seven weeks of rehearsal with singers, chorus, orchestra, extras, corps de ballet, *musique Sax*, stage machinery, sets, costumes and all the copying and printing etc., etc. Six months littered with incidents of every kind, as the *France Musicale* reported on December 23:

> There has been talk of incidents and a curious anecdote concerning the preliminary rehearsals for Verdi's new opera. The composer's patience has been most sorely tried; but finally, thanks to the ever conciliatory intervention of Perrin, all difficulties have been resolved, and we are assured that all the artists are now satisfied. It has to be admitted that the composers who work for the Opéra do not always tread on rose-strewn paths. More often than not, alas, they encounter thorns instead of flowers. Happy are they who can reach their goal without losing patience and having to fight some great battle.[9]

Incidents, anecdotes, interminable rehearsals, interminable toil and muted hostility . . . The author of the article, Claretie, detected these difficulties and is completely won over by the artist's character. Verdi, for his part, has already drawn his own conclusions; two and a half years later he expresses them unequivocally in a famous letter to Du Locle:

> [. . .] *Alas!! It's neither the toil of writing an opera nor the judgement of the Parisian public that deters me; it's the certainty of never being able to have my music performed in Paris according to my own wishes. It is very strange that a composer must always see his ideas thwarted and his concepts misrepresented! In your opera houses (this is not meant as an epigram) there are too many wise men! Everyone wants to pass judgement according to his own ideas, his own tastes and, what is worse, according to a system, without taking into account the character and individuality of the composer. Everyone wants to give an opinion, express a doubt – and when a composer has lived for a long time in this atmosphere of doubts, his own convictions must eventually be shaken, and he ends up by correcting, adjusting – or to put it better – spoiling his own work. Thus, instead of a work all in one piece, you are confronted in the end with a mosaic. And however beautiful it might be, it is still a mosaic. You will object that the Opéra has produced a string of masterpieces in this manner. Masterpieces they may well be, but permit me to say that they would be even more perfect if they didn't from time to time smack of being pieced together and repaired. No one, surely, will deny the genius of Rossini. All right – but*

despite all his genius, one detects in his Guillaume Tell *this fatal atmosphere of the Opéra, and sometimes, although more rarely than in the work of other composers, you feel that there is too much here, too little there, and that it doesn't flow with the honesty and sureness of* Il barbiere. *By this, I don't wish to disapprove of your method of work; I only mean to say that I simply cannot again crawl under the* Caudine yoke *of your theatres, when I know I cannot have a real success unless I write as I feel, free from all other influences, without having to remember that I'm writing for Paris and not for the world of the moon. Moreover, the artists must sing not in their fashion but mine; the chorus ("they have a very capable chorus at Paris") must display similar goodwill. In short, everything must be under my control, and one will alone must prevail – mine! Does that seem tyrannical? Perhaps it is. But if the opera is a whole, then the idea is a* unity, *and everything must work together to form this* unity. *Perhaps you will say that there is nothing to prevent one achieving this in Paris. No. In Italy it can be managed – at least I can always manage it. But in France, no. If, for example, I arrive in the foyer of an Italian theatre* [for the very first run-through of a new opera], *no one dares to express an opinion or judgement, before they have properly understood the work, nor would anyone venture to ask irrelevant questions. They respect the opera and the composer and leave the public to judge the work. In the foyer of the* Opéra, *on the other hand, after four chords everyone is whispering:* "Oh, ce n'est pas bon . . . c'est commun . . . ce n'est pas de bon goût . . . ca n'ira pas à Paris. . . ." *What on earth do these feeble words* "commun", "bon goût", "Paris" *signify, if you are dealing with a work of art which should be universal! The conclusion to all this is that I am not a composer for Paris. I do not know whether I have any talent, but I know that my ideas on art are quite different from yours. I believe in* Inspiration; *you believe in* Construction. *I admit your criterion for the purpose of discussion; but I require the* Enthusiasm, *that you lack, in feeling and in judgement. I want* art *in whatever form it manifests itself; I do not want the* compromise, *the* artifice, *or the* system *that you prefer. Am I wrong? Am I right? Whatever the answer, I am right to say that my ideas are very different from yours; and I would add that, unlike many other composers, I am not prepared to give way in spineless fashion and deny my profoundest convictions which are deeply rooted within me. Moreover, I should be most upset if I were to write an opera for you, my dear Du Locle, which you might have to withdraw after some dozen performances, as Perrin did with* Don Carlos. *– [. . .]*[10]

For the moment, however, Verdi is there, on the stage of the Opéra, surrounded by the musical Establishment made up of famous names such as the Belgian composer and musicologist Geväert, appointed four days previously to the post of *directeur de la musique*, Massé, Delibes, Cormon, Cadaux; Vauthrot, the *chef de chant*, was absent – perhaps forgotten by the journalist from *Le Figaro*, perhaps temporarily engaged elsewhere at other rehearsals. The date, we repeat, is 17 February 1867, and we are at a rehearsal of the great Act 3 scene from *Don Carlos*.

A rehearsal of Don Carlos – Verdi

I have heard an entire act of *Don Carlos*, which will be performed at the Opéra in ten days time, and I have seen Verdi.

It was from the back of a box, in the dark, that I managed to witness this scene. No one knew of my presence; I took care not to move, and remained there, spellbound, listening, looking, my eyes fixed on this pale man who had conceived, created and composed this great music drama.

The chandeliers were extinguished, the great auditorium was plunged into darkness and seemed quite devoid of life, apart from the stage and the orchestra whose number had been specially increased for this opera. Above their heads, above the violins and the sparkling brass instruments stood Georges Hainl[11] with his ruffled head of hair and bristly moustache. The conductor, baton in hand, like a colonel before the attack, contemplated his soldiers huddled in the trenches.

Opposite, mesmerizing him so to speak with his flashing eyes, sat Verdi, his great white hands resting on his knees, motionless, like some Assyrian God, musing, listening with all his soul, wholly absorbed in this music which had emerged vibrant and living from the depths of his being.

The man is tall, thin yet solidly built, with Atlas-like shoulders which seem capable of supporting the weight of mountains. His long, luxuriant, thick hair is thrown forward on to his brow in heavy locks, his beard is jet-black but white beneath the chin. He has two deep lines along his cheeks, a gaunt face, thick eyebrows, bright, electric eyes, a large, bitter and disdainful mouth, a proud, manly appearance, the attitude of a defiant tribune.

To the right, in a corner, in the glow of a little lamp, like confederates of some secret tribunal, the musicians – composers likewise – responsible for rehearsing the choruses, bend over the score or look questioningly at Verdi's eloquent gaze, read his thoughts from a single flash of his eyes or a single frown, take notes, attentive to the slightest gesture, the slightest word from the Maestro. And these are men such as Gevaërt,[12] Victor Massé,[13] Léo Delibes,[14] beloved and famous names, Cormon,[15] Cadot [sic];[16] they all attend to every note, follow each piece of music with finger and eyes, like a student would study a book – lieutenants enrolled in the company of this leader. Some conduct the male voices, others the female voices, and another (M. Cormon), baton in hand, walks to and fro, beating the time, leading a battalion of chorus-singers like an officer at the head of a parade. What movement!

And what exertion from every quarter! From the composer down to the extras. M. Perrin grows agitated in his box, steps from it, walks from the corridors to the wings, from the stalls to the stage, moves to the back of the auditorium to listen from further away, meets M. Du Locle, author of the libretto, makes some observations and receives others. Ah! The eve of battles! And amid all this agitation Verdi remains waiting in his place, alone, meditating.

But now the chorus strike up a magnificent, gripping march, without doubt a sudden moment of inspiration, an unexpected find, one of those creations which bursts forth and becomes popular over night, sweeping along audiences, galvanizing crowds.

Verdi listens; his entire being, the whole might of his iron-like temperament strains towards a single goal. His sense of hearing is doubly, triply acute. He questions everything. In this thundering harmony he can hear the faintest of notes. He can hear everything at the same time: the chorus, the brass, the aria and all that happens on and off the stage. He gets up, leaps about, valiantly spurring on all these groups, shouting with that Italian accent which lends charm to his voice:

"Il y a un trou là! . . . Allons! . . . Vite! . . ."

Some of the music is sung on the apron, but he now addresses the chorus at the back of the stage, almost leaping towards them:

"Eh! . . . eh! . . . Il y a un accent sur cette note-là!"

In one direction he cries: "Allons, presto!" In the other: "Piano! Con amore!"

He gets up, beats time, snaps thumb against middle finger, and this strident, bright, terse note, this noise like the sound of castanets is heard above the orchestra and the chorus, goads them on, drives them forward like lashes from a whip. Then he claps his hands. He radiates harmony from head to foot, he measures himself against his ideal, he instils his artistic genius into these men and women, kindling them with his fire, himself devoured by fire, beating the floor with his heels, running to the back of the theatre, stopping the singers and rediscovering his original conception among the chaos from which an ordered world will emerge.

This majestic march in the third act – played first by new brass instruments designed by Sax,[18] now clear and penetrating, now deep and low, then sung by the chorus appearing from the wings and by the regal voice of Mademoiselle Sasse,[19] then taken up by the orchestra, will always remain one of Verdi's finest inspirations. Those musicians – the chorus masters – overwhelmed by so many successive rehearsals, still wish to hear it twice and applaud it twice. Verdi hardly reacts, bows his head and seems to say: Let us continue!

The fact is that the following scene is simply overwhelming: the Deputies from Flanders demand their freedom from Philip II, protest against their violated rights and utter with ardour their cry of liberty. Don Carlos supports them; the King orders his arrest. No one stirs. The Marquis of Posa advances towards the Infant and seizes his sword. It is a splendid scene. Morère[20] and Faure[21] should be heard. Schiller could certainly not complain of not being understood.

You will recall this scene in Schiller's *Don Carlos*: "Sire, I have lately returned from Flanders and Brabant . . . so many rich and flourishing provinces! A great and vigorous people . . . and a good people too. To be father of a race like this, I thought must be divine indeed! And then I stumbled on a heap of burnt men's bones!" No dramatic action is more poignant or more beautiful. Well – into this chorus of Flemings, of basses singing in unison,[22] slowly like a hymn and muffled like a rumble of thunder, threatening, frightening, sublime, Verdi has poured the same repressed ardour, the same energy and vigour. The Flemings are prepared for the ultimate: sacrifice, death, torture. Theirs is the harsh call of stifled liberty that demands to live. And Verdi, like none other, has expressed the great griefs of the oppressed. All the sobs of his Italy were once uttered by the mouth of the Troubadour. That opera contained the tears of an entire generation. The Motherland cried and implored through the mouth of her son. In *Don Carlos*, sobs have turned into threats, laments into arms, supplications into protests, and I doubt whether the Deputies of the King of Spain can hear without emotion these courageous cries of freedom.

This third act is a masterpiece. I have so much still to mention: Sasse's performance was remarkable; Obin[23] and Castelmary[24] too were excellent; there was a wonderful duet for Faure and Morère. But I have said enough. The public will be overwhelmed and will wish to hear it again and again – for even hearing it without costumes, and in semi-darkness, with the knights dressed in overalls and the inquisitors in great overcoats, I was moved, overwhelmed, humbled.

In fact, one leaves such a performance with the feeling of being both more insignificant and yet, at the same time, greater. Greater, with new emotions, wide-open horizons and ablaze with heroism; and more insignificant, because one has measured oneself against genius.

Here, then, is a man who is rich, honoured, magnificent, who has nothing more to expect from his art but more toil, fatigue, crowns won at great cost, triumphs paid for with pain, insomnia and anger. He has an income of 80,000 lire. His name is now synonymous with freedom, a rallying cry for his homeland. This man has sat in parliament, has been dragged on to the stage, acclaimed, applauded, embraced. What more does he desire? It is you he desires, O sacred passion of beauty! It is you that he harbours in his heart, where you shall always dwell! He desires the Highest. He continues on his way, struggles, works.

He will sit down on this chair, and with strained ears will listen to these choruses for four hours on end. Having exhausted himself mentally, he will then exhaust himself physically till midnight sounds. And after this prodigious effort, on the evening of the first performance one of our colleagues, a journalist who has had a bad dinner, a wag searching for a paradox, a wit seeking a bon mot will exclaim: *What! Is this all!* Don Carlos! . . . *Oh, I don't like Verdi!*

It is fortunate that in the clamour surrounding him, the artist, the true artist remains absorbed by his idea, listening only to his conscience; and it is also fortunate that often, among those that surround him, there are people who can tell him how the future will judge him. This is the genius' revenge – it is not the present, but posterity for which he writes.

Verdi, on the other hand, without awaiting the judgement of posterity, will have experienced the extreme joy of what Alphonse Rabbe called *the glory of ready cash*. But he bears his burden like an athlete. "I am merely a peasant," he says, when one talks to him of his fame. So be it. He is one of those peasants who win battles or discover new lands.[25]

JULES CLARETIE

NOTES

1. U.GÜNTHER: "La genèse de *Don Carlos*, opéra en cinq actes [. . .], deuxième partie", in *Revue de Musicologie*, Paris LX, 1–2: 1974, pp. 87–158; see in particular the two plates between pp. 110 and 111, showing the list of rehearsals for *Don Carlos* from 11 August 1866 to 11 March 1867, the day of the first performance.

2. U. GÜNTHER, *art. cit.*, *loc. cit.*

3. U. GÜNTHER, *art. cit.*, pp. 123–55. Günther here gives an account of the eight different cuts, totalling in all 505 bars, that were replaced by 102 new bars. The most important cuts concern a "Prelude and Introduction" in Act I, a duet between Elisabetta and Princess Eboli and Philip's lament over Posa's dead body in Act IV – all of which have been restored in performances given recently, first at La Fenice, Venice, then at La Scala, Milan.

4. Except for a period spent by Verdi and Giuseppina at Cauterets in the Pyrenees between 20 August and 13 September 1866.

5. *Verdi intimo*, cit., p. 72.

6. *Verdi intimo*, cit., p. 73.

7. Autograph: Museo Teatrale alla Scala, Milan.

8. *Verdi intimo*, cit., p. 74. He had expressed himself in virtually the same terms on February 6 in a letter to Clarina Maffei; cf. A. LUZIO: *Profili biografici e Bozzetti storici* (new edition), Cogliati, Milan 1927, II, p. 522.

9. *La France Musicale*, XXXI, 51: 23 December 1866, p. 402 (reprinted in U. GÜNTHER, *art. cit.*, p. 118).

10. Autograph: Bibliothèque de l'Opéra, Paris (draft copy with variants in *I Copialettere*, cit., pp. 219–22).

11. François-Georges Hainl (Issoire, Puy-de-Dôme, 1807 – Paris 1873); already conductor at the Théâtre de Lyon, he was appointed in 1863, as we have already seen (see N. VII, p. 41) to replace Pierre Dietsch at the Opéra. Verdi could not have been greatly satisfied with Hainl's conducting in *Don Carlos*, since he writes to Du Locle a year later in a letter dated 14 March 1868:

> *Ah, if your orchestra could be persuaded that there are effects which they are unable and unwilling to render! It goes without saying that the Bologna orchestra, because it was conducted by Mariani, played better than yours; and even the Rome orchestra (a poor orchestra) produced effects that yours failed to give!* (autograph: Bibliothèque de l'Opéra, Paris.)

12. François-Auguste Gevaërt (Huysse, East Flanders, 1828 – Brussels 1908), organist, composer, musicologist. He owes his fame to his numerous anthologies of music history and to musicological publications such as: *Traité général d'instrumentation* (Gand 1863; new edition Paris – Brussels 1885), *Histoire et théorie de la musique de l'antiquité*, 2 vols. (Gand 1875–81), *Traité d'harmonie théorique et pratique*, 2 vols.

(Paris–Brussels 1905–7). Verdi esteemed him as a scholar (cf. N. XXVI). On 14 February 1867, i.e. four days before the dress rehearsal to which Claretie refers, Perrin had appointed him "Directeur de la Musique du Théâtre Impériale de l'Opéra" (cf. *L'Art Musical*, n. 12, 21 February 1867, p. 95).

13. Victor Massé (Lorient 1822 – Paris 1884), famous composer of elegant, melodic operas, of which *Paul et Virginie*, 1876, is considered his masterpiece. From 1860 he was chorus-master at the Opéra, and also, from 1866, teacher of composition at the Paris Conservatoire.

14. Léo Delibes (Saint-Germain-du-Val, Sarthe 1836 – Paris 1891), success-ful composer of the ballets *Coppélia* (1870) and *Sylvia* (1876) and the opera *Lakmé* (1883); in 1865 he had been appointed assistant chorus-master.

15. The reference is perhaps to Eugène Cormon, pseudonym for Pierre-Etienne Piestre (Lyon 1810 – Paris 1903); librettist and dramatist, he wrote libretti for Geväert and with Carré the libretto for Bizet's *Les pêcheurs de perles*.

16. In fact, Claretie must mean Justin Cadaux (Albi 1813 – Picpus 1874) opera buffa composer, arranger and conductor, who died of a mental illness in a nursing home; from 1866 he was at the Opéra as head of the music-copying department (cf. U. GÜNTHER, *art. cit.*, pp. 132–3).

17. Cf. N. VIII, note 7.

18. Adolphe Sax (Dinant 1814 – Paris 1894), the famous designer of instruments, whose name is connected with the invention of the saxophone (1840).

19. The soprano Marie Sasse, or Sass, or Saxe (Gand 1838 – Auteuil, Paris 1907) made her début in 1859 at the Opéra-Lyrique in *Le nozze di Figaro*, and in 1860 she moved to the Opéra, making her début there in *Robert le diable*; she also sang in the Paris première of *Tannhäuser* (1861) and the world première of *L'Africaine*. In 1865 she married the bass Armand Castelmary, who was also engaged to sing in *Don Carlos*, from whom she separated several years later. Verdi was not satisfied with Sasse's interpretation of the role of Elisabetta; a year later in the letter to Du Locle of 14 March 1868 (already quoted), he writes:

> *Ah, if only Sasse could be persuaded that the part is better than she believes. In Italy Stolz turned it into the main role.*

20. The tenor A. Morère, who sang the role of Don Carlos.

21. The baritone Jean-Baptiste Faure (Moulins, Allier 1830 – Paris 1914), one of the greatest French singers of the nineteenth century; he first made his mark at the Opéra-Comique (where he sang in the world première of Meyerbeer's *Dinorah*), and opera houses in London and Berlin; he then moved to the Opéra in 1861, where he was one of the principals in the first production of *L'Africaine* (1865). In 1868 he sang in the première of Thomas' *Hamlet*, and the following year in the new version of *Faust*.

22. Written for six basses, this music is usually sung not by the members of the chorus but by six soloists. For the Paris première, the Director of the Opéra, Perrin, requested Auber, the Director of the Conservatoire, in a letter dated 4 January 1867, to use six young Conservatoire students (see U. GÜNTHER, *art. cit.*, p. 134), some of whom were later to enjoy a successful career: Victor Maurel, who sang in the premières of the revised *Simon Boccanegra*, *Otello*, *Falstaff* and *Pagliacci*; Pierre Gailhard (Tolosa 1848 – Paris 1918), who made his début in 1867 at the Opéra-Comique, before moving to the Opéra some years later and becoming its director from 1884 to 1908; Jean-Louis Lassalle (Lyon 1847 – Paris 1909), one of the finest baritones at the end of the last century, who was admired not only at the Opéra but also on the most important international stages.

23. The bass Louis-Henri Obin, who sang Philip II.

24. The bass Armand Castelmary (Tolone 1834 – New York 1907); married to Marie Sasse, he had sung in the first performance of *L'Africaine* at the Opéra. He sang often and with success in Italy (Turin, Rome, Genoa, Trieste, Florence) and died during a performance of *Martha* at the Metropolitan. Contrary to what is stated in the *Enciclopedia dello Spettacolo*, he did not sing the part of the Grand Inquisitor in the première of *Don Carlos*, but that of the Friar. The role of the Grand Inquisitor was sung by the bass David, who had been originally cast as the Friar, but who replaced the bass Belval as Inquisitor, because the latter had refused to sing what he considered to be a role for second bass; he even brought an action against Perrin (cf. U. GÜNTHER, *art. cit.*, pp. 104–6).

25. Almost like a prophet, Claretie anticipates several ideas about the critic's task and the artist's duty to perceive "new worlds", that Verdi was to express a few months later, on December 23, to Vincenzo Torelli, so that the latter might convey these thoughts to his son Achille, a writer of comedies, who had just completed *I mariti*:

> *Let praise not puff him up nor censure alarm him. When confronted by criticism, even the most honest criticism, he must pursue his path. The critics are doing their job; they judge and must judge according to fixed rules and forms. The artist must peer into the future, perceive new worlds amongst the chaos, and if at the end of his long road he eventually discerns a tiny light, the surrounding dark must not alarm him. He must pursue that path, and if occasionally he stumbles and falls, he must rise up and continue. Sometimes it is a good thing that even the leader of a movement can fall . . .* (autograph: Biblioteca Lucchesi-Palli, Naples).

XI

VERDI'S HOUSE AT SANT'AGATA

1868

ANTONIO GHISLANZONI: "La casa di Verdi a Sant'Agata", in *Gazzetta Musicale di Milano*, XXIII, 30: 26 July 1868, pp. 242–6; *Il Trovatore*, Milan, XV, 30: 26 July 1868, pp. 1–3; *La Lombardia*, Milan, X, July 1868; *L'Universo Illustrato*, Milan, July 1868; reprinted by the author in his *Reminiscenze Artistiche. Scritti piacevoli*, Brigola, Milan, 2nd edit., 1870, pp. 25–49; then with addition of a note in his *Libro serio*, Milan, 1879, pp. 151–68, (reproduced in A. POUGIN, *op. cit.*, pp. 123–6; *id.*: "Verdi: Histoire anecdotique", cit., pp. 288–93; in *Verdi intimo*, cit., pp. 49–51; in part in *L'Illustrazione Populare*, Milan, XXIV, 7 (special *Otello* edition): 13 February 1887, p. 104, and XXX, 6 (special *Falstaff* edition): 5 February 1893, p. 86; in G. BRAGAGNOLO – E. BETTAZZI: *La vita di Giuseppe Verdi narrata al popolo*, Ricordi, Milan, 1905, reprinted 1913, pp. 252–4).

THIS IS ONE of the best known nineteenth-century articles on Verdi. Ghislanzoni (who two years earlier, in 1866, had been appointed director of the *Gazzetta Musicale di Milano* which had resumed publication after a three-year stoppage), penned it on his return from a visit he had made to Sant'Agata in the company of Giulio Ricordi in the late spring of 1868 – June, according to Ghislanzoni, but more likely at the end of May, as we can deduce from a letter from Mariani to Ricordi, and a further letter from Ricordi to Verdi.[1] Twenty years had passed since Ghislanzoni had last seen Verdi: he had first been introduced a long way back in 1846 by Andrea Maffei at the house of mutual friends in Milan. The visit to Sant'Agata had been suggested by Ricordi himself in the hope that Ghislanzoni, by meeting Verdi, might be stimulated into providing a new solution to the finale, that wretched "catastrophe", of *La forza del destino*, which had virtually caused the composer to withdraw the score that now lay at the publisher's in cold storage. Ricordi's hope was soon fulfilled; in the late autumn Ghislanzoni, urged on by Verdi, set to work revising the libretto, and the new version of *La forza del destino* was performed at La Scala on 27 February 1869. Ghislanzoni then completed the libretto of *Aida* (1871).

Posterity has treated Antonio Ghislanzoni (Lecco 1824 – Caprino Bergamasco 1893) strangely. His name today seems known only because of his activity as a librettist; and by a strange fate, his fame seems to rest almost entirely on the libretto which was only partially his own work and for which he merely provided the versification – *Aida* (see N. VIII, note 7). A boulevardier in spirit, by character a bohemian, he was a lover of paradox, a polemicist who was both arrogant and moralizing, ever ready to contradict and jest, with a sense of social obligation, and loyal to Republican ideals. He defined himself thus: "An odd fellow who does not recognize the power of any established authority."[2] The life of this human and artistic figure, who with genuine originality lived through the cultural events of Italian society in the first decades of political unification, has yet to be fully researched. A seminarist and doctor *manqué*, he was singer,[3] patriot, journalist, impresario,[4] poet, novelist, librettist,[5] literary and music critic, founder and director of newspapers,[6] all in "a bizarre rotation of often conflicting activity, rich in resignations and comebacks, desires and aversions, sailors' oaths and nostalgia. He lived the life of a perfect bohemian and also, due to a kind of obscure destiny, the life of a character straight out of opera".[7]

Verdi's house at Sant'Agata

Houses of illustrious men should remain inexorably closed to those indiscreet guests called journalists; but since Maestro Verdi, forgetting this wise advice, chose to invite me in June 1868 to spend several days at his villa at Sant'Agata near Busseto, I do him no wrong to suppose that, in according me such an honour, he was counting on my discretion.

I do not credit myself with greater discretion than others. And what journalist would have the moral courage to bury in the depths of his soul the agreeable impressions, the small but interesting secrets that it was my fortune to collect during my brief stay at the villa?

Besides, there is no way out. Great artists, like kings, like emperors, like famous commanders or ministers of State, cannot escape historical enquiry; and since the composer of *La traviata* and *Don Carlos* has already taken his own place in the history of Italian music, he must also subject himself, whether he like it or not, to the violations of biographers, commentators and portrait painters. After all, there can be no great harm in the biographer having known his victim at close quarters.

I had not seen Maestro Verdi for about twenty years. In 1846 or

1847 I had found myself in his company at a dinner with friends in Milan, and the features of that grave and pensive face had impressed themselves indelibly on my young imagination. Also present at that table, amid many journalists, men of letters, artists and *bon viveurs* of all types, was Cavaliere Andrea Maffei, the elegant translator of Schiller, Moore and Goëte [*sic*], the Virgilian poet whose poetry is music. Surrounded by our merry noise, the poet and Maestro maintained an awkward silence. Both appeared engrossed in weighty thoughts. At that time, I believe, the score of *I masnadieri* was in preparation, soon to be performed at His Majesty's Theatre, London.

Since that day I did not, I repeat, have the good fortune of meeting the Maestro again who, after a few months in Milan, left the city of his first triumphs and only returned about twenty years later, that is to say in early July 1868.

Neither the house where he was born nor the delightful villa where Verdi prefers to spend his summer holidays form part of the small town called Busseto. But if Busseto does not have the honour of being the birthplace of contemporary Italy's most energetic and fascinating composer, it has the greater glory of having given him his first musical education, of having understood and admired his budding talent. The house where Verdi was born lies about three miles from Busseto. I visited it with profound emotion. Imagine a sort of hut made of lime and stone, virtually isolated amid a fertile plain sown with maize and hemp. One understands how an artist born in this place must retain throughout his life a love of isolation. A few paces from this lowly hut, where today a good woman in her Sunday best sells wine to the peasants of the neighbourhood, there rises up a beautiful majestic church. In that church, at the age of fifteen, the young pupil of Busseto school used to play the organ continuously, intoxicating his fervid imagination with mystical inspirations. And from the church organ he returned to the spinet of his own home, and a whole world of hopes, illusions and sublime raptures paid court to the pale adolescent in that poor oasis of houses lost in a desert of endless fields.

I was shown the little room where the predestined boy used to live. Later, in the villa at Sant'Agata, I also saw the first instrument on which his child's fingers used to practise. That worthy spinet no longer has strings and it has lost its lid. The keyboard resembles the jawbone of a skull with long, corroded teeth. And yet, what a precious monument! And what memories it must hold for the artist who shed upon it the prolific tears of a tortured adolescence! And what lofty emotions it arouses in him who observes and questions it![8]

And question it I did. From the keyboard I raised one of the hammers which revealed an inscription, and I read the words, which were as simple as they were sublime, revealing a craftsman's generous gesture and, at the same time, resembling a scrupulous prophecy. My readers will be pleased to see reproduced here the text of that inscription in all its simplicity. It would be sacrilege to correct even one of the slight orthographical inaccuracies which make it adorable.

> *These jacks were renude by me, Stefano Cavaletti, and lined with leather, and I fited the pedals, for which I made no charge; as I also renude for free the said jacks, seeing the willingness of the young Giuseppe Verdi to learn to play the instrument – which is enough to satisfy me completely – Anno domini 1821.*

This good and acute workman, who was called Stefano Cavaletti, thus sensed the boy's musical instincts, revealing greater imagination than an eminent professor of the Milan Conservatoire who, a few years later, sent Verdi back to Busseto with a certificate of incompetence – a fact which will make posterity laugh.

You must know that there exists at Busseto a sort of Institute, part of the Monte di Pietà, where five or six boys from the town or elsewhere are given free musical education. It is thanks to this same institute that Verdi, son of a poor but most upright peasant, was able to begin his studies; and his compositions, written when he was very young, bear witness to his gifts and the rapidity of his progress. The Busseto band often plays a brilliant sinfonia, composed by Verdi at the age of twelve, a precious fragment of music which, with many others, constitutes the greatest glory of this Institute of music.[9]

But let us visit the villa at Sant'Agata. This, too, is situated about two miles from Busseto; this, too, is virtually isolated in the middle of a vast plain. The church, which bears the name of the saint, and two or three peasants' dwellings form the entourage of the Maestro's rich and elegant abode.

Nature has not bestowed any charm upon this locality. The plain is monotonous, covered only with prosaic corn, which gladdens the greedy farmer but says nothing to the imagination of the poet. Amid those long rows of poplars skirting a meagre ditch of water, you are suddenly surprised by the sight of two weeping willows leaning against a gate. Those two enormous trees, which elsewhere would not perhaps create such a vivid impression, are as striking to the spirit as an exotic apparition. The person who had these trees planted can have nothing or very little in common in terms of character or habits with the population of the plain through which you have travelled. The inhabitant of the house, which you glimpse not far away, must be an eccentric personality – an artist, poet, thinker, perhaps even a misanthropist. To approach that gate you need to cross a bridge, the sole connection between the artist's abode and that of other human beings. He who knows by name the inhabitant of that house imagines, when passing nearby at dusk, that he hears in the branches of those sad trees the whisper of the Trovatore's lament or the final gasp of a dying Violetta.

If a genius dwells here, you must naturally understand that he is the genius of sorrow, the genius of strong, aroused passions. A serried row of trees defends the house from profane glances on the side which overlooks the main road, while on the opposite side the garden runs down more cheerfully and smoothly to the bank of an artificial lake.

And yet one can foresee that when the young plantation gradually grows more luxuriant, shadows and sadness will utterly envelop that abode.

Beyond the garden stretches the Maestro's vast property, crossed by a long avenue fading into the distance, and dotted with peasant's huts and little well-designed farm-houses. The cultivation displays that perfect art one associates with foreign fields less favoured by nature. Verdi's acute mind has lavished on this land all the most advanced agricultural technique of France and England. While the willows of the garden, the dense trees, the dark arbours and the melancholy winding lake depict the artist's passionate nature, the cultivation of these spacious fields seems to reflect the ordered mind of the man, that practical and positive discernment which, with Verdi, is uniquely allied to an exuberant imagination and a lively, sensitive temperament.

This practical and positive discernment is particularly evident in the architecture of the house, the choice of furniture and everything that constitutes comfort and interior order for his family. There is but one single word, a musical word, which can express this wonderful order, this happy blend of art with the material necessities of life – *harmony*. The most exquisite taste and the most informed planning presided over the building of this place. Everything here is beautiful, elegant and of the greatest simplicity; but more important, everything corresponds to the requirements of wholesomeness, convenience and comfort. – My readers will not insist upon a minute description of the rooms, ornaments and pictures. No more can be said but that the house is worthy of an artist who has become a *grand seigneur* through the works of his own genius.

The Maestro usually composes in his bedroom – a spacious room on the ground floor, with plenty of air and light and furnished with artistic profusion. The windows and the glass doors give on to the garden. Then there is a magnificent piano, a bookcase and a massive writing–desk of eccentric shape which divides the room into two and displays a charming variety of *maquettes*, statuettes, vases and artistic trinkets. Above the piano hangs the portrait in oils of old Barezzi,[10] Verdi's loyal friend and patron, for whose name and venerable portrait he professes a kind of worship.

Verdi's first wife, whom he married when they were both very young, was the daughter of this excellent Busseto patriarch; but this is not the place to record all the memories of affection, sorrow, struggle and sacrifice which combine to make the name of such a beloved and beneficent relative so sacred to the Maestro. It is from this room, in the silence of the night, that the trembling harmonies burst forth from his creative genius. It was here that *Don Carlos* was composed, and this mighty opera, which rivals the most renowned masterpieces of French opera, was completed in the space of six months.

In one of the upper rooms I was shown his first piano, which replaced the wretched spinet described earlier; the sight of this would almost cause anyone devoted to art to faint in exultation. And near that piano I heard piquant anecdotes about Verdi's first compositions for the theatre, which differ radically from the usual fabricated accounts. There is little truth in what is generally claimed about the circumstances that preceded and accompanied the performances of *Nabucco*; but I shall only recount this story in all its details when I publish an extensive biography of Verdi which will include a critical study of all his operas.[11]

To conclude this sketch of the villa: everything that you see here, whether animate or inanimate, stationary or in motion, is beautiful, simple, attractive. As I stated earlier, the villa at Sant'Agata displays the luxury of a grand seigneur and the exquisite taste of an artist of genius.

Malevolent biographers, and above all that erudite ignoramus who goes by the name of Signor Fétis, not satisfied with having attempted to thwart the talent and glory of the celebrated Italian Maestro, with their reviews riddled with arrant sophistry, have also deigned to describe him as a moral and physical savage, one could almost say a bear.[12] Nothing is more foolish than caricature when it strikes wide of the mark.

Maestro Verdi is now fifty-five years of age. Tall, strong, slender, endowed with robust health and a robust, energetic character, he promises to keep his vigour for ever. When I met him for the first time twenty years ago, his entire appearance presented alarming symptoms. Whereas then his frail frame, pale face, sunken cheeks and deep-set eyes aroused ominous fears,[13] today you find nothing in that countenance but the glowing health and stability of a man destined for a long career.

And like his appearance, his character also seems to have changed for the better. No one could be more receptive, genial, expansive. What a difference between my taciturn table companion of 1846 and my lively and often high-spirited host of 1868! I have known artists who, in their youth, were light-heartedly and extravagantly cheerful and affable, and then became, with the veneer of glory and decorations, impenetrable and virtually intractable. Verdi, on the other hand, may be said to have proceeded through a career of triumphs and discarded after each one part of that hard and rough exterior, which characterized him in his younger years.

The villa at Sant'Agata is where Maestro Verdi still prefers to live. His prodigious physical and mental activity can develop here more freely than elsewhere. At five in the morning he walks along the avenues of his estate, visits the fields and farms, and amuses himself sailing up and down the lake in a small boat which he navigates skilfully.[14] He does not pause a moment. As respite from music, Verdi reads poetry; he finds an outlet for his strong emotions by seeking refuge in history and philosophy. There is no branch of human knowledge which his restless mind, avid for culture, does not research with rapture.

Signora Giuseppina Strepponi, his wife, who has an excellent mind and an affectionate heart, and is as cultured as she is lovable, shares with this Attic and gifted artist the pleasurable domestic duties. Harmony reigns in both their hearts and all that one sees around them.

And meanwhile, dispatches arrive from every corner of the civilized world, begging for operas, offering incredible sums of money, promising honours and triumphs. How long can Maestro Verdi resist such tempting offers of wealth and glory? I do not consider it possible for the composer of *Don Carlos* to exhaust the effervescence of his own genius, that overbearing need to express himself, which always spurs him on. The volcano has its moments of inactivity, but its latent fire must sooner or later erupt.

I could write at much greater length about the character, habits and way of life of this illustrious composer. But I shall halt here, convinced that I have already overstepped the bounds of discretion. Should Maestro Verdi not wish to pardon me for having, with great ingratitude, revealed the secrets of his abode, I shall take my revenge publicly, by divulging as much as I have already suppressed. Just try inviting these journalists to dinner – on the very next morning you will read in the paper a list of your dishes and wines!

ANTONIO GHISLANZONI

NOTES

1. There is a hint of this visit in a letter from Angelo Mariani to Giulio Ricordi, which Abbiati (*op. cit.*, III, p. 175) publishes without date, but which must go back to spring 1868:

   I shall do all I can to come to S. Agata, if only for a day, for I have the greatest desire to be with you, your family and dear Ghislanzoni at the home of the Maestro of Maestros.

   And there is a letter, dated 26 May 1868, from Giulio Ricordi to Verdi, thanking him for the welcome he received at Sant'Agata:

   I really cannot find words to express our gratitude and the pleasant, delightful feelings that will remain indelibly printed in our hearts; no, we shall never forget the great kindness with which you and dear Signora Peppina received us (autograph: Villa Verdi, Sant'Agata).

2. *Libro serio*, cit., pp. 27–28.
3. Expelled for bad behaviour from the seminary where his father, a doctor, had sent him to be educated, he enrolled for the faculty of medicine at Pavia university, where Antonio Stoppani was his friend and companion. On discovering he had a baritone voice, he left university to dedicate himself to the art of singing, making his début at Lodi in 1846. A year later he was at Milan's Teatro Carcano (where the young Angelo Mariani was conductor); when he refused to sing in a new opera by Uranio Fontana, in order to prevent the inevitable fiasco

that would have ensued (the date, fixed by the police for the première, gave no time for rehearsal), he spent several days in prison. He took part in the uprisings of '48, and founded two newspapers with republican ideas; having sheltered in Lugano and then in Tuscany when news broke of the proclamation of the Roman Republic, he endeavoured to reach Rome and join Garibaldi's troops, but was instead arrested by the French. Freed after four months' harsh imprisonment at Bastia, he resumed his singing career in that same city. Having landed at Marseille in March 1850, he appeared with touring companies in several provincial French theatres. After a performance of *Linda di Chamounix* in April 1851 at Rouen with Rossetti Sikorska and the tenor Antonio Giuglini, the following review by Amédée Mereaux appeared in *La France Musicale* (XV, 19: 11 May 1851, p. 151):

M. Ghislanzoni, the baritone buffo, played the part of the Marquis de Brisfleury with great comic verve. This artist gave a vivid demonstration of his talent as both singer and comedian.

On the evening of 2 December 1851 he made his début at the Théâtre Italien in *Ernani*, with Cruvelli and the tenor Guasco, without, however, creating a very favourable impression. It was during these days that the *coup d'état* was being prepared, which would lead to the birth of the Second Empire. Despite an attack of bronchitis which had damaged his voice, he continued to appear in French theatres (Rouen, Lyon, Poitiers, Limoges) with an opera company which he himself directed. He returned to Milan in 1854, and a year later he appeared at the Teatro Carcano, despite a now damaged voice, and was hissed. He himself wrote:

Throughout the various stages of my intermittent career, it had never been my lot to hear the sinister, shrill sound of hisses. I experienced this satisfaction – till then the only omission in my theatrical biography – five months ago in Milan: it was strident, relentless, worthy of me. The Teatro Carcano, which in 1847 had been my Marengo, was transformed eight years later into my Waterloo. The hisses, the screams, the abuse which assaulted me while I summoned in vain what remained of my expiring voice to sing the heroic part of Briano in *Il templario*, enjoined me to surrender. The morning after the rout, I resolutely decided to abdicate.

Exhorted by Giuseppe Rovani, the spiritual father of the ascendant Milanese Bohemianism, Ghislanzoni turned once and for all to journalism and writing, with only the occasional return to the theatre as impresario or assistant choreographer.

4. Besides his activities in France at the beginning of the '50s, he spent

some time on his return to Milan as a not very successful impresario at the Teatro di Santa Radegonda. He then returned to Paris for some time and collaborated with the choreographer Giuseppe Rota on several ballets, including *La contessa d'Egmont*.

5. He had already started to write libretti when singing in France. He wrote approximately 85; besides *Aida* and the revised version of *La forza del destino*, the following are worthy of mention: *I promessi sposi* (1869) for Petrella, *Il parlatore eterno* (1873) and *I Lituani* (1874) for Ponchielli, *Fosca* (1873) and *Salvator Rosa* (1874) for Gomes, *Papa Martin* (1871) for Cagnoni, *Edmea* (1886) for Catalani.

6. His first contributions were to the *Cosmorama Pittorico* of Milan, where he published in serial form his most famous novel, *Artisti di teatro*. In 1857 he helped found the humorous magazine *L'uomo di pietra*. He wrote for the *Italia Musicale*, published by Lucca, which ceased publication in 1859. He was director for several years of the *Gazzetta Musicale di Milano*, published by Ricordi, when it resumed publication in 1866. As literary and music critic he wrote for the main Milanese papers and magazines of the time. He founded and directed several newspapers, experimenting from time to time with new formulae, "always relying upon impulse and the inspiration of the moment" (G. MARIANI: *Storia della Scapigliatura*, S. Sciascia, Caltanissetta-Roma, 2nd edition, 1971, pp. 697–8.) In 1860 he founded *Lo Straordinario*, then *Il Lombardo* in 1861, the short-lived *Figaro* (for which Boito wrote theatre reviews) in 1864, the *Petite revue* which died at birth, in collaboration with Tarchetti in 1867, and so on until the *Rivista minima di scienze, lettere e arti* (1876), the *Giornale-Capriccio* in 1877, and finally the *Posta di Caprino*. The greater part of his literary output is to be found in the six volumes of the *Capricci letterari*, published between 1886 and 1889 by means of the subscription of numerous friends, Verdi included. His oeuvre includes, besides more than 2,100 articles and about 85 libretti, comedies, tragi-comedies, parodies of opera, chronicles (*Storia di Milano dal 1836 al 1848*), stories, novels, futuristic tales (*Abrakadabra*, 1883), eccentricities (*L'Arte di far debiti*), whimsical pieces (*Memorie d'un gatto*), autobiographical writings (*Memorie di un baritono*), humorous, political, fantastic and forbidden tales, etc., etc. . . . Mariani writes (*op. cit.*, p. 699):

> It is realistic humour that predominates in the writings of Ghislanzoni [. . .]; he is perhaps the only writer who portrays truthfully, with compassion, irony, smiles and bitterness, that *boulevardier* world, which is idle and aimless but intensely picturesque: sketches of layabouts ready to joke, failed writers, ruined second-rate actors, all of whom he describes in a wholly human way. And it is, I think, this description of the artist which we value most highly in the writings of Ghislanzoni – a description in which the sentimental, the pathetic, the paradoxical, the jocular, the comic and an angry social

commitment seem to blend, or rather harmonize in a belligerent
vision of life and art, drawn from his own experience as a journalist,
writer and artist.

7. E. GARA: "Peripezie di un librettista di Verdi", in *1941: Anno Verdiano.
   Chiusura delle manifestazioni*, Teatro Regio, Ass. Turistica Pro Parma,
   Parma 1941, p. 21.
8. This spinet is probably connected with an episode, related by one of
   Verdi's earliest biographers, Ercole Cavalli of Busseto, who also wrote
   the first biography of Verdi to appear in book form:

   > Verdi continued to live in Michiara's wretched house [the shoemaker
   > of Busseto, where Verdi, during his studies, had been sent to live
   > with full board by his father] and sorely missed a piano on which he
   > could practise and experiment to his heart's content; however, he
   > asked and pestered his father so much, that he finally consented. But
   > what a piano! It was one of those old spinets which did not cost a
   > single Milanese crown, that is to say less than five francs. Poor Carlo
   > had made an effort to please his son who, satisfied henceforth because
   > he could study at ease, played the instrument night and day. There is
   > a saying in Italy which runs: "The worst neighbour is a novice
   > studying music." I cannot keep silent about an event which, though
   > it vexed him at the time, was of great advantage to him later.
   > Opposite Michiara's house lived the carabinieri, whose chief was
   > called Giovannelli; and because the piano-playing had for many
   > nights disturbed his sleep, he complained to Michiara, insisting that
   > he let him sleep at night. The shoemaker told his lodger what had
   > happened; but since the latter took not the slightest notice of the
   > Chief of Police's command and continued his practice, the following
   > scene occurred one night. The Chief of Police, beside himself with
   > anger, leapt out of bed and, sword in hand, furiously summoned his
   > neighbour, threatening him that, if the racket did not cease and they
   > would not let him sleep, he would attack them with his sabre.
   > (H. CAVALLI: *Biografias artisticas contemporaneas de los celebres José
   > Verdi, maestro di musica y Antonio Canova escultor*, Imprenta de J. M.
   > Ducazcal, Madrid 1867, pp. 7–45.)

   Cavalli, who lived in Spain for a few years, dedicated his book to the
   tenor Gaetano Fraschini. Cavalli wrote another biographical sketch on
   the subject of Verdi's youth ("Giuseppe Verdi: Nuovi particolari inediti
   e interessanti") that appeared in *Il Pensiero di Nizza* on 29, 30, and
   31 December 1876 and 4 January 1877, but which with our present
   knowledge of Verdi's life is of relatively modest interest.
9. On 15 August 1868 (two and a half months after Ghislanzoni's visit to
   Sant'Agata), at the opening of the new Teatro Verdi in Busseto, a
   performance of *Rigoletto* was preceded by a youthful composition by
   Verdi – as we learn from the *Gazzetta di Parma* of August 16:

The orchestra, conducted by maestro Gaetano Bassoli, first violinist of the Busseto Orchestra, and made up for the most part by our own musicians [from the Parma orchestra], played the *Capricciosa*, a charming piece, composed by Verdi at the age of twelve.

Ghislanzoni is most probably referring to this work.
10. Antonio Barezzi had died the previous year, on 21 July 1867.
11. Ghislanzoni never wrote this work.
12. François-Joseph Fétis (Mons 1784 – Brussels 1871), musicologist, teacher and composer, considered to be one of the greatest music historians of his time. In September 1850 during a stay in Venice (in the months immediately before *Rigoletto*), he wrote two vicious articles about Verdi, which were published in the *Revue et Gazette Musicale de Paris* (XVII, n.37: 13 September 1850, pp. 308–10; n.39: September 29, pp. 322–5; see M. Mila: *Fétis e Verdi ovvero Gli infortuni della critica*, cit.). These articles were then printed in *Italia Musicale*, published by Lucca, in the *Rheinische Musikzeitung* of Cologne and in other periodicals, arousing lively controversy, from which Verdi wished to remain aloof. After the publication of the first article, he wrote to Giovanni Ricordi on 30 September 1850:

> I have read all your letters and the articles you sent me, and I have pondered your reasons, but I shall make no reply to Fétis' article. If you wish to reply, then do so in your own name, since I do not wish to be involved. He has behaved in an unbecoming and Jesuitic way, he has treated you disgracefully, but I shall not pen an article in reply. Escudier's article, though written with too much temper, contains truths that you will not always understand, since you are not perhaps sufficiently acquainted with all the subterfuges of that coterie, that continually hangs about the Opéra. We still cite that incident in Paris, when they dubbed Rossini Vacarmini, when we wish to ridicule over-emotional criticism. You know what Vacarme means in French [uproar, hubbub]. But if you want my opinion on the real merit of Fétis' article, I shall say that he could have done better. He could have tried harder, uttered rather fewer lies and not contradicted himself so often. He accuses me of total lack of originality and ideas, and further on he claims to have seen in your archives hundreds of dead scores, hardly born for lack of ideas. If these scores lacking ideas have failed, how come that my scores, likewise lacking ideas, are performed everywhere? Screams!! Good God! The champion of Halévy and Mayerber [sic] accuses me of screaming!! Control yourself, Signor Fétis! And besides, it is untrue that my effects are only produced through screaming. I do not know whether the Duet and Sleepwalking scene from Macbeth are beautiful, but I know that they produce an unusual effect, because in no age has it been usual to encore pieces three or four times. Well then! Where is there screaming? In the Ave Maria [I Lombardi] or the Duet between father and daughter in Luisa Miller? etc. etc. To compare my music with that of Bellini, Donizetti and Rossini is merely a

mendacious, puerile play of words. And as for implying that Italians scream and the French sing – that's arrant nonsense. And Signor Fétis calls himself a critic? Full of bad faith, he claims that the theatres are deserted – well, yesterday evening [at Bologna, where Verdi was staying for the production of *Macbeth*] *there was good proof to the contrary. But the cities are deserted, so why does he not state the cause?* [Verdi alludes to the changed political situation, after the failure of the '48 rebellion]. *So much for Signor Fétis!!* (Autograph: RAI – Radiotelevisione Italiana, Turin.)

In his article on Verdi, written in 1864, in his *Biographie Universelle des Musiciens* (2nd edit., Didot, Paris 1878, vol. VIII, pp. 321–5) Fétis pens this portrait of Verdi, to explain the composer's failure in the Milan Conservatoire exams . . .:

Those people who brought this action against the Milan Conservatoire are not aware that the Director then was Francesco Basili, one of the last Maestri produced by the great school of the eighteenth century, and an artist of great merit [. . .]. It is virtually certain that Basili searched Verdi's face for some indication of his artistic ability, because it is there that a Director can, in the majority of cases, appraise the potential of an aspiring student. Now, to anyone who has seen the composer of *Rigoletto* and *Il trovatore*, or merely his portrait, it is clear that a composer's physiognomy never gave less indication of talent. That cold appearance, that impassive expression and bearing, those thin lips, the general steeliness – all this could well indicate intelligence; a diplomat could be concealed behind such a countenance. But no one could discover there those impassioned emotions of the soul which alone preside at the creation of beautiful works of the most moving of all the arts.

Years later, à propos a short monograph by Monaldi (see introduction to N. XXVIII), Verdi wrote to Arrivabene in the following terms:

[. . .] *These writings repeat what has been said on the same topic by previous writers; when something is not known, it's invented – and that is how the Grrrreat Fétis proceeded. For all musicians he is an august personality; in fact, he is a mediocre theoretician, a very poor historian and a composer of enormous naïveté. I detest this great charlatan, not because he has said such hurtful things about me, but because one day he made me run to the Egyptian museum in Florence (do you remember, we went together?) to examine an ancient flute, on which he claimed (in his History of Music) to have discovered the system of ancient Egyptian music. A system equal to our own, except in the tonal quality of its instruments!!! Son of a bitch! That flute was nothing but a whistle with four holes, like our shepherds use. Thus* is history written! And imbeciles believe it! (Letter of 8 February 1878, in *Verdi intimo*, cit., p. 209.)

On the episode of the "Egyptian flute", see also N. XLIX, p. oo.

13. Indeed, Verdi was in rather poor health in 1846. The physical strain caused by intense work (three operas in nine months between autumn 1844 and summer 1845: *I due Foscari* at Rome, *Giovanna d'Arco* at Milan, *Alzira* at Naples, besides the staging of the *I Lombardi* revival at La Scala and *I due Foscari* at Venice etc.) was followed by frequent illnesses caused by rheumatic fever and gastric disturbances. The most serious crisis occurred in Venice in January 1846 during the composition of *Attila*, when there were fears for his life (see N. V, note 8). The illness left him somewhat debilitated; Verdi was forced to postpone several engagements (including a new opera for London, which had been agreed with the publisher Lucca) in order to take a long period of convalescence, which included a summer stay at Recoaro in the company of Andrea Maffei.

14. Little lake – or "puddle" in Giuseppina Verdi's words – which, almost exactly one year later, nearly proved fatal to both Giuseppina and Verdi. The account of the incident is contained in a letter, dated 18 July 1869, from Giuseppina to Clara Maffei:

> God be thanked that it's over now – it's thus unnecessary for me to attempt to give you a palpitatingly tragic description of it . . . but all the same, I can tell you that the puddle, the infamous puddle nearly became our tomb. The ancient proverb is right, when it says that still waters should never be trusted. Verdi was in the boat, holding out his hand to help me in. I had one foot in the boat, but in setting down the other the boat capsized and down we both went to the bottom – the very bottom of the lake! Verdi, thank God, chance or his presence of mind, feeling the boat brush against his head was able, by raising an arm, to thrust away that sort of coffin lid. This movement somehow helped him to get on his feet, and in that position he was able, with incredible strength and promptitude and with the help of Corticelli, to pull me out of the water, where I was unable to move, caught by my dreadfully distended silk garments, virtually unaware of my predicament, and thus making no attempt to save myself. I shall not describe the alarm, the despair of my poor sister who ran away crying "Help!", or the fright of all who saw us in that terrible moment. I hadn't had time, so to speak, to take fright, since losing my balance and finding myself with two fathoms of water over my head had all occurred in a flash. I was about to faint, when I opened my eyes and found myself supported by the arm of Verdi, who was standing bolt upright with water up to his throat, and I thought he must have hurled himself in on purpose to save me. It was only later that I learned how things had happened, and then I was seized with terror, thinking of Verdi and the consequences which that sorry involuntary bathe could have had for him and art. As for myself, being nothing to the world . . . but let's think no more of

*it . . . My sister, my mother . . . Gesu Maria, how many misfortunes if
. . . Tell Giulio* [Ricordi] *what happened, as I don't wish to repeat it over
and over again; but for the love of God, save us from the newspapers and
their lying exaggerations.* (A. LUZIO: *Profili biografici* [. . .], cit.,
pp. 558–9.)

XII

THE ORIGIN OF A THEME FROM *AIDA*

1869–1870

[STEFANO SIVELLI]: "L'origine d'un motivo dell'*Aida*", in *L'Italia*, Milan,
14 January 1941 (reprinted in *La Giovane Montagna*, Parma, XLII, 1:
15 January 1941; then in V. MARCHI: "Un'invocazione dell'*Aida*", in *Aurea
Parma*, XLIV, 2: April–June 1960, pp. 101–2).

WE HAVE HERE an eye-witness account which, though of compara-
tively recent date, is none the less reasonably reliable; it is certainly
the most credible of all the many versions known to us about the
incident concerning the local, home-grown sources of several
"Egyptian" themes from *Aida*. The "anecdote" was also included in
Bruno Barilli's volume,[1] ("who perhaps", observes Marchi in "Un'
invocazione dell'*Aida*", p. 103, "did not recall the incident in all its
details"); Barilli presents his thesis in a famous passage, but in a
somewhat fanciful style. The metaphor, however, which he uses to
comment on the incident, remains a classic: "Verdi can see the entire
Orient in one of our native fruits, such as the water-melon."[2] There
is another, slightly earlier account of the same subject, almost
unknown in Italy, which should, however, be approached with considerable circumspection. It appears in an article by BENNO GEIGER:
"Erlebnisse mit Giuseppe Verdi", in *Deutsche Revue*, Stuttgart,
XXIV, 1902, pp. 71–80 (reprinted in P. NETTL: *The Book of Musical
Documents*, New York 1948, pp. 302–3;[3] and O. ZOFF: *Die grossen
Komponisten gesehen von ihren Zeitgenossen*, Scherz, Bern 1952, pp.
257 ff.; and also in several dictionaries of opera, such as R. KLOIBER:
Handbuch der Oper, new edit., DTV-Bärenreiter, Kassel 1973, II,
p. 654). These "Erlebnisse", though signed by Geiger, are in fact the
work of Count Leopold Thurn von Valsassina, who was introduced
to him by "the kind mediation of Countess Contin [?] di Castel-
seprio", as Geiger himself, then twenty years old, informs us at the
end of the article.[4] The "Erlebnisse" concentrate chiefly on recalling a
visit to Sant'Agata, made by Leopold Thurn with his mother, when
Verdi was composing *Aida* and Thurn was still a boy. The phrases
attributed to Verdi in the course of these memoirs, some of which

are recorded in the original Italian, and several of the attitudes attributed to Verdi, seem to contradict openly so many well-known accounts of the composer's irritable character and laconic speech, and thus lack authenticity. A passage like the following, in which Verdi announces to Count Thurn's mother that he is composing another opera, is enough to make us query the reliability of these memoirs:

> "*You see, Signora Isolde,*" he began, turning to my mother, "*I now have to compose a new opera:*[5] Ismail Pascià, Khédive of Egypt, commissioned it from me not long ago for the opening of the Suez Canal. It will be an Egyptian opera. I myself have visited Egypt to gather the necessary material: at Luxor, on the Nile, in the Egyptian temples . . ."

There is no need to mention that Verdi was never in Egypt (indeed he states explicitly in the contract that someone should be sent at his expense "to conduct and direct the opera at Cairo");[6] and there is little point in recalling that *Aida* was not written for the opening of the Suez Canal, which had already been opened on 17 November 1869 – some time, therefore, before the negotiations for *Aida*, that effectively began in the spring of 1870.[7] It is true, however, that Verdi and several assistants collected many notes on ancient Egypt concerning ceremony, costume and musical instruments etc.[8] And it is therefore possible that 30 years later Count Thurn mistook this research for an actual journey to the land of the pharaohs.

For all these reasons Geiger's article/Count Thurn di Valsassina's memoirs have not been included in this anthology. Nonetheless, however inauthentic the words and attitudes ascribed to Verdi seem, there is one passage that rings reasonably true; as Gradenwitz remarks: "The narrator here recorded observations, the truth of which can be confirmed by any expert acquainted with how popular Italian tunes come into being through continual contact with oriental countries."[9] Here is the passage in question:

> [. . .] "*Now you shall hear something beautiful!*"[10] [Verdi] exclaimed once more, and sang a measured, unrestrained melody which, coming between the elegiac phrases of a chorus, seemed to ring out at intervals like an impassioned lament. Until this moment I had spoken little, if at all, with the Maestro, partly because my age did not permit me, and partly because my mother, more closely connected with him, was conversing with him

almost all the time. But I could not now prevent myself from exclaiming:

"*But professore, I know that tune,*[10] and I even know the words that are usually sung to it!" And Verdi replied:

"*Yes, yes, it is a song our mountain-folk sing in the Apennines as they return from work. You are right, Poldino, you are certainly right; it is a melody that suits this opera well.*"[10] And he continued, by way of explanation:

"The fishermen and sailors who in Italy are, strangely, for the most part mountain-folk, usually bring the songs from the East into our country: from Syria and Asia Minor to the summits of the Ligurian Apennines. They are then sung, adapt themselves to the region, and are inherited by future generations together with the songs of our own people. The melody that I have used here is, I think, one of those songs brought here by sailors from the East. To the Italian ear the augmented sixth, typical of oriental modes, sounded strange, and was thus naturally brought into line with the diatonic scale. Nonetheless, a tinge of languor, an oriental fragrance remains that I, as a musician, can recognize in this popular song."

And once again he played us the melody which we hear, perfectly adapted, in *Aida*. Who could imagine that the music which flows gently from everyone's lips in the first scene of the second act, when the love-lorn Amneris, surrounded by her slaves, prepares for the celebrations, had been so ingeniously gathered by Verdi from the lips of that very people who today still sing the same music as if it were their own?

[. . .] "And so I welcome this popular song in Aida," Verdi added, "precisely because of its oriental flavour." [. . .][11]

The remark – attributed by Geiger, alias Count Thurn, to Verdi – about Italian sailors and their mountain origins, does not appear entirely without foundation (recent research into the music of the Apennine valleys in the province of Parma confirmed how in some areas, especially the Val Ceno, there had in the past been a constant stream of inhabitants leaving the mountains for maritime professions: ship's cooks, stokers etc.). Nevertheless, the explanation concerning the "oriental flavour" of the songs that reached the Ligurian Apennines from across the sea and then spread to neighbouring regions, reveals the typical attitude of a trained musician towards a "different" culture with its own particular characteristics. Even if one cannot exclude the possibility of contact with distant peoples influencing the songs, it is the survival of modal characteristics in the folk-songs of the Apennines that makes them sound "oriental" to the trained musician.[12] This may or may not have been influenced by liturgical chant, but recent folk-song research has provided ample confirmation of their survival down to the present age in central-northern Italy, and scholars consider them particular to this region.[13]

But let us return to Sivelli's account, certainly more reliable than that of Count Thurn, published by Geiger. According to Sivelli, the incident dates back to autumn 1869, when Verdi was not yet thinking of Aida. It is possible that the composer, hearing the vendor of cooked pears sing his strange song, noted it down without having any immediate use for it in mind; but it is most probable that the episode took place in the autumn or late summer of 1870, when Verdi was already at work on Aida.[14]

Referring to the melody from Aida, in which he recognized the pear-vendor's song, Sivelli draws particular attention to the "invocation of the priestesses" in Act 3; but instead of quoting the text that they sing, he quotes the words given to the priests, thus fortunately misleading Marchi, who refers in his article to the melody in E minor of the male voices instead of to the melody in G minor of the women's voices:

It was fortunate that Marchi was misled, since, having this melody in his mind, he drew the analogy (that has escaped many scholars) with

the melody of the liturgical parody in the final scene of *Falstaff*:
"Domine fallo casto!"[14] That Sivelli was guilty of a slip in quoting
the wrong text, and yet was right to refer to the "invocation of the
priestesses" is shown by the following example, in which the text of
the pear-vendor's song, when compared with that of the priestesses',
reveals a substantial rhythmic similarity which is not so apparent
when compared with the priests' song:

It is surprising to note that Verdi's acute ear, almost as if obeying a
distant ancestral voice, had detected in the pear-vendor's song the
origins of the liturgical singing of psalms, restoring it to the atmosphere of the temple, albeit Egyptian, and bestowing upon it once
more the original character of a priest's refrain. But in connection
with this, see Marchi's arguments, *art. cit.*, inspired by Leo
Spitzer's[16] essay, which in turn was inspired by a most subtle
observation by Marcel Proust on the close similarity between the
vendor's cries that rouse Parisians from slumber and the chants of the
Catholic Church.

The origin of a theme from Aida

[. . .] The anecdote was told us by a friend of Professor Stefano
Sivelli, who played in the orchestra[17] in the first performances of
Aida at Cairo and Parma.[18]

In the autumn of 1869 – began Prof. Sivelli – on a cold, grey
afternoon, I was in Casali's shop, which sold earthenware goods, in
Via Farini (at that time Strada dei Genovesi), talking with the shop-
owner, poor Chitarrèn, one of the genial characters of old Parma.

Our conversation was interrupted by the entrance of a tall gentleman with grizzled hair, wearing a loose-fitting black jacket, a broad-
brimmed hat and a black neckerchief. He was accompanied by a
rather elderly lady, slightly bent, with a pale and suffering expression. The gentleman – whom I instantly recognized as the Maestro,
already famous and dear to the people of Italy – turned to Casali and
said in a baritonal voice: "Siòr Casali, bring me some bowls." Old

Chitarrèn promptly showed his customer, whom he did not know, the best articles on the shelves, and Giuseppe Verdi began to examine closely the various kinds of bowls, seeking advice from his pale and smiling companion, Signora Giuseppina Strepponi.

Outside in the street there was the usual silence of our peaceful afternoons. The solitary, faint and rhythmic sound of a monotonous, sing-song voice could be heard from time to time. It was Paita, the much-loved vendor of cooked pears, who was selling his wares to the accompaniment of a rhythmic refrain: "Boiènt i pèr còtt, boièèènt!" (Hot cooked pears, hooot!)

A brief pause . . . then again, closer and clearer, that slow, sing-song voice. Verdi looked up with bright eyes from the many-coloured bowls, and stood still for a moment, listening, as if pursuing his own thoughts.

Paita's voice, now clear and strong, rang out in the stillness of the empty street: "Boiènt i pèr còtt, boièèènt!" Verdi's face suddenly lit up with one of those flashes that often blazed in his eyes, he abandoned the bowls, his wife and Chitarrèn, took from his waist-coat pocket a little note-book, ran to the shop door and stared at old Paita, who was still beseeching people to buy his stewed fruit. Verdi rapidly scribbled a few lines in his notebook, returned merrily to the counter and accepted without discussion his angelic wife's expert choice of bowl.

Two years later, in the Khédive's theatre at Cairo, I was rehearsing for the first time the score of *Aida*, which Giovanni Bottesini had just handed out to the orchestra.

At the beginning of Act 3, when all of us already felt indescribably excited by this wonderful masterpiece, I was strangely struck by a familiar theme. It was the moment when, in the bright moonlit night, the invocation of the priestesses rises from the temple of Isis on the banks of the Nile:

> *O tu che sei d'Osiride*
> *Madre immortale e sposa . . .*

The mystical, melancholy theme was not new to me. But where and when had I heard it? And amidst the triumphant harmonies that rose from the sumptuous Egyptian theatre, I seemed to hear the hawker Paita's tenor voice repeating his refrain. Softly the strings repeated the prayer to the Goddess, and the vision of that distant autumnal morning loomed clearly before me, when Giuseppe Verdi heard the voice from the street, left the bowls on Chitarrèn's counter and hastily scribbled in his notebook. The refrain of our own Paita had been written down by our eminent Maestro and then immortalized in the sublime masterpiece.

From that moment on, Paita was for me no longer the good old man from whom, as a boy, I used to buy tasty fruit; he had become nothing less than an unknown collaborator of Giuseppe Verdi.

NOTES

1. B. BARILLI: *Il paese del melodramma*, Carabba, Lanciano [1930], p. 53 (new edit. edited by E. Falqui: Vallecchi, Florence 1963, pp. 114–5). M. MILA (in *Verdi*, Laterza, Bari, 1958, p. 85, note 1) remarks à propos the episode described by Barilli, that "whether true or invented, it well illustrates the strength and originality of Verdi's exoticism".
2. Cf. G. BALDINI: *Le acque rosse del Potomac*, Rizzoli, Milan 1967, in the chapter "Il Cocomero di Barilli" (1966), pp. 141–4.
3. But only partially, and quoted as a Verdi letter!
4. Art historian, poet, translator and political journalist, the Viennese Benno Geiger was a friend of Rainer Maria Rilke, Stefan Zweig, Hugo von Hofmannsthal, an acquaintance of Arrigo Boito and Lorenzo Perosi, and lived for many years in Italy. In one of his books of memoirs (*Memorie di un Veneziano*, Vallecchi, Florence 1958, published in a limited edition) he recalls the article on Verdi published in *Deutsche Revue*, and reaffirms that, although it had been attributed to him later on as a personal recollection of several encounters with Verdi, it was in fact based on confidences made to him by Count Leopold Thurn of Valsassina, who during his youth did indeed live at Busseto near Verdi (see P. GRADENWITZ: *Musik zwischen Orient und Okzident. Eine Kulturgeschichte der Wechselbeziehungen,* Heinrichshofen, Wilhelmshaven–Hamburg 1977, pp. 297–300, to whom I am grateful for the information concerning Geiger and his volume of memoirs). But here is what Geiger himself writes in his *Memorie* about his article and about his encounter (or rather non-encounter) with Verdi:

> I had previously written a long essay on Don Lorenzo Perosi in the *Deutsche Revue* and then in 1901, in the same paper, a commemoration of Verdi, whom I pretended to have known (in fact I merely related the memoirs, confided to me by an old gentleman, Count Leopold Thurn di Valsassina who, in his youth, had actually lived near Verdi in Busseto). Not as yet inflamed by the passion for Wagner and his wonderful operas, which restored to the world the pagan German gods, resurrecting them in poetry and music, emulating Homer's prototypes, I was still far from viewing Verdi – as I did later (what intolerance and unadmitted deficiency!) as the inventor of music for those instruments, that were activated by a handle and dragged along the streets by a mule, and designed to vulgarize

genius. I am aware that many people will not pardon me what I am
about to say, but I have never been able to tolerate geniuses with a
certain sort of white beard, designed to inspire confidence, neither
Garibaldi, nor Verdi. [. . .] Verdi, then, with all his undeniable
vulgar genius, is for me the prototype of Italian bad taste – as
represented by town bands full of trombones and drums (which
influenced him as a young man), and by those vendors of plaster
statues who sell his portrait abroad, shouldering it together with the
portrait of Giuseppe Mazzini. Italian taste can be sublime; in every
age right down to our own it thrives in the likes of Petrarch,
Leopardi, Poliziano, Foscolo of the *Sepolcri*, Palestrina and even
Perosi. But there is another type of taste, exemplified by people who
eat impolitely at table, cut fish with a knife which they put into their
mouth with or without the fish, who clean their nails with a
toothpick with which they also remove wax from their ears, who
bawl along the streets at night, striking up deafening serenades with
mandoline and guitar accompaniment – taste, which a hundred years
ago, well before Marinetti, anticipated the loudspeaker at cross-roads
and in churches, neon-lighting, the hooters of motor vehicles and
advertisement hoardings in the street. Verdi – when I am obliged to
listen to his music, or when a barrel-organ passes (I mean used to
pass) along the street – is for me the official representative, metaphor-
ically of course, of all this bad taste: nagging and wearisome (to my
ears, I repeat, not to other people's), like a "commercial" on the radio
at one o'clock in the afternoon. [. . .] And if I read the texts of his
librettist Piave, I ask myself: at what level did this genius operate?
What on earth could have incited him to set them to music, except an
absolute lack of even a modicum of literary taste? [. . .] Are not
I due Foscari, *Ernani* and *Simon Boccanegra* infinitely old-fashioned – as
indeed is basically the case with all the rest of Verdi's noisy operas?
The only exception is, perhaps, *Falstaff*, where the composer, the
equivalent of an Italian Meyerbeer, whiffed the Bayreuth perfume,
combed his white beard and, at death's door, mended his ways.
[. . .]

5. Italian in the original.
6. *I Copialettere*, cit., p. 225.
7. G. Carrara Verdi: *Preliminari di "Aida"*, cit.; U. Günther: *Zur
   Entstehung von Verdis "Aida"*, cit.
8. See, for example, Verdi's letter to Du Locle of 15 July 1870, in
   F. Abbiati, *op. cit.*, III, p. 376:

   *Thank you for the information on the Eygptian musical instruments that
   could be of use in several places [. . .] And tell me: Did Isis or other
   divinities have priestesses? In the books that I have leafed through, I find that
   it was more the men who officiated. Please inform me about this and think*

seriously about the costumes, which need to be excellent and authentic [. . .] (autograph: Bibliothèque de l'Opéra, Paris).

9. P. GRADENWITZ, *op. cit.*, p. 300.
10. Italian in the original.
11. B. GEIGER, *art. cit.*, pp. 75–76.
12. M. CONATI: "Il 'popolare' in Verdi e Verdi nel 'popolare'. Appunti e considerazioni", in *Atti della IX Sessione musicologica italo-polacca dedicata alla musica del tardo Romanticismo*: Warsaw, 4–5 October 1977, soon to be published.
13. For the popular songs of the mountainous regions near Parma, including some traditional liturgical songs, see M. CONATI: *Canti popolari della Val d'Enza e della Val Cedra*, edited by the Communità delle Valli dei Cavalieri, Parma 1976, with record enclosed.
14. Since the episode narrated by Sivelli refers to a melody from the third act of *Aida*, it will be as well to remember that the composition of this act was only begun at the end of September 1870, as two letters (September 28 and 30) from Verdi to Ghislanzoni reveal: *"This third act is very good, though there are passages which should, I think, be revised."* And *"I did not write immediately, because I wanted to compose the first scene of Act III. Because the tune that the chorus sings is weighty, eight verses are too many – six would suffice."* (*I Copialettere di G. Verdi*, cit., pp. 645 and 646.)
15. V. MARCHI, *art. cit.*, p. 103. An analogy between the burlesque cantilena from *Falstaff* and the spacious melody of the *Requiem*'s "Hostias" has been pointed out by CHARLES OSBORNE: *The Complete Operas of Verdi: A Critical Guide*, V. Gollancz, London 1969, p. 448.
16. L. SPITZER: *"L'etimologia di un 'cri de Paris'"*, originally in *Palatina*, Parma, n. 3, 1957, then included in the same author's volume: *Marcel Proust e altri saggi di letteratura francese*, Einaudi, Turin 1959, pp. 345–51.
17. *Aida* was performed at the Reggio di Parma on 20 April 1872 with Stolz, Waldmann, the tenor Giuseppe Capponi, the baritone Adriano Pantaleoni, conducted by Giovanni Rossi. Verdi himself supervised the rehearsals and staging.
18. His name also figures, as an ophicleide player, in the list of orchestral players that was printed on pages 4–5 of the first edition of the libretto to *Aida*, which was published in Italian and French (Tipografia Francese Delbos-Demouret, Cairo 1871).

XIII

A PORTRAIT OF VERDI
SKETCHED BY AN AMERICAN PEN

1871

ANON: "Ritratto di Verdi disegnato da una penna americana", in *Il Trovatore*, Milan, XVIII, 33: 17 August 1871, p. (2).

IT IS NOT known from which North or South American newspaper this portrait of Verdi was taken. It nonetheless appears authentic; sketched with just a few essential strokes, it is as lapidary as the composer's own style and needs no comment.

A portrait of Verdi sketched by an American pen

A broad, open face – more lean than fleshy; masculine, energetic features, reminiscent of a Salvator Rosa bandit chief. His gaze is fateful and legendary. Bushy eyebrows conceal his gray eyes in mysterious shade. From his small broad nose two deep wrinkles, like two furrows dug from disdain, descend to his chin.

A beard as black as coal hides an ever ironic smile; his broad, masculine brow is covered by a luxuriant crop of hair with artistically dishevelled locks. The general expression of his countenance is most severe, proud and arrogant. His features denote an indomitable will, fearlessness and suspicion – a true Rienzi, manly to the point of roughness.

Verdi is a man of proven honesty and proverbial shyness; he shuns society, obstinately refusing every invitation to dinners, parties and dances. He detests compliments and abhors *claques* above all else.

His character is bizarre, eccentric, problematic. Verdi is a stiff, hard, unsociable, impatient man with a constantly threatening appearance. To the uninterested he presents an ice-cold exterior and never expresses his own opinion, especially in musical matters. He shudders at the sight of an *album* or when asked to sit for a portrait. In short, he is indescribably eccentric. No one dares approach or interrupt him during rehearsals; he shows no pity towards the interpreters of his music and, if necessary, will make them repeat the same piece ten times over, without regard for their exhaustion, until he is satisfied. He flies into a fury at the slightest provocation, and the most insignificant incident excites his nervous irritability. In a word, Verdi is a nightmare for singers and players alike.

XIV

MY FIRST INTERVIEW WITH VERDI

1875

BLANCHE ROOSEVELT: *Verdi, Milan and "Othello"*. Being a short Life of Verdi, with Letters written about Milan and the new opera of *Othello*, Ward & Downey, London, 1887; see chapter XV: "My first interview with Verdi" [interview first published in *Chicago Times*, June 1875, pp. 75–84].

BLANCHE ROOSEVELT, SINGER, journalist, writer was born in Sanduski, Ohio, USA, in 1853, the daughter of a senator. Described by Victor Hugo as "the beauty and genius of the New World", she moved when very young to Milan to learn the art of singing; her first newspaper articles date from that period. She made her début at Covent Garden in 1876 in *La traviata* under the name of Blanche Rosavella, without creating a very favourable impression: her voice was rather ugly and her intonation unreliable; she was, however, a most attractive woman. Later on she sang in Milan, Belgium, Paris and America. She married an Italian, Signor Macchetti, who later succeeded to the title of Marquis of Alligri. At thirty she published her first book, *Stage struck; or, She Would Be an Opera Singer*, which amongst other things contained a description of the often eccentric method of many contemporary singing teachers, including that of the famous Lamperti, "based on the theory that the voice comes from the stomach". She died when still young in London in 1898, as a result of injuries sustained several months previously at Monte Carlo, when the carriage in which she was travelling overturned.[1]

At the time of her visit to Verdi, Blanche Roosevelt was 22, and for more than a year she had been living in Paris, completing her singing studies at the school of the celebrated Pauline Viardot. Although her article in the *Chicago Times* bears the date 5 June 1875, the interview must have taken place about a month before – i.e. before the composer left Paris for London on 5 June 1875, as Miss Roosevelt herself states. The interview can therefore be placed at the time of the revival of the *Requiem* at the Salle Favart in Paris (home of the Opéra-Comique, of which Du Locle was then director), the first stop of a tour on which performances of the *Requiem* were to have taken the composer and his four soloists (Teresa Stolz, Maria Waldmann, Angelo Masini and Paolo Medini) to London, Berlin and Vienna. After seven performances at the Salle Favart (the first took place on April 19), the *Requiem* was given at the Albert Hall, London, where it received three other performances. But because of a small financial loss, Ricordi, the publisher, decided to cancel the Berlin stage of the tour, to the great annoyance of Verdi who cherished the opportunity of performing the *Requiem* in Berlin. The tour proceeded to Vienna (June 11) and finished in Venice at the Teatro Malibran, where Franco Faccio conducted, since Verdi had in the meantime returned to Sant'Agata. Refusing to forgive Ricordi for cancelling the Berlin performances, he now wished to review all his contracts from *Rigoletto* onwards; a long dispute began, which was only settled when damages were agreed out of court and the publisher paid Verdi 50,000 lire. The inspiration for this tour is explained in a memorable passage, dated July 1875, from Giuseppina's diary – quoted here in Luzio's[2] succinct narrative (Giuseppina's words are in inverted commas):

"Verdi's aim was to play Italian music as he thought it should be played, in the hope of establishing it abroad, especially in Germany", a musical country of the highest rank. "If art could gain glory from this, the commercial gain for the publisher might be incalculable." But Ricordi preferred not to run the risk, as *Aida*'s triumph still seemed insufficiently European! "The glorious success of the *Requiem* in Paris caused him to think again of Germany and London. Verdi, who always cherished in his artist's heart the project that had failed once before,[3] agreed to the tour . . ." "After the splendid performances in Paris, we went to London. We neither wished to nor could get to know the country. Instead of taking many days off, we were obliged to give the greatest possible number of performances [. . .]. In that distant hall, in the horseracing season, in a city with a population of three million, the success of the first performance in the Albert Hall was simply not enough: it was necessary to repeat the *Requiem* the maximum number of times; the great mass of people who attended the fourth and final London performance proves the truth of what I say." However, the small financial loss incurred in London caused a panic "which, it must be said, made Verdi smile bitterly", but which also brought about the ill-considered decision to omit Berlin and make straight for Austria! "We travelled to

Vienna, a smaller, more attentive city, and extremely musical. The artistic success was as great as one could have wished (nor was there any cause for financial alarm)". On returning to Italy, however, Verdi's ill-temper could not help but turn against the instigators of the enterprise with the famous biblical cry: "homo modicae fidei quare dubitasti?"

In the interview with Miss Roosevelt, Verdi alludes to the improved performances of the *Requiem*, brought about by the presence of two new artists: the tenor Angelo Masini and the bass Paolo Medini, who had created the role of Ramfis in *Aida* at Cairo. The previous year, again at the Salle Favart, the *Requiem* had been performed immediately after the first Milan peformances (at the church of San Marco and La Scala), with Stolz, Waldmann, the tenor Giuseppe Capponi and the bass Ormondo Maini: there had been eight performances, the first taking place on July 9.

My First Interview with Verdi

Paris, 5 June 1875

The second season of Verdi's Mass at Paris, one morning the thought struck me, "I'll call on the great composer, and see what he looks like face to face." Learning that he was stopping at the Hôtel de Bade, I carefully noted down the address, fully intending to avail myself of a kind invitation, received a little time before from the Maestro himself, to call on him some day at his residence.

A hurried rush into the director's room after performance is never very satisfactory, and compliments, however earnest, must be very ingenious to be well said in a hurry; so, after the *au revoir* at the stage-door, I made up my mind to see the great master before he went to London.

The Hôtel de Bade is always graced by any amount of professionals, and we were not surprised in coming up before the entrance door to see a number of the stars lounging about in the sun. No. 79 is on the second floor, and after the *concierge* sent us up I fell to wondering whether Verdi would look like an ordinary man or not. A very smiling waiter elbowed his way past with a tray, and somehow it looked as though we ought to follow him, which we did, and we stopped before a door numbered 79. He went in, and we gave our cards to a smart-looking servant who came out of an inner room. Mamma and I sat down, waiting until we should be shown into the presence of the author of *Il trovatore*.

The ante-room was rather large. At one side was a table, at which was seated a young woman busily writing. She didn't look up, and I am sure she was not very interesting. I stared hard at her and then hard at the wall, which almost seemed to touch her left elbow. The wall was perfectly blank and dark-coloured, but some way I saw scores of music all over it; then it gradually became a stage, where musicians, chorus, and artists all seemed jumbled together in one confused mass. I looked harder, and they began to shape themselves. There was the orchestra at the back of the stage, and the chorus-singers, all dressed in white, with graceful drapery of black lace falling over head and shoulders. There was a murmur, and two dark gentlemen came forward with a look that said, "Behold the tenor and bass solo artists." They took two seats in front. Then there was a slight rustle, another murmur, and two queenly women, in long trailing robes of white satin, came forward, their faces lighted with pride and pleasure. Following them closely was Verdi himself. The three stepped forward to the footlights, and my imaginary stage seemed to tremble with the shouts and cries of welcome that rang on every side. The ladies sat down. Verdi took up the baton; there was a hush, and the music was about to begin. I seemed in dreamland; I could hear the first soft notes of the instruments as they commenced the opening number; I could hear the melody wind in and out, like the clear waters of a mountain brooklet. I looked at Madame Stolz, then at Madame Waldmann, and I wondered if there ever could be such lovely golden hair as she had, unless in a picture.[4] The threads seemed to shimmer and glow under the black Venetian veil she wore, like summer sunlight falling on a gilded harp. The music grew sweeter and louder; the wave of the baton was more vigorous, and the chorus was just about to come in, when I heard a decidedly waiterish voice say, in pure French, "Have the goodness to come into the large salon; M. Verdi will come in directly." I started and looked at my wall, but the musicians had faded away, leaving it blank as before. Evidently I had only been dreaming. The waiter's voice brought me to my senses. Imagination was very tame compared with the reality that was soon to be before me. I got up, but vouchsafed a last look at the *nonchalante* who sat at the table. She was still writing, and, as she never turned her head, we went into the grand salon.

Did you ever hear of a woman before who had so little curiosity? I thought she'd look up once at least; but no, she never moved, and we were allowed to enter the parlour, feeling that there was one person in that hotel totally unaware of the great importance and honour of making a morning call on Verdi.

The door closed, and we found ourselves in a richly-furnished room, with a square table containing a coffee-service on one side and an Erard piano on the other. Of course the piano took my eye first, and after that the china. I was wondering whether the one was up to concert pitch, and how *Traviata* would sound played by the master's fingers; then next, if the china was Sèvres or Dresden, when I heard as near by, "*Buon giorno, signorina,*" and the Maestro stood before us.

Yes, he looked just exactly the same as when he stood on the stage of the Opéra Comique.

His personal appearance is not striking; he is small[5] but very broad-shouldered, with a full, generous chest, and well-built body. He has large, laughing gray eyes, eyes that flash and change colour every instant. The face is strong, and shows very few lines for a man of his years. The features are large, the cheek-bones high, and the lower part of the jaw rather sunken; the chin and side of the face are covered with a short heavy beard, once black, but now slightly mixed with gray. The mouth is large and pleasant, but it is almost totally concealed by a dark moustache, which gives the face a very young look. The forehead is very broad and high, denoting great character and quickness of perception; the eyebrows are heavy, also gray and black. The hair is very long, lying lightly on the forehead; it, also, is slightly mixed with gray. There are a wonderful firmness and hidden strength in Verdi's countenance, which made me think of a picture I had once seen of Samson.

In one way I was disappointed in his looks. He has the air and figure of anything but an ideal composer. I do not know what I expected to find, but certainly he has the frank, social manners of an ordinary individual rather than the exclusive and sometimes painful diffidence characteristic of men of great talent. I cannot say he lacks dignity, but there was so utter an absence of self-consciousness in his bearing, and such a happy, gracious smile on his face, that I was charmed with his whole manner.

We arose as soon as he entered the room. He came forward with outstretched hands and pleasant words to greet us, and then begged us to be seated. Smilingly looking at the breakfast service, he said, "I haven't taken my coffee yet; will you excuse me, and perhaps you will also have a cup – you know one can always drink coffee in Paris."

We declined the proffered nectar, but looked at the god.

Verdi, looking quickly up, said, "Mademoiselle, how do you like Paris?"

"Paris! Why, dear Maestro, it's the most beautiful city in the world. Don't you think so?"

"Yes; it's too beautiful," said Verdi. "My time is always wasted here. I do nothing, and find that some way the hours fly while I am even thinking of work. Yes, it is far too beautiful for anything but pleasure. I never could compose here. I am very fond of the city, but, strange to say, I am more fond of the country – agriculture, roaming about the fields, through lone forests, where I can be quiet and admire nature with all its many beauties undisturbed. I do all my writing in the country; somehow there everything comes at once, quite without effort, and I am more contented."

"But," I interrupted, "you go soon to London; how do you like that great city?"

Verdi groaned. "Don't mention it," he said. "It's as much too sad as Paris is too gay. I think were I to live there more than three weeks that I should die."

Then he stirred his coffee vigorously, and I sympathized with him in his opinion of London, only I persisted that during "the season", for a time, it was very agreeable.

"O! I was speaking of 'the season', also," said Verdi; "but London is a sad, dreary place at all times."

"Aren't you pleased with the reception given you by the Parisians?"

"O, yes," said Verdi; "the French people are an amiable race, and I am sorry I cannot stay longer in Paris, but must go soon to London, as the rehearsals must begin in the Royal Albert Hall for the *Messa di Requiem*."

"Ah, that Mass," said I, "how beautiful it is! And then, too, Maestro, you are fortunate in being accompanied by such artists."

"You are right," said Verdi. "I am every day more thankful that the score is in such hands. But how do you find the male singers – the new tenor Masini, for instance?"

"I think I like him much better than the man who sang last year."

"O, yes," interrupted Verdi; "I think he has the divinest voice I ever heard: it is just like velvet. Then, too, he is very young, and he is not quite at his ease; but this is his first public appearance,[6] and I think he does very well considering. I find his tenor, from the highest key to the lowest, simply perfect, and he has great talent. And the basso – how do you find his voice?"

"O, it's magnificent! I particularly like the effect in the concerted pieces. It carries very well."

"Ah!" said Verdi, smiling, "so you have discovered it; that is the great thing in which he excels. I like him for that better than the artist of last year.* How do you compare this performance with those of the last season?"

"If possible, it is more perfect than the first representations were. I find the last trio faultless; and as for the ladies, well, Signor Verdi, I am sure they were never equalled before, and how divinely they sing!"[7]

Verdi looked upward, and the look said much more than I can ever tell you. "Have you met them?" he said finally. "I think I heard them speak of you?"

"O, yes!" I said quickly. "I had a delightful call on Madame Waldmann,† and she seems sweeter off the stage even than on. How modest she is, and so young! Mamma and I were talking with her sister, and she told us so many things about her: how she first studied in Vienna, where she was born, and how, after three years, she made her début in Milan at La Scala in *La favorita*;[8] but she said that she never would have her picture taken, and that she detested publicity of any sort, but she was very fond of singing, and she was truly pleased with her first success in Paris."

"O, yes," said Verdi, "it's all true; she is extremely retiring, but she cannot hide her voice and her great talents. You ought to see her in opera."

"Yes, indeed; I am most anxious to see her in *Trovatore*. She must be a superb Azucena. Madame Viardot thinks her wonderful. By the way, madame sent her compliments to you, and I will deliver them now."

"Madame Viardot?" said Verdi. "Ah, yes, my old friend. Did she ever tell you how she once sang for me? Well, I must mention it. It was during one of my first visits to Paris, and *Il trovatore* was to be given at Les Italiens.[9] Alboni was suddenly taken ill, and the next day being billed for the performance, I was in despair and really worried

---

* Masini, the celebrated tenor, and Medini, the basso, replaced Messrs. Capproni and Maini, who first sang the *Messa* in Paris.

† Madame Waldmann retired from the stage on her marriage with the rich Count Massari of Ferrara.

at the idea of putting it off. It was in the morning, and I happened to think of Madame Pauline Viardot, and hoping to find her at home, I rushed off at once to see her and beg her to undertake the part. I found her in her music-room at the piano, and I said: 'You must sing this for me. Madame Alboni is ill.' '*Il trovatore!*' screamed Madame Viardot; 'impossible! I never even saw the score, and I am very busy.' 'Let's look it over,' I said soothingly. 'Perhaps you can do it. And think of me.' Then madame laughed, took up the book, and –"

"And thought of you," I added.

Verdi smiled and said: "Yes; the same day, after having learnt the whole score in a few hours, she sang it after one rehearsal superbly, and I never can forget it.[10] She's a woman of great talent and altogether remarkable."

"She expects you this evening," I said, "at her grand farewell reception. Shall we see you?"

"O, yes," replied Verdi; "I look forward to this evening. But you study with her, I believe you said?"

"Yes," I answered proudly. "She is my teacher, and some day, Signor Verdi, I will sing opera for you."

"Good!" said the Maestro, laughing; "but it's such a child (*fanciulla*). When am I to hear you?"

"Not for some time. I am not yet ready to sing, and I never should have the heart to attempt *your* music until I could do it justice in some way at least."

After quoting an Italian proverb, Verdi said: "You have time in years from now; do not be in a hurry. Americans are so ambitious."

I felt my heart throb when he spoke of my compatriots, and said excitedly, "Who would not be ambitious to want to sing such music as yours? And they are very fond of you in America. When are you going there?"

"Now, don't mention that," replied Verdi; "I hate the water, and one is so long at sea; besides, I am getting too old now. I must rest. I shall give up composing and travelling. I think the *Messa di Requiem* will be my last work."

"Please don't say that. We will allow you to stay where you will. Only never give up writing."

"Suppose I am tired," he interrupted; "don't you really think I ought to stop now after so much –" (leaving the word unsaid, and indicating with one slender finger a pile of music near the piano).

"No, I don't," said I stoutly. "You are not a bit old, and you look as if you did not mean what you say. Isn't it true that you love composing and you will never give it up?"

Verdi sighed, and thoughtfully said, with a tiny French shrug of the shoulders: "*Que voulez-vous?* I suppose you are right. I am like the others."

"Dear me," said I, glancing at the clock, "Maestro, you are too kind; think how much of your time we are taking up. Much as we would like it, I dare not trespass longer on your amiability."

We were sitting around the table most socially. Verdi had finished his coffee, the tray had been pushed on one side, and I had never even noticed that the time had passed so quickly, as the call and conversation had been delightful, to say the least. We arose, and Verdi insisted that we need not be in a hurry; but he got up and added that he had nothing to do except to go to the box-office of the Opéra Comique, and he had plenty of time before twelve. Yes, it was twelve. Where had the hour gone to? Hastily saying *au revoir* to the great composer, we shook hands and parted. He smilingly invited us to come any time, assuring us that we would not disturb him. We then left our compliments for Madame Verdi and the artists of the *Messa*, and, saying "good-day", walked out.

"He's a dear," said I when we had reached the boulevard. "Just think of seeing so great a man, and finding him so simple, unaffected, and yet so kind! I have met many people, but never any person more agreeable than Giuseppe Verdi."

Then I reviewed his life in my mind: how he had commenced by writing comic operas, and how little hope of success he had in his young days. He was born in 1813, and now he looks scarcely as old as most men of fifty do. He lives in the country most of the time, in his beautiful country seat, "Sant'Agata"; there he writes all his operas. It is only when conducting an orchestra that Verdi seems possessed of unnatural power, and then his face looks as might that of Moses when he smote the rock with his rod. There is an inspiration in every move, in every look, and in the leader's chair one understands the completeness of Verdi's genius.

Of 20 operas that he has composed, the familiar ones of *La traviata*, *Rigoletto*, *Il trovatore*, and *Ernani* will never be forgotten. They say he will write soon a new mass to the memory of Donizetti, to be performed at the cathedral of Bergamo,[11] but he told me he would compose nothing new, so I cannot credit the *on dit*.

What words of mine can add to Verdi's greatness? He is known throughout the length and breadth of the land, and should we never meet again, I shall ever retain most pleasant recollections of my call on him in Paris. To my mind, had he never written anything else, the introduction to the last act of *La traviata* would immortalize him as an operatic composer. He has given more to the world than it ever can give to him; and while his name ever will be an inspiration to the young composer, his music cannot fail to awaken the same ambitious feelings in the heart of the singer.

That same evening my happiness was complete when I stood in Madame Viardot's parlour, and saw and heard what one hears and sees once in a lifetime: Gounod, Ambroise Thomas, Verdi, and Lamouroux [sic][12] listening in rapt attention to one of Mendelssohn's trios. Rubinstein[13] sat at the piano, Madame Viardot turned the leaves, and her son, the young genius, Paul Viardot,[14] a youth of fifteen, played the first violin.*

BLANCHE ROOSEVELT

NOTES

1. CH. MATZ: "Blanche Roosevelt", in *Opera News*, New York, XVII, 20: 23 March 1963, pp. 26–28.
2. A. LUZIO: *Carteggi Verdiani*, cit., II, pp. 43–44.
3. The "project that had failed once before", to which Giuseppina refers, was a tour of *Aida* in Germany and Austria. It recurs in the pages of Giuseppina's diary, dated 21 July 1872 (see A. LUZIO, *Carteggi Verdiani*, cit., II, p. 37), where she announces to Ricordi that she has stormed her husband and gained victory: Verdi would now go to Germany with *Aida*, provided that he was invited by the publisher and guaranteed model performances. Giuseppina noted:

   > *Verdi himself would conduct the first three performances. The first stop would be Weimar, then Berlin and Vienna. In this way it would be a veritable artistic event, establishing (I hope) well and truly our music in Germany. Verdi would derive individual glory from the tour, and Italy general glory. The two ladies would be the ones now performing* Aida *at Padua [Stolz and Waldmann] – since not only were they German, but they had acquired, while preserving the German quality of their voices, an Italian style. With these conditions, I could even guarantee that Verdi will not reply: "I in Weimar? Are you crazy?"*

4. An allusion, perhaps, to the pastel by F. Gariboldi, now in the Museo Teatrale at La Scala, Milan.
5. Clearly a matter of opinion (and who is to say that the beautiful Blanche

---

* Special correspondence, *Chicago Times*, 1875

was not very tall . . .). On the other hand, we have already seen
Escudier describe Verdi as being of similar stature to Donizetti (see
N. I), and we know that Donizetti was rather tall (cf. G. ZAVADINI:
Donizetti. Vita – Musiche – Epistolario, Ist. Ital. d'Arti Grafiche, Ber-
gamo 1948, p. 163); the correspondent of the *Allgemeine musikalische
Zeitung* (see N. II) describes Verdi as "medium-build"; while Monnier,
Claretie and Ghislanzoni state unequivocally that he is "tall" (see
NN. V, X and XI). And we shall see later how others also describe him
as tall. Gabriella Carrara-Verdi informs me that, according to her
family, Verdi was a little taller than the solicitor Angiolo Carrara,
father of Alberto, who married Verdi's adopted daughter and was
consequently great-grandfather to this same Gabriella. As we know
Angiolo Carrara to have been exactly 1,75 metres tall, Verdi must have
been about 1,78.

6. Perhaps he intended to say that this was his first appearance before a
foreign audience. Angelo Masini (Forlí 1844 – Forlí 1926) had made his
début in the autumn of 1867 at Finale Emilia in *Norma*, and had already
sung at Bologna, Mantua, Rome and Palermo. His triumph in *Aida* at
Florence's Pagliano theatre in October 1874 had attracted the attention
of Ricordi and therefore Verdi who, for the tour of his *Requiem*, had at
first considered the tenor Giuseppe Fancelli, who had sung in the first
performance of *Aida* at La Scala, then Luigi Bolis and Italo Campanini
(cf. F. ABBIATI, *op. cit.*, III, pp. 718–19). To his friend Giuseppe Piroli,
who had sent Verdi congratulations on the award of the Cross of the
Commander of the Legion of Honour, bestowed on him by the French
Minister of Education, Verdi made the following reply on 6 May 1875:

> [. . .] *The Requiem goes splendidly. The quartet of soloists is infinitely
> superior, since this year we have a tenor with a delightful and accurate voice.
> Oh, if only he were an artist! Tomorrow evening, Friday, will be the last
> performance, and on Saturday we leave for London* (autograph: Accademia
> Nazionale dei Lincei, Rome).

7. We quote here part of the review of Verdi's *Requiem*, dated "Paris June
12", that Roosevelt had sent to the *Chicago Times* a year earlier (and
then reprinted in her book *Verdi: Milan and "Othello"*, cit., pp. 68–74);
it also contains some interesting observations on the voices of Stolz and
Waldmann:

> Verdi conducting it in person was an added charm, and it was a
> pleasure to realize that the man before us was the author of such a
> work: that slender gray-headed man who stood up and wielded the
> baton with such decision; who watched with such anxious eyes the
> movements of the solo artistes, and whose white-gloved hand fairly
> spoke in its quick, gliding motions. I think now one of the ambitions
> of my life has been realized: to have seen Verdi conduct in person; to

have seen in Paris a new work brought out under the direction and sole leadership of the composer himself. [. . .] Madame Stoltz's [sic] voice is a pure soprano, with immense compass and of the most perfectly beautiful quality one ever listened to, from the lowest note to the highest. Her phrasing is the most superb I ever heard, and her intonation something faultless. She takes a tone and sustains it until it seems that her respiration is quite exhausted, and then she has only commenced to hold it. The tones are as fine and clearly cut as a diamond, and sweet as a silver bell; but the power she gives a high C is something amazing. She is said to be the greatest singer in the world; and I presume it is true, as I cannot possibly imagine any one greater than she. Her cultivation is absolute perfection in every way. Where nature has done everything, and art has done even more than nature, what more can you ever expect to hear? One is completely satisfied after listening to her. There is nothing more to be desired. She opens her mouth slightly when she takes a note, without any perceptible effort, and the tone swells out bigger and fuller, always retaining that exquisite purity of intonation, and the air seems actually heavy with great passionate waves of melody, that entrance the hearer and hold him spell-bound. She is a fine appearing woman, and dressed simply in white, with a veil of black lace falling from a shapely head. She had more grace and dignity than is usually seen in one of her years, and her manners were charming. But Madame Maria Waldmann, if possible, has a grander voice for a contralto than Madame Stolz has for a soprano. It certainly is rare to hear such quality of tone in any female voice. Many times one would think it the tenor, and only when one would look at her and see some slight quiver of the otherwise motionless form, could he realize that it was a woman singing. It is wonderful beyond anything I ever heard of, for a contralto, and she has as perfect cultivation in every way as Madame Stolz. She is a very lovely person, with golden hair and sweet oval face. She was also dressed in white, with great elegance and taste; but the dress didn't amount to anything – it was the singing. Both Stolz and Waldmann could stand up muffled in Indian blankets, and, after a few notes, have a world at their feet.

8. This is inaccurate: having made a name for herself in *Don Carlos* at Trieste in September 1869 with Stolz, and after a season at Moscow, Waldmann made her début at La Scala on 7 March 1871 as Zerlina in Mozart's *Don Giovanni*, and then a few days later sang Maffio Orsini in Donizetti's *Lucrezia Borgia*. She never sang *La favorita* at La Scala.

9. i.e. the Théâtre Italien.

10. Verdi is clearly a little confused here. It was Adelaide Borghi-Mamo who sang the role of Azucena for the first time at the Théâtre Italien (23 December 1854); she also sang in the November 1855 revival with Verdi still conducting, and performed it in French at the Opéra

(12 January 1857), again under Verdi's baton. Pauline Viardot took over from her at the Théâtre Italien for a few performances only from 24 February 1855, and was subsequently the first Azucena at Covent Garden (10 May 1855) alongside the tenor Enrico Tamberlick and the baritone Francesco Graziani. The episode to which Verdi refers in the interview occurred, therefore, most probably in February 1855 in Paris, where the composer had been living for several months, working on *I vespri siciliani*. Pauline Viardot (Paris 1821 – Paris 1910), daughter of Manuel García senior and sister of Manuel García junior and Maria Malibran, having studied piano with Meysenberg and Liszt, and singing with her brother Manuel, made her operatic début as a soprano in 1839 (in the role of Desdemona in Rossini's *Otello* at Her Majesty's Theatre, London, and then at the Théâtre Italien, Paris). The Opéra engaged her and she made her début there in 1849 in the world première of Meyerbeer's *Le prophète*, in the mezzo-soprano role of Fidès – a memorable interpretation. No less memorable was her interpretation of Gluck's *Orfeo ed Euridice* in 1856 at the Théâtre Lyrique, Paris. She retired from the stage in 1862, but still gave concerts (in 1872 she sang Delila in the first performance of Saint-Saëns' *Samson et Dalila*, given privately at his Paris home). She devoted herself to teaching, and among her pupils were Arkel, Artot and Brandt. She wrote several operettas to librettos by Turgenev, the great Russian writer, who was a very close friend.

11. Verdi had indeed received a request to compose a sacred work to be performed in September 1875 on the occasion of the removal of Donizetti's and Simone Mayr's ashes to the cathedral of Santa Maria Maggiore in Bergamo. He declined, however, and this gave rise to a little polemic by Pietro Cominazzi in *La Fama* of Milan in May 1875, which then appeared in the columns of the *Arte* of Trieste. Amilcare Ponchielli was called upon in his stead, and he composed a *Cantata* on a text by Ghislanzoni.

12. Charles Lamoureux (Bordeaux 1834 – Paris 1899), violinist and conductor; in 1881 he founded the Nouveaux Concerts, which were later named after him.

13. Anton Rubinstein (Vychvatinez, Podolia, 1829 – Peterhof, Petersburg 1894), pianist, composer and conductor who founded the Petersburg Conservatoire.

14. In fact Paul Viardot (Courtavenel 1857 – Algiers 1941) was at that time almost eighteen. He became a concert violinist of great renown and was also a conductor.

XV

VERDI IN VIENNA

1875

ANON: "Verdi in Wien", in *Neue Freie Presse*, Vienna, n. 3874: 9 June 1875 (reprinted in *Signale für die musikalische Welt*, Leipzig, XXXIII, 30: June 1875, pp. 465–7; partly translated into Italian in F. WALKER: "Verdi a Vienna", in *Giuseppe Verdi*, Scritti raccolti in occasione delle "Celebrazioni Verdiane" dell'VIII Settimana Musicale Senese, Accademia Musicale Chigiana, Sienna, 1951, pp. 52–54).

VIENNA, WHICH VERDI had not seen since the distant spring of 1843, was the final and for the composer perhaps the most prestigious and triumphant stage of the *Requiem's* European tour. He arrived in the Austrian capital from London via Paris on the evening of 3 July 1875, together with his four singers (Stolz, Waldmann, Masini and Medini), and took rooms with his wife Giuseppina at the Hotel Munsch. Franco Faccio, who had rehearsed the orchestra and chorus of the Hofoperntheater, had arrived before him. Verdi conducted the first full rehearsal on the morning of June 7, as we learn from a news-item in the *Neue Freie Presse*, n. 3872 of the same date:

> Maestro Verdi appeared at eleven o'clock today at the Hofoperntheater to conduct in person the first full rehearsal of his great *Requiem* for Manzoni. The celebrated composer was welcomed by the entire chorus and the Akademischer Gesangverein with ecstatic applause and cries of "Long live Verdi", which lasted for several minutes. Verdi thanked them courteously and then began the rehearsal, during which the musicians, at particularly striking moments, played the part of audience and broke out into loud applause. Verdi, who mostly speaks French to the musicians, is said to have been highly satisfied with the performance of both orchestra and chorus, and he repeatedly proclaimed that they had exceeded his highest expectations.

The first performance of the *Requiem* took place on the evening of June 11, with the composer conducting, in the presence of Emperor Franz Joseph. It was a rapturous success; three other performances followed. There were also two gala performances of *Aida*[1] with Stolz, Waldmann, Masini and Medini, of which the first took place on June 19. Before this performance the Emperor, who attended the entire opera, bestowed upon Verdi the highest possible cultural honour, the Comthurkreuz of the Franz Josef Order. Verdi wore the honour while he conducted the opera, which was received by the audience with unceasing applause.[2] If the Viennese public extended a triumphal welcome to composer and artists, Verdi, for his part, was astounded by the chorus and, in particular, the playing of the Viennese orchestra which remained for him the best orchestra he was ever to hear or conduct – a veritable touchstone. The day after the first performance of the *Requiem*, June 12, he wrote to his friend Piroli:

> *A greater success than anywhere else, and the performance was distinctly better than anywhere else. What a fine orchestra and what fine choirs, so agile and easy to direct! In short, a complete performance, the like of which we shall never see again. I know that you are going to Venice (I shall not be there),[3] but however fine the performance will be, it will seem very pallid compared to this one.[4]*

And on June 27 in another letter to Piroli from Venice, he reasserts

> *Everything, as you know, has gone well. What a fine orchestra, what fine choirs! A splendid performance all round! I think that this artistic dash has been a success for everyone. If only we had been able to perform in Berlin![5] Perhaps Ricordi was frightened, because the musical season was nearly over; but that was no reason to stint on a few thousand francs . . . but merchants will always be merchants![6]*

On June 26 Verdi left Vienna to return, via Venice, to Sant'Agata. Four months later the *Requiem* was revived at the Hofoperntheater under the baton of Hans Richter, the famous Wagner conductor, who that very year had been appointed *Musikdirektor* of the Viennese opera house. Although the quartet of soloists, comprising the soprano Marie Wilt, the mezzo Tremel, the tenor Walter and the bass J. B. Rokitansky could not compete with the soloists who had sung with Verdi conducting (yet Rokitansky, to judge from the critics, surpassed Medini in voice and diction), the performance was excellent and the success so great that two movements of the *Requiem* had to be repeated. Also present at that performance, in a box, were Richard Wagner and his wife Cosima.[7]

Verdi in Vienna

A personal friend of the composer has sent us the following article about Verdi. It is well-known that Verdi spends the greater part of the year in his modest villa at Busseto; belonging to the house are extensive estates, which he manages himself. He passes the winter in a rented apartment at the Palazzo Doria. On his travels he is always accompanied by his wife, the celebrated singer Strepponi, who frequently appeared in his early operas. Verdi visited Vienna for the first time in 1843, where on April 4 and 5 he conducted his opera *Nabucco* in the Kärntnertortheater. He still recalls that occasion with pleasure when, not yet 29 years old, he was honoured in most flattering fashion. Donizetti at that time was conducting *Linda* and *Maria von Rohan*, which he had composed especially for Vienna, and Verdi told me that the great Maestro from Bergamo, jealous and distrustful of Nicolai,[8] who was then Kapellmeister of the Kärntnertortheater, would never allow the latter to conduct his own operas. When our conversation turned to Wagner, Verdi remarked that this great genius had done opera an incalculable service, because he had had the courage to free himself from the tradition of the aria-opera. "I too have attempted to blend music and drama in my *Macbeth*," he added, "but unlike Wagner I was not able to write my own libretti. Wagner surpasses every composer in his rich variety of instrumental colour, but in both form and style he went too far. At the outset he successfully avoided mundane subject-matter, but he later strayed from his idealistic aims by carrying his theories to extremes, and committed the very error that he had originally set out to reform: and so the monotony, which he avoided with such success, now threatens to dominate him." The new opera house[9] pleased Verdi greatly, the architecture as well as the stage machinery and decoration; but he finds the slope of the stage too shallow: the perspective consequently suffers considerably in the great ensembles. He thought that the performance he attended of *Tannhäuser*[10] excellent, and he particularly admired the orchestra, chorus and production. Verdi has his own opinion on singers. "Germany has no lack of voices," he says, "they are almost more sonorous than Italian voices, but the singers consider the art of singing as a gymnastic exercise, concern themselves too little with the training of the voice and merely strive, within the shortest possible time, to acquire a large repertoire. They do not endeavour to render nuance, but concentrate

solely on emitting this or that note with great volume. Their singing
is therefore no poetic expression of the soul but a physical struggle."[11] Verdi was enchanted by Vienna, which he considers to be the
fairest city in Europe; the surroundings as well as the inhabitants
remind him vividly of Northern Italy. The enthusiastic reception,
even during the rehearsals of the *Requiem*, impressed him greatly. He
has resolved to return to Vienna soon to conduct the first performance of a new work. The Maestro politely declined an invitation to
conduct his *Requiem* at the National Theatre in Pest.

NOTES

1. ABBIATI, *op. cit.*, III, p. 753, is therefore wrong to deny that these
performances took place. He writes: "The notion of a Vienna *Aida* can
no longer be entertained; there had been inadequate time to rehearse."
The opera was performed in the German edition at the Hofoperntheater
on 29 April 1874 (cf. M. CONATI: "Cronologia delle prime rappresentazioni dal 1871 al 1881", in *Genesi dell'"Aida"*, edited by S. Abdoun, cit.,
pp. 159 and 161.
2. See an article in the Leipzig *Signale für die musikalische Welt*:
News from Vienna: before yesterday's performance of *Aida*, Prince
Hohenlohe, accompanied by Director Jauner, presented Maestro Verdi
the Comthurkreuz of the Franz Josef Order, that His Majesty the
Emperor had conferred on him. At the same time, Signor Ricordi
received the Ritterkreuz of the same Order. The members of the
Opera's orchestra and chorus also received an exceptionally rare mention of merit from Director Jauner, who had been specifically instructed
to express to both orchestra and chorus His Majesty's the Emperor's
highest recognition of their exemplary performances of Verdi's *Requiem*
and *Aida*. At the performance of *Aida* Maestro Verdi appeared on the
conductor's rostrum wearing the decoration conferred on him by His
Majesty. He was naturally greeted with great excitement. The opera
itself was, if possible, received with even greater enthusiasm than when
the composer first conducted the work. At the end of each act the
soloists had to take two or three bows, and the audience only settled
down when Verdi himself appeared with the soloists. (*Signale für die
musikalische Welt*, Leipzig, XXXIII, 32: July 1875, p. 503.)
3. The *Requiem*, with the same soloists as at Paris, London and Vienna,
but conducted by Franco Faccio, was performed in Venice at the Teatro
Malibran on 10 July 1875, and received four other performances. It was
then given with the same cast and conductor on September 19 at the
Principe Umberto Theatre in Florence, and then for another three
evenings at the Pagliano.
4. Autograph: Accademia Nazionale dei Lincei, Rome.
5. See introduction to N. XIV.

6. Autograph: Accademia Nazionale dei Lincei, Rome.
7. Cf. *Signale für die musikalische Welt*, Leipzig, XXXIII, 55: November 1875, pp. 867–8. Concerning the presence of Wagner at Vienna in May 1875 to conduct three concerts, and the welcome received in June by Verdi from the Viennese, see the August number of the *Monthly Musical Record*, London (quoted in F. WALKER: *Verdi a Vienna*, cit., pp. 55–56):

> Wagner and Verdi conducting almost at the same moment in the same town, and both filling the house to the top! Who would have believed it ten years ago? And this time Verdi has even out-run the former, as the third concert of Wagner (and that was still in the first days of May) was already beginning to show empty places, whereas Verdi, in the very heat of June, and in defiance of enhanced entrées, was strong enough to fill the great Opera House six times. Verdi's *Requiem* was performed four times, and his opera, *Aida*, twice; the receipts of those six evenings amounted to the sum of 48,000 florins.
>
> Not only the public in general seemed never tired of showing their sympathy for the Maestro and his works, but even the Emperor himself was so delighted with the representations, that he attended the *Requiem* three times, and sat out *Aida* to the end of the last bar. He honoured Verdi by granting to him the Commandeurkreuz of the Franz-Joseph decoration, and when Verdi thanked him in an audience, the conversation is said to have been uncommonly long and cordial. Verdi assured us that he was extremely pleased with our chorus and orchestra, and that he was very much touched by the kind reception of the Viennese.

8. Carl Otto Nicolai (Königsberg 1810 – Berlin 1849), founder of the Academy of the Vienna Philharmonic, the composer of *Die lustigen Weiber von Windsor* and *Il proscritto*, the libretto of which by Gaetono Rossi was given to him, on Merelli's request, by Verdi, in exchange for the libretto of *Nabucco*, which Nicolai had deemed to be of little interest.
9. The Staatsoper of today; built to replace the old court theatre of the Kärntnertor, by this time inadequate for modern needs, it was inaugurated on 25 May 1869 with a performance of *Don Giovanni*.
10. *Tannhäuser*, which had already been performed at Vienna, first at the Thalia-Theater in 1857, then at the Kärntnertortheater in 1859, had been recently given in the Paris version at the Staatsoper.
11. See the following chapter: "Verdi on singing".
12. On June 6, the Hungarian paper *Jelenkor* ("The Present") had announced Verdi's arrival at Budapest to conduct his *Requiem* with Stolz, Waldmann, Masini and Medini; but a week later the *Figyelö* ("The Observer") stated:

> Verdi will not be coming to the capital and so we shall not have the

opportunity of hearing his *Requiem*. He has written in reply to the National Theatre's invitation that the long trips he has taken recently and the hard work of rehearsals have so exhausted him that he cannot undertake to conduct the *Requiem* and *Aida* in Pest, and as the Vienna performances will be over on the 23rd of the month and a previous contract requires him to be in Venice by July 1, he must devote the remainder of the week to getting some rest. (P. P. VARNAI: "Verdi in Hungary", in *Verdi*, Bollettino dell'Istituto di studi verdiani, Parma, n. 5, p. 1027.)

XVI

VERDI ON SINGING

1875

ANON.: ["L'opinione di Verdi sul canto"], in *Signale für die musikalische Welt*, Leipzig, XXXIII, 33: July 1875, p. 521 (republished in F. WALKER: "Verdi a Vienna", cit., pp. 54–55).

A SHORT BUT interesting interview which supplements Verdi's statements on singing and singers which appeared in the *Neue Freie Presse* (see preceding chapter).

[*Verdi on singing*]

A Viennese journalist who visited Verdi writes: the Maestro praised the chorus and orchestra of our opera house. "I have seldom heard so many powerful young voices together. The chorus is admirable, the best I have encountered." We spoke of the singers who contributed to the brilliant success of the *Requiem*. "Austria is responsible for a portion of the success," said Verdi, "for the female soloists are, after all, Austrian. Nevertheless," he corrected himself with a little smile, "the success is not entirely due to them; the manner in which they sing is Italian. This they have learnt from us." I agreed. "Listen," Verdi continued, "Italian singers are often unjustifiably criticized for neglecting acting for the sake of *bel canto*. Yet how many singers are there who combine both, who can act and sing? In comic opera both are easily combined. But in tragic opera! A singer who is moved by the dramatic action, concentrates on it with every vibrant fibre of his body and is utterly consumed by the role he is portraying, will not find the right tone. He might for a minute, but in the next thirty seconds he will sing in the wrong way or the voice will simply fail. A single lung is rarely strong enough for acting and singing. And yet I am of the opinion that in opera the voice has, above all, the right to be heard. Without a voice true singing cannot exist."

NOTE

1. The *Wiener Fremdenblatt* of 22 June (reproduced in the *Gazzetta Musicale di Milano*, XXX, supplement to n. 27: 4 July 1875, p. 4), reports that for the *Requiem*, the Director of the Hofoperntheater, Jauner, "increased the chorus by adding many young and fresh voices from the other choral societies. Almost the entire Academic Choral Society (all young singers) addressed themselves with great enthusiasm to the work. Verdi said that in putting on this performance of his *Requiem*, he was greatly surprised by the quality of the immense chorus, which he called the best he had ever heard; in the same way he praised the courtesy of the students who rehearsed patiently and zealously for the successful performance.

XVII

A VISIT BY VERDI TO THE VIENNA CONSERVATOIRE

1875

ANON: ["Verdi in visita al Conservatorio di Vienna"], in *Wiener Fremden-blatt*, 23 June 1875 (republished in *Gazzetta Musicale di Milano*, XXX, supplement to n. 27: 4 July 1875, p. 5).

THIS VISIT WHICH took place in the afternoon of 22 June 1875, was also mentioned in the article in the *Monthly Musical Record* (see N. XV, note 7):

One day he [Verdi] visited the Conservatoire, where a performance of the pupils had been arranged. They played an overture and gave some arias and duets, Verdi sitting at the side of Frau Marchesi,[1] the Professorin of the singing-class. He praised her, the *ensemble* – playing by the pupils of Director Hellmesberger,[2] as well as her own pupils, who, he said, were to be found on all the greatest stages. Before entering the concert-room, Verdi asked to see the library of the Conservatoire, and was greatly interested when he heard that there were many autographs by Beethoven, whose handwriting he had never seen. He was shown the great man in letters, compositions, and sketches, in portraits and medals, in a very interesting cast (Gesichtsmaske, taken from life), and in an excellent bust, a masterpiece by Dietrich. But when he saw a copy of the *Eroica* with many alterations by Beethoven himself, he had no eyes for the rest, and looked, and examined, and dwelt on the parts he liked best, as the work was well-known to him.

The following account in the *Wiener Fremdenblatt* is much more detailed.[3]

[A visit by Verdi to the Vienna Conservatoire]

Verdi had promised to visit the Amateur Music Society and the Conservatoire yesterday at four o'clock in the afternoon; he appeared a quarter of an hour earlier, accompanied by Professor Marchesi.[4] He was received by Councillor von Mosenthal,[5] Director Hellmesberger, general secretary Zellner and several others who led him into the little hall, where the students had prepared pieces in his honour. The illustrious Maestro halted on the first step, turned to Mosenthal and asked him if the Conservatoire library housed any Beethoven manuscripts. Hellmesberger replied that there was a vast quantity of most important manuscripts by the great genius, whereupon Verdi descended the stairs and asked to be shown these treasures. Pohl,[6] the librarian, showed him many of the museum's portraits and autographs of Beethoven, which Verdi examined with great attention. He was especially surprised by autograph copies of the Violin Concerto and the *Eroica*; he discussed the former with Hellmesberger and the latter with Professor Ambros,[7] from which he read entire passages with an extraordinarily detailed knowledge of the work. He was also shown Schubert autographs.

Having visited the museum, Verdi went with the other gentlemen to the examination room, which was crowded with students of both sexes from the Conservatoire, who broke out in cries of hurrah! There was also a small group of most distinguished amateur musicians, including Prince Rad. Liechtenstein, Count Amadei and Prince Montenuovo who all greeted the Maestro warmly. Verdi sat down next to maestra Signora Marchesi, and Hellmesberger climbed onto the platform and conducted his select band, who performed Auber's overture to *Lestocq* with brilliance, accuracy and clarity. Verdi, astonished at such a performance from an orchestra composed for the most part of boys and girls from ten to fifteen years of age, who had only attended Hellmesberger's school since the previous October, congratulated them all most heartily. Signorina Bemstein then sang Azucena's great scena from *Il trovatore*. The young singer, a pupil of Marchesi's, has a most attractive contralto voice which modulates beautifully; she sang and gestured with great élan and theatrical verve. Verdi applauded loudly, and praised her teacher Marchesi highly. Signorina Gerster,[8] another of Marchesi's pupils, had no less a success and sang the great aria from *La traviata*, revealing the excellence of the school, particularly in the coloratura and staccato passages. When Verdi requested to hear a duet, Hellmesberger distributed the parts for the great duet for Count Luna and Leonora, which Dienersberg sang with Nawasawsky. Verdi was enthralled by the energy and assurance with which the young orchestra brought out every nuance, and the two singers also earned his applause.

When the performance was over, Hellmesberger did not let slip the opportunity of making a little humorous speech, which he delivered in French: "Comme directeur du Conservatoire j'ai le droit de proposer les thèmes pour le concours; j'espère, mesdames et messieurs, que vous me prêterez votre concours pour le thème, que je vous propose maintenant: *Vive notre maître Verdi!*"[9] Verdi left the little hall to enthusiastic shouts and entered the great concert hall. The sumptuous light from the large upper windows, the splendour of the hall and the beautiful symmetry delighted Verdi, who listened smilingly as he heard the low notes of the magnificent organ: the organist, Zellner,[10] was playing a wonderful improvisation on themes from Verdi's *Requiem*. The Maestro thanked the talented artist, enquired about the structure of the organ and its number of stops, and said that those sounds reminded him of his youth when he, still a boy back in his own homeland, had to officiate as organist.

Verdi then took his leave of the assembled company and expressed his delight to the Director of the Amateur Music Society, councillor von Mosenthal, that he had been introduced to such a splendid institution as the Vienna Conservatoire, which was not only of the greatest importance for the cultivation of music in its own country, but also for the musical countries of Germany, France and his own Italy, for which Vienna provides a large number of musicians and singers. Verdi then confessed that he himself owed a great debt to the same institute, since so many artists who sing his own operas with such success were trained there; he added that his best wishes would always go with that sacred institution, because, if it continued on the same path, its future would resemble its glorious past in the golden days of the great flowering of Austrian music, the great Viennese school. Verdi then thanked Hellmesberger for his kindness, where-upon the latter declared in jest that he would only accept written thanks, i.e. in the form of a new composition for the next season of the Amateur Musical Society's concerts; but Verdi, pointing to his hoary head, smiled and gave no reply. Amongst cries of hurrah, and after a visit of three hours, Verdi, touched, left the Conservatoire.[11]

NOTES

1. Mathilde Marchesi De Castrone, née Graumann (Frankfurt-am-Main 1821 – London 1913), wife of Salvatore Marchesi and mother of the singer Blanche Marchesi. She was a singer of the Rossini school, performing almost exclusively as a concert artist in Germany, Paris and London between 1844 and 1853. She excelled as a singing teacher, taught at the Vienna Conservatoire from 1854 to 1865 and from 1868 to 1878, and subsequently only gave private tuition, moving to Paris in 1881 and London in 1908. She was nicknamed "maestra di primedonne"; her pupils included Galli Marié, Fricci, Calvé, Krauss, Melba, Gerster, D'Angeri, Arnoldson, Eames and Kurz.

2. Joseph Hellmesberger senior (Vienna 1828 – 1893), violinist, composer and conductor. He founded a quartet that greatly influenced Viennese musical life between 1849 and 1891, drawing the public's attention, amongst other things, to their contemporaries Brahms and Bruckner. He was appointed Director of the Vienna Conservatoire in 1859, where he also taught the violin; from 1860 he was also first violinist in the Court orchestra.

3. An account of Verdi's visit to the Vienna Conservatoire can also be found in the *Neue Freie Presse* of 23 June 1875 (reprinted in *Verdi aus der Nähe. Ein Lebensbild in Dokumenten*, compiled and translated by FRANZ WALLNER-BASTÉ, Manesse Verlag, Zürich 1979, pp. 289–91).

4. Salvatore Marchesi, cavaliere de Castrone (Palermo 1822 – Paris 1908), husband of Mathilde, whom he married in 1852. He studied singing in Milan; having taken part in the revolutionary uprisings of '48 he was exiled and went to America, where he made his début at New York in *Ernani*. He then moved to London to complete his studies with Garcia, and began to make his name as a recitalist. In 1854, together with his wife, he was appointed Professor of singing at the Vienna Conservatoire. According to the *Wiener Fremdenblatt* of June 22 (reproduced in the *Gazzetta Musicale di Milano*, no. cit., p. 4), Marchesi acted as mediator in the negotiations between Ricordi and the Vienna Hofoperntheater for the performance of Verdi's *Requiem*:

> A few days ago, Professor Marchesi was granted an audience by His Majesty, and the Emperor remarked that Marchesi had earned the gratitude of all music lovers, having acted as mediator between the house of Ricordi and the Imperial Opera, thus making possible the beautiful performances of Verdi's *Requiem*. And nor had such a task been easy. As early as December, Marchesi had, as representative of the house of Ricordi, visited the Director of the Opera, Herbeck [Jauner's predecessor], offering him a performance of the *Requiem* at the Imperial Opera. [. . .] Nothing came of it. Director Jauner, however, immediately after his nomination, initiated negotiations

once more with great energy, and after a very long struggle the matter was clinched. [. . .] The Southern Railways laid on return trains, giving great pleasure to the holiday-makers and lovers of beautiful Italian music, and bringing them back after the performance to the tranquil shade of country-houses.

5. Salomon Herrmann von Mosenthal (Kassel 1821 – Vienna 1877), man of letters and librettist, who wrote the libretti of Nicolai's *Die lustigen Weiber von Windsor* (1849) and Goldmark's *Die Königin von Saba* (1875); in 1868 he was appointed Director of the Society of the Friends of Music in Vienna. In 1872 he founded with J. von Weilen a theatre and opera school at the Vienna Conservatoire.

6. Carl Ferdinand Pohl (Darmstadt 1819 – Vienna 1887), organist, teacher and musicologist, author of numerous publications, including a biography of Haydn in 3 volumes; in 1868 he was appointed archivist and librarian of the Society of the Friends of Music in Vienna.

7. August Wilhelm Ambros (Vysoké Mýto, Prague 1816 – Vienna 1876), one of the greatest scholars of aesthetics and music history of his time. He was the author of a monumental *History of Music*, which remained incomplete after the 5th volume, and was appointed Professor at the Vienna Conservatoire in 1872.

8. Etelka Gerster (Koschau, Hungary 1855 – Pontecchio, Bologna 1920) was to have a brilliant career. It seems that it was after this very performance of the aria from *La traviata* that Verdi recommended her to be engaged by La Fenice at Venice, where she made her début on 8 January 1876 in *Rigoletto*, and appeared a month later in the first Italian performance of Thomas' *Hamlet*. In 1877 she married the Italian impresario Carlo Gardini. Her career unfolded mainly in the United States, where she became well-known for her bitter rivalry with Patti. Leo Riemens in the *Enciclopedia dello Spettacolo* described her as possessing exceptional vocal agility and dramatic expression. "On stage she was an enchanting personality and a consummate actress; off-stage, however, her character was much less charming – she indulged in terrible outbursts of anger, which amongst other things led to the break-up of her marriage."

9. "As Director of the Conservatoire I have the right to propose the titles for the competition; I hope, Ladies and Gentlemen, that you will all agree to the title I propose: 'Long live our Maestro Verdi!' "

10. Most probably Leopold Alexander Zellner (Zagreb 1823 – Vienna 1894), organist, composer, teacher, who in 1868 had been appointed Professor of Harmony at the Vienna Conservatoire and had also become secretary of the Society of the Friends of Music. From 1854 to 1868 he was editor and owner of the periodical *Blätter für Theater, Musik und bildende Kunst*, for which he wrote several reviews of Verdi's operas that were not always complimentary.

11. For Verdi's presence in Vienna and in particular his enthusiastic account

of his visit to the Vienna Conservatoire, see an interview with Mathilde
Marchesi, published by the *Neue Freie Presse* of 27 June 1875 (reproduced in *Verdi aus der Nähe* [. . .] by F. WALLNER-BASTÉ, cit.,
pp. 291–3):

Verdi is still the principal topic of conversation of the Friends of
Music, and it is thus with especial pleasure that we print the following article on Frau Marchesi's dealings with the composer that the
celebrated Professor of Singing has today put at our disposal:

In the course of my frequent meetings with the so highly esteemed
Maestro Verdi, I could not help but think of Mendelssohn and
Rossini, of whom I saw much and who, like Verdi, were remarkable
both for their kindness and unpretentiousness. These divinely gifted
men bore not a trace of presumptiousness or arrogance. Verdi never
tired of expressing his great joy at the cordial reception he had
received in Vienna, which he said was so genuine and warm.
"Potrebbe credersi in Italia" [Italian in the original: "One might have
thought oneself in Italy"] he said. Of his visit to the Conservatoire he
told me: "Do you know that I was genuinely surprised by the
performances. And the great order that reigns in this institution must
benefit each student's development." The singing satisfied him
greatly and riveted his attention; he lavished praise on the young
orchestra and singled out in particular *l'attacco netto e preciso* [Italian in
the original: the accuracy and clean attack] of the violins. He seems
to have enjoyed himself greatly at the soirée given by Prince
Hohenlohe. "*Gran società*" [Italian in the original], he said, "*tutti
principi*, and my poor tenor (Masini) was so greatly impressed that he
was seized by a fearful panic and could hardly sing, indeed he left out
whole bars." For the first time in many years I saw Verdi's wife
again, the former celebrated singer Giuseppina Strepponi, who had
shown such interest in me during my studies with Garcia in Paris and
had encouraged my artistic aspirations. She is as simple and modest
as Verdi, accompanies him on all his journeys and, like him, loves the
solitude of their country home in Busetto [sic]. Verdi has no children
and has adopted his niece, who is at present at a boarding school in
Turin.

XVIII

VERDI AND THE PLAYS OF GRILLPARZER

1875

ANON.: ["Verdi e i drammi di Grillparzer"], republished from an unknown Viennese newspaper in *Gazzetta Musicale di Milano*, XXX, supplement to n. 27: 4 July 1875, p. 6.

A VERY SHORT interview, almost certainly incomplete and containing several errors[1] in the version printed by the *Gazzetta Musicale di Milano*, the original source of which has yet to be traced. Nonetheless, it deserves to be quoted in this anthology because, as well as containing a sentence in French which seems to have been plucked straight from the composer's lips, it confirms the interest that Verdi took in the plays of the great Austrian Franz Grillparzer (Vienna 1791 – Vienna 1872).

[*Verdi and the plays of Grillparzer*]

A newspaper gives this account of an interview with Verdi: "We spoke of the honour conferred on the Maestro by the Emperor, and I added that in his time the celebrated dramatist Grillparzer had also received this distinction. 'That Grillparzer also received it,' Verdi replied, 'can only increase for me the value of this decoration. I have read his works in translation, and *Libussa*[2] fired me most of all. I had once intended setting one of his plays to music, *Die Ahnfrau*.[3] The romantic plot aroused my excitement, and I had already prepared a sketch[4] . . . but it's so long ago now. First and foremost I was attracted by the figure of [Count] Borotin, but the text is too romantic – romanticism assumes monstrous proportions in this drama. Ça serait quelque chose pour l'Ambigu ou pour la Porte Saint-Martin.'[5] I spoke to the Maestro about *König Ottokars Glück und Ende*,[6] and recommended to him this huge romance. 'Be so good to write down for me the title of that play,' the Maestro said, 'I'll see if I can get hold of a good translation.'"

NOTES

1. A succession of "howlers" by the typographer of the *Gazzetta*: Barotin, Parte Saint-Martin, Fine e felicità di Ottocare . . . that have been corrected here.
2. Posthumous tragedy in five acts, written in iambic pentameters, probably completed in 1848, performed at Vienna in 1874; inspired by the Czech legend of the founding of Prague, it has as its heroine Libussa, a fabled character of supernatural origin. Grillparzer's tragedy blends fable, history and philosophy into a complex work of symbolic significance.
3. "Fatalistic" tragedy in five acts, written in 1816 and the first play of his that Grillparzer saw performed on stage (Theater an der Wien, 1817). The play could not help but excite the composer of *I masnadieri*, *Il trovatore* and *La forza del destino*, three operas from which several important themes (the life of the chivalrous brigand, the grandmother's curse, the fatal killing of the father and the belated recognition of brother and sister, etc.) seem as it were to merge into this "most romantic" drama of the Viennese playwright. In the autograph page of the *Subjects for Operas*, inserted in the *Copialettere* (see introduction to N. III), *Die Ahnfrau* is the sixth title of the list, following three tragedies by Shakespeare, Byron's *Cain* and Hugo's *Le roi s'amuse*. By 1846 at the latest, Verdi had already considered Grillparzer's tragedy; on August 13 of that year Muzio wrote to Barezzi:

> The Maestro is busying himself with the libretto for Florence; there are three possibilities: Die Ahnfrau, I masnadieri and Macbeth. He will choose die Ahnfrau, if he can get Fraschini [for whom the composer clearly intended the role of Jaromir]; if instead of Fraschini they give him Moriani, as seems probable, then it will be Macbeth [. . .] (G. Verdi nelle lettere di E. Muzio, cit., p. 258).

A year later, on 2 August 1847, Verdi, writing from Paris, suggested to Lucca a group of three operas, including once again *Die Ahnfrau*:

> I think I am bound to let you know that according to our existing contract of 16 October 1845, I am to write the opera for one of the leading Italian theatres, not later than the 1848 carnival. Till now I have considered the following subjects: Il corsaro [from Byron's eponymous poem], Die Ahnfrau (a fantastical German drama) and Medea, using Romani's old libretto. (I Copialettere di G. Verdi, cit., p. 42.)

A few months later, in about February 1848, Muzio informed the publisher Ricordi:

The subject of the opera that Verdi has written for Lucca is Die Ahnfrau, *a subject which has much in common with* I masnadieri; *it is taken from a German legend.* (F. ABBIATI, *op. cit.*, I, p. 762.)

In fact, Verdi had decided on *Il corsaro*, perhaps following Lucca's request, whom he had left to choose from the list of three subjects; but perhaps Muzio was *au courant*, probably from a letter that Verdi wrote him from Paris, stating that he had drawn up an outline of Grillparzer's tragedy.

4. Luzio states that "the outline" exists in 4 acts, "in the Maestro's hand, among the rough drafts in the Milan town-hall". (*I Copialettere di G. Verdi*, cit. p. 42, note 2.)

5. "That would be a suitable work for the Ambigu or the Porte Saint-Martin." Both these were Parisian theatres. The former, rebuilt in 1828 in boulevard Saint-Martin, was famous in those days for spectacular productions; the latter, built in 1781, also in the boulevard Saint-Martin, was a stronghold of the romantic movement (Hugo's *Marion De Lorme*, *Lucrèce Borgia* and *Marie Tudor* were all performed there) where ballets and, above all, *mélodrames* and *féeries* used to be staged.

6. An historical and patriotic drama, written in 1823 and performed two years later at the Burgtheater in Vienna.

XIX

A VISIT BY MARIA WIECK TO VERDI

1877–1878

ANON.: ["Una visita di Maria Wieck a Verdi"], in *Allgemeine deutsche Musikzeitung*, Cassel, V, March 1878 (republished in *Gazzetta Musicale di Milano*, XXXIII, 12: 24 March 1878, p. 109; then in *Svensk Musiktidning*, Stockholm, XXI, 9: 1 May 1901, p. 67).

MARIA WIECK (Leipzig 1832 – Dresden 1916), half-sister of the more famous Clara, the wife of Robert Schumann, was also a distinguished pianist. A pupil of her father Friedrich, she pursued her career as a concert pianist in Germany and abroad; she settled in Dresden where she taught singing and piano. Touring Italy in the 1877–78 season, she took the opportunity of a concert in Genoa to be introduced to Giuseppe Verdi, a name that after the *Quartet* and *Requiem* and above all the composer's successes at Vienna in 1875 and Cologne in 1877 was gaining ever greater respect in German-speaking countries. It is not without significance that the brief account of this visit appeared in the newly-founded but already authoritative *Allgemeine deutsche Musikzeitung* (*Allgemeine Musikzeitung* as from 1882). We give the version that appeared soon after in Ricordi's *Gazzetta Musicale di Milano*.

Fleeting mention is made of the previous year's Cologne festival. In May 1877 Verdi had been invited to conduct his *Requiem* at the 45th Niederrheinisches Musikfest; the invitation had been sent him by Ferdinand Hiller (Frankfurt-am-Main 1811 – Cologne 1885), the German anti-Wagnerian, the inspiration of Cologne's musical life and Director of the Cologne Conservatoire and the Gürzenich Concerts. Composer, conductor, pianist, music critic, a close friend of Rossini (who had helped him in 1839 to get one of his operas, *Romilda*, performed at La Scala), Hiller in his last years became an admirer and friend of Verdi, with whom he corresponded continually till his death in 1885.[1] Verdi's *Requiem* had already been given in Cologne two years earlier, but the importance of the performance on 21 May 1877 was increased by the composer's presence on the podium (virtually unprecedented in Germany).

August Guckeisen wrote an article on Verdi's qualities as a conductor in the *Kölnische Zeitung* (22 May 1877, no. 141); it is a rare and almost unknown document which, considering the virtual absence of accounts that give us an accurate and reliable description of Verdi as an orchestral conductor, must be quoted here. From the German critic's review, from his remarks, from his comparisons with other conductors during those years in Germany, there emerges the portrait of an interpreter whom today we would consider completely modern:

> Giuseppe Verdi is for the German people the composer of *Il trovatore*, and for the musical aristocracy the composer of the *Requiem*. In spite of his advanced years he had travelled willingly from his winter home in Genoa to our festival on the Rhine in order to conduct his *Requiem* in person. To see this man face to face, above all to see him in action would thrill any music lover. And I do not believe that anyone was disappointed. The fire, which burns in the decisive moments of his dramatic music, is also revealed undiminished in Verdi's whole being, as soon as he holds the baton in his hand. The singer or orchestral player knows at once: there stands the living interpretation of the work about to be heard. Verdi does not merely beat time, he conducts in the fullest sense of the word, he mirrors the musical ideas in his expression, his stance and the movement of his baton [. . .]
>
> It is now time to describe how Verdi's conducting affected the work. It was not just a question of a few different tempi or accents, that always arise when instead of the usual conductor the composer himself takes over the baton. This time the entire performance seemed strange, in the sense that it was far removed from our own national sensibility; for the most part this was to the work's advantage, even if in some passages it impaired the performance. In the first place Verdi chose much sharper, more strident nuances than is customary in Germany. In this respect we can learn something from the Italians, for one's response to music is to a very considerable degree sensuous, and the ear in any case demands, for a complete and intellectual understanding of music, sharper contrasts than the eye, which can take in contrasting colours with ease. Sensuous effects do not impair the intellectual beauty of a work; the former only become objectionable if they are devoid of intellectual beauty. Nor can the circumstance that Verdi allows himself a certain degree of rubato disadvantage a

composition, not even a German one. Rubato is an intrinsic part of declamation, in which the control of the musical content is reflected. Even Beethoven expressly demanded, as Schindler testified, that his compositions should be declaimed with greater freedom. But regarding declamation, Germans and Italians mean quite different things. In many passages we would allow a *morendo* to permit the solo voices to unfold in a more satisfactory and powerful manner – Verdi, on the other hand, never permitted this. To a considerably greater extent than we Germans, the Italians use the human voice instrumentally – and rightly so, because Italian voices are technically more assured. Solo voices are thus used in the same way as orchestral instruments: singers and players are treated as one large orchestra. This explains the quick tempo of the *Sanctus* fugue which was taken as a lively *alla breve*, and the equally quick tempo of the *Libera me Domine* fugue – both tempi hardly seemed fast enough for the composer. We are not accustomed to such treatment of fugues for voices. Our tempi in the choruses of Bach and Handel allow the somewhat rigid strength of German voices to unfold powerfully and fully, and we therefore instinctively expect a similar effect from a Verdi fugue – and are, quite simply, disappointed. Usually we pay less attention to the orchestra because the chorus dominates, but here the chorus plays in the orchestra. And so it is everywhere in the *Requiem*: the solo voice is given its own theme no more or no less than any other instrument of the orchestra. There can be no doubt about it: the choruses of *Die Jahreszeiten* [Haydn] are more sympathetic to German ears than Verdi's choruses. The choruses of German oratorios allow us, in their expansive development, much greater time to appreciate fully their beauty; a Verdi chorus is over, before one has had the time to listen properly.

For us Germans, therefore, it is the orchestra – and never the soloists – in the *Requiem*, that assume the most important rôle. And it is interesting to observe that Verdi's individual instrumental effects, however numerous they be, are in general less intrusive and more noble than is very often the case in German works. Verdi never allows the individual instruments to stand out more than is necessary for the general effect. In this respect he received significant support from the splendid wind-players, who are selected with extra special care for music festivals. And Verdi drew from the string section of the orchestra playing of the greatest possible power – a truly wonderful sound.

The above observation on the role of solo singers was endorsed by the difficulty the voices sometimes experienced in emerging from the full orchestra. The singer must possess an exceptionally powerful instrument for his voice to ring out loud and clear. Our soloists, at any rate, were absolutely first-rate, especially Lilli Lehmann[2] and Adèle Assmann (second soprano) who covered themselves in glory. They gave splendid accounts of the *Recordare* and the *Agnus Dei*. Their voices dovetailed beautifully, the tone was light, the voices rounded; the bright high notes of Miss Lehmann in particular soared wonderfully over the ensemble. And Verdi has another lesson for us Germans: his pauses are kept as short as possible, never destroying the sense of rhythm.[3]

During the 45th Rhenish Music Festival there was also a performance of Verdi's *String Quartet*, which had been heard four months previously in Cologne, on 13 December 1876 during the Gürzenicht Concerts. On May 22 Verdi wrote to Countess Maffei about these days in Cologne:

Although you will think me rather immodest, I must tell you that I have been well received and that the welcome surpassed anything I expected. Imagine the musical turmoil in these days of festivals: music and songs everywhere; orchestras, bands, quartets, serenades, mattinatas, invitations to luncheons and dinners. Above all, dinners: every performance must, whatever happens, be over by 10 in the evening, so that afterwards you can go to restaurants where you never find a bottle of water but beer, claret, hock, champagne and a great variety of things to eat. Yesterday after the concert – which was the last – the Festival Society invited us to dinner at the Casino. There were perhaps more than 500 present. Wine and toasts; and towards the end everyone was handed a printed song, and everyone, men and women, began to sing. It was very strange! Later on, another song was handed round, printed in Italian with the most charming misprints imaginable, and once again they all began to sing. Both songs had been composed in my honour. Finally, Hiller made a speech in French in honour of Italy and Germany, expressing the wish that we should always remain united as nations, in the same way as were now united through art etc., etc. There was a defeaning cry of hurrah . . . May we thus remain united now and forever – that, as you well know, is my ardent wish. As for the concerts, they were a magnificent success, and the music was well received. Excellent performances from choir and orchestra. The Members of the Festival presented me with a magnificent, enormous album with views of the Rhine [. . .]. And the Quartet, which was received with such condescension in Milan [it had been performed at the Conservatoire on 3 December 1876 by the Florentine Quartet], has been accepted here and is performed frequently. I have heard it myself very well performed. They also presented me with a little ivory and silver conductor's baton, inscribed with the letter V in little diamonds, and also with the words "the ladies of the choir". Also a most delightful crown of gold and silver; on each leaf was inscribed the name of one of the ladies from Cologne who presented it. Enough. There will be a concert in the gardens today given by six bands, and then farewell.[4]

And on the same day, May 22, he writes to Arrivabene:

[. . .] In the first place I can tell you that I am half dead with fatigue, not so much because of the rehearsals but because of a continual succession of excursions, invitations, visits, luncheons, dinners etc., etc., of which I've refused as many as possible. I was unable, however, to refuse an invitation to a concert given by a Choral Society, who performed for me several songs of their most famous composers. Marvellous performances. The Quartet Society wished me to hear my own, and that too was played quite marvellously. I have heard Rondes Lieder *etc., etc. Finally, yesterday evening, there was a performance of my Requiem with a chorus of 300 and an orchestra of 200 . Excellent apart from the four soloists. Resounding success. [. . .]*[5]

[A visit by Maria Wieck to Verdi]

The well-known pianist Maria Wieck, during her recent tour of Italy, visited Verdi in Genoa. The famous Maestro received the German artist in a splendid loggia of the Palazzo Doria with a magnificent veranda overlooking the sea. The Maestro's wife, a doctor and a niece[6] were also present. The furniture is Eastern, magnificent, many-coloured and Egyptian in style.[7] One of the paintings, representing an Egyptian woman in a veil, is impressive.[8] A cabinet (there is a similar piece of furniture in Liszt's house at Altenburg in Weimar) is packed full of silver and golden laurel crowns, conductor's batons and other trophies. It is said that Verdi does not like visits, yet he behaved most affably towards the German artist and conversed with great naturalness and without affectation.

The conversation – in Italian – touched on Cologne and Ferdinand Hiller (memories of the Cologne Music Festival), and Miss Wieck and her companion remained a full hour with the Maestro, who then accompanied them to his study and into his bedroom.[9] An Erard piano stood in the former. Verdi requested Robert Schumann's sister-in-law to play a little German music. Schumann's *Romance in D Minor, Evening* from *Phantasiestücke* op. 12, and a *Gigue* by Hässler pleased the Maestro greatly. On the music-rest lay Bach's *Preludes and Fugues*, clearly for Verdi's own use - which will be of great interest to those Germans who spurn Italian music. At Miss Wieck's request, he inscribed an album: *"To Maria Wieck in adoration, Giuseppi Verdi."*

(*Allg. deutsche Musik-Zeitung*)

NOTES

1. Cf. A. LUZIO: *Carteggi verdiani*, cit., vol. II, *Verdi and Hiller*, pp. 317–45.
2. Lilli Lehmann (Würzburg 1848 – Berlin 1929), one of the greatest German sopranos of the second half of the nineteenth century. The previous year she had taken part in the first performance of Wagner's *Ring* at Bayreuth (Woglinde, Helmwige and the Forest Bird).
3. As well as this interesting account from the *Kölnische Zeitung* of Verdi as conductor, there are two fragmentary reviews, published after the concert in commemoration of Rossini, given at La Scala on 8 April 1892, during which Verdi himself conducted – the *Prayer* from *Mosè*, for solo voices, chorus and orchestra – as an act of homage to the composer of *Guglielmo Tell*. *Il Commercio* of 9 April 1892 wrote:

Verdi conducted the entire piece standing up, waving the baton energetically and jerkily, staring at the players in the pit and the singers on stage, marking with his left hand – a white, diaphanous, almost waxen hand – the rhythmical development of the piece.

And *L'Italia del Popolo* of 9–10 April 1892 reports:

He conducted with ample, resolute gestures, while the fingers of his right hand rested on the stand and quivered nervously: with an imperious *ssss* he obtained a *piano* from orchestra and singers, while a movement of his whole body drew crescendos and tone from the players.

4. A. LUZIO: *Profili biografici e bozzetti storici*, cit., see chapter: *Il carteggio di G. Verdi con Clara Maffei*, vol. II, p. 538.
5. *Verdi intimo*, cit., pp. 203–4.

6. Maria (ex Filomena) Verdi, wife of Signor Carrara, at the time of Maria Wieck's visit pregnant with her first son.

7. Perhaps this is a reference to the so-called "Turkish Room", as it was generally called in Verdi's household. A "pen sketch drawn from life" of this room, executed around 1880, is reproduced in *Verdi a Genova: Ricordi, aneddoti ed episodi*, by F. RESASCO [. . .], Genoa 1901, p. 30. On p. 31 Resasco, describing a visit by the committee of the Circolo Filarmonico di Genova, writes:

> [. . .] One of us expressed the wish to see the Turkish Room of Verdi's abode. "Sala turca!" said Verdi, modestly, "it's only a little room with some hangings and carpets, more or less oriental, a painting called the Odalisque by Morelli, that I'm fond of and which is certainly precious, several pieces of furniture which are more or less byzantine. Anyway, come and see the sala . . . turca!" – And he led us into the drawing-room of truly oriental character which, except for Morelli's wonderful painting, was furnished with pieces made exclusively in Turkey and Egypt.

8. *The Odalisque* by Domenico Morelli, now in Villa Verdi, Sant' Agata.

9. For this room too, see the "pen sketch drawn from life", reproduced in *Verdi a Genova*, cit., p. 21.

XX

VERDI

1879

A. DE LAUZIÈRES-THÉMINES: "Verdi", in *Le Figaro*, Paris, XXV, 284:
11 October 1879 (republished as "Verdi in Busseto" in *Signale für die
musikalische Welt*, Leipzig, XXXVII, 56: October 1879, pp. 881–4).

THIS ARTICLE WAS written after a journey to Sant'Agata made by de
Lauzières, an old acquaintance of Verdi and his dogged supporter in
France,[1] in the company of the new Director of the Opéra, Auguste
E. Vaucorbeil, who had succeeded Olivier Halanzier scarcely three
months previously on 19 July 1879.[2] The aim of the journey was to
obtain Verdi's permission to stage *Aida* in French at the Opéra –
permission that he had obstinately refused to grant (preferring the
Théâtre Italien to all other Parisian theatres) – which he had made
clear on 24 August 1872 in a famous letter to Halanzier:

> *I thank you for the charming way in which you wished to open discussions
> with me. I am particularly flattered that you found the score of* Aida
> *worthy of the Opéra. But let me say at once that I know the personnel of
> the Opéra insufficiently well; and then allow me to confess: I have always
> been so very little satisfied in my dealings with your great theatre, that I
> do not now feel disposed to attempt a new adventure. – It is possible that
> later, if you are still kindly disposed towards me, I shall change my mind.
> But at present I do not have the courage to face once more all the quarrels,
> all the underhand opposition that prevails in your theatre, of which I hold
> distressing memories. – Forgive me, Sir, for having expressed my mind
> with perhaps too great frankness; but I wished to speak to you at once and
> with an open heart, to make the situation clear. [. . .]*[3]

The meeting between the two Parisian travellers and Verdi took
place at Sant'Agata from 3–4 October 1879; the composer finally
gave his consent, and on October 7 he wrote to Muzio:

> *As matters stood, even I saw that I could not have refused them* Aida; *but
> between you and me, I am not very happy about it. Either I shall not go*

*to Paris and the opera will be performed flabbily, feebly and fail to
impress; or else I shall go and destroy myself body and soul.* [. . .] *The
Italian newspapers will not approve my giving way over* Aida. *Only
yesterday the* Corriere della Sera *said that, after the incessant rudeness I
had endured, I would not give them permission to stage* Aida. *Who
knows what they will say when they know I have. The strange thing is
that I basically agree with them ten times over. Perhaps Capponi* [sic][4]
who has written to me about Aida *in Paris, can find the opportunity to
write something in the* Fanfulla *or* Perseverenza, *saying that for such
and such reasons I had no option but to do what I did etc., etc.*[5]

De Lauzières' article contains in the second half a concise account of
his visit to Sant'Agata in the company of Vaucorbeil.[6] Several years
later De Lauzières provided another account, more detailed and of
much greater interest, on the eve of *Otello*: see N. XXXI.

Verdi

We know the musician but not the man. His music – whether we like
it or not, whether we dote on it or debate it – we all know it; at least
partially, since about half of his operas have been performed in our
theatres. We have a similarly partial knowledge of his life.
Biographers have gossiped about the marital status of the Italian
maestro, have told of his obscure origins, recalled that, when he
applied to the Milan Conservatoire, it was stated that he possessed
not the slightest aptitude for composition[7] and would be wise to
abandon the idea; they have told us how his *Nabucco*, from the very
first performances, placed him in the front line of Italian composers –
for success is a little like that down in Italy as it is here in France: his
music was accepted like a wedge in a block of wood.[8] Fame was slow
in spreading his name to the four winds; and he forced her to sound
her trumpet – he would sooner have broken it on her back.

Besides, what can biographers know of his private life, since,
following the sage's precept, he conceals it? Only his friends – and
one must understand this word in its highest and truest sense – can
speak about it. For everyone else, Verdi is a "bear" – uncivilized too,
according to all those people whom he has offended. Agreed, he's a
bear. But before risking a paw-shake, let us start by visiting his cage.

He built it himself – just as he made himself. The old cliché "a self-
made man", if it may be used once again, is a perfect description of

Verdi in the 1850s

Teresa Stolz (pastel by Gariboldi,
Museo Teatrale alla Scala)

Verdi (photograph by Meulnier)

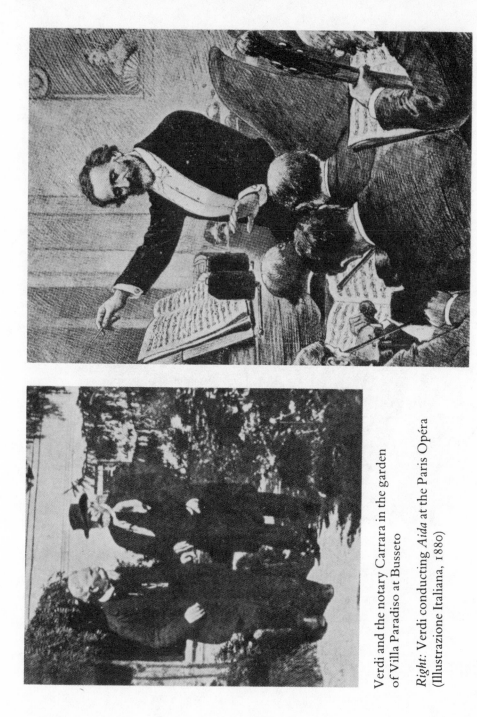

Verdi and the notary Carrara in the garden of Villa Paradiso at Busseto

Right: Verdi conducting *Aida* at the Paris Opéra (Illustrazione Italiana, 1880)

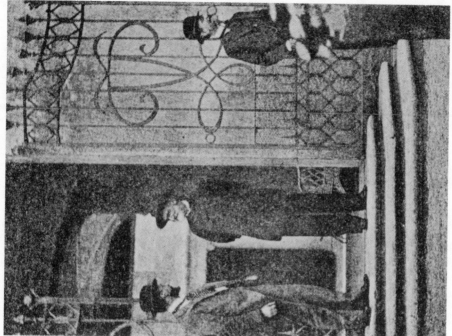

Giuseppe Giacosa and Arrigo Boito

Right: "Bricconi! . . ." ("Rogues"). Verdi and Tito Ricordi, Giulio's son; Giulio Ricordi is on the right (summer 1892, Perego garden)

"But it's all over". From left to right: Carlo Chessa, Arrigo Boito, Tito and Giulio Ricordi (summer 1892, Perego garden)

Giulio
Ricordi,
centre,
introducing
the painter
Carlo Chessa
to Verdi

Annie
Vivanti

The palazzo
Doria at Genoa,
Verdi's winter
residence from
1874 to 1900

Verdi in the summer of 1892, portrayed in the Perego garden,
Via Borgonuovo, Milan, where Giulio Ricordi lived.
This photograph was used by Chessa for his etching.

him. This famous cage is situated to the North of the peninsula, on the boot's "turnover", in that part of the country which was once so carved up and called the Duchy of Parma and Piacenza. There you find a straggling little town called Busseto, where Verdi was born 64 years ago from the day before yesterday.[9] His career at the outset was not easy. Without a maecenas to detect his brilliance, he would not have seen his first opera performed at La Scala. Initial success might not bring in riches, but at least it opens up the path to fortune. Verdi, who is a fine walker, set out on it and advanced at the double, as he had once promised himself to do – it had needed all his iron will not to break that promise. He can now say, with one of our great writers who also started without a sou and later wallowed in wealth:

> Un jour on comprendra quelle lutte obstinée
> A fait sous mon genou plier la destinée, etc.

Once fortune had arrived, the composer folded his tent and thought of creating a more durable dwelling. The choice was his; all Italy offered him the home of his dreams. Proud Genoa with its bay in the shape of an amphitheatre, where white villas resemble pearls set in green enamel; Naples with its emerald coast beneath a sapphire sky; Florence with her gently contoured hills where sunset clouds come to nestle and admire; Venice with her marble palaces reflected in her gondola-furrowed lagoons, where our dress is the only anachronism. Not one of the great cities tempted him. They only gave him glory and wealth. He preferred the modest little town which had been his cradle. He chose Busseto.

But where in this little town could he find enough land to stroll at his leisure? No problem, there. He went just a little further, and saw a vast stretch of land, almost wild. That's the place! he said to himself. He bought it and began by building a villa. Then he added a garden to the villa, a park to the garden, meadows to the park, woods to the meadows; and over the whole estate he dotted fine, beautiful farms – as many, I believe, as the operas he had composed! He had read in Virgil that farmers would be content if they knew the inherent worth of their property: *Sua si bona norint.*[10] He thought that if Virgil could, without detriment, busy himself with agriculture while writing verse, he could follow his example by combining agriculture and music. Verdi is both farmer and artist; harmony and agriculture occupy him simultaneously. He composes an opera and conducts a harvest. Loving landscape yet unable to be a landscape painter in the manner of Claude and Bril,[11] he created landscapes in nature. He did not paint, he planted. Yet the artist appears at every turn: in the design of his park, the outlines of his buildings, in the vistas that he conceived and above all in the interior decoration of his villa, the choice of antique furniture, hangings, pictures, etc.

But his love of art did not cause him to neglect his property. Let a few examples from hundreds suffice. The river Po (*Che guerra porti e non tributo al mare,* wrote Tasso),[12] floods in winter over a vast area. In summer, as it recedes, it leaves behind parched, grass-covered land where willows grow like daisies on a lawn. Verdi purchased part of this land and later sold the willows, whose tall, straight branches are in great demand as vine-props. His meadows did not lack water, but irrigation was laborious and difficult. He installed an irrigation machine, the model of which he had seen at some exhibition. He leased his land and woods, and to relax from agricultural work he set about rearing horses – an occupation he still pursues today. Between times, he composed *Il trovatore, Rigoletto* and *La traviata,* on the pretext of keeping his hand in. So much for the cage. It exhibits the product of his labour. Now for the bear.

Open the dictionary at the word "Bear", and you will read, among other definitions: "The bear is not only wild but solitary; instinctively he flees society; he avoids those places where humans roam, and only feels at ease in those areas which still belong to nature; there he will retire, alone, without emerging for months on end," etc. Ah! My dear Maestro, if that be so, then you are indeed the bear described by Buffon and the dictionary.

Verdi, however, does not live *alone,* he is not exactly a *solitary*: he has with him his faithful companion, Mme Verdi, a retired singer whom he married for love and for whom he has always retained an affection at least as great as that which she bears him. It is true that he does not extend invitations to his numerous acquaintances, but friends who visit Sant'Agata find the warmest hospitality. How did he acquire these friends? Reserved at first, Verdi waits for like-minded natures, a certain similarity of ideas and what Goethe terms *elective affinities* to form a friendship, which, from that moment on, remains firm, active and unshakeable. Ah, he is not accessible to all who sue for his friendship! It is not Mistrust that stands guard, but Work, which keeps out the inquisitive and the intruders, and opens the door only to the select few.

The bear also presides over the staging of his operas. He wishes the work to be performed as he conceived it, not as the performers conceive it. Does a general not behave a little like a bear during manoeuvres? Afterwards he invites the officers to his table and clinks glasses with them; rank and hierarchy give way to a spirit of good fellowship. This is the Maestro's way with artists and musicians, after the inevitable difficulties of rehearsals.

It has been said – and what isn't said – that Verdi loves money for money's sake. It is true that he takes a certain perverse delight – easily forgiven – in earning as much as possible by his composer's pen. But there is not a pauper for twenty miles around whom he has forgotten, or who has forgotten him! There is not a subscription which does not bear his name at the top, followed by a figure that is often discouraging for other subscribers. During the Italian war there was not a single sheet that remained in his house. I cannot vouch for mattresses . . . Some bear!

But you waste your time writing him flattering letters, and waste his time too. Although he doesn't lack savoir-vivre, he has an unholy horror of official invitations and society gatherings. He avoids crowds like the plague. Among a small gathering of friends, on the other hand, he is a witty and affable conversationalist. As a Deputy, he rarely spoke from the rostrum; as a Senator he takes excessive holidays. And you can be quite sure: the popular vote and the sovereign will did not bring him to parliament for his artistic talent, but for his civic virtues, his wisdom and practical expertise. For example – although he hides his life, he does not hide his thoughts! He expresses them frankly and clearly, and would declare them to kings, who hear the truth less often than most. He has a respect, bordering on a cult, for the great masters of art; but he does not disguise his aversion to shabby mediocrity. Some bear!

When I recently visited him with my excellent friend M. Vaucorbeil, to request something most difficult to obtain, the Director of the Opéra feared that he would not be able to converse at leisure with the Maestro who, he thought, would be surrounded by a host of friends or guests. We found him alone, walking in the garden, followed by an enormous dog called *Leda*, perhaps to mock those people who call him the *Swan of Busseto*. Mme Verdi, seated a little further away, was reading in the shade of an ash tree.

"Listen, my friend," said the Maestro, when I broached the important question next morning, "when I wish to stage an opera here, I am offered the most advantageous terms; all the great opera houses of Italy vie with one another in gaining my consent. The best artists are engaged, even at the cost of paying for broken contracts. The musicians fête me, the conductor hands me his baton, and singers compete with one another to give of their best. Why should I go abroad? To hear that I am ousting their own composers? But I don't wish to oust them. Let them leave me here in peace! Look about you – it is really quite comfortable here. If you knew what awaited me over there! . . ."

It would not have needed much for him to cry out, believing that his garden at Sant'Agata was the garden of Gethsemane: *Transeat a me calix iste!* It would have needed even less for me to say to M. Vaucorbeil, in view of the Maestro's magnificent property and his calm, contented life: "Forget your mission, the Opéra, everything, and let us raise three tabernacles here . . ." But we had not visited Verdi to surrender ourselves to biblical recollections. The Director of the Opéra and I therefore returned to our task of obtaining the Maestro's permission to stage his latest opera. He finally agreed. The bear was tamed.

I had thought that an opera by Verdi, already known, and not to be performed till next February,[13] would not have deprived our own composers of their rights. I also told myself that when Gounod, Massenet, Saint-Saëns went to Italy and were asked (very recently in the case of the last two) to compose a new opera for Milan and Turin, it was not said over there that they were ousting Italian composers. I did not think, therefore, that I was acting badly! . . .[14] Perhaps that is because, when I hear a military band pass beneath my windows, playing a tune that pleases me, I listen to it happily without wondering too much whether the flats in the key-signature are French, German or Italian.

But if anyone bears me a grudge, it should be Verdi, who had intended staying at Sant'Agata till it was time to leave for the Palazzo Doria in Genoa, where he would continue his patriarchal existence during four or five winter months! For Verdi is a mixture of child and patriarch; a patriarch before his time, and a child with a grey beard – a spoilt child, if you will, but it is the public who have spoilt him, and the public only spoil those whom they love. He combines great wisdom and strong principles with an indefinable *naïveté* in tastes and manners. A beautiful picture will delight him, like a new toy delights a baby. Did he not once amuse himself by gathering in his greenhouses every known species of grape? He loves birds and forbids any shooting in his gardens. The carp and eel in his ponds die of old age. He has a gondola in which he crosses his lakes, and one evening it capsized – he fell in the water and emerged, covered in weeds, looking like a river god. How we laughed![15]

As I admired the vigour of this man, his iron strength, his robust constitution, I wondered whether his active life, the seven months of the year he spends in the country, retiring early, rising with the dawn, working alternatively at the piano and in the garden, breathing in deeply the fresh air of the woods, rather than suffocating in theatres and drawing rooms – whether this kind of life was not the chief cause of his strong physique, his serenity of mind, his unabated vigour which survives so astonishingly into old age. And I left him, my heart full of regret.

A. DE LAUZIÈRES-THÉMINES

NOTES

1. This must presumably be the son of Achille de Lauzières, quoted in N. VIII, note 15, whose death, according to the dictionaries, occurred in 1875. An A. de Lauzières-Thémines wrote several articles of music criticism in French newspapers (*La Patrie*, *Le Figaro*, *Le Progrès*) up to the last decade of the nineteenth century.
2. Auguste-Emmanuel Vaucorbeil (Rouen 1821 – Paris 1884), composer, choral singing teacher at the Paris Conservatoire, from 1872 Minister for state-subsidized theatres, from 1878 Inspector of Fine Arts, he held the post of Director of the Opéra till his death.
3. A.POUGIN: *Giuseppe Verdi: Vita aneddotica*, cit., pp. 82–83 (note).
4. Jacopo Caponi, Italian correspondent in Paris of the *Perseveranza*, Milan, and the *Fanfulla*, Rome.
5. *I Copialettere di G. Verdi*, cit. pp. 312–13.
6. Another account, based on information supplied by Vaucorbeil himself, was published by F. de Lagenevais (pseudonym of Henri Blaze de Bury) in the *Revue des Deux Mondes* of 15 November 1879, pp. 460–5 (then reprinted in A. POUGIN: *Verdi: Histoire anecdotique*, cit. pp. 259–60).
7. On the contrary: it was precisely in composition that Verdi received fairly encouraging criticism. His failure was determined by a piano examination and by questions of a bureaucratic and administrative nature that were asked him; but see N. XLVIII, note 2.
8. A play on words in the original French text: "*Sa musique y est entré comme un coin dans le bois*".
9. In fact he was sixty-six.
10. *Georgics* II 548.
11. This very probably refers to the painters Claude (XVII century) and Mathys Bril (XVI century).
12. Italian in the original.
13. *Aida* was performed at the Opéra a little later, on 22 March 1880, under Verdi's direction with the soprano Gabrielle Kraus, the baritone Victor Maurel and others.

14. Contrary to what Lauzières thought, requesting Verdi's permission to stage *Aida* (which had already been given in Paris, at the Théâtre Italien in 1876 in Italian, and at the Théâtre Lyrique in 1878 in a bad French translation) at the Opéra, which usually staged works written expressly for it, did cause several French composers to feel that their rights were being ignored. Saint-Saëns (one of the three mentioned by Lauzières) in particular deplored the Opéra spending time and money on a work like *Aida*, which "after all was of less worth than *Les Huguenots*, *Guillaume Tell*, *Faust*, and even *Hamlet* and *Le roi de Lahore*, and would gradually disappear from the repertoire, as had been the case, one after the other, with *Jérusalem*, *Luisa Miller*, *I vespri siciliani*, *Il trovatore* and *Don Carlos*" (from the columns of *Voltaire* on 19 October 1879, and then reprinted in the *Gazzetta Musicale di Milano*, XXXIV, 43: 26 October 1879, p. 367). A polemic ensued both in France (where *Le Soir* and other papers defended Vaucorbeil and Verdi), and Italy, where the controversy was stirred up by Leone Fortis' *Pungolo* of Milan. Saint-Saëns replied on 3 November 1879 with a letter to the *Pungolo* (edition of November 7, printed two days later in the *Gazzetta Musicale di Milano*, p. 383), in which, modifying his own attack, he affirmed that his *Voltaire* article had not been aimed at Verdi, who was worthy of the highest regard, but rather at the Verdi fetishists of Paris. Saint-Saëns was at that time negotiating with the Teatro Regio in Turin for a performance of his own *Samson et Dalila* (an opera which was to remain unknown in France till 1890!), which two years previously had enjoyed a great success in Weimar; but the controversy surrounding *Aida* and the Opéra (which in turn reflected the increasing deterioration in Italian–French relations, that had begun after the Congress of Berlin of 1878 and flared up in 1882 when Italy joined the Triple Alliance) forced the Turin promoters to postpone the project to a later date (cf. G. DEPANIS: *I concerti popolari e il Teatro Regio di Torino*, S.T.E.N., Turin 1915, II, pp. 53–55).

15. See N. XI, note 14.

XXI

A VISIT TO GIUSEPPE VERDI

1881?

CATERINA PIGORINI BERI; "Una visita a Giuseppe Verdi", in *L'Illustrazione Italiana*, Milan, VIII, 44: 30 October 1881, p. 279.

CATERINA PIGORINI BERI (Fontanellato, Parma, 1845 – Rome 1924), sister of the famous archaeologist Luigi Pigorini, and wife of Commendatore Beri, mayor of Camerino, was a student of literature, ethics, art, politics and women's education. She wrote for many newspapers and periodicals (*Gazzetta di Parma*, *La Nazione*, of Florence, *Il Giornale d'Italia* of Rome, *L'Illustrazione Italiana*, *Il Fanfulla della Domenica*, *Roma Letteraria*, *Natura ed Arte*, etc.) and left behind stories, novels, critical essays and, of particular importance, several publications on folklore. She published about a dozen articles on Verdi and her meetings with him,[1] all suffused with a rhetorical sentimentality fairly common in Italian journalism of that era, and therefore somewhat lacking in real merit as documents on Verdi and his thoughts. The following article by Caterina Pigorini is chronologically the first, and less wishy-washy than her other articles. The writer, who in this article gives neither the date of her visit (it presumably took place in the spring of 1881) nor the names of her two "companions in adventure", also corresponded with Verdi; she published several of Verdi's letters to her in *Roma Letteraria* (10 February 1901), *La Nazione* (30 June 1912) and *Nuova Antologia* (16 October 1913); other letters were published in *Nuova Antologia* on 16 August 1928.

A visit to Giuseppe Verdi

We were fully aware of the difficulties to be overcome, if we were to gain entrance to the Maestro's residence. People said that he would let no one visit him, and that when taken unawares, he was so monosyllabic that never again would one wish to climb up to his delightful and celestial hermit's eyrie.

Perplexed, we stood for a while, and sought to hearten each other with encouraging looks, but our long, doubtful faces finally succeeded in robbing us of that bit of courage each one of us believes he has in reserve for the great events in life. We were a stone's throw from Sant'Agata, a single bridge separated us from that historic sanctuary but we felt how distant the cup still was from our lips. And yet we demanded nothing, not even a reception. I had already said: *if only I could touch the hem of his coat!* . . .

We had already equipped ourselves with passports and letters of introduction, prepared for a battle, wearing a coat of mail like Dante da Castiglione, and a velvet coat adorned with ermine, and a plume in our hats like Ettore Fieramosca. It was an adventure, an exploit, a foray – something between impudence and fear . . . we behaved like the nocturnal traveller, dying of terror, seeing apparitions in every bush and graves under every colonnade, singing loudly to display a lion's heart.

Our carriage halted before the bridge. It had fallen down, and the workmen who were labouring to repair it looked at us, without stirring, with amazed and inquisitive eyes, as if to say: But can't you see, no one approaches beyond this point.

We took the long route to cross the Ongina by the public bridge. Within me resounded the song of the mountain girl:

> Misi lo piede e mi manco il terreno,
> Dico d'avvicinarmi e m'allontano.[2]

Before me lay the garden with its indistinct and confused fragrance of a thousand flowers, the soft murmuring of enamoured birds, the breeze of the *foresta imbalsamata*, the palace rising serious and sad, like a great silent personage amid a feast of flowers and light – all this disturbed and attracted me strangely. This must be how sailors feel when they hear the bewitching song of the sirens. All of a sudden the carriage stopped before a closed gate: a gardener, who was waiting for our timid ring, opened it, smiling at our embarrassment. The sky had darkened and from time to time those large drops of spring rain fell – April, sweeping the air with a smell of whipped-up dust. The gardener walked silently in front of us until we reached a wide courtyard; a manservant came forward and rang a bell – another bell rang in answer. The first perhaps meant: trouble ahead for the Maestro. And the second certainly replied: may the Maestro's will be done – for we were admitted.

We passed through several rooms. Who would now remember

them? I caught sight of a billiard table, paintings, plants, dark walls and spotless floors as shining as mirrors; there was neither too much nor too little light. At last, we could look around, and we could see that art here held indisputable sway, that the man who lived here needed the great harmony provided by the colours, the light, the fragrant flowers in the window-boxes, the furniture that adorned the rooms, the paintings, their frames and a thousand tiny details. And does not every art have its own harmony?

The drawing-room, where we waited for Mme Verdi to lead us to him, was as grave as the other rooms. The upholstery was dark-red, the furniture black, or so it seemed. Wide velvet door-curtains hide the doors; and the paintings – what paintings! – gleam on the walls between half-closed windows, as though the light streamed from them. On a small oblong table lay . . . but what? I have forgotten . . . Surely there was an *Orlando furioso* illustrated by Doré, with a red binding, incised with fantastic gold figures taken from the text of that most imaginative of poets. But who could think of looking around?

We were about to realize the most daring dream of our lives, to be absolved from the vows of an artistic pilgrimage that had always been most difficult, and therefore most ardently desired. In that severe, almost solemn room, surrounded by charming trinkets and magnificent furnishings, he had perhaps conceived and created those ineffable melodies which hold sway over the world, civilize it, sweep from our thoughts the coarseness of earthly life and raise us aloft to an apparently inaccessible goal. Who could have thought of anything but this?

The rustle of a silk gown roused us from our reverie. There could be no further doubt – we had already entered the atmosphere of that glorious meteor. The gentle messenger who arrived, with her reassuring smile, lovely grace, sharp mind, her vivacious and ready ingenuity, her simple, black, high-necked and tight-fitting dress, her benevolent gaze and soft voice, banished the great problem that still perturbed us: the introduction. A minute later we were already embraced by an intimacy that was more affectionate than ceremonious. It was evident that she fully understood our commotion; and we were grateful that her unconstrained courtesy would free us from the anguish of our initial timidity.

Our letter of introduction was read with a tender and smiling solicitude; she was clearly already enjoying the prospect of seeing us in his presence, lost for words, not daring to look at him, frightened of what we had done . . . Truly, we must have been a singular sight!

"The Maestro will be here shortly," she said.

And in fact, after a few moments we heard a man's footfall upon the resonant floors. He walked briskly, like one who has been called for and knows he is expected. Only the Maestro could walk thus in a house where the few who manage to pass the threshold walk on tiptoe and whisper as if in church. We all rose together, as if a spring had been released, even before we saw him. The blood throbbed in our veins, we remained motionless, the Maestro appeared in the doorway and stopped to gaze at us.

The curtains of red velvet, held back by broad loops, under which he stood, and the light streaming in from the room behind him, made him appear as though framed in a luminous painting. In his hands he held a wide-brimmed black hat, which he had doffed when greeting us, and he wore his habitual buttoned jacket, bordered with silk braid, which broke the severe lines of the dark cloth. His pale, serious face with its full beard, grizzled like his thick, luxuriant hair, is still young, if one can so describe a face which neither has, nor could have, nor could have had anything in common with either present or past centuries. His smile is gentle and sad, those lips could never open in noisy laughter. No one will ever be able to reproduce the expression of those eyes – one might as well try to capture a ray of sunlight in one's room. Raphael, Michelangelo and Dante must have had those flashing eyes; as you approach him, he seems to grow in height like the Egyptian pyramids, from whose summit 40 centuries seemed but a flash to Napoleon. I believe that if he wished to measure himself against someone else, his eyes would only meet infinite space and shadowless light. He has a tall, well-proportioned, aristocratic frame; *aristocratic* in the Greek meaning of the word: perfect. Not a single one of the millions of people we meet on this earth resemble him even remotely. Once you have seen him, you cannot possibly forget or confuse him with another. He is Giuseppe Verdi. His voice is low and quiet; its inflection is not difficult to grasp, but impossible to reproduce. His speech is neither slow nor hasty, but measured, moderate, kind and graceful. He seems unaware of the effect his presence produces on people. He is Giuseppe Verdi, and appears not to know it.

As he approached and held out his hand in welcome, inviting us to be seated, we could not utter a word. Our embarrassment had vanished. Very rapidly our feelings had changed: we had imagined ourselves frightened, but in fact we were moved. He sat down in front of us, very naturally, as if he were someone other than himself. His wife, with her usual encouraging smile, sat quietly and good-naturedly next to me on an ottoman in a corner between a window and a door. A little table stood like an altar between us and the Maestro.

The world at large likes to imagine Verdi as cold and stern, shunning the public whom he exalts and transports. But where was this Verdi, now that he was conversing with us? Where was that almost misanthropic austerity which is always attributed to him?

How could those dissatisfied and inquisitive types, who attempt to solve great mysteries solely for the vanity of discovering and belittling them, hope to penetrate those reaches where genius withdraws before returning down to earth with revelations from the inaccessible and infinite heights of art? Numa sought refuge on the Sacred Mount to hearken to his inspiring goddess, and the Tables of the Law were handed Moses on the mountain in a luminous mist. Who has ever known a genius who was not withdrawn, silent, concealed in solitude – that gentle and loving enchantress who restores the soul?

Without solitude, without secrecy, without meditation, neither art nor love could ever come into being, and yet there we were, absorbed and pleasantly agitated by that great personality who had glittered like a beacon through so many epochs, splendours and destinies, and remained with a modesty so unusual that it seemed pride, a kindness so natural that it seemed learnt in the ubiquitous flattery of newspaper advertisements, and an indulgence that seemed nonchalance to those who do not know that *tout comprendre c'est tout pardonner*.

We felt ourselves transported into a fragrant, select and ecstatic atmosphere, as if we had always known him, living for one instant the luminous experience of the fly, who, dazzled by a ray of sunlight, reflects the colours of the rainbow in its transparent, mother-of-pearl wings.

The conversation was long, but time passed in a flash. His words will remain enclosed in our hearts, diligently, jealously and selfishly guarded; not a syllable will be uttered nor a word written – because the pilgrim who absolves a vow cannot, must not, lift the veil that covers certain ineffable mysteries.

Three times we made our adieus and three times the flashing eyes of the Maestro commanded – stay. And when it was our duty to insist, and he graciously permitted us to part, the lord and lady of the villa expressed the wish to accompany us to our carriage which had remained outside the wide gates. Nor did the same small drops that an indiscreet and importunate cloud let fall on the parched earth deter them in their courtesy. Our umbrellas covered those two heads, and their faces in that weather still bore the most perfect and sweet expression of kindness.

The Maestro had put on his black hat, tilted to one side like a troubador's – an artist even here, since he can be nothing else. And his smile, at seeing us so bewildered by the favours that descended upon us from such heights, seemed to say: Let me do as I wish; can you not see that I am a king who occasionally amuses himself with such whims? And he opened the door of our carriage, proffered us his arm, chivalrously waved his hat, shook hands again, and we departed.

A stone's throw from the villa many carts were blocking our way, and we were obliged to descend. Without saying a word, my two companions and I took one another by the hand and ran, as though crazed, over the bridge. When we looked at each other we had something in our eyes that resembled tears. One of us, who pretended to be strong and perhaps was so, expressed surprise at that unaccustomed phenomenon. Not I, because in my memory there had dwelt a most delicious emotion, since the time when a distant music had played to my heart and mind – *Va, pensiero, sull'ali dorate!* . . .

. *Idolatry*, I know, *is not the prevailing religion at Sant'Agata*; but since the worship of all that is beautiful and great in the world is permitted there, I cannot suppress that ardent enthusiasm, from which precisely those cults are born, which sometimes produce idolaters, but which more often, raising the human mind *to the summit of the glorious mountain*, offer man the ideal for which he is ever questing.

CATERINA PIGORINI BERI

NOTES

1. There follows a list, which does not claim to be complete, of other articles published by Pigorini Beri on the subject of Verdi: "Giuseppe Verdi e le litanie lauretane", in *Fanfulla della Domenica*, Rome, XV, 14: 2 April 1893; "Una visita a Giuseppe Verdi" (practically the same as the article in the *Illustrazione Italiana*) in *Strenna della "Gazzetta di Parma" per l'anno 1898*, Parma 1897, pp. 61–71; "Giuseppe Verdi e Jacopa Sanvitale", in *Gazzetta di Parma*, XLII, 38: 8 February 1901, pp. 1–2; "Giuseppe e Giuseppina Verdi", in *Roma Letteraria*, IX, 3: 10 February

1901, pp. 58–60; "Verdi intimo" (taken partly from the article in the *Illustrazione Italiana*) in *Natura ed Arte*, Milan, X, 3: 15 February 1901, pp. 19–26; "Per l'epistolario di Giuseppe Verdi: Reminiscenze", in *La Nazione*, Florence LIV, 182: 30 June 1912, "Giuseppe Verdi in casa sua", in *Giornale d'Italia*, Rome, 8 August 1913 (reprinted in *L'Illustrazione Popolare*, Milan, L, 44: 2 October 1913, pp. 691–3); "Giuseppe Verdi a Sant'Agata. (L'ultima volta!)", in *L'Illustrazione Italiana*, Milan, XL, 40: 5 October 1913, pp. 342–8; "Verdi intimo", in *Nuova Antologia*, Rome, vol. 251, 16 October 1913, pp. 543–60; "Un giorno a Sant' Agata", in *Falstaff*, an illustrated review for the Festeggiamenti Verdiani, Busseto, n. 9–10: 25 December 1913, p. 2; and finally, "Lettere inedite di Paolo Mantegazza, Cesare Correnti e Giuseppe Verdi a Caterina Pigorini Beri", in *Nuova Antologia*, Rome, 16 August 1928.

2.   I set down my foot but the ground fell away,
          I think I approach but wander farther off.

XXII

CONVERSATIONS IN VERDI'S VILLA

1883?

A. VON WINTERFELD: "Unterhaltungen in Verdis Tuskulum", in *Deutsche Revue*, Stuttgart, XII, 1887: pp. 327–32 (reprinted with variants and cuts as "Persönliche Erinnerungen an Verdi", in *Neue Musik-Zeitung*, Stuttgart–Leipzig, XXII, 5 [special Verdi number], 1901: pp. 57–58).

IN THIS INTERESTING account Winterfeld recalls two meetings with Verdi, the first at Genoa and the second, about eight days later, at Sant'Agata. He does not state the year; but since at one point he mentions the "almost 70-year-old Maestro" and had previously spoken of a "beautiful April day" for the visit to Sant'Agata, it is likely that these two meetings took place at the beginning of spring 1883, when Verdi was sixty-nine and a half. In that year he moved from Genoa to Sant'Agata on about April 5 or 6 – the meetings can therefore be safely traced back to either side of those dates.

Conversations in Verdi's villa

When I leaf through my travel notes, I linger with particular pleasure over those passages which describe my meetings (which I reproduce here) with Giuseppe Verdi, because they, unlike the frequently disappointing encounters with famous men, have left behind nothing but pleasant impressions.

My first encounter with the great Maestro took place several years ago in Genoa, in the house of the senator, Count D., on the occasion of a farewell dinner given in honour of Verdi, who was very shortly to leave the town and move for the summer to his country estate at Sant'Agata near Busseto.

I was his neighbour at table.

To judge from the impulsive, fiery character of Verdi's music, I would have expected the composer to be a lively, passionate man who enjoyed a lively social life.

I was therefore not a little surprised to find my famous neighbour very calm, silent and almost embarrassed, so that the task of starting a conversation at first seemed difficult and virtually impossible. However, I did not allow myself to be deterred by the short, cool answers I received, and took care, although I wished to steer the conversation towards music, not to indulge in banal compliments, and kept to more general topics. I had the satisfaction of seeing my neighbour gradually emerge from his shell. He showed interest when I spoke of the German musical scene, thawed more and more, and asked animated and stimulating questions.

It was not long after his visit to Vienna, and he spoke vivaciously about his impressions.

"Theatres, in the sense of your stable German Court theatres, do not and cannot exist in Italy," he said; "that is because of our climate, our national institutions and social customs. Our winter is not long, and our opera is still the short-lived child of the Carnival, in the impresario's care. This of course causes many disadvantages, but there are advantages too. I admit that we lack stability, permanent orchestras, choirs and soloists. On the other hand we do not find ourselves in the situation of having to hear, year in and year out, the same singers who have been engaged for eternity or at least for many years, even when they are long past their prime. By the same token, we are, it is true, deprived of hearing our favourites once again during the next season. Our impresarios must see to it, that new stars are always rising in the operatic firmament.[1]

"The same is true with music in general; it must be thoroughly national. I greatly appreciate and admire German music, and owe much to it: your great Giovanni Sebastiano Back"[2] – for so he pronounced Bach[3] – "is still my master. But I will not for that reason compose German music, any more than a German will compose Italian music. If the genius of a nation is not discernible in the music, it will be without charm or worth."[4]

About Wagner, who was at that time still living, Verdi expressed himself with a certain restraint – understandably so if one bears in mind the former's opinions on Italian music. He merely said that there was much to be admired in *Tannhäuser* and *Lohengrin*,[5] but that Wagner in his recent operas seemed to be overstepping the bounds of what can be expressed in music. For him "philosophical music" was incomprehensible.

Of German singers, he said that their voices were not inferior to those of their Italian counterparts, but that they attached too great importance to power and too little to beauty of tone[6] – a criticism that can be endorsed without reservation.

The table rose, and we were unable to continue our conversation, for the Maestro was surrounded by other guests.

My kind host congratulated me on my "conquest of Verdi", as he termed it, adding that it was in no way easy to approach the much flattered artist. "Verdi," said the count, "is by nature and through experience very reserved and cautious, almost mistrustful. But if your ideas and judgements conform to his and he is attracted to you and convinced that your opinions are based on truth and accuracy, he will be a constant and reliable friend, kind, witty and frank; whereas he appears taciturn and almost awkward beneath the constraint of official celebrations, in other words when he is the hero."

Instinctively we turned towards Verdi who, a picture of discomfort and impatience, stood silently holding his cup of coffee, surrounded by verbose, cliché-ridden admirers, and only occasionally lifted the spoon to his mouth. The whole group illustrated the count's words in such drastic fashion, that neither of us could suppress a smile.

Meanwhile Verdi had finished his cup of coffee, broken through the surrounding crowd and approached our host to take his leave, reminding him of his promise to visit him before long in Busseto. Whereupon he turned to me and said most sincerely: "Should you care to accompany our mutual friend, you would give me great pleasure."

As surprised as I was delighted, I promised to accept the invitation, and Verdi left.

"Was I not right about your conquest?" exclaimed the count, laughing. "I know Verdi; very few people are invited to Busseto, for his door remains obstinately closed to the curious and obtrusive, who pursue fame unrelentingly."

About a week later, on a beautiful April day, the count and I set out from Parma, that desolate, former seat of government which contains several old buildings not unworthy of inspection, for the little town of Busseto, which lies within the territory of the former Duchy.

We soon arrived and made our way at once to the estate of Sant'Agata, which lies just outside the town.

Although the landscape, if strict standards are applied, has nothing special to offer, it was a pleasure to travel through the fields, meadows and tree plantations, all resplendent in the first green of spring. As soon as we had arrived at the estate, we saw a man in the distance who, judging from his dress, was a farmer, moving towards us, accompanied by a large dog. It was only when he drew near and doffed his broad-brimmed hat that we recognized Verdi; having welcomed us in his earnest and friendly way, he led us to the farmstead in the middle of his estate.

Surprised at the meticulous cultivation I saw about me, I expressed my admiration. Verdi seemed pleased, and we were soon engrossed in a keen conversation on agriculture, during which I recognized that the famous composer was a passionate and knowledgable farmer, for whom the yield of a field of maize seemed to be of no less interest than the success of one of his operas.

He showed us his estate with great zeal. "Do not think," he said, "that I found everything here as you now see it. It is the fruit of many years' work. When fortune smiled on me and I was in a position to build a home in the most beautiful region of my fatherland, I purchased this land (which at that time was neglected, barren and *brutta natura*),[7] because it was situated near my birthplace and the town where I spent my youth, and possessed for me a native charm and gave scope for my creative energy. To have settled in a well-ordered property or a petite villa would have given me little pleasure. First of all these fields had to be cultivated, the orchards planted, my house and barns built, and my park – once a jungle – landscaped. The results of my efforts were more than once devasted by the flooding of the Po[8] – but the river is now conquered. I have built dams which the floods will not break and therefore not devastate my fields."

Meanwhile we had entered the park, whose broad, dew-fresh lawns and splendid tree-clumps gleamed in the spring sun. Everywhere one recognized and admired the refined and artistic taste of its creator – in the choice of views, the beautiful lines and lay-out of the park. Out of the chaos and destruction Verdi had indeed created here an ideal park landscape, just as in music he has created harmony out of disharmony; Prince Pückler could have done no better.[9]

When I expressed my amazement how he was able to practise two such disparate activities as composition and agriculture, he exclaimed: "Precisely because the one gives me strength for the other. If I leave my study mentally exhausted, I am refreshed by the intimate communion with nature which agriculture affords, and which restores to my imagination and mind the vigour that is necessary for artistic creation."

When we were close to the simple, tasteful and villa-like house, we noticed a lady reading in a chair beneath an evergreen oak. It was the Maestro's wife, a pleasant, matronly figure, who gave us a warm welcome.

Inside the house, which we had now entered, everything breathed the same beneficial influence of noble and refined taste. Ostentatious splendour, extravagance and tasteless excess were nowhere to be seen; instead there were genuinely beautiful works of art, paintings and sculptures – always uplifting and delightful to behold.

In Verdi's study there stands, in addition to a large grand piano, an ancient, worm-eaten spinet in a corner, which aroused my curiosity.

"Yes, I began my studies on that harpsichord," said Verdi, lifting the lid and revealing the keyboard with its black lower keys and yellowed upper keys, "and for my parents it was no small sacrifice to acquire for me this instrument, which even then was old, and which made me happier than a king."

He then lifted the cover and pointed to some Italian words, written in pencil, on the inner wall of the case, which according to my notes read:

"These jacks were renude by me, Stefano Cavaletti, and lined with leather, and I fited the pedals, for which I made no charge; as I also renude the said jacks, seeing the willingness of the young Giuseppe Verdi to learn to play the instrument – which is enough to satisfy me completely – Anno domini 1821."

Verdi's parents were poor, simple people from the nearby village of Roncole, where the old church organist[10] taught the organ to the young Giuseppe Verdi.

"My greatest ambition," the Maestro recounted, "was to become my teacher's successor, and after three years I had actually reached the point of being able to stand in for him, which filled my parents and me no less with considerable pride.

"When my father brought me to Busseto to receive a better school education, I walked back to Roncole every Sunday to fulfil my duties as organist – a position I had been given, for a salary of 40 lire, after the death of old Baistrochi. The paths in winter were often unpleasant, and once I fell in the dark into a deep ditch, where I would have probably drowned, if a peasant woman on the path had not heard my cries and pulled me out."[11]

Although at first it made Verdi very unhappy that his father refused to consider the idea of a career in music and, instead, apprenticed him, when he had left school, to a businessman in Busseto, named Barezzi – this was to advantage him in two ways.

For Barezzi was a great lover of music, even skilled in counter-point, and when he noticed his apprentice's gift for music, he took him to the concerts of the "cerculo [sic] filarmonica [sic]", of which he was president.

It was here that Verdi heard good music for the first time; he copied out the scores of works that were to be performed, and was given lessons both by the village-organist, Giovanni Provesi,[12] who had taken a liking to him, and by his master, who probably initiated him more into the secrets of counterpoint than those of double-entry book-keeping.

Fortune also smiled on the young Verdi at Barezzi's house in the guise of his master's beautiful and very musical daughter, Margherita, with whom Verdi fell in love and who later became his wife, after she had for several years enjoyed fame as a singer.[13]

And it was Barezzi, who not only obtained a scholarship for the young artist, so that he could continue his training in Milan, but also gave him generous financial support.

After the simple and excellent meal, during which our host and hostess both showered us with kindness, Verdi proposed a drive to Roncole, where we soon arrived, drawn by two spirited black horses, "from my own stud", as he stressed with pride.

In Roncole he showed us not far from the church the simple cottage of his parents, where he was born on 12 October 1813 – the correct date of his birth, according to the entry in the church register that I saw.[14]

"Up there," said Verdi, pointing to the old bell-tower, which stood in Italian style away from the church, "my mother, holding me in her arms, sought refuge in 1814 from the Russians, whose rioting caused the inhabitants of Roncole 24 hours of anxiety and terror; during all that time she hid up there in the bell-cage, accessible only by ladder, terrified that I might betray our hiding-place by crying. Fortunately I slept almost continuously and laughed with great satisfaction when I woke."[15]

Verdi also told us of an eccentric wandering musician, named Bagasset, whose violin-playing had given him his first idea of music, and to whom he had listened raptly when still a little boy.[16]

Verdi indulged in childhood reminiscences with visible enjoy-ment. I had to admire the intellectual and physical freshness and sprightliness of the nearly 70-year-old Maestro, whose character reveals a mixture of patriarchal dignity and child-like *naïveté*. He loves flowers, animals – no bird may be killed on his estate – and not least, people, as his great charity (of which many examples were cited to me) bears witness. He has often been criticized for too great a fondness for earning money; in fact, he only seeks to earn a lot, so that he might give more abundantly – which he, an enemy of every kind of ostentation, does with almost comic secrecy, as Count D. told me.

The fading day forced us to think of our return journey, and Verdi insisted on driving us to the station in his gig. On the way we met a party of fieldworkers, who were returning in the sunset from their day's work. Catching sight of the Maestro, they stopped beside the path, doffed their caps and sang, with that innate vocal talent of Italians, the beautiful male chorus from *I Lombardi*,[17] as we drove slowly past.

This quite spontaneous, unaffected homage seemed to please the Maestro, who waved briskly to the singers in greeting and thanks, much more than any of those celebrations in his honour, which he avoids only too willingly and whenever possible.

Our visit to Verdi's villa, where he spends the greater part of the year, thus ended in harmonious fashion. There is, after all, no greater pleasure than discovering that a great artist is also a noble and lovable human being.

A. VON WINTERFELD

NOTES

1. On 5 February 1876 Verdi wrote to Arrivabene:

> *The best thing would be a repertory theatre, but I doubt whether it could be achieved. The examples of the Opéra and Germany have very little value for me, because the performances in all those theatres are deplorable. At the Opéra, the productions are splendid, the historical accuracy of their costumes and their good taste are superior to those of any other theatre, but the musical side is awful. Singers are always very mediocre (except for Faure a few years ago), the orchestra and chorus lazy and lacking in discipline. [. . .] In Germany the orchestras and choruses are more attentive and conscientious; they play accurately and well, although I have seen deplorable performances in Berlin. The orchestra is loud but sounds coarse. And then the singers . . . oh they are bad, downright bad. [. . .] In Vienna (which is now the leading German theatre) things are better in the case of chorus and orchestra (quite excellent). I have attended various performances and have found the chorus and orchestra very good, the productions second-rate and singers third-rate. But the performance usually costs very little; the audience (who are made to sit in the dark during the performance) sleeps or is bored, applauds a little at the end of each act, and after the performance goes home neither displeased nor elated.*

That is all very well for these Northern natures, but just try putting on a performance like that in one or our theatres, and see what a din the audience will make! Our audiences are too excitable and would not be content with a prima donna who costs only 18 or 20 thousand florins a year, as in Germany. They want the prima donnas who go to Cairo, St. Petersburg, Lisbon, London etc., who cost 25 to 30 thousand florins a month. But how could we pay them? [. . .] Now I ask you, whether with our audiences, it would be possible to maintain a stable company for at least three years! And then, are you aware what a company such as the one now at La Scala would cost per year? [. . .] (Verdi intimo, cit., pp. 186–7.)

2. Italian in the original.
3. *Back* in German comes from the verb *backen* (to cook) and is used with other words to denote food that is cooked in the oven (e.g. *Backbirne-* = cooked pear).
4. On 2 February 1883, hardly two months before the probable date of this meeting, Verdi had written to Piroli:

> *I admire the Minister's wish to reform our music schools, but in the final analysis I do not think he will succeed. Nowadays one can no longer find either composers or pupils who are not infected by the teutonic outlook, and it would be impossible to form a Committee untainted by the disease, which like other diseases must run its course [. . .]. Europe and the world once had two schools of music: the Italian and the German (from which all others derive). We have been bewitched by foreign charms and have renounced our own, and chaos has resulted! [. . .] Our music, unlike German music, whose symphonies can exist in concert halls and quartets in private apartments – our music, I say, is rooted principally in the theatre. But our theatres, without governmental assistance, cannot exist. That is an undeniable fact.* (Autograph: Biblioteca Nazionale dei Lincei, Rome.)

Some years later, on 14 July 1889, Verdi wrote to Franco Faccio:

> *Our young Italian composers are not good patriots. If German composers, setting out from Bach have arrived at Wagner, they have acted as good Germans, and that is fine. But if we descendants of Palestrina imitate Wagner, we commit a musical crime and create useless, or even harmful works.* (I Copialettere di G. Verdi, cit., p. 702.)

And on 14 April 1892 he wrote to Hans von Bülow:

> *If the artists of the North and South exhibit different tendencies, it is good that they are different! They should all preserve the character of their own nation, as Wagner quite rightly says. You are fortunate in still being the sons of Bach! And we? We too, sons of Palestrina, used to have a great tradition, and our own! It has now become bastardized, and ruin threatens us! If only we could go back to the beginning?!* (Ibid., p. 376.)

For similar ideas, see N. XXVIII.

5. It is well-known that Verdi travelled to Bologna to attend the first Italian performance of *Lohengrin* (19 November 1871), conducted by Angelo Mariani. Equally well-known are the glosses (drawn up in minute detail by F. ABBIATI, *op. cit.*, III, pp. 508–11) that the composer made during the performance on a copy of the score that is still preserved at Sant'Agata; the majority of these glosses have been remarked upon several times – the adverse critical comments, however, concern more the performance than the worth of the opera itself. The uproar that surrounded these Bologna performances and the interest of the national press were such that the term *lohengrinata* entered Verdi's regular vocabulary to denote the publicity campaign that usually surrounds a première; see, for example, the postscript of his letter to Ricordi of 25 December 1871:

> *Take care not to publish or have published my telegram from Cairo. –*
> *Corticelli asked me to give it to the* Movimento [Genoan newspaper] . . .
> *but I roared at him: "Per Dio; non voglio Lohengrinate." Poor Corticelli*
> *took flight and is still running* . . . (autograph: Archivo della Casa Ricordi, Milan).

6. The same ideas about Wagner and German singers had been expressed by Verdi at Vienna in 1875 to a journalist of the *Neue Freie Presse* (see N. XV, p. oo).

7. Italian in the original.

8. The River Po had flooded disastrously in early June 1879; Verdi wrote to Piroli about it on June 11:

> *Our misfortunes are not as great as in the regions of Mantua and Ferrara, but the crops are almost entirely destroyed. The mulberry trees are ruined, the hay almost entirely ruined, only one seed of wheat remains, two at the most. Maize grows poorly and rots. Grapes virtually entirely wiped out. There will be famine and deaths this winter. I know that grain will arrive from abroad [. . .] And all while the government contrives to raise taxes, increase armament spending and build railways of low priority, under the pretext of giving work to the people. It truly is a mockery! For goodness sake, if you have millions, spend them on repairing the rivers, before they submerge us all!* (Autograph: Biblioteca Nazionale dei Lincei, Rome.)

On June 30 Verdi conducted his *Requiem* at La Scala in aid of the inhabitants of the flooded regions – a performance which marked the extraordinary return of Stolz and Waldmann (whose property in the Ferrara region had also been damaged), and in which the tenor Barbacini and the bass Maini also sang.

9. Hermann L. H. Pückler Muskau (Muskau, Silesia, 1785–Branitz, Kottbus, 1871), nominated Prince in recognition of his patriotism.

When residing in his castles of Muskau and Branitz, he tended the great gardens of these seats with considerable originality, became an authority on the art of gardening and published in 1834 *Andeutungen über Landschaftsgärtnerei*. He enjoyed popularity as a writer of travel books.

10. Pietro Baistrocchi who died in about 1823.
11. This episode is narrated in one of the first biographies of Verdi, which appeared by instalments in 1857 in *Il Fuggilozio*, a Milan periodical, managed by Carlo Viviani, who probably used Giuseppe Demaldé's *Cenni biografici* of 1853, which remained partially unpublished until our age and was only recently published in toto, edited by M. J. Matz in *Verdi Newsletter*, American Institute for Verdi Studies, New York, n. 1 and 2, 1976, and n. 3, 1977:

> It is said that, as a little boy hardly eight years old, he had to walk each day from his village to school in Busseto. One winter's day he decided to defy the frost and the snow, which completely covered the road; half way to Busseto, however, he fell into the ditch that ran alongside the road, and because his delicate limbs were so numbed he could not get up, he would have died of cold, if a peasant who was passing by had not picked him up and carried him home. (*Il Fuggilozio*, Milan, III, I: 2 January 1857, pp. 14–15.)

An account of the same episode can also be found in an unpublished biography, illustrated by the famous caricaturist Melchiorre Delfico, published in part in F. ABBIATI, *op. cit.*, I, p. 10.

12. Provesi's first name was, in fact, Ferdinando.
13. Winterfeld here obviously confuses Margherita Barezzi and Giuseppina Strepponi. This passage was later omitted in the 1901 reprint of this article in the *Neue Musik-Zeitung*.
14. October 12 is not the "correct date" of Verdi's birth, though this was the date of the civil registration of his birth, drawn up in French, in line with a Napoleonic regulation of the time. October 11 was the official date of his baptism, however: "[. . .] *hac mane baptizavi Infantem natum heri vespere hora octava* [. . .]". Winterfeld has obviously confused the two registrations or has read the date of the parish register inaccurately. For the actual date of Verdi's birth (October 9, as the Maestro himself always maintained, or else October 10) see N. I, note 8.
15. This episode, narrated here with greater brevity and liveliness, can also be found, like the subsequent one about the wandering violinist, in Delfico's unpublished biography (cf. F. ABBIATI, *op. cit.*, I, pp. 5–6).
16. This episode also appears in the biography, already quoted, by Ercole Cavalli, of Busseto, who probably heard it directly from Verdi's mother:

> The little boy was reasonably good-natured, gentle and obedient; but he was very introspective and loved solitude. His mother was seldom

obliged to reprimand him; but whenever they passed barrel-organs or wandering musicians, it was impossible to restrain him, and it was necessary to use force to bring him back home. His poor mother used to say to her friends: "This boy could not be better-behaved, but if he hears a barrel-organ, he won't leave me in peace." (H. CAVALLI, *op. cit.*, p. 8.)

The presence of popular musicians during Verdi's infancy is also indicated by another episode, related by the anonymous biographer of *Il Fuggilozio*:

[. . .] An old man of the village of Roncole related, as though alluding to a prophecy that had come true, that the godfather of the newly-born child, as a harbinger of happiness, had wanted the joyful fanfares from a group of wandering musicians to accompany the child to the sacred font. ("Giuseppe Verdi", in *Il Fuggilozio*, cit., p. 14.)

17. "O Signore dal tetto natio" – if this is the chorus to which Winterfeld refers – is in fact a chorus for mixed voices.

XXIII

VERDI AT HIS VILLA (NOTES)

1884

GIUSEPPE GIACOSA: "Verdi in villa (Note)", in *Gazzetta Musicale di Milano*, XLIV, 48, special supplement (for the Verdi jubilee): 27 November 1889, pp. 774–5 (republished in *L'Illustrazione Popolare*, Milan, XXVI, 50: 15 December 1889, pp. 790–1; in "Verdi e il *Falstaff*", Special Edition of the *Illustrazione Italiana*, Treves, Milan (February 1893; reprinted 1913), pp. 17–18; in *L'Illustrazione Popolare*, Milan, LXIV, 45: 9 October 1913, pp. 706–7; in A. ROVERSI: *Gli artisti di ieri: Storia della vita di Giuseppe Verdi* [. . .], Bologna, 1939, pp. 25–29; in G. CENZATO: *Itinerari verdiani*, 2nd edit., Ceschina, Milan, 1955, pp. 55–57; in *Carteggio Verdi-Boito*, cit., pp. 326–8; with variants and additions in "Verdi e il *Falstaff*", special edition of *Vita Moderna*, Milan, II, 12 February 1893, pp. 50–52).

THIS DESCRIPTION OF Verdi's life at Sant'Agata refers to a visit by Giacosa to Verdi's villa, accompanied by Boito, in the autumn of 1884. "You don't imagine I want you here with Giacosa!" Verdi had written to Boito on 26 September 1884.[1] The two men of letters arrived at Sant'Agata on 29 September (cf. *Carteggio Verdi-Boito*, cit., pp. 77–78) and departed a week later. For Boito's association with Giacosa (Colleretto Parella 1847–1906), the successful author of *Partita a scacchi*, *Tristi amori* and *Come le foglie*, see P. NARDI: *Vita di Arrigo Boito*, Mondadori [Milan], 1942.

Verdi at his villa (Notes)

The Maestro is accustomed to spend five or six months of the year at Sant'Agata, near Busseto, in strenuous pastoral indolence. The quiet and spacious villa, concealed in a great thicket of very tall trees, betrays the long-standing habit of hospitality, that both creates and satisfies the refined needs of good-living without seeming to be obtrusive and continually over-attentive. No sooner have you entered, than you feel that the house is your friend; when you have been a guest for half an hour, you will know your way about, as though you had lived there for a decade. And even though it is neat and elegant, not a single part of it appears new, nor do I suppose it ever did, even in its earliest days.

It was planned and built by the Maestro. At first there were four or five rooms, and as Verdi's work and prosperity thrived, so the rest of the building was gradually added. The Maestro sometimes regrets having kept these original rooms intact, because the rest smacks of adaptation; but I believe he is speaking with the modesty of an owner and architect, for there is not a part of the house that betrays any sign of additions or adaptations: everything is homogeneous and seems to have been conceived and built at the same time. The décor is rich, but without ostentation or false modesty: it is rich with the composed and tranquil richness that pays no heed to opinion. There are paintings by Morelli and Michetti, old prints, inlaid and carved furniture, a beautiful library, rare editions, the quaintest of *albums*, collections of souvenirs – but all arranged in an unobtrusive manner. No one would dream of suggesting to the owner a tour of admiration – which is the equivalent of import-duty in certain grand villas. In the course of your stay, as you walk through a room, meditate in the library, await your turn at billiards or sit conversing in a drawing room, you gradually discover about you further examples of artistry and intellectual activity.

The owner is like the house; hospitable without striving to flaunt hospitality. Your natural anxiety to avoid being a burden, is allayed by the end of the first day, after which you are glad to see that he does nothing to change his way of life for your sake. But on the second and third day, when you realize each time you wish to find him that he appears, that you can see him at all hours through open doors intent upon work, which it is not intrusive to interrupt, that he gives you a friendly greeting as he passes you in the room next to his bedroom – you notice then how he practises at all times a watchful and considerate courtesy, conscious of your reserve and resolved to allay any suspicion you might have of causing trouble.

Verdi is reputed by many to be uncivil and disdainful. But anyone who considers the great volume of his work must concede that he is a man who has wasted less time than most. Now, if a man is too accessible he wastes an incalculable amount of time – but to hear those individuals who award diplomas for courtesy and affability, it is clear that in their eyes you have to be too accessible to be accessible at all. He who becomes such a celebrity so early in his career – as was Verdi's lot – is soon assailed by thousands of petitioners: the inquisitive, the vain, the philanthropic; dealers, misunderstood geniuses and zealous advisers; people with new, miraculous artistic methods. Although each one asks for no more than ten minutes, together they

would use up ten hours of the day. And to persuade them that he has
no time would take as much time as it would to give them a hearing.
If you then add his public duties, the honorary assignments with
which he is inundated, the tedium of official duties and the invitations and the letters – then tell me if, in trying to accommodate even
half of those who besiege him so politely, Verdi wouldn't have
deprived the human race of half of his masterpieces. If you wish to
avoid, without discourtesy, so many opportunities of losing time,
you need a general principle of conduct: to withdraw into your shell
and earn yourself an undeserved reputation of bearishness. Those
who know Verdi well, also know that he submits unwillingly to this
painful necessity. The Maestro loves to converse and shows an
interest in all aspects of human thought. He is unaffected and affable,
not through artificial modesty but genuine goodness of soul. But he
is profoundly convinced that an artist must above all, whatever the
circumstances, always attend to his art.

The table. – Verdi is a gourmet, not a gourmand; the table he
keeps is truly hospitable, that is magnificent and cultured. The
cuisine at Sant'Agata would be worthy of a standing ovation: it is so
picturesque, lavish and varied, resembling a laboratory of sublime
Pantagruelian alchemy. There is no danger of going without dinner,
because the cook is indisposed. At Sant'Agata, in addition to the
regular cook, there are emeritus cooks in the shape of the gardener,
the coachman and the serving-woman: *uno avulso non deficit alter*. It
should be noted that all this apparatus has an essentially hospitable
function. Verdi is not a great eater, nor is he difficult to please. He
enjoys food like all healthy, wise and moderate men, but above all he
loves to see his guests display that sincere and keen joy which
accompanies and follows beautiful and exquisite meals. Verdi is a
man of discipline, and as such he believes that every activity in life
must at times prevail over other activities; he is also an artist and as
such he considers, quite rightly, that a dinner is a work of art.

Verdi is a concise and lively raconteur. I recall the evening he told
us of the first performance of *Rigoletto* in Venice. The senior member
of the chorus was a certain individual who had once been a leading
player in provincial theatres, and considered his joining the ranks of
the chorus a colossal act of condescension. The poor fellow assumed
the dignified air of a misunderstood and persecuted genius, so typical
of those actors who had high hopes and on whom fortune did not
smile. In the storm scene the Maestro required the chorus to utter
a sort of muffled roar, an indistinct sound through closed lips,

accentuated merely by dynamics, to render the rise and fall of the wind. But he had to teach by example and rehearse the scene a hundred times. Our singer could not convince himself that it was this and not something else that was required of him, and when finally he could no longer doubt the composer's intentions, he advanced proudly and placed himself firmly in front of the Maestro, angrily summoning his malevolent star to witness such an outrage, saying: "You mean I'm even expected to be the wind!" Whereupon he returned to his place with the stride of an Aristodemus.

Verdi also recounted the astonishment and dismay of certain old gentlemen at Florian's who, on hearing how the role of Rigoletto sometimes bordered on the comic, all but considered La Fenice dishonoured and the artistic tradition of the Serenissima offended. But such fears were expressed on the eve of the first performance; at the première, those old moralists were themselves forced to applaud from that sincere and unprejudiced feeling for art, which is the privilege of our country's great musical public.

In the evening there is a game of billiards or cards. One evening, immediately after dinner, we went out into the courtyard. Verdi and his wife sat down on the steps that lead up to the house, Miss Stoltz, Boito and I stayed in the open. The moon was shining and divided the courtyard neatly in two: silvery brightness here, dense darkness there. I forget who first started it, but a tune from *Ernani* was definitely heard. One of us took up the tune from the other, and what with the help of the shadows, the warmth of the dinner, the nocturnal exaltation and the rarefied theatrical atmosphere – the three of us ended up by singing and acting scenes from that opera. Verdi and his good lady Giuseppina laughed and applauded.

At one point I finished my aria with a certain tremulous embellishment, which seemed to me the *non plus ultra* of bel canto, and the Maestro, to whom I had that day for some unknown reason mentioned my home town, mocked me gently by saying: "You heard that sung at Ivrea." That was the last straw, and the curtain fell.

GIUSEPPE GIACOSA

In a later version of the article, published in a special Verdi number of "Vita Moderna" (see page 157), Giacosa inserted the following passage before the final paragraph:

But the sacred hours came in the afternoon, when we would

gather in the Maestro's study to discuss his new opera. It was then that I heard several scenes from the first act, and the most delightful chorus in honour of Desdemona – played by the Maestro at the piano. Discussions then arose, not, of course, about the music, but the expressive importance of some word and the accentuation it should be given. Verdi would sometimes clutch the libretto and read several pieces aloud. Boito and I looked at each other, our gazes expressing our great admiration:[2] the voice, the accent, the cadences, the force, the anger expressed in that reading betrayed such an ardent kindling of the soul, magnified so immeasurably the sense of the words, that the source of the musical idea was clearly revealed to us. With our own eyes we saw, as it were, the flower of the melody blossom, and the words, given by his voice their utmost power, transmuted into waves of sound, sweeping away the endless anguish that sometimes assails the human soul.

The great artist drew from his serene and vigorous old age a cheerful view of life. I remember how a few days after the first performance of *Otello*, certain of Verdi's words had filled my soul with a profound sadness – we were speaking, of course, of the opera and its triumph. At one point the Maestro, who had already grown pensive during the discussion, said: "How painful to have finished it! I shall now suffer such loneliness. Till now I used to wake each morning and return to the love, anger, jealousy, deceit of my characters. And I would say to myself: today I have this scene to compose, and if it did not progress according to my wishes, I would arm myself for the struggle, confident of victory. And then, when the opera was finished, there were the rehearsals, the uncertainties, the task of explaining my thoughts clearly to the actors, to make them move on stage as I wished; and then the new ideas for the staging, that I was forever thinking up in the name of representational realism . . . and I would arrive home, still excited by the glorious life of the theatre, happy at the goals I had reached, thinking about those I intended reaching tomorrow, and I was not conscious of fatigue and I did not feel my age. But now? Since *Otello* now belongs to the public, it has ceased to be mine, it has become totally detached from me; and the place that it occupied within me was so great, that I now feel an enormous void, which I think I shall never be able to fill."[3]

What sadness these words caused me! I recalled the touching way that Gibbon addressed his work, after writing the final pages of his History. So this is the reward for such noble endeavour! A few hours after the delirious applause of an audience, which included some of the most distinguished minds in the world, had died away, while their endless acclamations still echoed on, and the great cities of Italy, the king and the sovereigns of half Europe were sending the Maestro their grateful congratulations, the Maestro saw in his newly achieved glory a cause for disheartened thoughts and regrets.

NOTES

1. In a new version of this article, written three and a half years later for the Milan periodical *Vita Moderna*, Giacosa wrote: "I had the great fortune to be Verdi's guest a few months before the first performance of *Otello*. I was with Boito and we spent a week at Busseto." This suggests that the visit took place in the course of 1886; but an examination of Verdi's correspondence with Giulio Ricordi and Boito shows no visit of a week's duration by Giacosa and Boito together at Sant'Agata during that year. That the visit actually took place at the beginning of autumn 1884 is documented by the Verdi–Boito correspondence and confirmed by a lecture, entitled *The Art of Reading*, which Giacosa gave in the Sala della Minerva at Trieste in May 1885, as is proved by a passage from the same lecture, reported by the *Corriere della Sera*, and later by the *Gazzetta Musicale di Milano* on 17 May 1885, pp. 176–7:

> Giacosa then spoke of the dramatic arts, remarking on their decline, which he said was because the spoken word was no longer studied; and having begun an argument about modern theatre, he spoke of authors, actors and audiences, deploring the fact that art should be so content with superficiality. "For goodness' sake," he exclaimed, "let us once again study the spoken word, which is daughter of spoken thought." To prove, as he said, how the word only really takes wing when spoken by man, Giacosa narrated this interesting episode:
>
> "One of my most perfectly satisfying spiritual experiences was listening to Giuseppe Verdi read from the drama that he is at present setting to music. In the company of Arrigo Boito, I had the great honour of being his guest at the villa of Sant'Agata. This was last October. While I listened, the great Maestro discussed with Boito several parts of the libretto that the latter had written for him; together they worked their way through Shakespeare's drama, which Verdi discussed with profound dramatic perspicacity. He ended up reading entire scenes from the drama. Boito and I looked at each other, and our gazes expressed the devout feeling of admiration that filled our souls." [. . .]

2. Cf. preceding note.

3. On 18 December 1886, the composer had written to Boito:

I have just handed Garignani the last two acts of Otello! *. . . Poor Otello! He will not come here again!!!* (Autograph: Istituto di studi verdiani, Parma.)

XXIV

HOW I MET THE MAESTRO

1885

EDIPI: "Come conobbi il Maestro", in *Scena Illustrata*, Florence, XLIX, 21 (Verdi number): 1 November 1913, p. 36.

THIS IS THE account of a casual meeting in Cremona between the anonymous journalist, accompanied by Carlo Gomes, and Verdi. The latter often travelled to the city of the Great Tower, the nearest large town to Sant'Agata, to shop or see to other matters; his wife Giuseppina went to Cremona even more often to visit her sister Barberina. The meeting can hypothetically be traced back to one day towards the end of October 1885, on the basis of a note, dated October 11, that Verdi sent Boito: "*All right; and I shall expect you on the 16th. Any later would be impossible, because Peppina, as usual, must visit her sister.*"[1] In Cremona that is. Verdi was at that time finishing the composition of *Otello*. As for Carlo Antonio Gomes (Campinas, San Paolo, 1836 – Belém, Pará, 1896), he was going through a rather critical and familiar phase of his life as an artist: after the failure of his *Maria Tudor* at La Scala in 1879, he had not produced a new opera; he was, however, composing *Lo schiavo*, and in the spring of 1885 there seemed to be a hope of having this, his penultimate opera, performed at Bologna's Comunale theatre. He was also busy with *Oldrada*, to a libretto by Ghislanzoni. But then relations with his wife deteriorated, and appalling economic conditions made it difficult for him to stay in Villa Brasilia which he had built in Maggianico near Lecco as long ago as 1878. On October 29 he wrote from Milan to Tornaghi, manager of the Casa Ricordi: "*For some time now I've had certain troubles that make my mind dull and unfit for* harmonies . . . *I shall tell you of my misfortunes in person.*"[2] It appears that Verdi had said of him, after his triumphant *Guarany* at La Scala in 1870: "This young man is beginning where I leave off . . ."[3] The phrase seems a little bold for Verdi, who was usually so cautious when judging his own contemporaries. Nonetheless, Gino Monaldi states:

A composer for whom Verdi, immediately after *Guarany*, predicted a splendid future – which never occurred – was Gomes. And this can be explained. In the music of *Guarany*, Verdi recognized much of himself, in so far as the ardour and dash of the Brazilian composer reminded him of the brilliance and excitement of his own youth. And Gomes was very much aware of the great Maestro's liking for him and faith in him; in his last years when, after *Il Condor*, he felt all his bold hopes finally evaporate, he felt infinitely bitter. "You see" – he told me one day in a moment of great dejection – "what grieves me most is my failure to live up to his prophetic words and become his successor . . ." "What genius!" he continued, growing excited – "after *Otello*, I can no longer begin to measure it . . . It frightens me!" [4]

How I met the Maestro

In the autumn of 1885, the year before the death of poor Ponchielli, [5] I happened to be in Cremona for business reasons, writing the occasional article for the *Provincia*, edited by the much lamented Ettore Sacchi, namesake and cousin of the Radical minister, and a great hope of the party from the moment Felice Cavallotti introduced him enthusiastically to the Chamber.

I had formed a close friendship with Alfonso Mandelli, [6] the worthy founder of the Children's Hospital in his town, and, with Pini and Baiardi, a great propagandist for paediatrics in the whole of Italy. Mandelli, who rented a villa in Maggianico opposite those of Amilcare Ponchelli and Carlos Antonio Gomes, had introduced me to the composers of *La gioconda* and *I Lituani*, *Guarany* and *Il Condor*.

And through my journalistic and literary perpetrations, I had also struck up a friendship with Antonio Ghislanzoni, the last hothead of Lombard bohemianism, actor, novelist, librettist of *Aida*, *I Lituani*, *Salvator Rosa*, author of *Capricci letterari* and other works, and even for a time hotel-owner in Caprino Bergamasco. [7]

Ghislanzoni was a constant contributor to the *Scena*, in which he published, among other things, his marvellous *Violino a corde umane*.

Cremona was fanatical about Ponchielli – and I was scowled at for daring to assert that I preferred *Mefistofele* to *La gioconda*.

During that autumn, a beautiful and famous singer with copious curvilinear charms was on holiday in Cremona – and Gomes often visited her from Maggianico to instruct her, I think, in a role she was to sing in Rio de Janeiro. Although the composer of *Guarany* was no longer young, he was still most handsome with his mane of grizzled hair, his open, imperious expression and sparkling eyes. A veritable enchanter. We were walking together one evening in the Corso Campi, when we saw Giuseppe Verdi in front of the window of a bookseller and music-dealer.

He was dressed in dark grey and wore a loose-fitting jacket, a tattered old hat – also grey – a black tie that fluttered in the breeze, he held his hands behind his back, and in his hands a . . . melon of vast proportions.

I asked Gomes to introduce me, but Don Carlos appeared a little irritated. But when he greeted Verdi, as he passed close by him, I plucked up my courage, approached him and said that Antonio Ghislanzoni had requested me to pass on his good wishes.

The Maestro immediately enquired after his collaborator's health . . . and showed a keen interest in the hermit from Caprino; but suddenly his face darkened, and he looked at me with some suspicion.

"And how could Ghislanzoni have known," the Maestro asked me with an ironic little smile, "that you would see me here in Cremona, since I only arrived this morning, without a word to anyone, and shall leave almost immediately for Sant'Agata? Who could possibly have guessed that I would stop here, especially since it was only during the journey that I suddenly decided to consult a book in the local library and buy a melon from the *mellonera* outside the Porta Milano?! . . ."

I could have replied, with impudence, that Ghislanzoni's request had been made some time ago, and that he had told me to convey his greetings at the first opportunity; but no – I preferred to confess candidly that I had resorted to this little stratagem in order to hear the *voice* of the Maestro, whose melodies had delighted the whole world, and . . . to have the honour of carrying his vast melon to the train, if he would be so kind as to entrust it to my care. And while he defended himself, as I tried to wrest from his hands the vast pumpkin, I added, in order to conquer all resistance:

"And then . . . I love you dearly, Maestro, because my father – a composer, too, but of sacred music only – resembles you in a most extraordinary manner! . . ."

And it was for this that the Maestro forgave me; he shook my hand and entrusted his most precious fruit to my care.

And so it was that Gomes, who also seemed timid in the presence of the great Maestro, and your humble author had the honour that evening of accompanying him to Codogno station, where I religiously deposited the melon on the luggage-rack in his carriage.

As for Gomes, he was, I think, at that time composing *Lo schiavo* for Emperor Don Pedro of Brazil, who had just abolished slavery. A fine action – most modern and humane – which none the less contributed, perhaps, to his downfall!

EDIPI

NOTES

1. Autograph: Istituto di studi verdiani, Parma.
2. *Antonio Carlo Gomes: Carteggi italiani*, raccolti e commentati da G. N. Vetro, Nuove Edizione, Milan 1977, p. 185.
3. M. CONATI: "Formazione e affermazione di Gomes nel panorama dell' opera italiana. Appunti e considerazioni", in *A. C. Gomes: Carteggi italiani*, cit., p. 49.
4. G. MONALDI: *Verdi nella vita e nell'arte (Conversazioni verdiane)*, Ricordi, Milan [1913], pp. 187–8.
5. Or rather, a few months before Ponchielli's death; the composer of *La gioconda* died suddenly, struck down by severe pneumonia on 16 January 1886.
6. The Cremona lawyer Alfonso Mandelli, apart from his legal activities, was a theatre and literary critic with a special interest in comedy and libretti; he was for some years mayor of Cremona. His friendship with Gomes is attested by numerous letters addressed to him by the Brazilian composer (see *A. C. Gomes: Carteggi italiani*, cit.).
7. Cf. N. XI.

XXV

VERDI IN PARIS

1886

PAUL FRESNAY: "Verdi à Paris", in *Voltaire*, Paris, 29 March 1886.

ON 17 MARCH 1886, accompanied by his wife and Emanuele Muzio, Verdi travelled to Paris and remained there until April 11, taking rooms, as was his wont, at the Hôtel de Bade in the Boulevard des Italiens. One of the reasons for this journey was the composer's wish to hear for himself – with a possible performance of *Otello* in mind – the vocal form of Victor Maurel, about whom he had heard conflicting reports.[1] On the eve of his departure he wrote to Arrivabene:

> *I'm off to Paris!!! What do you say? You will be amazed, but certainly no more than I! I shall meet Saint Joseph en route [. . .] So I'm going to Paris, without really knowing why. Partly to hear Maurel, partly to see if they are still as crazy as they used to be, and partly to get some exercise. I shall be there for two weeks, three at the very most! Otello is progressing, slowly but surely! Will I finish it? Perhaps. Shall I have it performed? Even I find that difficult to answer. In the meantime, let us proceed. Amen.*[2]

Several days later, on April 4, he informed Piroli:

> *Never ever a moment of peace; and what's more, I go to the opera almost every evening. I simply must!! I need to hear these young artists I do not know. And to tell you the truth, they are not at all bad. There's a tenor at the Opéra with a stupendous voice . . . and two ladies, whose voices are a little thin but who have talent. In short, I repeat: not at all bad! [. . .] I travel all over Paris, spend money and go to the opera . . . that's all!*[3]

It is from this visit to Paris of 1886 that Boldini's two famous portraits date, mentioned by Caponi in the next chapter. As for *Otello*, we know that the libretto was finished and the score nearing completion. By the end of January it was common knowledge that the composer had promised to have the opera staged (if he completed it) at La Scala, and had declined the offers of Gailhard, Director of the Opéra. A few weeks later the *Gazzetta Musicale di Milano* announced:[4]

We believe that we commit no indiscretion in saying that Maestro Verdi has confirmed with our distinguished Mayor Negri [of Milan] that the opera is not yet finished and still requires a great deal of work, but that if his health permits him to complete it, he will be most happy to have it performed at our La Scala.[4]

Verdi in Paris

A coincidence: the simultaneous visit of two great and very different composers, of two utterly dissimilar men.

Liszt – the extraordinary virtuoso, whose life since the age of nine has been nothing but a long succession of triumphs, whose star is now shining with renewed brightness – a man who has benefited from his background and *savoir-faire*.

And Verdi – the composer of genius, who has dedicated his entire life (he was born in 1814 [sic]) to the great cause of art. He travels strictly incognito and courts neither applause nor celebrations.

He has taken rooms unostentatiously at the hotel, whose rooms look out on to the Boulevard that he likes to visit once or twice a year.

I went to call on Verdi and our conversation, which for me was most instructive, began immediately; I gained little information, however, about Verdi, for the composer's life is as uncomplicated as his art.

"What is the truth about your new opera?" I asked the Maestro. "Shall we have the première or will it be performed at La Scala?"

"*Otello*," he told me, "is far from finished; perhaps I shall complete it by the end of next winter, perhaps later. In any case, it is an Italian work. Boito, seeking inspiration from Shakespeare, has fashioned me a libretto which would lose greatly in translation. Should I finish my opera, it will perhaps be given in Milan, assuredly in Italy."[5]

I then asked the Maestro how he had conceived his opera; whether he would bring a new spirit or new creative processes to bear on its composition, whether he would write it in the style of *Les vêpres siciliennes* or *Aida*.

"I cannot answer you," he told me. "I write as I feel, the method does not concern me; if I think a certain style conveys my thought, I use it, even if it means composing in a new style. That is the way I have always composed."[6]

Since I was putting questions to the Maestro about his ideas, I asked him for his opinion of Wagner, Liszt, Gounod etc.

"Music," he told me, "is a universal language. There is, I maintain, no such thing as Italian or German or French music,[7] but rather different men with different temperaments, who feel in different ways. It is not a question of method. I have never written music following fixed ideas, and I have never followed or wished to found a school. For example, you will find in passages of my *Requiem*, which you mentioned just now, methods which are not at all Italian and which, when used lavishly in Wagner, amazed the audience. I had no hesitation in writing three successive parallel fifths in a certain passage.[8] And if I did commit this error in harmony, that an ordinary pupil at the Conservatoire would avoid, it was because it was necessary for the effect I wished to produce.

"As for my opinion on Wagner – there have been many anecdotes, very often untrue. I admire him greatly.

"He has been true to *himself* and has had new ideas. Whatever is said, there is much melody in Wagner; but you must know how to find it. I confess that I prefer his earlier operas to his later style, and consider that none surpasses *Lohengrin*.

"I knew Berlioz well; I regard *La Damnation de Faust* to be his masterpiece. He could have led a charming life, but was always unhappy, because of his melancholy character. He was a great man, although not everyone can understand his music.[9]

"As for Gounod, whom I know personally, his is a refined and charming talent; his *Faust* is a first-rate work, although he has neither followed nor rendered Goethe, unlike Boito in *Mefistofele*."[10]

I then asked Verdi if he had in mind to visit the opera again.

"Oh! I've been to your Parisian theatres three days running – they are so hot, and I need to rest. But I hope to hear *Sigurd*, about which I've had enthusiastic reports.[11]

"Yesterday I heard *Guillaume Tell*. Ah, Rossini! He was a man, and *he was himself*! He possessed a quality that is now lost, that none of us now have: he knew how to write for the voice. Look at the trio from *Guillaume Tell*!

"But those are an old man's ideas, no one thinks in that way any more. What is now written is often heavy. It is not the singers who sing any more, but the orchestra. *Le Cid* [12] is very beautiful, but I find that the orchestra dominates; it is very difficult to understand."

"And Liszt?" I asked Verdi. "I neither saw him nor heard him play," he replied. "I am therefore unable to speak about him; moreover I know none of his works."

I then took my leave and was accompanied to the door by the Maestro, who told me several times:

"Do not write much or talk much about me, write very little."

PAUL FRESNAY

NOTES

1. Cf. *Carteggio Verdi-Boito*, cit., pp. 344–5. At that time Maurel was singing in Hérold's *Zampa* at the Opéra-Comique. Considered as one of the greatest baritones of the second half of the nineteenth century, Victor Maurel (Marseille 1848 – New York 1923) took part in almost all the Verdi premières from the composer's maturity to his old age. He was, as we have seen (see N. X, note 22), one of the six Flemish deputies in the première of the Paris *Don Carlos* in 1867; thirteen years later in 1880 he was Amonasro in the first French performance of *Aida* at the Opéra; the next year he took part in the première of the new version of *Simon Boccanegra* at La Scala; then in 1887 he sang in the first performance of *Otello*, and in 1893 the première of *Falstaff*. And in 1894 he sang in the first French performances of *Falstaff* at the Opéra-Comique and *Otello* at the Opéra. He wrote about his Verdi experiences in two publications: *A propos de la mise en scène du drame lyrique "Otello"*, Bocca, Rome 1888, and *A propos de "Falstaff"* in the *Revue de Paris*, I, 8: 15 May 1894, pp. 211–24, which both then appeared in his volume *Dix Ans de Carrière*, Dupont, Paris 1897 (anastatic reprint: Arno Press, New York 1977).

2. *Verdi intimo*, cit., pp. 331–2. Alberti dates this letter March 19, but this must be an error, made perhaps by Verdi himself, since the latter was then already en route for Paris, as one can deduce from a phrase in the same letter: "I shall meet Saint Joseph en route." Saint Joseph's day, Verdi's name-day, falls, as is well known, on March 19.

3. Autograph: Biblioteca Nazionale dei Lincei, Rome.

4. N. 9 of 28 February 1886, p. 63.

5. Verdi had already expressed analogous ideas in a letter, dated 16 August 1882, to Boito, concerning a request by Blaze de Bury to assign him the translation of the libretto *Iago* (not yet *Otello*) with a view to a possible première at the Paris Opéra:

> Un jour ou l'autre Iago (*not Iago*) existera. . . . *This confidence of the Baron's surprises me, because I . . . I personally do not know if it existera. It surprises me considerably more that a man of letters of Blaze de Bury's*

calibre, France's most authoritative critic, as you so rightly say, should wish to condemn himself to such drudgery by translating an Italian opera into French – a much more arduous task than translating from French into Italian. [. . .] But I repeat, why talk now of a work that does not exist, that will be Italian in scale and Italian in God knows what other way (Tremble, o ye mortals!)? . . . Perhaps a few melodies, if I can find a few . . . And melody is always Italian, essentially Italian, and can be nothing but Italian, whatever its source. Furthermore: it will be an opera without mise en scène! *And without a* ballet! *Just imagine: an opera at the* Opéra *without a ballet!!!*
(Autograph: Istituto di studi verdiani, Parma.)

Two days before leaving for Paris, in January 1886, Verdi had received a visit from the former baritone Pierre Gailhard – one of the "Flemish Deputies" of the première of *Don Carlos* at Paris in 1867 (see N. X, note 22), who in 1884 had been appointed joint-Director of the Opéra. He had travelled to Genoa to obtain from the composer permission to stage the première of *Otello*; on January 26 Verdi himself had informed Boito:

As you know, Gaillard [sic] was here, and I'm surprised I wasn't told that he had first of all spoken with you. – I told him that the opera was not yet finished, that it was written in Italian, in good Italian, and that the première should be in Italian. – All this talking and writing about Iago!!! *I reply in vain that* Otello, pas Iago, n'est pas fini, *but they go on writing and talking about* Iago, Iago!! [. . .] *If you agree, let us begin to baptize the work* Otello [. . .] (autograph: Isituto di studi verdiani, Parma).

6.   On page 599 of *I Copialettere di G. Verdi*, there is an interesting account of Verdi's creative process, taken from the memoirs of Quintino Sella, the famous Minister of Finance (Biella 1827–1884) and author of the notorious "tax on flour":

"In 1861 and 1862" (Sella recounts) "I had the honour of occupying a seat in the Chamber of Deputies next to that of an indisputably famous man, Maestro Verdi.

   "One day I asked him: When you compose one of your wonderful operas, how does the thought present itself to your mind? Do you first of all think of the principle theme, and then arrange the accompaniment, studying the best combination of the instruments, whether it should be flutes or violins and so on? No, no, no, the famous Maestro interrupted me vehemently, the thought presents itself whole, especially the feeling whether flute or violin be the suitable accompaniment. The difficulty is always writing it down fast enough to express the musical thought in its entirety, precisely as it came into my mind.

   "Since I am one of those people who can, perhaps without great difficulty, grasp a theme, but must then hear the score a second time in order to associate part of the accompaniment with the main tune, and then hear it several more times to appreciate the texture of the notes and the beauty of their association, you will understand how greatly I used to admire that man's rare ability to perceive simultaneously and effortlessly so many different sounds. I always said to myself: I would be quite unable to compete with such a man. I should never reach such realms of perfection, which he attains so naturally."

7. Years previously he had written to Arrivabene (16 July 1875):

> *Some wish to be melodists like* Bellini, *some harmonists like* Meyerbeer. *I wish to be neither one nor the other, and I wish the young composers of today would not think about being melodists, harmonists, realists, idealists, futurists or any other of these devilish pedantries. Melody and harmony should only be used by the artist as a means of making music; and should the day ever dawn when people no longer talk of melody or harmony, or German schools or Italian schools, or the past and the future etc., etc., etc., etc., then perhaps the kingdom of art will begin. (Verdi intimo, cit., p. 182.)*

8. Verdi is probably referring to a passage from the *Dies irae* in his *Requiem*, "Oro supplex et acclinis" (see bar 510 of the score), containing a series of parallel fifths. Many years previously, on 4 March 1869, he had written to the music critic Filippo Filippi:

> [. . .] *when I write something that sounds irregular, it is because the strictly regular is not what I want, and because I don't believe that all the rules hitherto adopted are correct. The treatises on counterpoint need revising* (autograph copy: Archivio della Casa Ricordi, Milan).

9. Verdi's opinion on Berlioz, expressed in a letter to Arrivabene on 5 January 1882, is well-known:

> *Berlioz was a poor sick man, furious with everybody, acrimonious and malicious. He had a great talent, and a feeling for instrumentation. He anticipated Wagner in many orchestral effects (Wagnerians don't admit it, but it's true). He lacked moderation. And he lacked the calm and, I would say, the equilibrium that produces complete works of art. He always went to extremes, even when creating something praiseworthy. His present successes in Paris are for the great part justified and merited, but reaction has even more to do with it. He was so badly treated when he was alive!!! Now he is dead! Hosanna!!! (Verdi intimo, cit., p. 295.)*

And three years earlier, on 14 April 1879, he had written to Ferdinand Hiller:

> *And so your performances of Berlioz were utter failures! Poor Berlioz has*

become fashionable, having been so badly treated in the past. I also knew him well and heard the Enfance du Christ the first time it was performed under his direction, at the Sala Herz, I think. There are certainly marvellous things in his work. Lofty inspiration, but his compositions are contorted, confused and stilted. (Autograph: Historisches Archiv, Cologne.)

Berlioz held the Italian composer in high esteem, as is confirmed by this extract from one of his letters to August Morel (dated June 2):

"Verdi is always at loggerheads with everybody at the Opéra. Yesterday he created a terrible scene at the dress rehearsal. I feel sorry for the poor man, and put myself in his place. Verdi is a worthy and honorable artist." H. BERLIOZ: *Correspondance inédite*, Paris 1888, p. 229);

and by his review of *I vespri siciliani* in the *Journal des Débats*, of 2 October 1855. The two men were well acquainted and would sometimes visit each other; at Sant'Agata in the album of autographs, there is an undated invitation to dinner, addressed to Verdi:

Jeudi soir 4/ Mon cher Monsieur Verdi/ Voulez-vous nous faire le plaisir de venir dîner à la maison Lundi prochain à 6h. 1/2 avec quelques uns de vos amis? Je serai bien heureux qu'il vous soit possible d'accepter cette invitation tout sans cérémonie./ Votre bien dévoué/ H. Berlioz. (C. MINGARDI: *Verdi e Berlioz* [. . .], in "Biblioteca 70", Busseto, I, 1970, p. 46, with facsimile.)

10. Also well-known is Verdi's opinion on Gounod, expressed in a letter to Arrivabene, dated 5 February 1876:

Gounod is a very fine musician, France's leading composer, but he lacks dramatic fire. Wonderful, charming music, magnificent details, the words almost always well expressed – the words, you understand, not the situation – the characters are not well drawn, and the drama or dramas have neither colour nor individuality. (*Verdi intimo*, cit., pp. 185–6.)

Two and a half years later, on 14 October 1878, he repeats the observation, again to Arrivabene:

[. . .] We must not delude ourselves but consider people for what they are. Gounod is a fine, very talented musician, whose chamber and instrumental works are most individual and superior. But he is not an artist of dramatic fibre. Even Faust, though successful, has been diminished in his hands. This is also the case with Romeo and Juliet and will be true also of Polyeucte. In short, he excels in the intimate piece, but always dilutes the dramatic situation and delineates his characters weakly, like so many others. Don't *accuse me of slander; I'm simply giving my sincere opinion to a friend, to whom I do not wish to be hypocritical* (*Verdi intimo,* cit., pp. 221–2).

11. *Sigurd* by Ernest Reyer (Marseille 1823–Lavandou, Hyère, 1909), composer of Wagnerian tendencies. After its première at Brussels in 1884, it was staged at the Opéra on 12 June 1885.

12. *Le Cid,* after the eponymous play by Corneille, the most recent opera of Jules Massenet (Montand, Saint-Etienne, 1842 – Paris 1912), which had been performed at the Opéra on 30 November 1885. Verdi had attended a performance on March 26, as an article from Paris, signed A.A. in the *Gazzetta Musicale di Milano* (XLI, 14: 4 April 1886, p. 108) informs us:

> *Last Friday* [*Verdi*] *was in a grand tier box at the Opéra* [. . .]*, attending a performance of Massenet's* Le Cid; *but abhorring the limelight, he sat at the back of the box, calm and unobserved.* [. . .] *But how his arrival in Paris has excited the journalists and galvanized their imaginations! Some of them state that he is visiting Paris to hear this or that singer with a view to casting his* Otello; *others say that Verdi has come to reach agreement with the Directors of the Academy or the Opéra-Comique about performing* Otello *in French – even before it has been performed at La Scala in Italian!* . . . [. . .] *For my part, I shall merely say that while I was with the Maestro, the Director of the Opéra came to ask him if he would give his consent to a performance at the Opéra of his* Requiem, *and if he would conduct it. He also suggested singers for the quartet of soprano, tenor, contralto and bass. But Verdi said that there would be insufficient time for rehearsals, since he had to leave during the first week of April or at the very latest at the end of that month, and particularly since the artists and the chorus did not yet know a note of the* Requiem.

XXVI

VERDI IN PARIS

1886

JACOPO CAPONI: "Verdi à Paris", in *Le Figaro*, Paris, 17 April 1886 (also in *La Perseveranza*, Milan, April 1886).

THIS ARTICLE CONTAINS further information about Verdi's stay in Paris between the end of March and the first few days of April 1886. Mention is also made of the portrait of Verdi by Giovanni Boldini (Ferrara 1842 – Paris 1931) in his studio in Place Pigalle, no. 11 – the famous painting that today hangs in the Giuseppe Verdi Home for Musicians in Milan. Boldini was, nonetheless, dissastisfied with the portrait. Camesasca recollects: "Giuseppina Strepponi, Verdi's wife, whose impatience seemed to make the painter nervous, and Maestro Muzio, with whom the model continued discussing professional business, were also present – and it was for these reasons that Boldini was dissatisfied with his work. The painter himself presented it to Verdi in 1893, after the success of *Falstaff*[1] with the following dedication: "To Maestro Verdi from his admirer and friend Boldini." Despite Verdi's reluctance, Boldini painted another portait. This is the even more celebrated painting of the composer wearing a top hat and scarf; the date "Paris 9 April 1886" in the top right hand corner refers to the day of the one and only sitting which, as Camesasca notes "was requested by the painter to 'make amends for' the poor result of the previous work. Verdi, we know, went unwillingly to the *atelier*; but after two hours the painting was so far advanced that the Maestro was impressed and agreed to stay for luncheon and another two-hour sitting – after which the portrait was finished. Boldini loved it dearly and refused to sell it, not even to the Prince of Wales. He showed it at many exhibitions, beginning with the Universal Exhibition of Paris in 1889, the first Venice Biennale and his one-man exhibition in New York (1897). In 1918 he presented it to the Gallery [of Modern Art in Rome] through the intervention of Princess Letitia of Savoy."[2] There are several unpublished sketches of this second portrait in the E. Piceni Collection in Milan.[3] Abbiati publishes a letter from Boldini to Verdi which dates back to that

Parisian visit of the composer; it bears the date April 1886, without giving the day:

> *A thousand thanks for the beautiful flowers, they have been very much admired, and my wife has instructed me to say a thousand things, et que tu est [sic] mignon tant plein! . . . But I have toothache and a swelling that makes my face look like a moon – just see how pretty I look* [Boldini here draws a caricature of himself]. *Before my attack, I went to hear* Il Cid, *and I rather think that it was this which gave me toothache, so much noise of every kind did I hear: dissonances, kettledrums, bells, bass drums – that my gums' nervous system has been assailed* [. . .][4]

Verdi in Paris

The Parisian press has published sufficient material to fill five or six volumes on Liszt's arrival and sojourn in Paris: we have read everything about him, from his infancy to the advanced age that he has now attained. He has been invited to social gatherings, dinners and meetings of every description, and no prima donna has ever received as many flowers and garlands as the porter at the Hôtel de Calais for the great abbé. While all that was happening, Verdi too had arrived, and in stark contrast he has avoided the public gaze almost entirely.

He avoids publicity as assiduously as Liszt revels in it. If, therefore, I have something interesting to report from my interview with Verdi, I owe it to the kind and friendly reception with which he once again honoured me.

Verdi, following his well-established habit of twenty years, stayed at the Hôtel de Bade which, although lacking the lavishness of the large modern caravanserais, has the advantage of being situated in the heart of Paris. The Maestro occupies the four little rooms on the mezzanine, from where he can at any moment plunge into the sea of Parisian life. When visiting Verdi you do not have to wait in ante-chambers, and there is absolutely no sign of clients and courtiers. You knock, and almost immediately, having crossed the first draw-ing-room, you hear the Maestro's familiar voice: Entrez! – and very often he will open the door himself.

More often than not Verdi is quite alone, reading the latest Parisian novelty, the latest novel, or skimming through the compositions that rain in on him with the customary "as a token of esteem". One day I found him browsing through Gevaert's *Traité de composition*[5] and heard him say: "That is an excellent work, useful and practical." In a corner of the room is a piano which, could it but speak, would tell you more than I. As at Genoa, in the Palazzo Doria, there is always manuscript paper on the piano, covered in the clear writing, resembling printed type, that has been Verdi's handwriting since *Oberto San Bonifazio*, his first opera. They are pieces from *Otello*, that work which finally exists but is known only by one or two privileged individuals, such as Boito and Muzio.[6]

To all those people who, after a thousand circumlocutions, finish by asking Verdi the aim of his trip to Paris, he replies good-naturedly and very shrewdly: "I come from time to time to keep in touch. One cannot afford to neglect Paris for long . . . And also – I simply had to talk to my tailor."

Sometimes he ends with a confession: "I do not deny that I was curious to hear some of the artists who are presently in fashion." It is this confession that generally causes the interviewer to forget his self-imposed discretion and let slip the inevitable: "And *Otello*?"

"*Otello*?" comes the immediate reply; "we shall talk of that when it is finished. At present it is not."

And Verdi, staring with his deep, large eyes at the intrusive interviewer, as if wishing to hypnotize him, repeats: "It is not, I assure you."

The Maestro is playing with words. *Otello* is finished, as finished as it could be, perhaps not all its notes are yet 'committed to paper, but that does not matter, the work is finished. How attentively I listened to the little he wished to tell me! To be frank, I am only guessing, but I would say that his choice of singers for *Otello*, while not known yesterday, has been made today. "The majority of my operas," Verdi told me, "were written with this or that artist in mind. With *Otello* this was not the case, which has its advantages and disadvantages: the composer is not restricted by any obstacle and can give free rein to his ideas; yet, once the opera is finished, it is more difficult to find singers to perform the work as the composer intends. And so it is with *Otello*; it is for this reason that I have told the impresarios at La Scala: engage whoever you wish . . . and then we'll see."[7]

"Is it true there are no choruses in *Otello*?"

"Who told you that? There are." And Verdi, smiling at my indiscreet questions, added: "There are choruses, duets, trios, a quartet, a finale . . . are you satisfied? What there is not," he continued, adopting a serious expression, "is a *divertissement*. There is none, and there will be none; a *divertissement* would harm the unity of the drama; it would be an hors d'oeuvre, spoiling the general impression. Anyhow, I don't know where the devil I could put it."

I understood very well that he wished to reply indirectly, not to me, but to certain opera-house directors who had perhaps requested him to follow tradition. In the past Verdi had always complied – for example, by developing the ballet in *Aida* for the Opéra[8] and inserting an entire *divertissement* into *Jérusalem* for the same theatre. But this time he refuses to make any concessions – on this point he has very clear ideas, from which he does not wish to depart.[9]

Verdi never ceases to praise the libretto that Boito has written for him. He finds the verse quite admirable and considers that it will be very difficult to translate into French. Nevertheless, this translation will be made, and I think I can state that the work will be entrusted to M. du Locle, the translator of *Aida*.[10] Boito has followed Shakespeare faithfully from the second act onwards,[11] Shakespeare's first act being entirely omitted in the new opera, which will have four acts, starting with the storm, when Otello arrives in Cyprus with Desdemona, i.e. when the real drama begins to develop.

As for the music, how can I speak of it when I have not heard a single note? What I think I have understood is this: though *Otello* might not be the rigorous application of the Maestro's famous motto *let us return to the past*,[12] he has none the less been won over to the idea of returning to the truth of lyric drama, according first place to the drama and making the orchestra its servant, not its master. In a word, *Otello* will be a melodic and a dramatic opera, it will serve as a salutary example and a lesson to the *young* composers, who are at present merely concerned with the orchestra – to the point of forgetting the drama. *More sauce than fish!*

It's all very well for the Maestro to say that he has come to Paris to order an overcoat from his tailor; it is, however, crystal clear that, like all great artists, he is utterly absorbed by his work. It is his sole preoccupation! One day I heard him arguing with a German journalist, as to whether Otello should have a black complexion, as he is played in Vienna, or a deep brown one as in the classic interpretations of Rossi and Salvini. He is equally preoccupied with the costume of his hero. – "Is it absolutely necessary for him to be dressed in an oriental manner? Is he not rather a general and admiral in the employ of the Republic of Venice? Why should he not wear that uniform? We must now discover what his uniform was and whether it conforms to the aesthetics of the theatre."[13] To tell the truth, I – a Venetian – had to confess that I had no knowledge of the Serenissima's military costumes and had seen no book that described or drew them, whereas the costumes worn by senators and magistrates are familiar to everyone.

It was clearly because of his preoccupation with *Otello* that Verdi attended several performances at the Opéra and the Opéra-Comique. At the Opéra he heard *Le Cid* and *Sigurd*; at the Opéra-Comique *Zampa*.[14] He was also present at Gayarre's[15] début in *L'Africaine*. There can be no doubt that in these two theatres he was searching for his future singers. He was most keen to hear Maurel again – and was very satisfied. He found him as he was several years ago, with his faults and his great qualities – the future and, as yet, undisclosed Iago that Verdi was seeking. The two theatres just mentioned are fighting over – it is the *mot juste* – the new opera. Rose Caron, an artist of great merit, a truly dramatic prima donna,[16] and M. Duc,[17] a new tenor with a superb voice, who impressed Verdi greatly, are the Desdemona and Otello who would make him choose the Opéra; the Opéra-Comique, with Talazac[18] and Maurel would offer another outstanding Otello and Iago. But the Maestro will make no decision before the Italian première, which will certainly take place in Milan.

During his final days in Paris Verdi received a flood of visitors. Close friends – those people who pay genuine homage to the great Maestro were to be seen there, but also the flatterers and autograph hunters.

Music publishers were also present, and I learnt that one of them had offered the Maestro a sum approaching a hundred thousand francs for the copyright of *Otello* in France and Belgium. "I have done business with Ricordi for forty years," Verdi replied, "I have no reason not to continue . . ." – a reply that is worthy of the Maestro and also honours the house of Ricordi.

The continual stream of visitors and the almost daily visits to the theatre eventually tired the Maestro a little. "I have no time to do anything,'" he said, "especially now that I must pose for my portrait." This was news to me, but news that I had expected. Boldini, the famous Italian painter, is one of Verdi's most passionate admirers. Two years ago, being unable to paint the Maestro's portrait, he contented himself with that of his loyal pupil, Muzio, and produced a genuine masterpiece. I have rarely seen so small a work make such an impression: Muzio, conducting an invisible orchestra with a baton in his hand, is quite life-like.

Verdi one day found this masterful painting over one of the fireplaces of the Palazzo Doria. It is one of the most precious jewels in his possession.[19]

It was quite natural that the Maestro, finding himself in Paris for some time, should in his turn pose in Place Pigalle.

"Give me two sittings only," Boldini had told him.

But the sittings multiplied; there were about ten.

The portrait, however, is superb, and will be greatly admired at the 1887 Salon.

I cannot go on ad infinitum. I shall therefore conclude by saying that this journey to Paris by the composer of *Aida* probably anticipates a performance of *Otello*. My most ardent wish is that this piece of "Verdiana" is, in turn, an anticipation of the triumphant article that *Le Figaro* will devote to the première which the musical public of France and Italy await with impatience.

J. Caponi

NOTES

1. E. Camesasca: "L'opera completa di Boldini", in the series *Classici dell'arte* n. 36, Rizzoli, Milan 1970, p. 103, n. 141.
2. E. Camesasca, *op cit.*, p. 103, n. 142.
3. See the reproduction in F. Abbiati, *op. cit.*, IV, p. 256.
4. F. Abbiati, *op. cit.*, IV, p. 281.
5. Cf. N. X, note 12.
6. A few days before leaving for Paris with Verdi, Muzio wrote to Ricordi:

   Boito entered the Maestro's study at the very moment he was playing to me at the piano, for the second time, the final duet of the first act, the only piece Boito had not yet heard, since it had only recently been finished. After breakfast and before Boito had arrived, I spoke to the Maestro about the French translation, and he told me that he would be very happy for Boito himself to undertake it [. . .] (F. Abbiati, *op. cit.*, IV, p. 279).

7. The impresarios at La Scala were at that time the brothers Cesare and Enrico Corti, sons of Lorenzo Corti, who for many years had been Director of the Théâtre Italien in Paris.
8. In the original version for Cairo and La Scala, the act 2 ballet which follows the famous "march" played on stage by "Egyptian trumpets", consisted of the first 52 bars of the present version, followed by a repeat of the initial theme in C minor (staccato triplets on the strings, flutes and piccolos above the cellos and bassoons) for a total of 69 bars (cf. the

first Ricordi edition of the score for voice and piano, bearing the number 42602, or the first Ricordi edition of the score for solo piano, no. 4286–42526). Verdi "developed" the ballet, inserting before the repeat, i.e. after the first 52 bars, another 52 bars of new music (what is now the central section which begins in B flat minor: of semiquaver triplets given to the woodwind over a staccato bass), followed in turn by the repeat of the theme in F minor, played by oboe and piccolo, for another 88 bars (cf. the orchestral score, published by Ricordi in 1958, no. P.R. 153, from the last two bars of p. 172 to the bottom of p. 188).

9. It was Boito who first placed the *divertissement* in act 2 of the opera; on 29 October 1886 Verdi replied to him:

> *The ballet is fine in the second act, if that will satisfy them. But it goes without saying that the ballet will only be performed at the* Opéra. *For other theatres* Otello *will remain as it is now – or rather, as it will be tomorrow or whenever the orchestration is finally finished* . . . (autograph: Istituto di studi verdiani, Parma).

And on 25 March 1887, when *Otello* had already been performed at La Scala, Verdi wrote to Ricordi:

> *As for the ballet, or rather the* Divertissement, *why publish it? It is a cowardly concession to the* Opéra *that the authors were wrong to agree to; artistically speaking, it is a monstrosity. Interrupt the full fury of the action by a ballet?!!! The opera must stand as it is, it's therefore a waste of time publishing the ballet* (autograph: Archivio della Casa Ricordi).

Verdi composed this ballet seven years later, on the eve of the French performance of *Otello* at the Opéra; rather than in the second act, as agreed in 1886, it was inserted in the third act, before the finale (cf. *Carteggio Verdi–Boito*, cit., pp. 455–7).

10. Du Locle was entrusted with the translation of acts 1 and 2; the other two acts were translated by Boito (cf. *Carteggio Verdi–Boito*, cit., pp. 356–7, 360–1, 371 and 443).

11. A propos this cut, cf. the *Carteggio Verdi–Boito*, cit., pp. 346–7.

12. The famous motto – *Let us return to the past: that will be progress* – appeared in the closing lines of a letter, dated 5 January 1871, from Verdi to Francesco Florimo, and caused an uproar in Italian music circles of the period, and has exercised Verdi critics at great length (and perhaps, to no great purpose). Verdi himself tried to explain its significance to Giulio Ricordi in a letter, dated 26 December 1883:

> *You know as well as I do that there are some people who have good sight, and like bold, strong and genuine colours. There are others who have a slight cataract, and like faded, dirty colours. They are in fashion, and I do not disapprove of following fashion (because an artist must be a product of his*

age), but I would prefer to see it accompanied always by a little judgement and good sense! So, neither the past nor the future! It is true that I said "Let us turn to the past"! But I mean the past which is our basis, fundamental and solid. I mean that past which has been deliberately ignored by modern exuberance and to which we are bound to return sooner or later. For the time being, let us allow the tide to rise. The dams can be built later (autograph: Archivio della Casa Ricordi, Milan).

13. The question of the costumes for *Otello* will be tackled the following May; see Boito's letter to Verdi, dated 16 March 1886 in *Carteggio Verdi-Boito*, cit., pp. 106–7 and 354.
14. By L.-J.-F. Hérold (Paris 1791–1833); the baritone Victor Maurel sang in this revival of Hérold's masterpiece, that had been performed for the first time at the Opéra-Comique on 3 May 1831.
15. Julián Gayarre (Valle de Roncal, Navarra, 1844 – Madrid 1890), one of the most popular tenors of the second half of the nineteenth century; he first made his name in 1870 at the Carcano, Milan, and then at the Regio, Parma, before finally establishing his reputation in 1876 in *La favorita* at La Scala. His début at the Opéra had been during these first months of 1886.
16. Rose Caron (Monerville, Seine-et-Oise, 1857–Paris 1930). She had already appeared in the première of *Sigurd* at Brussels in 1884 and at the Opéra in 1885; she was the soprano chosen by Verdi for the 1894 performance of *Otello* at the Opéra.
17. Joseph Duc, born at Béziers in 1858; he was a much admired singer but controversial actor, who had made his début at the Opéra the previous year in *Guillaume Tell*. He left the Opéra in 1893 to sing in other major Italian and Spanish theatres, including, in 1896, La Scala.
18. Jean Talazac (Bordeaux 1853–Chatou 1892) made his début in 1877 in Reyer's *La Statue* at the Théâtre Lyrique, and moved the following year to the Opéra-Comique, where he remained till 1888; he specialized in light, lyrical tenor roles, and excelled particularly in *Manon* and *Lakmé*.
19. It was not "two years ago", but about four years previously, in 1822, that Boldini had painted Emanuele Muzio; the picture now hangs in the Museo Teatrale at La Scala (cf. E. CAMESASCA, *op. cit.*, p. 98, n. 85).

XXVII

REHEARSALS FOR *OTELLO*

1887

Ugo Pesci: "Le prove dell' *Otello*", in *Verdi e l'Otello*, Special edition of the *Illustrazione Italiana*, compiled by Ugo Pesci and Ed.° Ximenes, Fratelli Treves, Milan. (February 1887; reprinted 1913), pp. 39–40.

VERDI ARRIVED IN Milan on 4 January 1887 to begin rehearsing *Otello*; the general rehearsals (as the *Gazzetta Musicale di Milano* of 30 January 1887 announced on page 41) began on January 27; the dress rehearsal took place on 3 February, and two days later the first performance was given with Franco Faccio conducting and Romilda Pantaleoni, Francesco Tamagno and Victor Maurel in the main roles.

Rehearsals for Otello

[. . .] The principal singers of *Otello* had each received their parts by the beginning of the autumn, and had had every opportunity of learning them thoroughly by the day Verdi arrived in Milan, when he went almost immediately to La Scala to start the piano rehearsals.[1] The excellent Cairati[2] had been rehearsing the chorus for two months.

That first day, after Boito, Faccio, Maestro Coronaro[3] and Giulio Ricordi had all exchanged the usual compliments (briefly, because Verdi is not by nature loquacious), as people who have not seen each other for some time are wont to do, the Maestro approached the piano and requested the artists to sing through the great ensemble of act 3, scene 8.[4] The sheer excitement of finding themselves in the presence of Verdi defeated them all: the Maestro was not pleased, the ladies were frightened and the men exchanged questioning looks. The second time, however, the piece went better, and a smile of satisfaction appeared on every face.

In addition to the usual hall for the harpsichord rehearsals, the theatre management had prepared another room, especially reserved for Verdi, with a fine Erard. And there the Maestro went with the principal singers. He himself sat at the piano to run through the solo numbers and duets; he gave advice and encouragement, and every now and then uttered one of those words which are worth more to an artist than any triumph. Verdi was anxious, however, to fuse singing and acting as soon as possible, and he could teach actors as well as singers. He would insist upon the greatest degree of naturalness, and with a keen eye he studied every movement, every gesture to discover what seemed to him most natural and true. Pantaleoni sang the willow song sweetly, interrupting it with the words that Desdemona must address to Emilia, who helps her take off her jewellery. She sings the lines

> *Scendean gli augelli a vol dai rami cupi*
> *Verso quel dolce canto . . .*

and then to Emilia: "Riponi questo anello." ["Put away this ring."] The Maestro pointed out that, to make the interruption seem less brusque, she should let the ring be seen on her finger, as she made the gesture with which she indicated so gracefully the birds flying down from the boughs. . . . With such a Maestro, is it possible to interpret a role with anything but great refinement?

Tamagno's turn came. At the end of the final scene Otello must fall. Verdi required a tragic fall à la Salvini. Tamagno rehearsed it several times, but the Maestro was not completely satisfied. Seeing that the artist was tired, he postponed rehearsing the fall to another day; and meanwhile, adoring children as he does, he went to cuddle and play with the famous tenor's little daughter, who had come to La Scala to collect her daddy. Tamagno fell ill and had to stay at home for several days. Giulio Ricordi stood in for him, singing softly in the ensembles. But Giulio Ricordi during these days is needed by everyone at La Scala; he is called away and Verdi himself takes his place in a scene with Desdemona, in which he considers the embrace to be too cold, too restrained. Changing roles for a moment, the Maestro demonstrates to Pantaleoni a fervent, passionate embrace.

Many will not believe it, yet it is true: at five o'clock in the afternoon, when the singers, Faccio, Coronaro and even Giulio Ricordi are exhausted, Verdi, with all of his 73 years, descends as fresh as a rose into the courtyard, which opens onto Via Filodrammatici, and climbs once more into the carriage in which he arrived at midday, to return to the Hôtel de Milan.

The general rehearsals of *Otello* began on January 27, and took place at the same time as the stage rehearsals. It is easy to imagine

how the excellent La Scala orchestra listened with affectionate respect
to Verdi's occasional observations. For the chorus and extras, the
opera does not present any great problems of staging, except that in
the first act the various phases of the storm must be accompanied by
crowd movements on stage. The chorus and extras only appear again
at the end of that act, for a few moments in the second, and then in
the great finale of act 3. Apart from its other great merits, Verdi's
new opera has the additional advantage of being stageable even in
smaller theatres, without the need of enormous stage machinery . . .
provided the singers are good.

Despite numerous requests, Verdi has remained adamant in his
policy of admitting no intruders to either the rehearsals or the dress-
rehearsal, as he knew they would not keep silent about what they had
seen and heard. His wish is that the audience should receive an
impression that has not been coloured by the gossip of the privileged
few. And he is absolutely right.

For any lover of art, the sight of Verdi conducting a general
rehearsal has something truly awe-inspiring about it. The eye can
hardly make out the long rows of empty seats in the vast, dark and
empty stalls. The silk curtains of many boxes are drawn, thus
increasing the general air of respectful mystery. The orchestral
players are in their places several minutes before the fixed hour; they
talk in whispers; and as you would expect, they talk of the opera and
the Maestro. Not a soul to be seen or heard in the wings [. . .].
Chorus and extras wait in their large rooms to be called on stage.
The principal artists are in their dressing-rooms, which every now
and then emit a trill or a phrase repeated many times, as if the singer
wished to study the effect. [. . .]

At half past eight the Maestro arrives. Boito, Giulio Ricordi and
Faccio are already present and have gone to meet him at the entrance
on the Via de' Filodrammatici side. The Maestro is dressed as usual
in his fur coat, with a silk scarf around his neck. On stage he
unbuttons his coat and loosens his scarf a little, and sometimes
removes it. [. . .] He sits down; Faccio is already on the rostrum
and has twice rapped his desk to gain the attention of his players. It is
the normal custom – but the players are already intent upon the
music and ready to begin. [. . .]

UGO PESCI

NOTES

1. Both Pantaleoni and Maurel had rehearsed their roles alone with the composer. Pantaleoni (then engaged to Franco Faccio), whom Verdi, with Boito's agreement, had chosen for the role of Desdemona, despite Giulio Ricordi's preference for Gemma Bellincioni, had visited Sant'Agata in October (cf. *Carteggio Verdi-Boito*, cit., pp. 353–4); Maurel had visited Verdi in Genoa in December (cf. F. ABBIATI, *op. cit.*, IV, pp. 302–3).
2. Giuseppe Cairati (Milan 1845–1915), oboist and singing teacher, was chorus-master at La Scala from 1881–1897.
3. Gaetano Coronaro (Vicenza 1852 – Milan 1908), composer, was assistant conductor to Franco Faccio at La Scala from 1879–1890.
4. Beginning with Otello's words: "(Ecco! E lui! Nell'animo lo scruta.)"

XXVIII

AN INTERVIEW WITH VERDI

1887

GINO MONALDI: "Un colloquio con Verdi", in *Il Popolo Romano*, Rome, n. 45, 15 February 1887.

MARQUIS GINO MONALDI (Perugia 1847 – Rome 1932), composer, music critic and impresario was the author of numerous publications on music and the theatre, including about a dozen books on Verdi. One of these – a most popular monograph, published in 1889 (and translated into German) – was based on rather vague documentation and contained errors, which still leave their mark on Verdi historiography.[1] His first published writings date from 1870, when he worked as a music critic on the *Gazzetta d'Italia*, which published in serial form his first monograph on Verdi, *Verdi e le sue opere*, a single 82-page volume in 1877. Monaldi sent several copies to Verdi at Sant'Agata and Genoa; the composer replied on 5 December 1877:

Signore! Several copies of your volume have already arrived at my country-house near Busseto, and now I receive another five here, which you have kindly sent me. You have produced a large tome from meagre subject-matter, and I am in all respects grateful; but permit me to refrain from giving you either my impression or my opinions. It is an old habit of mine never to pass judgement, even on music. I have so little faith in the judgement of others, that I can scarcely have faith in my own![2]

Verdi expressed his feelings, however, privately to Arrivabene some time after, on 8 February 1878:

I too have read, or at least glanced at Monaldi's volume. It is full of inaccuracies! It goes without saying that this sort of book can never be anything but a mass of errors, even if the author is genuinely inspired by his subject, because his amour-propre or at least his vanity, will cause him to conceal the bad and exaggerate the good. How few men are honest and high-minded. And so it is that this book repeats what previous books said on the same subject; and what they don't know, they invent.[3]

On 22 June 1878 Verdi refers again to Monaldi's volume in a letter to Florimo:

I want to tell you a funny story. Last November, just before leaving for Genoa, I received from a certain Sig . . . six copies of a new biography about me. I did not reply. And no sooner had I arrived at Genoa, when I received another six copies from the same man, with an offer of many more (as if it were my task to distribute my own biography) and a request for my opinion on his volume. To avoid further consignments I hastened to reply, thanked him warmly and apologized for withholding my judgement: "I have so little faith in the judgement of others, that I can scarcely have faith in my own . . ." *This letter was published! Had I been him, I'd never have done that! Would you?*

After a period on F. Torraca's *Rassegna*, Monaldi joined the *Popolo Romano* in 1887 as music critic. The interview with Verdi took place at the Hôtel de Milan on the morning of 7 February 1887, two days after the première of *Otello* at La Scala (see also Blanche Roosevelt's meeting with the composer in N. XXIX).

An interview with Verdi

The porter at the Hôtel de Milan, having delivered my visiting card, returned and said: "Maestro Verdi begs you to come tomorrow morning at eleven o'clock."

The next day – Monday the 7th – at the arranged hour I climbed up the two flights of stairs to the first floor, where the Maestro is wont to stay when he visits Milan [. . .]. I was shown into a large drawing-room where, to my surprise, I found myself immediately in the presence of Verdi, who approached me with outstretched hand.

He holds his handsome figure erect and moves in an agile, easy manner; his face blooms with health and nothing about him hints at his renowned old age, except for a trace of pearl-grey in beard and hair.

"I merely wish to shake you by the hand," I said immediately, hardly touching the Maestro's hand, who shook mine vigorously, "I know that your time is precious and . . ."

"Not a bit of it!" he replied, smiling affably. "Please sit down." And to avoid any hesitation on my part, he set an example, which I then followed.

"And so you too are in Milan? For a long stay?"

"I should already have left, but I couldn't bring myself to commit such sacrilege after only a single performance of *Otello*!" The burning topic had involuntarily escaped my lips.

"Oh, you would have missed nothing," the Maestro added at once, with a natural and sincere modesty that impressed me. I stammered some compliment, and seeing that I had been too direct, I changed the subject at the first opportunity and said: "Yesterday, Maestro, you must have felt your ears burning – so many of us were talking of you, close by." [4]

"I would have liked to come down for a moment, but I was feeling a little tired."

"You were with us in spirit. Giulio Ricordi said everything in his quite excellent toast."

"Did Mayor Negri also speak? He is a most effective speaker. If he were in the Chamber today, he would, I think, be one of the best." [5]

"And yesterday, though he spoke in French, his speech was full of pithy thoughts expressed in warm, poetic language. It was a sort of masonic toast . . . and to think that Milan's democrats cannot abide him . . ."

"That's right, because of Negri's enthusiastic support for the monument to Napoleon III." [6]

"This wretched democracy – it attacks intolerance in others, and is often little more tolerant itself. They have destroyed old privileges and replaced them with new ones, which are even worse."

"Exactly as in music!" the Maestro exclaimed with a certain warmth of feeling.

I was dumbfounded. What! He, Giuseppe Verdi, was throwing down the challenge, throwing the first card on the table! You can imagine that I was not slow in playing mine.

"Oh!" I exclaimed. "After *Otello*, privileges no longer exist: the revolution is complete. You, Maestro, have demolished the last bastions of conventions and formulae. Your opera is truly a new departure."

"Who knows . . . who knows! You would need to ask the future."

"From this very moment you could be sure of the answer."

"In any case, each person does what he can; and he will always achieve something, if he writes as he feels, and according to how nature prompts him. What I can tolerate least of all is for an Italian to write like a German, and a German like an Italian. An Italian must write as an Italian, a German as a German. Their natures are too different for them to blend. It is true that music is universal, but the men who write music are different, according to where they were born. It is useless to argue: man is, and always will be fashioned by the country in which he lives, and whatever he does, he will not be able to change his nature completely." [7]

"But our country of Italy seems to have lost much of its creative fertility, not as regards the quantity, but the quality of its works of art."

"That is not true," the Maestro continued with increasing animation. "There is still great talent, it is not this that today's young artists lack, but sincerity! Yes, they are not sincere: they do not write as they feel and how they would wish – they set about tormenting their own imagination, running behind stars which they neither see nor discern, but which they merely seem to sense. This is merely a pose – and quite unnecessary; for their natural talent, I repeat, would counsel them much better, if they allowed it to run its natural course. Tastes obviously change, and it is therefore necessary for artists to profit from and use shrewdly all those discoveries which are being made in art-theory every day. Such progress is necessary; but the artist needs to heed these changes without betraying his own character and individuality. And he must above all protect the sovereignty of the human voice and song. It will be said that the human voice is also, basically, an instrument, and it is therefore wrong to concede it too great a supremacy. Yes; this is true, in part. But young composers must remember that the human voice, apart from being the finest of all instruments, is not merely a sound; *poetry* is wedded to this sound, and poetry requires an ideal form of expression that is both lofty and always intelligible. Today's young artists forget this rule too easily."

While he spoke I was so spellbound that, when he stopped, I forgot to rekindle the Maestro's precious eloquence. His voice fell silent, and his deep, gentle gaze looked at me, as if to gauge the effect of his words. I tried a final question.

"And do you not think, Maestro," I said, "that part of the blame and responsibility for leading astray the talent of young composers must lie with the public, whose tastes have become so strange and recondite, that one no longer knows how to satisfy them?"

"No! you are wrong to accuse the public – who always judge with a sense of proportion. Oh, I have faith in the public, for without them I would not write. I speak naturally of the great publics who have been civilized by art. In the final analysis, such a public will be right."

Athough I could easily have continued this interesting conversation, and noticed that the Maestro was not averse to continue, I did not have the courage to insist, and wishing to show that I too still possessed moderation, I arose and took my leave. He also got up, accompanied me to the door, shook my hand and said "till next time". These words seemed to me a promise, an omen, a hope . . .

GINO MONALDI

NOTES

1. Cf. M. CONATI: "L' 'Oberto conte di san Bonifacio' ", cit., in *Atti del I Congreso internazionale di studi verdiani.*
2. Autograph: Biblioteca Piancastelli, Forlí.
3. *Verdi intimo*, cit., p. 209.
4. The morning following the first performance of *Otello*, Tito Ricordi invited to a lunch at the Hôtel de Milan all the Italian and foreign journalists, VIPs and artists who had attended the première. Present were: Mayor Negri, the Prefect, Boito, Faccio, the Corti brothers (impresarios at La Scala), Muzio, Caponi, Gailhard, Giacosa, Depanis, the American singer and journalist Blanche Roosevelt (seated between Boito and Noseda), Bellaigue, Bazzini, Martucci, the playwright Paolo Ferrari, Panzacchi, the German music critic Ehrlich (see N. XXXIII & N. XLIII), Pascarella, D'Arcais, Sivori, Boldini, Amintore Galli, Count Zorzi (a Verdi fanatic), Michetti, Cameroni, Ernest Reyer (the composer of *Sigurd*), Eugenio Checchi, Treves, D'Ormeville, Edwards, Filippi, Hueffer and many others. The seating plan can be seen on page 186 of *Otello* [. . .] *Giudizi della stampa italiana e straniera*, Ricordi, Milan [1877]. Verdi, of course, was absent. The same book quotes the two speeches, both given in French, by Giulio Ricordi and Mayor Negri.
5. Gaetano Negri (Milan 1838–Varazze 1902), politician, writer, active for many years in the Ministry of Education, Milan, then Mayor from 1884–1889; he was elected Deputy for the 12th legislature, then Senator from 1890.
6. Napoleon III died in exile in 1873, and Negri was among the organizers of a public subscription to erect a monument in his honour. Verdi, who had met Napoleon III during the latter's exile in London in 1847, always remembered his intervention in 1859 on the side of the Piedmontese against Austria, and subscribed 200 lire, thus provoking a reaction from Francesco Guerrazzi. The composer justified his action in a letter to Arrivabene, dated 22 March 1873:

But is this Guerrazzi a raging maniac? What is Guidicini's letter to him? And why should he object to 200 lire towards a monument in honour of Napoleon? Politics had nothing to do with this. I have always believed, and still believe that Napoleon was the only Frenchman to love our country. What's more, he risked his skin for us! This is quite enough to justify my modest little sum! (Verdi intimo, cit., p. 154.)

7. Cf. N. XXII, note 4.

XXIX

A VISIT TO VERDI AFTER THE
PREMIÈRE OF *OTELLO*

1887

BLANCHE ROOSEVELT: "Verdi, Milan and 'Otello'", cit.; v. chapt. XVI, pp. 247–9.

AT THE END of her book, the American journalist and singer gives an account of her final meeting with Verdi, after the première of *Otello* at La Scala (5 February 1887). Tamagno, the Otello, was suffering from an inflammation of the throat and had kept everyone in suspense on the eve of the much awaited première; it took place, however, as planned. But a worsening of the tenor's condition had caused the postponement of the second performance, which could only take place about a week after the première. In the meantime, Giuseppina Verdi wrote to Marietta Calvi in Carrara, Maria's – Verdi's adopted daughter – husband's stepmother:

Thank the Lord that Verdi – who has been utterly exposed to everyone's embraces, so many discreet and indiscreet requests, praises, speeches and hurrahs of a great number of good people and also a great number of fools[1] – is well, bearing up, eating with a good appetite and sleeping peacefully for many hours on end the sleep of the righteous, which is a true description of this great and respected man. This consolation and the sight of his courage and forbearance in these difficult circumstances give me the strength to hold out, and await with less impatience the moment of calm and general stability. Tomorrow, if other disasters do not occur, will be the second performance of Otello . . . *and then the third?!! . . . then all artistic toil will cease, and we shall hope for clearer skies and return to Genoa until the blessed moment arrives, when we leave for the country. Your husband will have told you all that happened on that memorable evening of February 5. The excitement was deafening and bordered on frenzy . . . I confess I was moved, because this admiration, this passionate demonstration is an expression of the high esteem and great affection that has accompanied Verdi throughout his long career. It was in Milan that he first gave evidence of his great talent, and it was in Milan that he wished to perform the final work of his genius! Verdi's genius is part and parcel of Italy's Resurrection!* [2]

[*A visit to Verdi after the première of* Otello]

Milan, 11 February 1887

Everything is over, and we leave Milan tonight: this afternoon I had a last chat with Verdi. I need not say he was most amiable, and that I found him the same old Verdi I had known in Paris, only a little quieter, perhaps a little more staid – shall I say it? – a little more gentle than before. There was a something sad in his manner: I could see that he was deeply chagrined about something, and that something is the big poster at La Scala, saying "Riposo".[3] Verdi is tired, worn, and nervous; can you wonder at it? At his time of life, to pass through such a series of emotions would be enough in themselves to render a younger and stronger man ill. Also the weather has changed – cold rains, hailstorms, and biting winds send people spinning and shivering through the Piazza;[4] faces are downcast, and the city seems in mourning. Even the triumph of last Saturday is far away, one of those vague delicious dreams, which, on awakening, leave a sense of having walked through perfumed meadows, but in a strange land. There is always some bitter to Verdi's sweet. Milan has always been destined to be the scene of his greatest triumphs, but also of his greatest humiliations. The King has given him another smart decoration, but if the sovereign could heal Tamagno, I think the composer would be more indebted than even to be allowed to call his Majesty cousin.[5]

Sounds of many voices came to us from the adjoining chamber. Crowds were in there – a delegation come to bring Verdi – the earth, as we would say in America – simply many honours, more triumphs, but most – municipal bores.[6] I think Verdi is proud enough, but rather tired of it all. This is Thursday, and there is no second performance tonight. It seems a farce, quite like *Le Locataire de M. Blondeau*, a piece I once saw at the Palais Royal theatre: still – the tenor is ill. That unfortunate artist is obliged to lay up, and the

other singers must remain *in statu quo* until he gets better. I asked
Verdi if it was hoarseness, temper, or tenor.[7] He raised his eyes and
said:

"Tenor? Perhaps! But you know he is really suffering."

"It is a thousand pities."

"Yes, it is at least *one*."

Verdi spoke absently.

I can see the Maestro is longing for the quiet of Sant'Agata. Even
those amiable joyful voices in the next room are enough to grate on
tender nerves. Honours! Honours mean fame and glory, but a great
many disagreeable things besides. The Maestro would leave Milan
today if he could, but etiquette and the La Scala commissioners
require that every composer shall personally assist three times if
living – *à la* Edmond About – I don't know how many times if dead
– at the first performances of his work. Verdi in this must do as
others have done, and as he himself has always done. He made a
precedent in the matter of rehearsals which has brought down envy
and annoyances – not on his head, it was well protected, but on the
heads of the Ricordis, the theatre managers, &c., and things are bad
enough without the composer fleeing the camp. Now, a word once
and for all about theatrical shortsightedness. Can you imagine a great
opera house like La Scala calmly paying twenty or thirty thousand
pounds to produce a new opera, and refusing to pay forty or fifty
more to engage substitutes in case a principal singer falls ill? Could
one believe such a state of things?[8] Not only that, but the *Othello*
artists have been singing *Aida* all the season, and by stopping it for
the new work took off the only paying opera; hence the theatre is
closed in mid-Carnival. Times have sadly changed when the greatest
traditional opera-house of the world is reduced to such management
and such straits. Naturally the loss to La Scala is enormous. I don't
say who deserves this, but I do say such impresarios certainly merit
no sympathy.

Of course you realize that it is also a real misfortune for the critics,
especially they who felt called upon to judge a second performance of
Otello. I don't need to hear a second; my mind is made up. I repeat,
the opera is Verdi all over; it is as Italian as the Lake of Como, and as
beautifully put together as the cathedral. Verdi's *Otello* is, indeed, a
Gothic structure and the crowning effort of his life.

But the Maestro.

We talked and talked, and I said: "They tell me your next work
will also be Shakespearean. Don't say no. I am going, but it is not

good-bye. On the contrary, I shall return to Milan to assist at your *next* great triumph."

I could have gone on for hours – most women can, and do, but I had to go. However, I reiterated my last words.

Verdi smiled – he smiled all over his face and eyes, as the children say. He came with me out into the passage, and only as my foot was on the staircase did he speak.

"Au revoir," he said, still smiling; then added, mysteriously coming closer to me, "another opera? Mademoiselle, connaissez-vous mon acte de naissance?"⁹

BLANCHE ROOSEVELT

NOTES

1. Turlurû (Lombard dialect): fools. Giuseppina was born in Lodi and always remained faithful to her native dialect.
2. F. ABBIATI, *op. cit.*, IV, pp. 325–6.
3. Italian in the original.
4. Italian in the original.
5. At the première of *Otello*, Umberto I had conferred upon Verdi the insignia of the Gran Croce dell'Ordine dei SS. Maurizio e Lazzaro. The right to style oneself King's "cousin" was only accorded to the holders of the highest royal decoration, the Collare dell'Annunziata.
6. Roosevelt had been present at the luncheon given by Tito Ricordi on February 6 at the Hôtel de Milan to the foreign and Italian journalists, the VIPs and the artists, who had attended the première of *Otello*. She was seated between Boito and Aldo Noseva, critic of the *Corriere della Sera* (see preceding chapter, note 5).
7. Allusion to a well-known theatrical saying, usually attributed to Hans von Bülow: *Tenor ist schon Krankheit . . .*
8. A pity that Roosevelt (who shows herself to be on intimate terms with Verdi, and is at pains to remind us of the ease with which she spoke to him) did not put these questions to the Maestro himself and report his reply, which would assuredly have been most interesting.
9. "Signorina, do you know when I was born?"

XXX

A VISIT TO VERDI

1887

ERCOLE ARTURO MARESCOTTI: "Una visita a Verdi", in *Il Teatro Illustrato*, Milan, VII, 76: April 1887, p. 58. (The author published an almost identical account, with the exception of an inaccurate date, in *Il Palcoscenico*, Milan, IV, 38: 22 October 1900, p. 5; republished in *L'Aurora Italiana*, II, supplement to n. 104 (Verdi number): 1901, pp. 5–6; and in *Lissone a G. Verdi*, Monza, August 1913, p. 2. The author also refers to this visit in a commemorative article published in *Ars et Labor*, Milan, LXII, 1: January 1907, pp. 11–17; and in *San Marco*, Venice, 4 February and 4 March 1939.)

THE REASON FOR this visit – which Marescotti erroneously dates back to 1888 instead of 1887 – was provided by the initiative of an "honourable Milanese firm", Melzi, who, as Marescotti relates years later in *Il Palcoscenico*

had gathered in a sumptuous album more than thirty thousand signatures, which they wished to present to Giuseppe Verdi on his name-day [. . .] The representatives of the Genoese press, including the undersigned, had been entrusted with the task of presenting it to the distinguished composer. [. . .] We had been assured that the Maestro would not be at home. However, when we had rung the bell at the Palazzo D'Oria [sic], we learnt from the servant, who opened the door, that Verdi was at home [. . .] We handed the servant our visiting cards, and after a while we were shown into the drawing-room where the distinguished Maestro receives his guests. The room was enormous and grand; what immediately caught the eye were two elegant and artistic pieces of furniture, antique in style, but light and glass-fronted, in which I admired a profusion of gold, silver and filigree crowns, and a vast and varied collection of innumerable precious gifts. Beyond them, on *étagères* and little tables, lay albums and souvenirs of every kind that testified to the glorious career of the distinguished Maestro [. . .]. Next to the fireplace, on one side of which stood a magnificent, open Japanese screen, were some delightful armchairs of damask cloth, arranged in a semi-circle around a tiny lacquered table. We were feasting our eyes on every object in that drawing-room, when a door to the right opened and Giuseppe Verdi appeared and came smiling towards us, stretching out his hand with unaffected naturalness.[1]

The visit therefore took place on March 19, Saint Joseph's day, 1887. Verdi had in fact returned to Genoa on March 2 from Milan, where on February 5 the world première of *Otello* had been given at La Scala. Indeed it was *Otello*, and even more the alleged *Iago*, that was the topic of conversation during that visit. When between 1881 and 1882 the press first began to gossip about the new opera that Verdi was composing to a libretto by Boito taken from Shakespeare's *Othello*, the opera was being christened *Iago* rather than *Otello*. And *Iago* was still the topic of discussion in the spring of 1884, on the occasion of the famous interview with Boito by a Neapolitan journalist, that was published in the *Roma* of May 24[2] and reported by other periodicals, and caused such a misunderstanding between composer and librettist that the composition of the opera[3] seemed jeopardized:

> Questioned about *Iago* which he [Boito] had written for Verdi, Boito mentioned how at first he had been unwilling to tackle such a theme, but that when the libretto was completed he felt sad that he himself would not be the composer destined to set the work to music.

Iago was the title (as we see from Marescotti's article) that the composer of *Mefistofele* had at the outset proposed giving the opera, either to highlight the dominant position of Iago in the drama (à propos the finale of act 3 he had written to Verdi on 24 August 1881: "*The main lyrical role is that of Desdemona, the main dramatic role that of Iago*"),[4] or else to underline perhaps the new character that the drama was acquiring, as it was transformed from Shakespeare's tragedy into opera. But as early as 16 August 1882, in his reply to Boito about a request from Blaze de Bury, Verdi was objecting, albeit in parenthesis, to the title of *Iago*:

> Un jour ou l'autre Iago (*not Iago*) existera . . . *This confidence of the Baron's surprises me, because I . . . I personally do not know if it* existera.[5]

More than three years later , on 21 January 1886, he was again writing to Boito:

> *All this talking and writing about* Iago*!!! I reply in vain that* Otello, pas Iago, n'est pas fini, *but they go on writing and talking about* Iago, Iago!! [. . .] – Iago, *it is true, is the devil, the driving force; but it is* Otello *who acts* = He loves, he is jealous, he kills and kills himself. *It would therefore seem hypocritical of me not call the work* Otello. *I'd sooner people say* "He wanted to do battle with the giant but was crushed" *rather than* "He wished to hide behind the title Iago. – *If you agree, let us begin to baptize the work* Otello, *and inform Giulio immediately.*[6]

And Giulio Ricordi, taking the opportunity of denying that there was any news regarding singers' contracts at La Scala for Verdi's new opera, immediately set about baptizing the work not *Iago*, but *Otello*.[7]

A visit to Verdi

Genoa, 26 March 1887

On Saturday the 19th, commissioned by the Melzi of Milan, I arrived at about two o'clock with three other journalists, Panizzardi, Scolari and Guastavino, at the Palazzo Doria where, as you know, Maestro Verdi is living, in order to present him with a sumptuous album, bound in red leather with most beautiful gilt edges and a raised coat of arms between the initials of the distinguished composer of *Otello*; this album contained more than thirty thousand signatures, gathered from all over Italy, with the help of a good many Maestri, by the Melzi who now very kindly wished to dedicate the book to the great man on his name-day.

We were welcomed by the illustrious composer with the utmost affability in the grand, enormous drawing-room where he receives guests. He was much moved, and having thanked us for the Italians' expression of admiration, which he termed greater than his own merits, he conversed with us about art, literature and journalism. The subject of *Otello* was then raised, and while we, confused by the great emotion we felt, could not find words to express our admiration, he interrupted us and said:

"But what have I in fact achieved? . . . it is nothing less than my profession. I write music, just as you gentlemen write articles."

And when asked about the story that Tom (Checchi) of the *Fanfulla* had circulated concerning the second opera *Iago*, which according to Checchi had been composed at the same period as the recently staged *Otello*,[8] Verdi smiled and with the utmost affability replied:

"Mere tales; there's not the slightest truth in such an assertion. One opera on one libretto is quite enough – even that is too much. He must be quite ignorant of the first elements of music to spread such rumours. It's clear that this Signor Checchi needed twenty lines or so to fill his newspaper column. But the misunderstanding most probably arose from Boito's indecision in naming his libretto, which he had originally wished to call *Iago*. But then, why *Iago* rather than *Otello*, which after all was Shakespeare's title? Besides, if in the drama Iago is the devil, the driving force, it is Otello who acts, and the dramatic action must of course be named after him."

When asked whether he intended to rest on his laurels, he replied with that sweet and lovable smile:

"I shall now enjoy absolute rest. I am 74 and, as you see, no longer young and . . . after all, I think I have some right to rest."

We then asked him if the newspaper stories were true, which claimed that he was composing something for the children of Busseto, and he replied, still smiling,

"I would do anything for those dear children, except write music. Rest, absolute rest . . ."

As we took our leave from him, he shook us heartily by the hand, and we could only repeat:

"Maestro, of all our days in journalism this is the finest, and one which we shall not forget."

And there are those who say that Verdi is ill-tempered, wild, almost unmanageable. No unfairer accusation than this was ever levelled at the great Maestro, who is sweetness and kindness personified.

Ercole Arturo Marescotti

NOTES

1. From *Il Palcoscenico*, 22 October 1900, *art. cit.*
2. Reprinted in *Carteggio Verdi-Boito*, cit., pp. 320–1.
3. Cf. *Carteggio Verdi-Boito*, cit., pp. 69–76 and 319–22.

4. *Ibid.*, p. 58.
5. *Ibid.*, p. 65.
6. *Ibid.*, pp. 99–100.
7. Cf. a short article, signed G.R., published in the *Gazzetta Musicale di Milano*, XLI, 4: 25 January 1886, p. 28, and reprinted in *Carteggio Verdi-Boito*, cit., p. 339.
8. In the Roman newspaper *Fanfulla* an article had appeared in the edition of 15–16 March, signed by *Tom*, the pseudonym of Eugenio Checchi, entitled *Il nuovo Iago di Verdi*, including alleged gossip on the two musical versions of *Otello*. He claimed that Verdi had set Boito's libretto twice; that one opera was entitled *Iago*, the second *Otello*; that it was in *Iago* that the Maestro's hand was most clearly in evidence, and that it was the composer's intention to stage the opera in the winter of 1888 at La Scala. . . .

XXXI

VERDI AT THE OPÉRA

1879–1887

A. DE LAUZIÈRES-THÉMINES: "Verdi à l'Opéra", in *Le Figaro*, Paris, 17 September 1887.

THIS ARTICLE CONTAINS a brief description of a conversation with Verdi in Paris between March and April 1886 (see NN. XXIV and XXV) and, still more interesting, a description of a visit to Sant'Agata with Vaucorbeil in September 1879 to obtain the composer's permission to perform *Aida* in French at the Opéra: a much more detailed account than de Lauzières' first version, published in *Le Figaro* on his return from Sant'Agata (see N. XVIII). In the present article there is a reference to the terrible fire, which on the evening of 25 May 1887 destroyed the Salle Favart, at that time the home of the Opéra-Comique, claiming around 400 victims. The Opéra-Comique was compelled to move temporarily to the Théâtre-Lyrique in Place du Châtelet, until the third Salle Favart was opened in December 1898. After the fire a Comité de la Presse was formed, presided over by the editor of *Le Rappel*, Vacquerie, who organized a concert at the Opéra for the benefit of the victims, in which Victor Maurel, leading baritone at the Opéra, took part. For this occasion Maurel wished to perform the "Credo" from *Otello*, for which Verdi's permission had to be sought. The composer replied to Vacquerie on May 30 with the following telegram:

> *Maurel is mistaken. It is an error to sing this piece at a concert and in a foreign language. But given the circumstances I cannot refuse. I shall write as much to Ricordi, but he as the actual owner might withhold his permission.*[1]

The piece was not performed, as Boito informed Verdi in a letter, dated June 9:

> *I was pleased to hear that Iago's Credo will not appear in the programme at the Opéra. It would have been a grave error.*[2]

Verdi always refused to stage *Otello* in Paris, before it could be performed in a French translation, and with a suitable company; and that was not until 12 October 1894.

Verdi at the Opéra

Will Verdi's *Otello* be performed here in Paris? And if so, where, when and how will it be performed? All these questions are put to me, under the pretext that I did my best to get *Aida* performed at the Opéra – but I shall take good care not to answer them in detail, probably because I have no answers.

Except that I know that if it is given, it will be at the Opéra, unless it is performed elsewhere. To be sure, I was not even certain about the Opéra a short while ago, and this is why:

The last time Verdi came to Paris[3] (he had not quite completed *Otello*, though very little remained for him to do), I wanted to spy out the land. The Maestro's replies were very evasive. He first of all told me that, having shaped his music to Boito's vigorous and Dantesque verse, he feared that in a French translation this subtle, vigorous, even slightly harsh language would grow slack.[4] I did my utmost to overcome this fear, which must by now have been allayed: for the translation has been carried out beneath the eyes of the Italian poet, with his agreement and almost with his collaboration.[5]

But the Maestro hesitated even more when faced with the choice of one or other of our two great opera houses.[6] "My opera," Verdi told me, "is a drama of passion, not a spectacle; it is almost an intimate drama. I even intend to reduce the size of the La Scala stage for the last act. I fear that the Opéra stage will be too vast for *Otello*." It would have been easier for me to reply to this objection, if I had not been aware of or sensed in the Maestro an even greater fear: namely that he would be asked to compose the inevitable *divertisse-ment* and dance music.[7] When the libretto could accommodate it, as in *Les vêpres siciliennes* or *Don Carlos* – a work, this latter which the Académie de Musique were wrong to drop from their repertoire[8] – he willingly consented; but when the libretto was originally con-ceived without a *divertissement*, and a *divertissement* was none the less insisted upon, he would be insistent. The Italian word *appiccicato* is even more expressive.

It is well-known how difficult it was to persuade Verdi to extend –

and not by much – the dance music in *Aida*.[9] As for *Rigoletto*,[10] apart from the brief little dance tune for the merry-making at the end of act I, he wondered with reason where an excuse for dancing could be found.

However, everything appeared to sort itself out; appeared to, I say. The Opéra would stage *Otello*. The question of the principal singers then arose. Mme Caron's contract had not been renewed, and it was to her that the Maestro, it was said, had assigned the role of Desdemona.[11] I confess with all due deference that I did not see in this a serious obstacle. Had Verdi seen a means of escape that he wished to turn to his own advantage? I dare not assert such a thing; but the fact remains, that a thorough search of the Opéra company would have revealed a singer, who would have sung the role at least as well as Mme Pantaleoni, who created the part in Milan.

I have no scruples about insinuating that the Maestro, still haunted by the fears, more or less founded, that I mentioned above, would have decided in favour of the Opéra-Comique. They would engage Mme Caron, Maurel would be readily available, Talazac[12] would make an excellent Otello. So much for the three main roles. The others are all less important. But though this had been mere supposition on my part, the fire at the theatre reduced it to nothing,[13] or at least postponed the outcome indefinitely.

As regards insinuations, however, there is one thing that I would like to put straight, and it concerns those individuals who judge questions of art according to Roger's account books.[14] They seem to state that Verdi would be proud and happy to give *Otello* at the Opéra, because of the fine royalties that the work would bring him there. I shall not allow myself to insult Verdi by defending him. I shall merely recall that *Otello* has already been performed in several theatres abroad,[15] and with success; that it is about to be performed on many other stages (so much for *amour-propre*), and that Verdi possesses as many rich farms on his vast estate of Sant'Agata as the operas he has written (so much for the question of money). And if that is not sufficient, let it be remembered how very difficult it was to persuade him to give *Aida* at the Opéra.

Poor Vaucorbeil,[16] when I suggested that he should accompany me to Busseto, hesitated greatly. He feared a refusal. It is true that his fears were more than founded by a very explicit letter that our papers had published and which made it absolutely clear that Verdi never intended to have any further dealings with the Opéra. He needed to be accompanied at sword-point to Busseto. At the Gare de Lyon he asked me yet again if his presence there was really necessary.[17]

When we arrived at Sant'Agata, he did not wish the coachman, who had driven us to the Maestro's estate from the station, to drive away. He did not even have our two suitcases unloaded. "Verdi," he said, "might suspect the aim of our visit and leave a message that he has gone away." I began to laugh but he still persisted.

We entered the beautiful garden which leads to the villa. Verdi came towards us with open arms . . . and his customary expression. I introduced Vaucorbeil. He showed us our rooms, had our luggage brought up, and as it was six o'clock in the evening, informed us that dinner would be soon. Half an hour later we were at table.

Aida, of course, was not discussed during the entire dinner, even though the Maestro could have no doubt about the reason for our journey. Besides, M. Muzio must have wired him. We talked about a great variety of topics, even music.

Very early the next morning I heard a knock at my door. I was already up. It was Verdi offering me a cup of black coffee, made – without playing on words – by his own Maestro's hand. He then said: "Let us go down into the garden, we can talk more easily there."

And there, sitting in front of a beautiful grotto completely covered with greenery, we began to discuss *Aida*. At first I found Verdi quite determined to refuse permission. For each reason he put forward to explain his decision, I did my utmost to find a counter-argument. The conversation lasted for several quarters of an hour, and I was afraid that I was going to experience Rabelais'.[18]

Vaucorbeil's arrival accelerated proceedings. As we saw him emerge from a path, Verdi said "There he is; am I to tell him yes?" – "Of course," I replied. He then got up, and moving resolutely towards his guest, he spoke the following words: "Vaucorbeil, I've slept on it: *Aida* is yours."

Vaucorbeil's only reply was to throw his arms round the Maestro's neck.

"Let us now talk seriously," said Verdi, taking hold of Vaucorbeil's arm.

My mission was complete. I left them to talk and went to wish Mme Verdi good morning, who seemed astonished when I told her that her husband had finally decided to offer his work to the Director of the Opéra.

When we took our leave, the Maestro had not decided which artist would sing the role of Aida. It was a long time since he had heard Mme Krauss.[19] He hesitated, but when he came to Paris and heard her in *Der Freischütz*, he was won over, without her suspecting his presence in the theatre.

Aida has long since received over two hundred peformances at the Opéra. Just work out the royalties which Verdi receives in their entirety, since the libretto in both French and Italian versions belong to him – not to mention the honours that have been conferred on him, such as his promotion to the rank of Grand-officier de la Légion d'honneur, and the golden crown presented to him by the Italian community in Paris etc., etc!

And to think that I had so much difficulty in persuading him to part with his *Aida*!

I hope it is now clear that it will never be financial profit that will decide him to give *Otello* in France.

As for conducting the orchestra himself, should he decide to stage *Otello* in Paris, he told me he would not have conducted *Aida*, if Faure [*sic*: he clearly means Faccio!], who was very familiar with the tempi, had been present.

Is Vianesi[20] familiar with the tempi of *Otello*? I do not know. My impression is, though, that Verdi will give his new opera at the Académie de Musique, but not conduct the performances. But it is not my responsibility. Once those gentlemen Ritt and Gailhard[21] have made up their minds, they will not relent. But that point has not yet been reached.

A. DE LAUZIÈRES-THÉMINES

NOTES

1. Cf. *Carteggio Verdi-Boito*, cit., p. 368.
2. *Ibid.*, p. 125.
3. Between the end of March and the first few days of April 1886; see NN. XXV and XXVI.
4. In the letter to Boito of 16 August 1882, cit., in note 5 of N. XXV, Verdi wrote of the difficulty of translating the libretto of *Otello* into French:

> *We use blank verse, and they, being obliged to use alternating masculine and feminine rhyming couplets, will be virtually unable to preserve the literal sense, especially with the music's accents and phrasing. In this connection I said a few weeks ago to a translator of one of my operas: "Why do you*

translate the recitatives and dramatic moments in rhyming verse?"
*But the nature of their poetry does not permit them – or at least no one dares –
to write blank verse.*

5. The translation had been completed the previous April (cf. *Carteggio
   Verdi-Boito*, cit., pp. 121–4 and 361–2); cf. N. XXVI, note 10.
6. The Opéra (or Académie de Musique) and the Opéra-Comique.
7. Cf. N. XXVI, note 9.
8. After 43 performances, *Don Carlos* disappeared from the Opéra's
   repertoire, and did not return until about a century later . . . on
   8 March 1963.
9. Cf. N. XXVI, note 8.
10. *Rigoletto* had already been given in Italian at the Théâtre Italien in Paris
    on 19 January 1857, and then in French at the Théâtre Lyrique on
    24 December 1863; it was performed for the first time at the Opéra on
    27 February 1885, naturally in French translation.
11. Cf. N. XXVI, note 16.
12. Cf. N. XXVI, note 18.
13. See introduction to this article.
14. Roger was the general agent in France of the Société des Auteurs et
    Compositeurs Dramatiques.
15. When this article was written, *Otello* had not yet been performed
    abroad: after the performances at La Scala, it was given at Rome's
    Costanzi theatre (16 April 1887), La Fenice in Venice (May 17),
    Brescia's Grande (August 11) and Parma's Regio (September 13). The
    first performances abroad – apart from a pirate edition of an adulterated
    score at City of Mexico on 18 November 1887 – took place simul-
    taneously on 8 December 1887 in Budapest and St Petersburg.
16. He had died on 2 November 1884.
17. For this visit to Sant'Agata, which took place on 3–4 October 1879, see
    also Lauzières' previous article in N. XX.
18. "Le quart d'heure de Rabelais" means the bad moment when the bill is
    presented, and, by extension, the unpleasant final moment of anything.
    The expression does not occur in Rabelais but in an eighteenth-century
    anecdote about his inability to pay the bill in an inn where he was
    staying. [Translator's note]
19. Gabrielle Krauss (Vienna 1842 – Paris 1906), a pupil of Mathilde
    Marchesi, had made her début at the Vienna Opera in 1859, remaining
    there till 1867, when she moved to the Théâtre Italien, where she made
    her début on 6 April 1867 in *Il trovatore*. At the outbreak of the Franco-
    Prussian war, she sang in Italy (at La Scala and elsewhere, giving the
    first performances there of *Lohengrin* and Gomes' *Fosca*). She
    returned to the Théâtre Italien in 1873, and two years later moved to the
    Opéra, where she virtually ended her career in 1887.
20. Augusto Vianesi (Leghorn 1827–New York 1908), a celebrated conduc-
    tor, active for several years at London's Drury Lane, then at Moscow,

St Petersburg, Madrid, Trieste (first performance there of *Tannhäuser* in 1878); he finally returned to London as successor to Michael Costa at Covent Garden. After a period of activity in the United States, he was appointed Principal Conductor of the Opéra in the summer of 1887 (making his début on July 1 in *Les Huguenots*), a post he held till 1891.

21. Co-Directors of the Opéra.

XXXII

A VISIT TO VERDI

1890

ÉTIENNE DESTRANGES: "Une visite à Verdi", in *Le Monde Artiste*, Paris, April 1890, republished by the author in his anthology: *Consonnances et Dissonnances: Études musicales*, Libr. Fischbacher, Paris, 1906, pp. 465–8 (reprinted in *Carteggio Verdi-Boito*, cit., pp. 395–8).

CONNECTED WITH THIS interview is a letter from Boito to Verdi, dated 7 April 1890:

Today or tomorrow a certain Signor Rouillé-Destranges will arrive in Genoa – a Frenchman, but one of the nice ones, who gave me proof of his most unselfish warmth, when Mefistofele *was performed at Nantes;[1] I do not know him personally, only through correspondence; but from his letters I have become aware of the man's goodness. It is this gentleman's fervent wish to meet you, that is, to be admitted for a few minutes into your drawing-room at the Palazzo Doria. One hundred individuals must have asked me this favour, and I have refused them all. But I haven't the heart to say no to this good Frenchman. He has nothing to ask you, he merely wishes to pay his respects; I do not know whether he is a musician, but I know that he has a deep and broad knowledge in matters of art. I beg you to tell me, either by letter or note, whether I may inform Signor Rouillé-Destranges that his request has been granted. Should the answer be yes, I shall wire him the good news at the Hôtel de la Ville (where he will be from today or tomorrow). I believe he will be staying in Genoa for several days.[2]*

Verdi – who from Boito's description was expecting a courtesy visit and not an interview – replied laconically on April 8: "Send the Frenchman whenever you like."[3] The interview, as will be seen from the final paragraph of Destranges' account, created quite a stir in France and elsewhere. Verdi, moreover, must have been both surprised and bitter to have read in the press several statements that he had made to a "French gentleman" who, according to Boito, had "nothing to ask *him* and "merely wished to pay *him* his respects" . . .

(And who knows whether the tone of the following note, sent by Verdi to Boito and bearing no date, is not connected with Verdi's bitter surprise: "If you are passing the Hôtel de Milan, and should care to climb the stairs . . . Read the enclosed article – I only send it to tell you to take the necessary precautions, when you next speak to that gentleman whom you introduced to me. Superfluous to tell you that everything in that article is distorted.")[4]

Étienne Rouillé-Destranges (Nantes 1863–1915) was a music critic who espoused the Wagnerian movement from its very outset. In his native town, where he worked as a journalist, he founded the review *L'Ouest-Artiste*, in 1890, wrote for the *Guide Musical* and the *Monde Artiste* and published numerous articles of music criticism, particularly on Wagner, and more than twenty thematic opera guides. One of these publications, a small work which first appeared in serial form in *L'Ouest-Artiste*, deserves mention: *L'Evolution Musicale Chez Verdi: Aida – Otello – Falstaff*, Libr. Fischbacher, Paris 1895; it concludes with these words:

> Wagner has greatly influenced Verdi – of that there can be no doubt – but he has influenced him beneficially. He has not destroyed the Italian Maestro's personality by causing him to compose in servile imitation, which is fatal for true art. If Wagner had not existed, Verdi would certainly not have written *Aida*, *Otello* and *Falstaff* – which is not to say that *Aida*, *Otello* and *Falstaff* are Wagnerian works; they are more, they are masterpieces in different genres.
>
> Of the operas prior to *Aida*, a few beautiful pages will survive, but no complete score. This will not be the fate of his last three operas. These constitute Verdi's true claim to lasting glory.

A prophecy which complements a critical comment, made fifteen years later by Giannotto Bastianelli, who passes this judgement on the art of Verdi:

> always primitive in content, though often perfect in form, profoundly sensual with dazzling colours and a somewhat florid sentimentality, but often frank and sincere – it is an art already perhaps in its decline, but not destined to oblivion. It deserves to be rigorously, dispassionately edited to be included in a sort of anthology, containing the finest pages of our nineteenth-century composers [. . .].[5]

We quote here the 1906 reprint of the interview with Verdi, together with Destranges' brief introduction and his final note (both in italics), which discusses the controversy his article aroused.

A visit to Verdi

During April 1890,[1] when travelling in Italy, I was given the opportunity of paying a visit to Verdi. As soon as I had left the home of the composer of Falstaff, I ran to scribble down the account of my interview and dispatched it to the "Monde-Artiste". Here is that article:

Last week, when passing through Genoa, I learned that Verdi had not yet departed for his villa at Sant'Agata. This time I took care not to let slip the opportunity of seeing the famous composer.

I am far from being a follower of the Italian school and many of the works of Verdi himself have a particular knack of getting on my nerves. Nonetheless I profess, in spite of everything, a sincere and profound admiration for the musician who, having written *Nabuco* [sic], *Il trovatore* and *Ernani* could compose *Aida* and *Otello*; and for the artist who, having scaled the heights of his profession, at least in his own country, did not rest on his laurels, as sadly Gounod has done in France. Verdi openly recognized that, while he was writing with great natural facility so many scores, which have for the most part already been forgotten, art had taken great strides forwards along the new path opened up by the Bayreuth Titan's genius. The composer of *Rigoletto* did not shrink from this fact. Without hesitating he set to work again, *mugged up* with a most youthful enthusiasm the new treatises on harmony and instrumentation, studied assiduously the scores of the great German masters, partially re-educated himself and finally, to the amazement of the musical world, composed *Aida*. Anyone who offers such an example of artistic conscience is no ordinary man, and although he belongs to a different school, one has absolutely no reservation in bowing respectfully before him.

A recommendation from M. Arrigo Boito, the composer of *Mefistofele*, opened for me the door of the Maestro's home.

Throughout the winter Verdi lives in Genoa, occupying part of the first floor of the beautiful Palazzo Doria. At first one enters a vast ante-chamber, whose walls are hung with colour prints, modestly framed, of the type that English newspapers offer as free gifts to their subscribers. I then passed into the very tall drawing-room, decorated with a beautiful ceiling and lit by large windows, which open on to a terrace that overlooks the Palace gardens and offers a splendid view of the harbour. While I waited for the composer, I quickly examined the drawing-room: red curtains, gilt chairs, mantelpiece ornaments in gilded bronze, two or three pieces of Boule furniture, and finally, in a corner, a couch with a cushion, tapestried in garish colours and representing a pheasant. Oh, such a cushion would tempt a country priest!! Everything in this room breathes an atmosphere of profound bourgeois luxury. How different from the majestic severity of *Wahnfried*, the great artistic order of Gounod's residence, the picturesque, oriental jumble of Reyer's bachelor abode! To the left of the fire-place, Verdi's innumerable decorations are displayed in a glass case, containing souvenirs of very different kinds: medals, laurel crowns in gold or silver, with the names of his operas engraved on the leaves, a conductor's baton in ivory, and finally the magnificent sceptre of ivory and gold, adorned with precious stones, which was presented to the composer at the première of *Aida* in Milan.

Verdi appeared. He carries his sixty-seven years lightly. He holds himself erect, his beard and hair are not yet entirely white. The face is intelligent, expressive, rather Olympian; his very broad forehead is deeply lined. As he looks today, the great Italian composer bears a striking resemblance to Victor Hugo around 1875.

I was accorded a most sincere and warm welcome.

"And Saint-Saëns?" Verdi asked me after several minutes' conversation.

I did not, of course, give him any precise information.[7]

"He must be mentally ill! An artist such as he cannot dissociate himself like that from his own work, the daughter of his own thought! It is not human nature. I do not know M. Guiraud;[8] he is said to be a man of talent, but he cannot have replaced the composer entirely." *

I longed, however, to broach a more interesting topic.

"And *Romeo and Juliet*, Maestro, when will that be finished?"[9]

"Never!"

"But it has been said . . ."

---

* *Ascanio* had just been given at the Opéra and *Samson et Dalila* for the first time in France, at Rouen. Saint-Saëns was away on his travels, but no one really knew where. [Author's note]

"Nothing but gossip that I don't even bother to deny. I can assure you that *Otello* is my final work. The decision is irrevocable. At my age, you see, it is better to be silent. I have made up my mind. My task is finished.[10] I leave the stage and become, in turn, a member of the audience. And yet *Romeo*! What a tempting subject! I envisage the work, I live this work. It is there in my head. Background: hatred, bloody strife between Montagues and Capulets. Foreground: the tragic love of the two children. Then there's the entire comic side, which Gounod ignored. "I would have wanted to create a more spirited work with greater contrasts, not a long duet."

Verdi had grown excited, but quickly regained his customary calm.

"What point is there in telling you all that, since I shall not write *Romeo and Juliet*."

"But you are dying to."

"I am too old. And then, I should hate to distract Boito from his *Nerone*. It's time he finished it."

"Shall we at least have *Otello* in Paris?"

"I doubt it. Brussels is more likely.[12] Ritt and Gailhard have delayed too long, and also I would have wanted Mme Caron. I heard this artist in a great and beautiful work, *Sigurd*. Both music and singer made a profound impression upon me. Yes, Mme Caron would make a beautiful Desdemona!"

The name of Ambroise Thomas was mentioned in the course of our conversation . . .

"And his *Tempête*?"[13] Verdi asked.

"Very poor, a deserved flop."

"What do you expect? He is old like me, and finished."

"With this difference, Maestro, that you compose *Otello*, and he writes *Françoise de Rimini*[14] and *La Tempête*."

"Well, there are several beautiful things in *Françoise*. But fancy tackling Dante! and with such a libretto!!! My favourite work of Thomas is *Mignon*. As for *Hamlet*,[15] most of it is not successful. If you wish to set Shakespeare you must not hesitate, as the French say, to take the bull by the horns. What musical situations there are in *Hamlet*, and how I would have loved to tackle them."[16]

"There is still time."

"You are forgetting my age. I do not forget."

And so the conversation continued, jumping from one subject to another, but always returning to the art of music. At one moment I steered it towards Wagner. I was curious to know what Verdi thought about the composer of *Parsifal*. The aged composer replied in just two words: "Ah him!" uttered in the tone one uses, when talking of giants like Bach or Beethoven.

Verdi is charmingly unsophisticated. Unlike so many others, he neither poses nor pontificates. The two hours I spent in his company seemed very short, and I shall preserve an excellent memory of them.

This article caused a stir that I hardly expected. The leading newspapers of France, Germany, Italy, England and even America printed it with passionate comments.[17]

In France the press treated Verdi very harshly, accusing him of insulting French composers.

I protested in "Le Monde Artiste" against these malicious insinuations, and I still consider it good to protest against them today.

In my opinion, the Italian composer felt no animosity or petty jealousy towards his French colleagues. To find Roméo a little monotonous is not to insult Gounod. Rossini, on the other hand, was much harsher when he said of this work: "It is a duet in three parts: one before, one during and one after."[18] With regard to Ambroise Thomas, the French press – most of whom suppressed a vital part of the phrase – reproached Verdi, in varying degrees of bitterness for having described Thomas as "finished".

Now, Verdi, when he said "he is old like me and finished", certainly had no intention of insulting the composer of Mignon.

As for Saint-Saëns, the illustrious old Verdi had uttered these words: An artist such as he! *in such an admiring tone, that there could have been no doubt about his feelings for the composer of* Samson et Dalila.

While the French press accused Verdi of vilifying our musical glories, the Italian press claimed that I had insulted their most famous contemporary composer, because the drawing-room in the Palazzo Doria had struck me as bourgeois!

But that was the period of tense Franco-Italian relations, when journalists of both countries sought every opportunity of exacerbating national hatred.

Since then everything has changed.

ÉTIENNE DESTRANGES

NOTES

1. In April 1887.
2. *Carteggio Verdi-Boito*, cit., p. 168.
3. *Ibid.*, p. 168.

4. *Ibid.*, p. 281.
5. G. BASTIANELLI: *Pietro Mascagni*, Ricciardi, Naples 1910, p. 6.
6. The visit must have taken place between approximately 10–14 April 1890, i.e. after Verdi's reply to Boito (April 8) and before Boito's letter to the composer (April 15), thanking him for having "courteously received" the Frenchman he had "recommended".
7. At that time Saint-Saëns had practically disappeared from circulation, and no one had news of him. The death of his mother in December 1880 had demoralized him so profoundly that, leaving Paris on medical advice for a while, he took refuge in Algeria. On his return to Paris, his depression worsened considerably; he removed all the furniture from his apartment, that caused painful memories, and leaving all his artistic belongings in Dieppe, he set out on a long voyage in Spain, and then the Canary Islands (where he was during Destranges' stay in Italy), leaving his friend Guiraud to supervise the rehearsals of *Ascanio*, which was premièred at the Opéra on 21 March 1890. A few weeks earlier, on March 3, *Samson et Dalila* had been performed for the first time in France, at Rouen.
8. Ernest Guiraud (New Orleans 1837 – Paris 1892), composer and author of a treatise on instrumentation, is well-known for having composed the recitatives of Bizet's *Carmen*, and completed the orchestration of Offenbach's *Les contes d'Hoffmann*.
9. The press had spread rumours several months earlier of a future *Giuletta e Romeo* by Verdi. To Waldmann, who had asked for confirmation of the rumours, the composer gave the following reply in January: "*Don Chisciotte, Giulietta e Romeo* and *Re Lear* sleep the sleep of the righteous.*"
   (F. ABBIATI, *op. cit.*, IV, p. 395.)
10. Verdi does not reveal that in early July he had resolved to compose *Falstaff* . . . (cf. *Carteggio Verdi-Boito*, cit., pp. 142–7). But this was still a secret between him, Boito and Giuseppina . . . On 10 July 1889 he wrote to Boito:

    I too wish to keep this a most strictly guarded secret – a word that I too underline three times, to tell you that no one must know anything! But shh! . . . Peppina, I think, knew before we did . . . But don't worry: she will keep the secret; when women have this quality they have it in greater measure than we.

    News of a *Falstaff* by Verdi only became common knowledge in November 1890 (cf. introduction to N. XXXV).
11. Having been performed at the Théâtre Lyrique in 1867, Gounod's *Roméo et Juliette* was given at the Opéra, with the addition of a ballet, on 28 November 1888.
12. Where Rose Caron, destined by Verdi to become the first French Desdemona, was then engaged, and where Gevaert, much respected by

Verdi, was working. But it was not until 1902 that *Otello* was performed in French, at La Monnaie in Brussels.

13. *La Tempête*, fantastical ballet in three acts on a theme taken by Jules Barbier from Shakespeare's play, the last work for the theatre by Ambroise Thomas, had been performed at the Opéra on 26 June 1889.

14. *Françoise de Rimini*, taken from Dante by J. Barbier and Carré, had been staged at the Opéra on 14 April 1882. A few days later, on 29 May 1882, Verdi had written about it to Ferdinand Hiller:

> *But I have been several times to the Opéra to hear works I did not know. In* Francesca da Rimini *there is a most beautiful prologue of excellent quality, and the last act, too, is good. All the rest is done with great, even too great, care, but is of little interest.* (Autograph: Historisches Archiv, Cologne.)

15. Also by Thomas, to a libretto by Barbier and Carré, premièred at the Opéra on 9 March 1868.

16. Shakespeare's *Hamlet* is second on the list of *Opera Subjects* (after *King Lear* and before *The Tempest*), drawn up by Verdi on the verso of a page from the autograph *Copialettere*, dating from about 1849 (see introduction to N. III). On 17 June 1850, the composer wrote to Giulio Carcano, playwright and translator of Shakespeare:

> *I would dearly like to associate my name with yours, since I know that if you are proposing I should compose* Hamlet, *the adaptation will be worthy of you. Unfortunately, these vast subjects demand too much time, and I have also had to postpone* King Lear *for the time being* [. . .]. *Now, if* King Lear *is difficult,* Hamlet *is even more so* [. . .] (*I Copialettere di G. Verdi*, cit., p. 482).

According to Luzio, it was in deference to Thomas, that Verdi abandoned the project, cherished for so long, of composing *Hamlet* "with the greatest of respect for Shakespeare's magnificent conception". (A. LUZIO: *Carteggi verdiani*, cit., II, p. 52, note). When he heard about the imminent performance of Thomas' opera, Verdi wrote to Escudier on 14 January 1868, requesting information:

> *How is* Hamlet *going? Is it true they've inserted two ballets?* Hamlet *and dance tunes!! How incongruous! Poor Shakespeare!* (Autograph: Bibliothèque de l'Opéra, Paris.)

Having received the libretto, he once again wrote to Escudier, on March 12:

> *I've read the libretto of* Hamlet. *Impossible to do worse. Poor Shakespeare! How they have ill-treated him! Only the scene between Hamlet and the*

Queen succeeds – it is both theatrical and suitable for setting to music. The rest . . . Amen. (Autograph: Bibliothèque de l'Opéra, Paris.)

And two days later to Du Locle:

Thank you for the news and the libretto of Hamlet. *Poor Shakespeare! How they have ill-treated him! And what have they done to that great and original character of Hamlet? And where is that grandeur, that breadth, that sublime rarefied and strange atmosphere one breathes when reading the English* Hamlet? . . . *This libretto seems an* opéra comique *that takes itself seriously. Thomas has achieved a great deal if he has had a success with a libretto that is wholly unsuccessful, apart from the Act 3 duet between Hamlet and the Queen, which is well handled.* (Autograph: Bibliothèque de l'Opéra, Paris.)

17. The *Gazzetta Musicale di Milano* ignored Destranges' article and the subsequent polemics; but the following short article, published without a signature and bearing the title *Pleasant reading* (XLV, 19: 11 May 1890, p. 301), seems to reflect the dispute:

A so-called arts journal, which calls itself *Monde Artiste*, would like to involve us in a disgraceful polemic, quite foreign to our newspaper and even more so to our readers, who are educated people with absolutely no interest in the words of writers who to us seem drunkards! The *Monde Artiste* threatens to continue its abuse: to them it is a diversion like any other, and everyone will have their own amusements – we certainly do not wish to descend to their level, for fear of soiling ourselves with filth. Continue, then, for as long as you will, we shall take care not to lose time by replying. And bray away in every edition, if you wish – heaven will not harken to a donkey's braying.

18. For a precise statement, made by Verdi several years later, concerning his opinion of Gounod's *Roméo et Juliette* that he expressed during Destranges' interview, see N. XL.

XXXIII

VERDI ON MASCAGNI

1892

HEINRICH EHRLICH: "Verdi über Mascagni", in *Berliner Tageblatt*, XXI, 208: 25 April 1892 (republished in part in *Die Signale für die musikalische Welt*, Leipzig, 1, 34: May 1892, p. 536; in F. WALLNER-BASTÉ: *Verdi aus der Nähe* [. . .], cit., pp. 313–5).

THIS INTERVIEW DATES back to April 1892, about a year before *Falstaff*. That April witnessed two significant events in Verdi biography. The first concerned the commemoration of the centenary of Rossini's birth, promoted by the Lombard Association of Journalists; invited by the committee and exhorted by the ex-mayor of Milan, Senator Negri, Verdi consented to go to Milan during the great festival, held at La Scala on the evening of April 8, and conduct the "Prayer" from *Mosè*.[1] The second event concerns Hans von Bülow's act of contrition, expressed in a letter, dated April 7, in which the German musician makes amends for his scathing criticism of the *Requiem*, on the eve of its first performance in Milan's St Mark's – a letter to which Verdi replied from Genoa on April 14.[2]

It must, then, have been between these two events or, more likely, immediately after them, that Heinrich Alfred Ehrlich (Vienna 1822 – Berlin 1899), the Austrian musicologist, pianist and composer, visited Verdi. Ehrlich was music critic of the *Berliner Tageblatt* from 1878 to 1898, and of the Berlin magazine *Die Gegenwart* from 1872–1892; he also contributed to other reviews, including *Die neue Berliner Musikzeitung*, the Stuttgart *Deutsche Revue* and the Breslau *Nord und Süd* and was the author of several novels and, above all, books of music criticism, particularly on Wagner. He was also very well informed about the Italian musical scene, which he followed with great interest, periodically visiting the peninsula to assess at first hand the boom of so-called "verismo" opera at the beginning of the 1890s. He was early on attracted to the Wagnerian movement, which he followed assiduously and with conviction, but at the same time he greatly admired the work of Verdi, at least from *Aida* on; above all he admired the Italian composer's unusual capacity for maintaining the independence of his own musical development, despite the fierce arguments on music, which were spreading like wild fire during those years. He attended the première of *Otello* in Milan,[3] and two years later, on the occasion of the Verdi Jubilee, he wrote a short critical biography of the composer, which appeared in *Nord und Süd*,[4] that can be considered as one of the most serious pieces of writing dealing with Verdi's life and work to have appeared up to that time in Germany. Verdi was also interviewed by Ehrlich five years later (see N. XLIII).

Verdi on Mascagni

Genoa, April.

It was with some apprehension that I entered Verdi's drawing-room in the ancient Palazzo Doria. I was excited by many thoughts. How would I find the nearly 79-year-old composer? In the previous year, his bearing had been as erect as in 1887 at the première of *Otello* in Milan, except that his head was slightly bowed. And another year at his age can make a substantial difference. How would I find him today? And lo and behold! The old Maestro came towards me, fresher and stronger than at our last meeting – indeed his head was even more erect. His eyes shone and grew more animated as our conversation progressed.

We discussed every possible musical topic, but I avoided mentioning Mascagni, since I knew from previous occasions that Verdi did not like to be asked his opinion about contemporary composers.* A strange coincidence, however, suddenly brought precisely this very delicate subject to the fore. The Maestro had read about a violinist from Germany, who was winning great success in Milan and other North-Italian cities, but Verdi could not remember his name, which was difficult to pronounce. After many wrong guesses I hit upon Ondricek – and sure enough it was he. I was now obliged to say which school he belonged to, what movement he followed,

---

*Years ago a young Italian author wrote a book about contemporary composers, which he sent to Verdi, requesting his opinion. This the Maestro refused to give: "Musicians cannot judge one another properly. Read what Schumann wrote about Meyerbeer and you will see what I mean" etc. I wrote about this two years ago in *Nord und Süd*, mentioning the author's name and the date of his letter. I can no longer recall them here in Genoa.[5]

and which famous artist he most resembled in tone and interpretation; the Italian newspapers were almost ranking him on a par with Joachim.[6] A whole procession of violinists, past and present, were now mentioned: Bazzini, who had long since exchanged bow for baton at the Milan Conservatoire,[7] Ernst, Vieuxtemps and Sarasate, whom Verdi had heard in Cologne when he conducted his *Requiem* at the festival; finally I enquired about Sivori, who had given many concerts during 1863 in Berlin, both at Court and in the Kroll theatre, and who now lives in Genoa. "He is still playing," said Verdi, "and very well too, despite his age – he must be 74 or 75 years old.[8] He was here as my guest only a few weeks ago and, surrounded by intimate friends, he sent for his violin and amazed us all. Did you know him?"

"Certainly. We gave concerts together in Paris in 1853; he played Gounod's melody on a prelude by Bach, which had then only just been published."

"Ah, you mean the *Ave Maria*?"

"Yes, that's how it was rebaptized, when violinists no longer wished to play it, and sopranos discovered that with harp accompaniment and ecstatic grimaces it made a splendid show-piece. But as I said, in 1853 it was called *Mélodie sur un prélude de Bach*, and I can assure you that at that time it was almost as frenetically applauded as the Intermezzo from Mascagni's *Cavalleria*."[9]

"Ah, Mascagni," exclaimed Verdi, "have you heard *L'amico Fritz*?"

"Certainly; I have written about it too."[10]

"Well, what is your opinion?"

"That Mascagni possesses great dramatic, but no lyric talent."

"Yes," said Verdi with great vigour, "Mascagni possesses a very great talent, he composes and invents with admirable ease, spontaneity and *élan*; but I believe" – and here he spoke somewhat slower – "that we, the old school, from Rossini on, studied music more, acquired a more thorough knowledge of harmony and therefore had at our disposal a greater variety of expression for different situations, without which one runs the risk of employing identical effects for different emotions."

"That is only too true, and *L'amico Fritz* confirms it utterly; even now I cannot forget the strange impression that scene made on me, when the infatuated Suzel runs off in shame after the Rabbi has asked her a particular question, and the orchestra illustrates this emotion with a chromatic passage for trombones and tamtam. But what

amazes me even more is the eternal change of time signature in one
and the same number – have you seen the piano score, Maestro?"

"Certainly!" [11]

"Well, you will remember how on one page you change from
three-four time, to four-four, two-four, three-eight ad infinitum –
almost as in Wagner's deeply tragic *Tristan und Isolde*."

"Even more so. And in *Tristan*, the alternation mirrors the most
terrible and raging (*poignantes*) passions. But in *L'amico Fritz*, in this
picture of rural life (*vie de paysage*),[12] I do not understand such things;
there was one moment, where I held my head in my hands," (Verdi
accompanied these words with the corresponding gesture) "and
asked: Why all this? Nonetheless, he has a very great talent, and has
invented a most effective genre: short operas without pointless longueurs.
Our mistake, you see, was to write interminable, large operas, which had to
fill an entire evening. We were always compelled to consider how we could
fill the four and half hours with music: this meant great choruses, which had
precious little to do with the drama, elaborate scenery, solo arias with all
kinds of incidental episodes – all of which slowed down the action. And now
along comes someone with a one, or two-act opera without all that pompous
nonsense, and the action develops speedily. The composer possesses,
moreover, a great, inventive talent – that was a happy reform, which the
public received enthusiastically."[13]

This pronouncement is so surprisingly modern and accurate, that
it should interest the entire musical world.

HEINRICH EHRLICH

NOTES

1. *Carteggio Verdi-Boito*, cit., p. 420.
2. Partially quoted in note 4 of N. XXII.
3. He reviewed it in *Gegenwart* (XXXI, 8: 19 February 1887, pp. 124–5)
   and then in an article on the development of opera in Italy, that
   appeared in *Nord und Süd* (n. 126, pp. 409–20).
4. Vol. 51, n. 152, 1889, pp. 197–220.
5. The episode, to which Ehrlich refers, is described in a note from his
   portrait of Verdi (see note 4) on p. 216, which we quote here:

   He [Verdi] is excellently informed about German musical life. An
   Italian musicologist, Leopoldo Mastrigli, sent him a book on the
   great composers, requesting his opinion. He replied: "*In matters of*
   music and works about music, I set no store by opinions – neither my own
   nor others. Remember the opinions of Weber, Schumann and Mendelssohn on

Rossini, Meyerbeer and others, and tell me honestly whether you can trust a composer's opinion." And the author of this letter is supposed to know nothing about Wagner?!

The book that the music historian and composer Leopoldo Mastrigli (Albano Laziale 1856 – Lausanne 1914) sent to Verdi for his opinion was, in all probability, *Gli uomini illustri nella musica da Guido d'Arezzo fino ai contemporanei. Cenni storico-biografici. Materiale pratico ad uso degl'istituti, delle scuole, dei collegi e delle famiglie,* published by Paravia in 1883. The handbook was a great success and went into a second edition at the end of the year (dictionaries are wrong to assign the second edition to 1886). Verdi's letter, quoted above by Ehrlich, was published in E. CHECCHI, *Giuseppe Verdi,* cit., p. 109, and bears the date: "Sant'Agata, 20 October 1883".

6. František Ondříček (Prague 1859 – Milan 1922) was at that time completing a tour of Italy: on March 22 he had given a concert in Milan with resounding success. His father and uncle were violinists, and he was a pupil, first at the Prague Conservatoire, then with J-L Massart in Paris, making his début as a soloist in 1879 during the Concerts Pasdeloup and very soon establishing himself as one of the greatest virtuosi of the age.

7. He had been appointed Director of the Milan Conservatoire in 1882.

8. Born at Genoa on 25 October 1815, he was now 76, two years younger than Verdi.

9. At that time the Intermezzo from *Cavalleria rusticana* was enjoying immense popularity in German-speaking countries, and was often played at symphony concerts (cf. M. CONATI: "Mascagni, Leoncavallo, Puccini & C. in Germania: Contributo per un' indagine sull' 'opera verista' nei teatri di lingua tedesca" (1890–1895), in *Discoteca Alta Fedeltà,* Milan, XVII, 162: August 1972, pp. 18–25.

10. *L'amico Fritz* was premièred at the Costanzi in Rome on 31 October 1891. The German première took place at Frankfurt-am-Main on 12 March 1892; a week later the opera was also performed at the Berlin Hofoper, also in German (cf. M. CONATI: "Mascagni, Leoncavallo, Puccini [. . .], cit.).

11. Indeed, while Mascagni's new opera was being performed in Rome, Verdi, in the tranquillity of Sant'Agata, was reading the score that Ricordi had sent him; and on 6 November 1891 he wrote to the publisher:

Thank you for the score of Fritz you sent me. I have in my life read very, very, very many bad libretti, but never have I read such a half-witted libretto as this. As for the music, I have made some headway, but I soon tired of so many dissonances, those false modulations, suspended cadences and tricks, and then, so many changes of tempi in almost every bar – all most appetizing, but they offend one's sense of rhythm and hearing. The setting of words is generally good; but the music is never dramatically convincing. It is not difficult to hit the target a little too high or a little low, but it is difficult to score a bullseye, as Manzoni said; and so his characters are not well drawn. The music might be very beautiful, but I have my own view of things . . . However, I am old and old-fashioned; or rather, old but not so old-fashioned (autograph: Archivio della Casa Ricordi, Milan).

12. The French words, quoted in parenthesis in the original text, indicate that the conversation was conducted in French.
13. The editor of the *Signale* made the following comment on Verdi's final remark: "At long last an authority has pronounced against the interminable length of modern opera!"

An opinion expressed by Verdi on Mascagni was quoted by Monaldi in his *Verdi nella vita e nell'arte. Conversazioni verdiane*, cit., p. 187:

While the Roman audiences were swept off their feet by *Cavalleria rusticana*, I happened to meet Verdi at Genoa. "Well then," he said, catching sight of me, "*Cavalleria* has enjoyed a great success at the Costanzi. Tell me something of it." It was the first time for many years that I had seen the Maestro take such a lively interest in any musical event. About a year later I met Verdi again, and at a certain moment he interrupted the conversation, saying: "You know, I've heard *Cavalleria*." – "Well?" I exclaimed with curiosity. – "Ah, a fine moment of sincerity, my word!" and that was all he said. A few years later, when Mascagni had already written *Fritz, I Rantzau, Silvano* and *Ratcliff* [therefore about 1895–96], Verdi, speaking of the young and successful composer, expressed himself thus: "What a pity! What a pity! He is a young man, whose feeling for music exceeds his knowledge of it . . . He could achieve much . . . but . . . I think he has now lost his way."

XXXIV

VERDI PHOTOGRAPHED

1892

ANON: "Verdi fotografato", in *Verdi e il "Falstaff"*, special edition of the *Illustrazione Italiana*, Treves, Milan (1893; reprinted 1913), pp. 15–16.

ONE OF THE most famous photographs of Verdi portrays the composer standing, with hands akimbo, next to Arrigo Boito. In fact there are two such photographs; one shows Verdi in profile, head held up; the other, perhaps the best known, portrays him three-quarters on, head slightly bowed. This last photo was the subject of a caricature in the *Guerin Meschino*, entitled *The new pose of the young school of Italian music*, depicting Mascagri, Leoncavallo, Franchetti and Puccini in the same pose as Verdi, hands akimbo . . .[1]

There is hardly a book or magazine on Verdi, which does not publish one of these two photos with the following caption: "Verdi and Boito at Sant'Agata", or "Verdi and Boito in the garden at Sant'Agata", or even "Verdi and Boito at Sant'Agata at the time of *Otello*", or simply "Verdi and Boito at the time of *Otello*". . . Incorrect, every one. Neither Santa'Agata nor *Otello*. Both photos were taken, with others, in the Perego garden in Milan, in Via Borgonuovo, the home of Giulio Ricordi, at the time of *Falstaff*, or more precisely in the summer of 1892, as this article shows.

Verdi photographed

Verdi does not care for poses of any kind, not even for photographs; and the portraits of him, taken from life, are very few, if you consider his long and glorious career as a composer.

Last summer, Arrigo Boito, Giulio Ricordi and other close friends expressed their wish that the composer (during his brief stay in Milan)[2] should pose for a new photograph, particularly as it would be rendering an almost indispensable service to a Piedmontese artist, Chessa,[3] who intended taking part in the competition, advertised by the Ministry of Education, for an etching of the great Maestro.

"I am not averse to being photographed," Verdi said with his natural affability, "but, my dear friends, I cannot stand still . . . I do not know how to pose . . . Seriously, it would be a torture for me . . ."

"But Maestro, we shall take the photograph without subjecting you to this torture," said Ricordi, "you will be photographed by surprise . . . without noticing it. . . . In the meantime, will you honour me by lunching with us tomorrow. . . ."

The next day Verdi lunched with Giulio Ricordi, Arrigo Boito and Tito, Giulio's son.

The Ricordi house stands in Via Borgonuovo and looks out on to the Perego garden, an ancient, most extensive garden, one of the most beautiful in Milan.

Behind the green bushes, behind the flower-pots, Ricordi had positioned several cameras, camouflaged, concealed like cannons behind the trenches. Each cannon was manned by a photographer, with precise instructions.

Lunch went by cheerfully. Verdi was happy, filled with all that gaiety, with which he had infused his last artistic creation. There was much discussion about *Falstaff*, none about photography.

"We could take coffee in the garden, don't you think, Maestro?" Giulio Ricordi said with great seriousness.

"By all means, in the garden!" Verdi added with a slight smile, which meant to signify: I follow your meaning!

And down they went into the garden. Giulio Ricordi had gone on ahead, and with a rapid look about him, had given the alert . . .

The Maestro, who was making his way down, hands, as usual, akimbo, stopped for a moment at the garden gate: "Rogues!" he was saying to young Tito . . . when suddenly the first shot was fired. But Verdi did not notice.

Chessa, the painter, then came up. Giulio Ricordi asked the Maestro's permission to introduce him. Verdi spoke for several minutes with the young artist; he appeared pleased to make his acquaintance and, in his good-natured and paternal way, gave him words of encouragement. At one point, a smile flickered across Giulio Ricordi's face. He had noticed the second shot . . . The Maestro, listening intently to Chessa, had noticed nothing . . .

Meanwhile Boito too had come down; Verdi joined his loyal collaborator and continued down the path.

"Rogues!" he exclaimed suddenly, "it's a trap!" And with a nod of the head he showed Boito a camera that he had finally discovered

. . . The third photo had been taken, the one which groups in a single frame the poet and composer of *Falstaff*.

"Come, then," said Verdi, still in the best of humour, "come; since you wish me to be tortured, let us climb the scaffold . . . I see, here . . ."

And he sat down on a chair, to the side of which stood a white sheet, so that the Maestro's face would stand out clearly against the background . . .

"Quick, don't prolong my torture . . ."

"But it's all over!" said Giulio Ricordi.

In fact, two cameras had been levelled at him, one focussing on the whole group, the other concentrating on the great Maestro's serene and vigorous head.

And that is the story of the photographs, from which the plates reproduced on this page and the great portrait on the front page of this number were made, and from which Chessa created his etching of Verdi, which brought him victory in the State competition. (Photos by U. Campanari and A. Ferrario.)

NOTES

1. Reproduced in G. BOCCA: "Verdi e la caricatura", in *Rivista Musicale Italiana*, Turin, VIII, 2: 1901, p. 359.
2. During the summer of 1892 Verdi was in Milan twice. First with his wife Giuseppina at the end of June to July 5, when he left for his now customary sojourn at the baths of Montecatini. The second time he came alone, in order to hear the soprano Emma Zilli, a possible Alice for *Falstaff*; this second stay lasted from July 28–31. Given the absence of Giuseppina at Ricordi's luncheon, a reference to which is made a little further on in this article, it is more likely that these photographs were taken during one of the last days of July.
3. Carlo Chessa (Cagliari 1855 – Turin 1912), painter and etcher, father of the painter Luigi, who founded the "Sei pittori di Torino", a group with impressionistic leanings.

XXXV

VERDI'S *FALSTAFF*
A VISIT TO THE COMPOSER

1892

[ANNIE VIVANTI]: "Verdi's *Falstaff*. A Visit to the Composer" (from a correspondent), in *The Daily Graphic*, London, 14 January 1893.

ONE DAY IN the autumn of 1892 at Genoa (it was the time of the Columbus Festivities, organized by the Ligurian town), Verdi received a visit from Giosuè Carducci, accompanied by an English journalist who, remaining anonymous, gave an account of the meeting in the *Daily Graphic*, of London. In 1906, on the occasion of Carducci's receiving the Nobel Prize, the Anglo-Italian authoress, Annie Vivanti, wrote a profile of the poet, to whom she had been both friend and muse, for the *Nuova Antologia*, containing amongst other things a re-evocation of a visit to Verdi, made in Genoa in the company of Carducci, on the eve of *Falstaff*. The contents of this article (quoted here on page 239), though briefer and omitting some incidents, correspond to those in the *Daily Graphic* piece, so that it seems legitimate to consider that the author of the latter is the same Vivanti, then aged twenty-five, who in those years was sending articles from Italy to several English newspapers. Annie Vivanti (London 1868 – Turin 1942), daughter of an Italian exile who had married a German wife, studied singing in Italy and subsequently made her operatic début in New York. On her return to Italy she met Carducci and became a close friend. In 1902 she married John Chartres and travelled the world, propagating the cause of Irish independence. The first fruits of her literary activity was a collection of poetry, *Lyrica* (Milan 1890), for which Carducci wrote the introduction. She was the author of two plays, several novels, but it was above all as a short-story writer that she made her mark.

Her account of that visit to Verdi begins by mentioning *Falstaff*, then in its final stages of composition, and Verdi recalls the day when Boito had officially announced the opera's existence, during a dinner at the Hôtel de Milan. Following this announcement, news of

Verdi's latest opera was given in the *Corriere della Sera* of 27 November 1890. Until that time *Falstaff* had remained a secret, jealously guarded by Verdi, Boito and Verdi's wife (cf. N. XXXII, note 10). The news in the *Corriere della Sera* was quickly confirmed by Giulio Ricordi in the *Gazzetta Musicale di Milano*:

> For many years now and on several occasions, the Maestro has expressed his wish to several close friends to write a comic opera; but he always considered the difficulty of finding a genuinely comic subject virtually insurmountable. We know, in fact, that Verdi had read the entire Italian and French comedy repertoire without finding a subject that met all his requirements. While Verdi was in Milan in the summer of last year, 1889,[1] he discussed this very topic of comic opera with Arrigo Boito, who took the bull by the horns and suggested a subject – he did not merely suggest, however, but with astonishing rapidity, within the space of a few hours, outlined a plot which he presented to Verdi: *Falstaff*, drawn from the various Shakespeare plays in which this character appears. The proposition delighted Verdi, but he made it quite clear that he would only accept the new libretto, if this did not distract Boito from other work, because, Verdi said, "I do not wish to have on my conscience even an hour's delay of your new opera, *Nerone*." Following Boito's assurance on this point, Verdi accepted the proposition [. . .].[2]

And here is how that *Mephistopheles of a Boito* divulged the secret and officially announced Verdi's new opera, as described by a reporter in the *Teatro Illustrato*:

> These are the genuine, authentic details. The day before yesterday [November 26] the entire family of Commendatore Giulio Ricordi – including his son-in-law and married daughter – were invited by Verdi to dine at the Hôtel de Milan. Arrigo Boito was also present. There is no need to talk of the dinner; suffice it to say, that Verdi was very cheerful and had never seemed younger or more genial. Everything about him – his appearance, conversation and manner – suggested that he was happy and content. And Giulio Ricordi, it should be noted, was quite unaware that Verdi had a new opera virtually completed. The secret had been jealously guarded; indeed, to guard it better, Verdi – who when composing normally uses manuscript paper supplied for him by

Ricordi – acquired it on this occasion from elsewhere. And so when the champagne had been poured, and everyone was in excellent spirits, Boito rose to make a toast and said:

"I drink to the health and triumphs of *Paunchy!*"

General surprise. No one understood Boito's allusion. Ricordi was the most astonished of all. Boito then repeated:

"I drink to the health of *Falstaff!*"

Renewed surprise from Ricordi, who still failed to understand. But Signora Giuditta Ricordi, who was sitting opposite Signora Giuseppina Verdi, did understand, or, more accurately, anticipated the revelation, and leaning over to Signora Verdi, she whispered in her ear:

"A new opera?"

And Signora Verdi, more with her head than her lips, indicated that this was so. You can imagine Ricordi's delight when he realized what had happened.

Once the secret had been revealed, Verdi supplied such detailed information about his new opera, that we are in a position to provide a summary, as if we had heard the details from his own lips.

For a long time now – as has often been said – Verdi has had a great desire to compose a comic opera; but he has always sought a subject in vain. Five or six years ago he asked Ricordi to buy him the complete plays of Goldoni, and these he read and re-read attentively without finding what he was looking for. Last year he spoke of his project to Arrigo Boito, expressing his ambition and regret at not being able to give free rein to his idea. Boito said nothing; but having left the Maestro, he returned home and fashioned straight from his head and within 48 hours the outline of a libretto, which he showed at once to Verdi, who was delighted. Th plot concerned Falstaff, Shakspeare's [sic] famous character, and Boito had created a completely comic libretto from the two histories and the three [sic] comedies of Shakspeare [sic] in which Falstaff appears.

It seems that the libretto was excellent, for Verdi declared that it was nothing less than a masterpiece, and so comic that it even made him laugh as he composed. This new opera of Verdi's has a baritone as protagonist, and many other characters; it requires a small but select chorus, and the singers need to be first-rate, almost all of soloist stature, fifteen men and thirty ladies at the most; and finally some young girls to dance.

Verdi said that he had already completed more than half and that the opera would be quite finished in a few months, so that it could be staged at La Scala during the 1891–1892 season. [. . .]

As for Arrigo Boito, when questioned about *Nerone* he replied that, being busy with the libretto of *Falstaff*, which was to be produced in the coming year, he had deemed it his duty to leave *Nerone* for the moment, as he wished to contribute all he could to *Falstaff* in his capacity as a poet. But he gave assurance that *Nerone* would without fail be ready for the following season, that is to say for 1892–1893. [. . .][3]

The announcement of Verdi's new opera had naturally aroused great interest, and not merely in the musical world. It almost seemed as if the Risorgimento cry of *Viva Verdi* would become fashionable again, as Leone Fortis pointed out in an article entitled *The old Maestro*, published at that time in the *Gazzetta Musicale di Milano*, in which he expresses his amazement that the over 70-year-old composer had "still not closed his glorious career", but still had "such energy and strength in both mind and heart to attempt a task that was as noble as it was difficult – the resurrection of Italian opera buffa." Fortis' article – a tribute to the mental and physical fitness of the composer – contains two vignettes of Verdi (one dating back to April 1889 at Genoa station, the other to the day before the announcement of *Falstaff*), which are not without interest in this collection of eye-witness accounts:

[. . .] Verdi – not merely through the music of his last opera, but also by virtue of his physical appearance – inspires admiration, affection, veneration even: that veneration which is and must be reserved for the old. Yet no, that is not accurate, for Verdi is certainly not old, and it will be a long time before he grows old, if indeed he ever does. Healthy and strong, he is at the peak of his manhood, which the dictionary defines as between youth and old age, between 38 and 50. Here, if anywhere, one could speak of the gallantry of a Dumas character towards a lady of 50. It can be said of Verdi – and to Verdi – that he has lived not for 76 years, but for two periods of 38 years.

And in this sense, my admiration for his physical condition matches my admiration for his art.

It is three years now – he was almost 74 – since *Otello* was premièred at La Scala. He astounded the audience with the robustness

and stamina of his genius and imagination; and he had already
astounded the artists with the robustness of his physical constitution, which enabled him to sit at the piano for four consecutive
hours, until the singers begged him for mercy and rest, while he,
as fresh as if he had only just begun, asked them with genuine
surprise: *What! Already tired? But we have only just begun.*

And at the orchestral rehearsals he was always on his feet for
four or five hours at a time, climbing on to the stage then down
again, to arrange the chorus, see to the extras, walk the singers
through their exits and re-entries – so that they might enter and
exit according to his wish. And when the rehearsal was over, he
would take the arm of his friend Giulio Ricordi – to stretch his legs
as much as to take a rest – and with quick, sure steps would drag
him for a long walk, to work up an appetite.

Last year, one day in April, I was passing through Genoa
station, having returned from Rome. There were many people on
the platform, and I noticed a group surrounding a sprightly,
cheerful gentleman who was speaking animatedly, with great
liveliness of gesture. He was wearing a large, floppy, black,
broad-brimmed hat and an overcoat slung across his shoulders,
although the temperature was anything but mild. This gentleman
moved away from the group to greet someone – and I recognized
him: it was Verdi who, on recognizing me, came to the wagon to
greet me. A foreigner – a Frenchman – who was in my compartment, noticing the deference with which I addressed the
gentleman, who had been surrounded by so many people, asked
me who he was. I replied:

"Verdi."

"A relative of the famous Maestro?" the Frenchman replied.
"Son fils, peut-être?"

"Non, Monsieur, le Maestro lui-même."

"Ce gaillard-là? Pas possible, puisque le Maestro est un
vieillard . . ."

"Pourtant! . . ."

And I do not think that he was convinced. Nor would I blame
him. I should not have been convinced either, had I been in his
place.

Some days ago, just before *Falstaff* was announced so unexpectedly and suddenly at an intimate family dinner, I was in Giulio
Ricordi's study, discussing musical matters.

To enter Giulio Ricordi's study from the entrance hall, you

descend a short flight of steps, which produces a somewhat theatrical effect to the visitor at the top of the stairs. [. . .]

The study has a secret little door – a sort of safety-valve, which was once perhaps used for mysterious entries but is now used for prudent escapes.

All of a sudden there was a knock at this little door; a fine-looking man appeared on the threshold, with a rosy complexion and a frank, smiling face, kind and serene, with flashing eyes, an unembarrassed manner, and with the nimble movements of a man with an upright, buoyant bearing.

It was Verdi.

No doubt about it! This was the *venerable old man*, as certain newspapers were describing him.

A *venerable old man* . . . to my mind that suggests a white-haired man, bent, with a slow gait and slow speech, a hollow voice and half extinguished eyes, who moves with slow, majestic steps – quite the opposite of the man now before me.

I was so stunned by his ever youthful figure, that I was unable to conceal my surprise. Like that Frenchman in Genoa, I too would have said: *Ce gaillard-là? Pas possible.*

My surprise revealed itself in a thought which flashed through my mind and which I could not check:

"*Maestro, when are you giving us a new opera?*" I asked him almost instinctively, just as I would have asked Puccini, Franchetti or Mascagni, if I knew him, for it seemed to me the most natural thing in the world that his vigorous health and strength were far from declining.

The Maestro smiled:

"*Ah, there are so many operas! . . .*"

"*Too many,*" I replied, "*that's why we need a new one from you.*"

Another smile flickered across Verdi's face, and his eyes flashed.

And in that smile and those flashing eyes, I believed I glimpsed a tacit assent – from which I sensed something . . . that was fulfilled on the morrow. [. . .]

A few days after the announcement of *Falstaff*, on December 3, Verdi replied to Gino Monaldi, who had asked him for information about the new opera, in the famous letter with its quasi official tone (he knew from experience that Monaldi, as had happened once before,[5] would be unable to resist the temptation of making it public – which he did, immediately):

What can I tell you? For 40 years now I have wished to write a comic opera, and for 50 years I have known The Merry Wives of Windsor. *However, the usual ubiquitous "buts" have always prevented me from fulfilling my wish. Boito has now swept away all the "buts", and has written me a lyric comedy that bears no resemblance to any other. I'm enjoying myself composing this music; I have no plans for it and do not even know whether I shall finish it. I repeat: I am enjoying myself. Falstaff is a rogue who does all sorts of wicked things . . . but in an entertaining manner. He is a* CHARACTER! *There are so many different characters! The opera is entirely comic. Amen.*[6]

A month later, on 1 January 1891, the composer wrote a letter to Giulio Ricordi, who now craved to see the opera printed and performed; Verdi, however, was of a different opinion:

[. . .] *and now we come to* Falstaff. *It seems to me that all these plans are crazy, truly crazy! Let me explain. I began writing* Falstaff *simply to pass the time, without pre-conceived ideas, without plans – I repeat, to pass the time! Nothing else! But these discussions, the proposals – however vague – and the statements they cause you to make, will all turn into obligations and commitments which I absolutely refuse to accept. I have told you, and I repeat: "I am writing to pass the time." I told you that the music was approximately half-finished . . . by which I meant "half sketched out". The most troublesome half remains to be done: the arrangements of the parts, the revisions and adjustments, not to mention the orchestration which will be extremely tedious. [. . .] When I was young I could, although frail, stay at my desk for ten or twelve hours!! working constantly, and more than once I started work at four in the morning and ended at four in the afternoon, with only a cup of coffee inside me . . . working constantly, without drawing breath. I cannot do that now. In those days I was in command of my health and my time. Now, alas, I am not . . .*[7]

The same day he wrote to Boito:

Paunchy is making no progress [. . .] *I am upset and distracted. Very sad months have passed* [in November the loyal Muzio and his friend Piroli had died], *and the present cold, the celebrations etc. etc. have knocked me off balance.*[8]

It was in these months that progress on *Falstaff* was halted – Verdi only resumed composition in April. At the time of Carducci's visit the opera was already practically complete, and the staging being arranged for the coming performance at La Scala.

Verdi's Falstaff
A visit to the Composer
(FROM A CORRESPONDENT)

A great deal of mystery is being observed respecting Verdi's new opera, *Falstaff*, which is to be produced at Milan next month. Press representatives are being excluded from all the rehearsals, and little or nothing will be known about the *mise en scène* until the actual production before the public. This secrecy is due to the express wish of the composer himself; indeed, if he could have had his own way, his first comic opera would have burst as a surprise upon the musical world in its complete and final form instead of being made the subject of anticipation and discussion for at least two years beforehand. So he himself told me in an interview which I had with him recently at Genoa.

"That Mefistofele of a Boito"
"This is the last work of my life," he said angrily, striding, a tall, gaunt figure, up and down his large drawing-room, and pushing back the long grey hair from his wrinkled forehead with an impatient gesture. "I am writing it for my own amusement. The public would have known nothing about it had it not been for that *Mefistofele* of a Boito! (*quel Mefistofele di Boito*)."[9]

This little joke of his own, more perfect in Italian than in English, put him into a good humour again, and on my asking what his complaint was against his clever librettist, he told me the whole story. They had been dining at the Hôtel Milan with Ricordi, the music publisher, his wife and one or two more. When dessert was on the table Ricordi, turning to Boito, inquired when his "Nerone", an opera for which the Italian public has been waiting for the last five years, would be ready. Boito replied that it had been laid aside in view of a work of much greater importance, and then rising with his glass in his hand looked towards Verdi and said laughing, "Here's to your fat-paunched hero." Inquiries, of course, followed, and in this way the subject of the new opera became known. "I should not have forgiven Boito his indiscretion," Verdi continued, "had he not written me a first-rate libretto. The music that I have put to it is in some passages so droll that it has often made me laugh while writing it."

At the Piano

I thought of the splendid death scene in *La traviata*, and then of Aida's mournful "O terra, addio", and wished that the old *Maestro* had not lived to employ his magificent genuis for the purpose of making himself or others laugh. My reflections were interrupted by Verdi inviting us into his *sanctum sanctorum* – the little, scantily-furnished study in which so much of his splendid music has been written. The other visitor present was Carducci, the Tennyson of Italy, who is in literature what Verdi is in music, and it was owing to the fact that I had been introduced by him that Verdi, usually harsh and un-approachable, had received me with marked kindness and cordiality. To be allowed – nay, asked – to enter his study was a special mark of favour. It is a tiny apartment, opening off the drawing-room, and more than half-filled by a grand piano on which, when I saw it, the manuscript of the new opera, written, as is the composer's custom, in pencil, and in very minute characters, was lying or standing in heaps. A writing-table in the window, a music-stand filled with music-paper, and a single chair completed the furniture of the room. On the mantelpiece stood a small portrait of Mascagni, and some volumes of poetry were lying about, for Verdi, though writing very indifferent Italian himself, has a strong taste for poetry, and reads his favourite authors continually. I asked him to touch the piano. He hesitated for a moment, and then with a smile, no doubt at the boldness of my request, sat down and ran over a wonderful staccato passage which he had just completed, and the notes of which, scarred with corrections, stood on the desk before him. Then he rose, and throwing open the high French windows, led us out upon the terrace.

The Composer's Flowers

"That," he said, pointing to the view that lay stretched out before us, "that is my inspiration."

The terrace overlooked a large neglected garden at the back of the old *palazzo*[10] in which the composer lives. Beyond a slight elevation of ground, which hides a dusty road that intervenes, lies the open expanse of the Gulf of Genoa, closed towards the right by villa-covered hills, and towards the left by the busy town and the docks crowded with shipping. The deserted overgrown garden, with its irregularity of surface, its pillars lying where they have fallen from their places in the portico below, and its moss-covered, dried-up fountain is seen cold and grey and still against the brilliant colouring of the sea, studded with its passing steamers and white-sailed yachts. It is here that Verdi lives and works for half the year, the remaining six months being spent at Busseto in his native province of Parma.

The terrace on which we stood was lined with pots of camelias and geraniums. They presented rather a decrepit and dried-up appearance, but Signora Verdi had previously told me that they were her husband's special weakness and that he always insisted upon watering and tending them himself. She went, indeed, so far as to say that the composer was far less angry with Mascagni for appropriating some of his melodies than he had been with a certain English visitor, bearing a well-known name, who had gained admission during Verdi's absence, and, anxious to carry off some souvenir, had possessed himself of a half-withered blossom. Bearing these facts in mind, I was duly impressed when Verdi now plucked one of the flowers and presented it to me with the grandest air in the world.

The Story of a Rehearsal

Then the conversation turned once more upon music. The inevitable organ-grinder had struck up the equally inevitable selection from *Il trovatore* on the roadway some distance off. I asked the composer whether he did not find this method of rendering his music peculiarly irritating.

"No," he replied, "on the contrary. It pleases me."

Then he turned suddenly to the poet.

"Carducci, how should you like to hear the people massacring your songs and poems through the public streets? You would eat them alive, *non è vero?*"[11]

The great Republican poet, whose classicism has always rendered his writings *caviare* to the general, shook his leonine head.

"No," he replied, "not at all. I love the people, though I love them as an ideal, not as an assemblage of ignorant and vulgar individuals, and perhaps that is why they do not understand me. With you it is very different. Your melodies have become part of the national life."

"Ah," said Verdi, "the people have always been my best friends – from the very beginning. It was a handful of carpenters who gave me my first real assurance of success."

I scented a story and asked for details.

"It was after I had dragged on in poverty and disappointment for a long time at Busseto, and had been laughed at by all the publishers, and shown to the door by all the impresarios.[12] I had lost all real confidence and courage, but through sheer obstinacy, I succeeded in getting Nabucco" – so the title of *Nabucodonosor* is commonly contracted in Italy – "rehearsed at the Scala, in Milan. The artists were singing as badly as they knew how,[13] and the orchestra seemed to be bent only upon drowning the noise of the workmen who were busy making alterations in the building. Presently the chorus began to sing, as carelessly as before, the '*Va pensiero*', but before they had got through half-a-dozen bars the theatre was as still as a church. The men had left off their work, one by one, and there they were, sitting about on the ladders and scaffolding, listening! When the number was finished they broke out into the noisiest applause I have ever heard, crying '*Bravo, bravo, viva il maestro!*',[14] and beating on the woodwork with their tools. Then I knew what the future had in store for me."[15]

"Not Yet"

His keen, blue eyes assumed for a moment a gentle look such as is rarely seen in them. Ordinarily Verdi views the world from under his grey, shaggy eyebrows with a stern and forbidding expression, and he rarely speaks about himself. He shrinks habitually from anything that tends to bring him into any but the most formal relations with his fellow men, and so far does he carry this peculiarity, that he likes even those who know him best to pass him in the street without saluting him, or showing that they are aware of his presence.

When we took our leave, Verdi accompanied us to the door. I mentioned that I was starting that evening for Sicily, the country of the *Cavalleria rusticana*.

"*A proposito*,"[16] I asked, "have you heard what everyone is saying about you? They say you have declared that you can die happy now that Mascagni's opera has been written.[17] Is it true, *Maestro*?"

Verdi shook his head rather gravely. "Ah, no," he said. "Not yet. Not yet."[18]

As mentioned above, in 1906 Annie Vivanti published a profile of Carducci in the *Nuova Antologia* of August 1; on pp. 378–9 there is a re-evocation of the visit she made to Verdi in 1892 in the company of the poet (reproduced in *Il Caffaro*, Genoa, n. 284: 2 August 1906; and in *Centocinquantesimo anniversario della nascita di Giuseppe Verdi*,

Teatro Regio, Parma 1963, pp. 79–80). Written years after the event, it appears less detailed and immediate, and is tinged by a streak of rhetoric. The visit to Verdi has more the literary tone of an encounter between two "bears", with Carducci more in evidence. Carducci's "bearishness", however, is shown to be more superficial, academic – an indication of a certain insecurity of character and shallowly rooted conviction. Not so Verdi's; as disdainful as ever, he is conscious of his own strength, and is in no way embarrassed to offer the poet a flower. . . .

[*Carducci and Verdi*]

[. . .] "Come. I'll take you to Giuseppe Verdi. Be sure to dress suitably in his honour. I shall wear yellow kid gloves."

And he did. But whether to honour Verdi or hide his malformed hand, I do not know.

Speaking of music we made our way to the Palazzo Doria, where Verdi was completing *Falstaff*.

To tell the truth, Carducci does not understand much about music. Like Victor Hugo, he has a greater sense of metre than melody. His favourite song is the *Lorelei*, with its simple, popular refrain. "Sing the 'Lorelei gethan','" he would say to me when I was a young girl.

And years later he said to my little girl, who was standing in front of him, tiny and serious, with a violin beneath her chin: "Play the 'Lorelei gethan!'" But

> quando Wagner possente mille anime intona
> e i cantanti metalli, trema agli umani il core[19]

he wrote; and he told me more than once: "If I had not been a singer of barbaric odes, I would have composed gigantic music, like Wagner." In fact, the enormity of Wagner's musical ideas almost arouses the poet's envy, who only has the word to express his boundless thoughts, wonderful ideas and limitless dreams.

Our visit to Verdi was hardly conventional. The magnificent old man, tall and handsome, came to meet his friend and embraced him with his clear, sky-blue sparkling and tender eyes. Carducci immediately went out on to the vast terrace overlooking the port, and sat down, pensive and silent. Verdi called me, sat down at his piano and began to play – fluently and easily, like running water or wind – sweet, fleeting music. He then got up, and together we went

out on to the terrace, where Carducci was still sitting and gazing at
the sea.

We sat down next to him and for a long time no one spoke. On the
dancing water in the sun the sails fluttered, shining and bright,
bowing and curtseying towards the distant blue. Carducci suddenly
said:

"I believe in God."

Verdi nodded with his white head, in solemn affirmation.[20] Then
Carducci – unexpectedly as always – stood up and said farewell.
I remember that Verdi who, like many men of genius, had his
childish side, detained us to show us his flowers.

"Look," he said proudly, pointing to a row of vases on the terrace,
containing strange plants of wretched, plucked appearance. "Look,
I planted and grew them myself. It requires much time and patience."

I looked reverently at the meagre plant, and asked what it was.

"But they are camelias!" said Verdi.

And Carducci turned furiously to me, saying: "But can you not
see that they are camelias?"

Verdi hastily disappeared and returned immediately with a large
pitcher full of water and set about soaking and inundating the meagre
vegetation.

Carducci was most impressed when Verdi, bending his white head
over one of the dripping vases, picked and offered him the only bud
that seemed anywhere near flowering.

I do not think the two friends ever met again.[21]

As we returned, Carducci was silent and bad-tempered. Many
people on the street recognized him and turned round to gaze; some
turned back and walked in front of him to get a better view. He
muttered darkly into his beard. All of a sudden he stopped:

"What are you looking at?" he shouted, flashing his eyes at the
people who had stopped to gaze. "I am neither a prima donna nor a
tenor. Nor am I here to amuse the inquisitive." [. . .]

ANNIE VIVANTI

NOTES

1. More precisely, during the last days of June and the first few days of
   July, while travelling to Montecatini,
2. G. RICORDI: "Un'opera nuova di Giuseppe Verdi", in *Gazzetta Musicale
   di Milano*, XLV, 48: 30 November 1890, p. 757.

3. *Il Teatro Illustrato*, Milan, X, 120: December 1890, p. 189, entitled: "Una futura nuova opera di Verdi. *Falstaff.*"
4. L. FORTIS: "Il vecchio Maestro", in *Gazzetta Musicale di Milano*, XLV, 49: 7 December 1890, pp. 773–5.
5. Cf. introduction to N. XXVIII.
6. G. MONALDI: *Verdi* (1839–1898), Bocca, Turin 1898, p. 285 (reprinted 1943).
7. Autograph: Archivio della Casa Ricordi, Milan.
8. Autograph: Istituto di studi verdiani, Parma.
9. Italian in the original.
10. Italian in the original.
11. Italian in the original.
12. Verdi clearly exaggerates here; indeed from the autobiographical sketch he gave Ricordi (reproduced in A. POUGIN: *G. Verdi. Vita aneddotica*, cit., pp. 40–46) we learn that the impresario of La Scala at that time, Bartolomeo Merelli, in no way lost faith in him after the fiasco of *Un giorno di regno*, and insisted that he compose *Nabucco*.
13. Including Giuseppina Strepponi! . . . Despite poor vocal form at that time, Strepponi had a personal success in Verdi's opera. There exists, however, a letter from Donizetti to his brother-in-law Antonio Vasselli, dated 4 March 1842 (i.e. five days before the première of *Nabucco*), that contains a surprising statement about Strepponi:

> *Tell him* [a Roman impresario] *that this singer made such a furore here in* Belisario, *that she was the only soloist not to be applauded: and Verdi did not wish her to sing in his opera, but the management insisted* (G. ZAVADINI: *Donizetti*, cit., p. 580).

14. Italian in the original.
15. The truth of Verdi's story is confirmed in the article "Verdi. Milan – Paris" in *La Grande Dame, Revue de l'Elégance et des Arts*, Paris 1894, which contains on pp. 156–7 a similar account that the author of the article, Comte L., claims to have heard at the première of *Falstaff* at La Scala from a "voisin de fauteuil [qui] a eu la bonne chance d'être reçu par le maître à Gênes, tout dernièrement" (perhaps Carducci himself or Vivanti, who were both present at the première).
16. Italian in the original
17. Some similar phrases attributed to Verdi began to go the rounds in the Italian press, following the triumph of *Cavalleria* at the Costanzi. One of the first to print it was the journalist Pilade Moretti, who wrote from Leghorn to the *Corriere delle Puglie* (n. 159, 18 June 1890):

> In a period of artistic decline in Italy and, I should say, throughout the world, a genius springs up, and Giuseppe Verdi writes: *Now I can die content.* These are the words of a genius approaching the grave, who extols the triumph of the rising star, in whom the Maestro

senses the successor to his school – one who will hold high the name and traditions of bel canto and the musical supremacy of Italy. (D. CELLAMARE: *Un cinquantesimo glorioso: Mascagni e la "Cavalleria" visti da Cerignola*, Palombi, Rome 1941, p. 87.)

A few months later in a letter dated 30 December 1890 to his friend Giuseppina Negroni-Prati Morosini, Verdi himself made the following observation:

> *They have attributed to me a phrase about* Cavalleria *which, had I expressed an opinion, I would have reversed:* Now I can live (*not die*) content *etc. etc. . . . .* (autograph: Museo Teatrale alla Scala, Milan).

About 40 years later, commemorating the 30 years since Verdi's death in an article for the *Lettura* of Milan, Mascagni denied that this phrase had ever been spoken, and attributed the origin of the "legend" to a "pleasant and affectionate episode", whose reliability rests entirely on a story told him by Giulio Ricordi, who had witnessed that "episode" (see N. XLV).

18. For an analogous denial, see the interview published in the *Journal des Débats* (N. XXXIX).

19. From "Presso l'urna di Percy Bysshe Shelley", published in *Odi barbare*, 1884.

20. This passage did not fail to attract the attention of two priests, writers on Verdian matters, who were keen to mitigate, if not debunk the traditional image of an anti-clerical and unbelieving Verdi: Lorenz Alpino (cf. his interview with Vivanti in *Stampa-Sera*, Turin, 11 February 1941) whose crude untruths about some Verdi letters, aimed at proving Verdi's piety, have been revealed by F. WALKER, *op. cit.*, pp. 484–7; and Ferruccio Botti (cf. "Verdi, Carducci e Annie Vivanti", in *L'Avvenire d'Italia*, Bologna, 28 January 1951, and in *Spigolature d'Archivio: Spigolature Verdiane*, terza serie, Battei, Parma 1963, p. 17).

21. Carducci attended the première of *Falstaff* at La Scala on the evening of 9 February 1983; when the opera was over he went to the Hôtel de Milan to pay homage to the composer; cf. *Gazzetta dell'Emilia*, Bologna, 10 February, 1893:

> I have spoken of the reception accorded Verdi when he returned to the Hotel. He was contented and satisfied; his handsome face was lit with a smile. Verdi accepted with pleasure the congratulations of his friends, and forgot none of those who were present. He gave Carducci a great welcome and spoke with him at length.

XXXVI

VERDI'S *FALSTAFF*

1893

EDUARD HANSLICK: "Verdis *Falstaff*", in *Neue Freie Presse*, Vienna, April 1893 (republished in *Musical Courier*, New York, XXVI, 21, n. 690: 24 May 1893, p. 8, entitled "Hanslick and Verdi", published in part in *Signale für die musikalische Welt*, Leipzig, LI, 31: May 1893, p. 492; reprinted by the author in *Aus meinem Leben*, Berlin, 1894, vol.II, pp. 281–3).

ROME WAS CHRONOLOGICALLY the third city, after Milan and Genoa, in which *Falstaff* was staged. The opera was given at the Teatro Costanzi (the present Teatro dell'Opera), whose management had been taken over for a period of three years from Lent 1892 by Gino Monaldi.[1] Singers, conductor, sets and costumes were the same as they had been at La Scala and Genoa. The score, however, differed from that used in Milan and Genoa, the composer having made two important revisions: in the concerted piece at the end of the second act, and the end of the first part of Act III.[2] Both alterations were then incorporated in the definitive edition. The first Rome performance took place on 15 April 1893 in the presence of the composer, who thus returned to Rome in his capacity as composer after an absence of 34 years, i.e. from the time of *Un ballo in maschera* (he had been in Rome very briefly during November 1875, but only as a recently elected Senator to take the oath in the Senate). Verdi arrived in Rome on the evening of April 13, to the reception of more than 2000 enthusiastic people.[3] His stay was brief, the reception triumphant. A recollection of those days in Rome can be read in Ugo Ojetti's interview with Pascarella (see N. XXVII).

It was in Rome that the most authoritative music critic of the time, the author of the famous and much debated *Vom Musikalisch-Schönen* (Leipzig 1854), the friend of Brahms, the man whom Wagnerians identified as the Beckmesser of music criticism – in short, Eduard Hanslick (Prague 1825 – Baden, Vienna, 1904) saw *Falstaff* for the first time. The article he dispatched to the *Neue Freie Presse*, the Viennese daily newspaper to which he had contributed for about 30 years, is not strictly speaking a review of the opera; it merely contains a few immediate impressions, biographical data and some statements made to him by Verdi during a short interview. From the 'fifties on, though criticizing him severely and accusing him of a "perverse aesthetic will", Hanslick professed his admiration of Verdi; but his true appreciation only came with *Aida* and the *Requiem*. He defended the Italian composer against accusations of Wagnerism and emphasized his original artistic development. He admired *Otello*, but without enthusiasm; *Falstaff* astonished him. Extracts from his Verdi criticism (which apart from the snippets published by Mila[4] and Della Corte,[5] are still not generally known in Italy) can be read in his nine-volume work, *Die moderne Oper* (1875–1900).[6]

Verdi's Falstaff

Sorrento, April.

It was not to hear music but to escape it, that I fled Vienna for a time. All kinds of melodies from recent operas and concerts fluttered like tiresome seagulls around my head and in the wake of our ship. For the time being I fervently wished to hear no more music. But there was one thing that I did wish: to see the aged Verdi once more and hear his *Falstaff*. The latest opera of the 80-year-old composer already belongs to musical history and its first Rome performance was a memorable event. Verdi had avoided Rome for years. In need of rest and sated with fame, he shunned fresh ovations and presentations at court. Even after his appointment as Senator, he refrained from thanking the King personally. But the first performance in Rome of his *Falstaff* drew him to the capital once more. What an evening! A national celebration, an *affaire de coeur* for the whole people! The enthusiasm that greeted Verdi's appearance on stage can hardly be imagined in Germany. And the applause was even more thunderous when Verdi appeared in the Royal box and took his seat to the right of the King. To see a very aged, very famous artist fêted in such a way is infinitely uplifting and moving, even for a foreigner. And all the artists were swept along by the force of this atmosphere. One will probably never hear a more intoxicating performance of *Falstaff* than on that evening of April 15 in the large and splendid Teatro Costanza [sic]. Being quite unprepared for this experience, I can only describe the immediate impression which the opera made on me personally. The imminent Vienna performance will permit me to give a more detailed and perhaps a revised account of my opinion.

Of Italy's famous composers, only Bellini and Verdi have given us no comic opera. All the others have composed both comedies and tragedies with equal enthusiasm and, mostly, with equal success – from Pergolesi, whose *La serva padrona* represents the first budding of opera buffa, and Piccini, in whose *Cecchina* the bud begins to blossom, to Rossini and Donizetti who alternated continually between comedy and tragedy. Only Bellini and Verdi, both extremely emotional and sentimental natures, seemed not to be made for and unable to write comic opera. Bellini died young; Verdi, at the age of 80, now presents his astonished public with this, his first comic opera. What an unexpectedly beautiful and significant turn of events, that the aged man at the close of his life should free himself from tragedy and, with the wisdom of happy old age, let his gaze rest on the sunny and serene side of existence!

When I expressed similar thoughts to Verdi on the day of the *Falstaff* performance in Rome, he replied that it had been his lifelong wish to write a comic opera. "And why did you not do so?" – "Because no one showed any interest (parce que l'on n'en voulait pas)." He had only composed *Falstaff* for his own amusement. He denied that he had already begun writing a *King Lear*. "I am not twenty years old," he said with a smile more roguish than painful, "but four times twenty!"[7] The simple warmth with which Verdi, who is virtually inaccessible to foreigners, received and welcomed me, moved me deeply, especially as I still had on my conscience many a sin committed against him in my youth. Something infinitely gentle, modest and yet distinguished radiates from this man, whom fame has not made vain, honour not arrogant and old age not cantankerous. His face is deeply furrowed, his dark eyes are deeply sunk, his beard white – yet his upright bearing and harmonious voice make him seem less old.

Verdi replied somewhat evasively to the suggestion that he had been influenced by Wagner: "Song and melody should always remain a composer's prime concern." In fact this is not the case in *Falstaff*, in the absolute sense of song and melody, as illustrated in the earlier Verdi operas; but compared with the operas of Wagner's second period, *Falstaff* illustrates well those words. Nowhere in *Falstaff* is the voice suffocated or swamped by the orchestra, nowhere is the memory spoon-fed by leitmotivs, nowhere is emotion cooled by sophisticated reflexion. And yet the music of *Falstaff* possesses more the character of animated conversation and declamation than that of distinctive melody weaving its own beauty. That he knew how to blend this latter type of music perfectly with the flowing music of comedy, is proved by the second act of his *Un ballo in maschera*. Comparing this with *Falstaff*, one can see evidence of Wagnerian influence in the latter, but only in the very widest sense of the term. *Falstaff* certainly exhibits an invaluable method for composers of genius who have the experience and technique of many years, but no longer the burgeoning imagination of youth. [. . .]

EDUARD HANSLICK

NOTES

1. With the express purpose of bringing *Falstaff* to Rome, Monaldi had become an impresario, by virtue of a binding letter that Verdi had written him on 11 January 1891:

   Should I ever decide to finish Falstaff *and have it performed, you may then stage it at the Teatro Costanzi in Rome, always provided that I consider you have all the necessary elements for a first rate performance. (I Copialettere di G. Verdi, cit., p. 362.)*

   .Nonetheless, managing the Teatro Costanzi brought about the financial ruin of Monaldi who, already by the time of *Falstaff*, was compelled to enter into partnership with the impresario Piontelli and, "pro forma", with Canori too (cf. G. MONALDI: *I miei ricordi musicale*, Ausonia, Rome 1921, pp. 133–5.)

2. Cf. *Carteggio Verdi-Boito*, cit., pp. 215–6 and 431–5.

3. Cf. *Verdi e Roma*, compiled by A. Belli and Ceccarius, Teatro dell'Opera di Roma, 1951, pp. 32–4.

4. M. MILA: "Verdi e Hanslick", in *La Rassegna Musicale*, Rome, XXI, 3: July 1951, pp. 212–24; reprinted by the author in *Giusepppe Verdi*, Laterza, Bari 1958, pp. 340–62. Mila justly laments the lack of an outline of contemporary Verdi criticism:

   To trace and place at scholars' disposal the main body of the Verdi writings of Filippo Filippi, D'Arcais, Alberto Mazzuccato, [. . .], Gian Giacomo Manzutto of Trieste [. . .] and many other minor critics and journalists of the period, would be a more useful task than the publication of official hagiographies.

   The same might also be said of French, English and German criticism. Unfortunately, 30 years after Mila's pronouncement, the situation remains substantially the same. Publishers are still more inclined to accept the increasingly useless "hagiographical writings" than documents indispensable to research.

5. A. DELLA CORTE: *La critica musicale e i critici*, U.T.E.T., Turin 1961, pp. 352–64.
6. Volume I (*Die moderne Oper: Kritiken und Studien*, Hoffman, Berlin 1875) contains on pp. 217–55 a critical summary, from *Oberto* to *Aida*, bringing together some reviews that appeared in the *Wiener Zeitung*, *Die Presse*, and *Die Neue Freie Presse*; vol. 2 (*Musikalische Stationen*, Berlin 1880) contains on pp. 3–12 reviews of the *Requiem*; vol. 3 (*Aus dem Opernleben der Gegenwart*, Berlin 1884) on pp. 22–30 those of the revised *Simon Boccanegra*; vol. 4 (*Musikalisches Skizzenbuch*, Berlin 1888) on pp. 319–35 those of *Otello* at La Scala; the fifth volume (*Musikalisches und Literarisches*, Berlin 1889) contains reviews on pp. 69–79 of *Otello* in Vienna; the eighth volume (*Am Ende des Jahrhunderts*, Berlin 1899) those of the *Quattro pezzi sacri* on pp. 302–6. And finally, the ninth volume (*Aus neuer und neuester Zeit*, Berlin 1900) contains on pp. 175–97 a biographical and critical sketch: *Verdi: Zur Geschichte seines Lebens, insbesondere seiner Jugendzeit*. For *Falstaff*, see *Aus meinem Leben*, cit., II, pp. 281–9.
7. The pun in the phrase, that Verdi certainly spoke in French, is lost in the German version: quatre-vingts = four times twenty = eighty.

XXXVII

GIUSEPPE VERDI AND
CESARE PASCARELLA

1887–1893

UGO OJETTI (Tantalo): "Giuseppe Verdi e Cesare Pascarella", in *Il Corriere della Sera*, Milan, XLVIII, 4 December 1923 (republished by the author in *Cose viste, 1923–1924*, vol. II, Treves, Milan, 1924, pp. 169–79; reprinted by Mondadori (Milan), 1942).

UGO OJETTI (Rome 1871 – Florence 1941), man of letters, critic, orator, journalist, impresario, owed his fame principally to the seven volumes of *Cose viste* – a collection of the articles that appeared in the *Corriere della Sera* (of which he became editor) from 1921 onwards, considered to be excellent memoirs of our era, written with lucidity and elegance.

Cesare Pascarella (Rome 1858 – Rome 1940), one of the most authentic and attractive of Italy's poets who wrote in dialect at the close of the nineteenth century, was greatly admired by Carducci and, with some misgivings, by Croce. After a restless youth he devoted himself to painting and drawing. In 1881 he began to publish his first sonnets in Roman dialect in the *Cronaca Bizantina* and *Capitan Fracassa*. On his return from a journey in India, he published in 1886 his first epic poem, *Villa Gloria* (discussed in Ojetti's interview), considered with *La scoperta dell'America* to be his masterpiece. He admired Verdi and dedicated to his music one of the finest sonnets, entitled *La musica nostra*:[1]

> Ma tu parla co' Nina la mammana,
> Che de' sta roba se n'intenne a fonno,
> Be', che dice? Che l'opera italiana
> È la piú mejo musica der monno.
>   E tu che soni appena la campana,
> Me venghi a di' che er frocio sia profonno?
> Pe' me tu poi canta' 'na settimana
> Tanto nun me rimovo, e te risponno
>   Che senza che ce fai tanto rumore,

Er pius urtra piú su, caro Marvezzi,
La musica piú mejo è er "Trovatore"
    Antro che 'sti motivi verd' e mézzi!
Quela pira . . . Divampa er mio furore.
Sconto cór sangue mio . . . Quelli so' pezzi.

He met Verdi in 1887 at the time of *Otello* and very soon became one of the composer's intimate friends. Verdi invited him, Boito, the painter Carlo Mancini and a few other friends to celebrate New Year's Day 1901;[2] at Sant'Agata a note is preserved from Pascarella to Verdi, dated 1 January 1901, 27 days before the composer's death:

My dear Maestro, My sincerest thanks for your kind invitation, which I most gladly accept! I shall be with you at 6.30. I kiss your hand [. . .].[3]

Luzio, who knew Pascarella, gleaned from him the following information and wrote:

Verdi too urged Pascarella to finish quickly his poem on the Risorgimento, and argued that his neurotic pursuit of unattainable perfection should not provoke him to sacrifice the great beauty and goodness that he could already bestow on Italy. "Get it down on paper," Verdi exclaimed, "finish and publish immediately all the new and inspired things you have to say; for goodness' sake do not imitate him (and he pointed to Arrigo Boito) who through ruminating and overtaxing his powers will end up by producing nothing."[4]

Giuseppe Verdi and Cesare Pascarella

Rome, 12 November

[. . .]
And as we chatted peacefully about this and that, we eventually mentioned Verdi too. Pascarella had met him in 1887. The previous year Pascarella had written *Villa Gloria* and Giosuè Carducci had crowned him with laurel: "Never has poetry in an Italian dialect risen to such heights." [. . .]
    Cesare Pascarella is still, apart from his countrified clothes, the same as he had been then, firm and muscular, with a free spirit and

resolute gestures. But tonight he began his story without gestures and with a soft voice:

"After *Villa Gloria* Benedetto Cairoli sent me Federico Napoli. 'Cairoli,' he tells me, 'wants to have you knighted.' 'Have me knighted?' I reply. 'Tell him that if he dares, I'll never visit his house again.' Then in comes Peppino Turco.[5] 'Did you know that Cairoli wants to give you a gold watch?' 'A gold watch?' I answer, 'what am I to do with that? Tell him that if he dares, I won't speak to him again.' Federico Napoli returns and says: 'Cairoli is going to Gropello.[6] He wants you to go with him.' 'Now we're talking,' I reply, and I leave for Gropello with Benedetto Cairoli."

There flashes before my memory the image of Pascarella when, his head hung low, his glance dull, his hand raised with difficulty, he uttered with a sigh the prayer of the wounded Cairoli:

> . . . Si camperete, ve scongiuro,
> Dice, de facce seppelli a Groppello.[7]

Pascarella continued: "In Groppello, naturally enough, I wanted to visit Milan. I had been there only once before, very fleetingly, for an exhibition. So I go to Milan. I enter the Café Cova[8] and sit down at a table. I was dressed, you know, in 'uniform', that is to say, in my own style, with a checked scarf, a flat cap on my head and a pipe in my mouth. As soon as I sit down, this very tall, very thin fellow appears in front of me, with a face rather like a skull. I had seen him somewhere before. You know how fashionable caricatures were in those days. I recognized him, and I knew that he recognized me too, from the same source. He stares at me repeatedly, comes towards me and announces: 'You are Signor Pascarella.' 'And you are Marco Sala,'[9] I answer him. And he sits down. We have a coffee, a drink, another coffee. Tosti[10] comes in, Giulio Ricordi comes in. It was as if I were a magnet, drawing all those friends out of their homes and compelling them all to collide against that little table. We all addressed each other as 'Tu'. 'You must stay,' they tell me, 'you're not returning to Groppello. You must come and meet the Maestro.' 'What Maestro? What for?' 'Verdi, Verdi.' 'I must go to Verdi? You must be off your heads.' 'You must,' they insist. 'No,' I insist. 'We'll all go to the Hotel Milan and you shall recite him *Villa Gloria*.' 'But I have to be in Groppello by this evening!' Well, they put me between them, two of them on each side of me, as if I were a prisoner and they the guards, and off we go to Milan. What a man Verdi was, my friend. What a man! Pascarella? Pascarella – yes, he had heard of me.

He looks me over from top to toe, which, tall as he is, doesn't take him very long, and speaks to me with these very words: 'Ah, you are Pascarella? Then let's hurry,' as if he had to have a tooth out and I were the dentist. The others arrange the chairs. Verdi sits alone, on one side, in an armchair. I sit alone, on the other side, opposite an empty sofa. The others sit all together at the back. What could I do? In my place, you too would have recited. And recite I did. One sonnet, two. He starts moving about. I can see him, I can hear him. But by the time I reach the death of Enrico Cairoli – you remember – and of Mantovani, he is sitting quite still, looking at me fixedly. I also look at him. Two big tears roll down his cheeks, over his beard. When I have finished, he picks me up under the arms as if I were an animal, lifts me up to the level of his face and gives me two big kisses. And that was it; from then on he was my friend."

Pascarella rose. I can still hear the even rippling of the water, as solemn and imperturbable as time itself. "Verdi, Boito, Tosti, Ricordi, Sala, all are dead." And he stroked his shaggy beard. "All dead."

I too rose. We head towards Monte Cavallo, a few steps away and a nice place to rest.

"And did you see Verdi again?" I asked him.

"Many times. He came to Rome for the première of *Falstaff*. The following evening he invited me to dinner at the Hotel Quirinal. Boito was there, and Ricordi with 'Sister Giuditta', and Strepponi. After dinner, Mascheroni, whom they all called Piccinella,[11] came in and showed the Maestro a long article by Montefiore in the *Tribuna*:[12] a regular hosanna. He looks at the title and folds up the newspaper. 'Praises, praises. What use are they to me? If my music is good, it's good. If it's bad, will it be rescued by praises?' And he starts walking up and down, humming 'Quando ero paggio del duca di Norfolk . . .' What a giant he was! Suddenly someone comes in and says 'Over there by the Costanzi theatre there's a great crowd under the window, applauding and asking for you.' 'For me?' says Verdi. 'Then let's go.' We process down a long corridor the length of the whole hotel. Verdi's wife leads the way, majestic, with the gait of a *carabiniere* on parade. He follows behind her. Waiters, chambermaids, foreigners – all stand outside their doors, applauding. There's a tall, blonde American lady, her shoulders bare to here. Not the type who stands on ceremony. As Verdi reaches her she lunges forward, throws her arms about his neck and gives him two big kisses. You should have seen how his wife turned around. He shook his head as if to get rid of those two kisses. But who could have removed them? And so he walked on for a few steps, very serious, and then turned round to have a look at that American lady, as if to size her up. As we reach the end of the corridor music is heard. The Costanzi orchestra had come out on to the terrace of the theatre over the main foyer entrance. 'What are they playing?' he asks. 'The prelude to *La traviata*,' explains Giulio Ricordi. 'Ah . . .,' he replies, as if it weren't his own work. Over there, fireworks had been lit. Verdi's face is transformed. He is as happy as a boy. 'Come and see. Come and see the fireworks!' We go out on to the balcony and shrink back. He salutes people right and left. I could almost hear him: had he been able to speak, he would have said 'Oh please, another firework . . .' We returned to the hall. He was still standing, as merry, erect and lively as a twenty-year-old. He comes and stands, with his hands on his hips, in front of Boito, who is sitting beside me. 'Boito,' he says, 'you must write me another libretto, at once.' 'In fact, I've already thought of a subject,' answers Boito, peering at him over his glasses. 'What?' 'Cleopatra' – and Boito turns to me and starts telling me the story.[13] But Verdi is inexorable. 'You chatter too much, you poets. Write me that libretto at once, instead of chattering!' Boito, who was rolling – you remember? – one of those little cigarettes as thin as a straw, answers: 'These things take time.' 'Time? That's precisely what I haven't got.' 'I have another libretto ready, if it meets with your approval.' 'And what might that be?' '*Nerone*.' Verdi did not even thank him. He could only think of himself, of his age, of his work. 'If only I were ten years younger, I'd accept it immediately.' And he turned his back on us."

Pascarella also turned his back on me. He had imitated all the gestures, all the voices, all the expressions, all the mannerisms of the various characters, as much a painter as a narrator.

"You who knew Carducci so well, whom do you esteem the more, Verdi or him?" I asked.

Pascarella halted, shook his head from right to left, from left to right. "That . . . that would be hard to say. Verdi was a different breed . . . how shall I put it? . . . he was no normal man. With Carducci – and God only knows how devoted I was to him after all he had done for me – with Carducci it happened once or twice in the heat of conversation that I put my hand on his shoulder. But Verdi? No one ever put a hand on *his* shoulder. He . . ." Pascarella stretched out his hand and raised it aloft, and looked up as if to question whether there would ever again be room between heaven and earth for a being of such stature. Then he shrugged his shoulders, as if to free himself of too many memories, and murmured to me happily: "What a day. It's so soft, it seems like spring."

TANTALO

NOTES

1.   You go ask the wet–nurse, Nina –
On such matters she of course knows best.
And what does she say? That Italian opera
Is the finest music in the west.

And you go claiming the effete is deep?
You who can barely ring a bell?
Go ahead. You can cross me for a week
And I won't budge. Let me tell

You, there's no need for all your squawking.
The plussest plus ultra, dear Maluezzi,
The most best music is *Il trovatore*.

Leave off with your rank intermezzi!
Quella pira . . . Divampa il mio furore.
Sconto col sangue mio – now you're talking!

2. Cf. *Gazzetta Musicale di Milano*, LVI: 3 January 1901, p. 6: Cesare Pascarella is in Milan: the remarkable and brilliant poet spent the first evening of the 20th century with Giuseppe Verdi, together with Arrigo Boito, Carlo Mancini and a few other friends.
3. A. LUZIO: *Verdi e Pascarella*, in *Il Corriere della Sera*, 10 July 1940, p. 3.
4. A. LUZIO: *art. cit.*
5. Neapolitan playwright, parliamentary journalist, author of the words of the famous song by Denza, *Funicolí funicolà.*
6. Now Gropello Cairoli, near Pavia.

7.   . . . If you survive, I beg of you,
He says, to have us buried in Gropello.

(The battle of Villa Glori, which took place near Rome on 22 October 1867, claimed the lives of Giovanni and Enrico Cairoli, who were then buried in their native town, Gropello, which today bears the name Gropello Cairoli.)
8. Famous café in Milan, beside La Scala, on the corner of Via Manzoni and what is now Via Verdi.
9. Composer and amateur violinist (Milan 1842 – Nervi 1901), friend and contemporary of Boito, "belonged to an offshoot of Bohemianism, that we shall call "Bohemianism *doré*" (P. NARDI: *Vita di Arrigo Boito*,

p. 159); he won a certain popularity with his characteristic pieces which earned him the title of the "Strauss of Italy".

10. Paolo Tosti (Ortona 1846 – Rome 1916), the famous composer of drawing-room songs, who was already singing-master at the English court.

11. Verdi used to call him "Farfarello" (imp) (cf. *I Copialettere di G. Verdi*, p. 716).

12. Tommaso Montefiore (Leghorn 1855 – Rome 1933), composer, music critic, he wrote articles for numerous Roman newspapers, often using pseudonyms (Thom in the Florentine *Fieramosca*, Puck in the *Eclettico*, Rastignac in the *Tribuna*). His review of the Rome *Falstaff* appeared in the *Tribuna* of 17 and 19 April 1893.

13. Years before, Boito had translated Shakespeare's tragedy *Anthony and Cleopatra*, adapting it for Eleonora Duse, who performed it at Milan's Teatro Manzoni on 22 November 1888. Those performances were famous in the theatrical annals of the age.

XXXVIII

TWO INTERVIEWS WITH GIUSEPPE VERDI

1894

J(ULES) H(URET): "Deux interviews – Giuseppe Verdi", in *Le Figaro*, Paris, 5 April 1894.

IN ANTICIPATION OF the Paris performance, *Falstaff* was translated into French during 1893 by Arrigo Boito; he called in Paul Solanges (Paris 1846 – Multedo, Pegli 1914) as collaborator, who had already translated the libretti of *Mefistofele* and *La gioconda*. At Boito's request the translation was then revised by Camille Bellaigue.[1] The score, too, was retouched slightly by the composer: after the twelve-bar orchestral passage before Nannetta's song "Sul fil d'un soffio etesio", he wished to add a few short phrases for Alice, Nannetta and the fairies.[2] *Falstaff* was performed at the Opéra-Comique[3] (the Opéra in Verdi's opinion being too vast); the composer arrived in Paris with his wife Giuseppina on the morning of April 4, Arrigo Boito having arrived at the end of March. The dress rehearsal took place on the 16th, the first performance on the 18th with Maurel (Falstaff), Soulacroix (Ford), Grandjean (Alice), Marie Delna (Quickly), Land-ouzy (Nannetta), Chevalier (Meg), Edmond Clément (Fenton) in the main roles, and the performance was conducted by Jules Danbé. After the third night Verdi and Giuseppina returned to Genoa. Verdi's presence in Paris once again aroused the curiosity of several journalists.

Two interviews – Giuseppe Verdi

The announcement that the composer of *Falstaff* had arrived in Paris, has unleashed storms of curiosity. While there are those who see in this nothing but the customary excitement that accompanies any Parisian event of any importance, there are those who, knowing that fashions do not last long in France, claim to detect an incipient reaction against Wagnerian zeal. I do not know – but the fact remains that for three days now M. Carvalho's[4] ante-room has been packed; and that M. Boito, the distinguished librettist of *Falstaff*, M. Ricordi, Verdi's wise and shrewd publisher, and the baritone Maurel have all been besieged by the regular army of our colleagues, as if Wagner himself were returning to conduct *Parsifal*.

Yesterday afternoon I spent two hours, for the sake of art, in the corridors and wings of the Opéra-Comique and in M. Carvalho's study. "Verdi's in there, Verdi's in there . . ." That was obvious from the quick banging of doors and double-doors, the rapid comings and goings, the rustling of hangings, the strictness of the ushers, who challenged every intruder who didn't know the password; obvious too from the searching and threatening gaze of the artists who stood in front of the foyer door, through which Verdi had entered, and seemed to say to whoever arrived: "No entry!" They could not enter either. Yesterday, Verdi was rehearsing the ladies, and had insisted that the other artists went away; he had said to M. Carvalho: "I hope that these gentlemen will leave us . . ."

The Italian Maestro is, in fact, inflexible on this point. In Milan, during the rehearsals of *Falstaff*, he had flown into a rage and threatened to leave, if outsiders were admitted to the auditorium; when he rehearses, he wants no one else around him but those who are rehearsing – each group must await its turn. Yet I succeeded in catching a momentary glimpse of him among his Merry Wives of Windsor. Sitting sideways in a large armchair, chin supported on right hand, he observed and listened to Mlles Landouzy, Delna,[5] Grandjean[6] and Chevalier, his wives. As he turned his back to the window, his staring, deeply set eyes lent his grey head, immersed in shadows, a severe, hard, almost wild expression. Sometimes he would interrupt the singing and keep correcting: "No, not like that!" He did not tire of starting again ten, fifteen, twenty times, until the phrase was sung to perfection.

Sitting beside the accompanist, he explains and analyses a nuance, indicates accents by tapping the piano. Then he sings the phrase as he wishes it to be sung; he takes the pianist's place, corrects the metronome markings which were too vaguely indicated on the score. From time to time he exclaims "I beg you, ladies and gentlemen, I beg you, do not lapse into sentimentality! Gaiety! Gaiety! That is the essence of *Falstaff* . . . There, that's good, good, like that, like that."

In the meantime the chorus has been rehearsing on stage: the masquerade in the Forest of Windsor. M. Ricordi, the publisher from Milan, directs the ballet energetically – and he it is who shows

Mlle Bernay how the ballet was performed in Milan; since there are only twelve ballerinas, a few figurantes have been added, who flit about the stage to give the illusion of a considerable corps de ballet; and you can hear "Forward now with the six ladies portraying the crowd!"

Five o'clock sounds. The rehearsals are over; the artists leave, and Verdi, accompanied by Carvalho, Boito, Ricordi and Danbé,[7] rests for a while in the Director's office. The Maestro has the proud look of a 50-year-old in perfect health – and he is 82! Upright, sturdy, with his pink face, less wrinkled than a 35-year-old woman's, framed by a white beard, he gives the impression of being miraculously young. His expression is no longer tense, forbidding and sombre, as it was in rehearsal; it is now the pleasing, almost ingenuous expression of a gentle, austere patriarch.

"I am very flattered," he told me, when I had been introduced by M. Carvalho, "by the compliments *Le Figaro* pays me. *Le Figaro* is for me an old and sympathetic acquaintance. I shall do my best to carry out the wishes you bring to me on its behalf – I am hopeful that I shall succeed, aided as I am by artists such as Carvalho, Maurel, Delna and Danbé. Today I rehearsed the Wives – and I am very satisfied with them; tomorrow it will be the turn of the men. I suppose we shall need four or five orchestral rehearsals . . ."

"Oh, I beg you," M. Carvalho interrupts him smilingly, "let us not discuss the date too much . . . let us wait a little . . . I beg you . . . you will see that things move quickly . . . but whatever you say, Maestro."

And the conversation became general.

"I do not wish you to lose a single day on my behalf," said Verdi.

And although he had alighted that very morning at seven o'clock, having spent a sleepless night on the train, the famous composer was at the Opéra-Comique at half-past one and set to work immediately!

He was soon speaking of his memories of Paris.

"When I think," he said, "that exactly 30 years ago, in 1864, my word, on the same stage where *Falstaff* will soon be staged, *Rigoletto* and *La traviata*[8] (with Nilsson making her début) were being given!"

"And *Macbeth*!" exclaimed M. Carvalho.

"And *Macbeth*, that's right," said Verdi, correcting himself. "And it was you, M. Carvalho, who introduced my opera to the hearts of the people of Paris! Until then it had only been given at the Théâtre Italien[9] . . . where I received no royalties. It is thanks to you, that my work has earned me some money in France."[10]

"And we were sold out every night," M. Carvalho added, not without pride.

"When were you last in France, Maestro?"

"Eight years ago;[11] I had asked M. Carvalho to let me hear Maurel in *Zampa*. It was after this performance that I gave him the role [of Iago] in *Otello*.[12] I recall that with pleasure . . . The time before was fourteen years ago, to conduct *Aida* at the Opéra. Oh, I love France and Paris. I have never been abroad to mount a production of my operas, neither to London,[13] Germany or anywhere.[14] I don't much like travelling, I am a *bear*, as you French say; but I have a weakness for Paris. The fact is that people are so kind to me here; I feel that everyone in this theatre wishes to be agreeable! The performance is almost ready. It just remains for me to hear the orchestra, but I suspect that with M. Danbé there will be very little for me to do . . ."

And interrupting himself, he said:

"By the way, M. Danbé, do you not think that the conductor's desk should be placed nearer the audience. It seems to me that the conductor would then benefit from being able to take in all his orchestra at a single glance . . ."[15]

M. Danbé explained that he thought it preferable for the conductor to be seen by all the performers, which would be impossible if he were nearer the audience.

". . . which perhaps explains the mishaps that occurred at the Opéra," M. Danbé added.

Since we were talking again of *Falstaff*, Verdi asked:

"Do you know what *Falstaff* is? It is nothing other than an ancient Italian comedy, written in a very ancient language long before Shakespeare! Shakespeare took the material and added the character of Falstaff, who in the original comedy was a mere village braggart. He replaced this braggart by an English general who, during the Hundred Years War, continually thwarted the plans of General Talbot, and he called him Falstaff. The rest of the play is practically identical. Boito wanted to return to the original source, and translated directly from the ancient Italian language, which was far from easy . . ."[16]

It was six o'clock, time for dinner. Verdi rose, shook hands and went on his way. "Till tomorrow!" Before climbing into his carriage, he wanted to take the air a little and "regain possession of Paris". He walked for half an hour around St Jacques Square with Boito and Ricordi; he was radiant, sprightly and happy as a child.

"Do you think it will be a great success?" I asked M. Carvalho.

"Greater than at Milan. In the vast spaces of La Scala, which is none the less a wonderful theatre, many things, many details – and the work is full of them – were lost; I think they will be shown to better advantage here."

J. H.

On April 18, the day of the first performance of *Falstaff* at the Opéra Comique, the same columnist from *Le Figaro* published the following account of a rehearsal of the opera with singers and orchestra, which was attended by Verdi:

A *rehearsal of* Falstaff

The auditorium, completely empty, is immersed in shadows, only the orchestra pit is lit; the back of the stage is in semi-darkness. Verdi, wearing a large silk hat, slightly tilted back on to his ears, and the rosette of the Legion of Honour in the buttonhole of his black coat, sits on a wicker chair by the prompter's box, a score in his left hand. He listens to the opening bars – his eyes, full of life, seem to follow in the air the invisible web of melodies, his fingers beat time imperceptibly. At the back of the stage, against the scenery, the artists in their everyday clothes either stand, or sit on wooden stools, awaiting their turn.

The four Wives move forwards. Miss Delna, bare-headed with her tangled medium length hair, resembles a big, happy, unsophisticated girl; she wears a black velvet bodice over a mauve stomacher; she does not stay still, but jumps, gesticulates, pulls funny, solemn and farcical faces. Miss Landouzy, dressed in dark clothes, looks cantankerous and grumpy; she sings reluctantly, as if as a favour, and immediately has an observation to make: a pause is too long, she runs out of breath; she points out that she is out of breath, strangled. Verdi smiles and looks at Danbé, the conductor, and they begin again at exactly the same bar; but this time the singer nods approvingly and makes a gesture, as if to say: "It's better like that . . ." Then comes the turn of Mlle Chevalier and Mlle Grandjean, who, like Mlle Delna, sings with enjoyment and spirit, and whom the Maestro compliments.

"From the beginning," says Verdi. He raises his hands, beats time with extraordinary vigour, singing: ta-ta-ta-ta, ta-la-la-la-, i-di-i-li-i.

And now Maurel. At first he sings mezza voce, so as not to tire his voice, but gradually he gets carried away in spite of himself, and finishes by tilting his hat at a great angle over his ear and acts the conquering, swaggering Falstaff, as he will act it on the first night. When he has ended his lightning aria "Quand j'étais page . . ." the whole orchestra rises to its feet and applauds. Maurel bows his thanks. "He was worried about finding the right tempo, which is very difficult," M. Carvalho told me, "but now he has found it and is content."

Miss Grandjean is about to sing a delicious melody off-stage; Verdi strains his ears, and with a pleading voice and tender gestures he exclaims: "Very softly, very softly, like a flute!"

The scene has just changed.

An enchanted, fantastically half-lit park is suddenly entered by a band of women, dressed in old-fashioned hats and faded costumes, with one of them in deep mourning, covered in crape from head to toe; they move rhythmically, silently and anxiously, and gently sway the branches of violet flowers which they bear on their heads. It is easy to imagine oneself transported into a mad world; the orchestra plays a mysterious melody, Miss Landouzy, with an expression of blackest hypochondria in every gesture, sings delightfully a song about the moon. Other women arrive; in one hand they brandish monstrous butterflies or little lances of gilded wood, with the other they lift up their skirts, which are too long, move this way and that, turn about and become entangled. In their midst, a man with white whiskers, completely dressed in black, prods them, beats the rhythm, dances, sings with them, threatens them with the stick he brandishes: "*Allons!* one, two! one, two! ta, ta, ta, ta . . . *Allons!* You there, don't look sad, smile with your eyes and lips . . . smile! *Allons!*" They obey, as though hypnotized, submissive and over-whelmed – and with their awkward, weary steps they move through the enchanted landscape.

Verdi pulls out his watch, it is nearly four o'clock. He makes a sign, everything stops. Applause breaks out from the orchestra and the stage, the Maestro doffs his hat and bows. The rehearsal is over.

"We are ready, you know," Carvalho tells me; but the closer the première, the more the Maestro wishes to work – he's indefatigable, and would rehearse from morning till evening, and from evening till morning. He's not a man, he's a force of nature!"

"Since this morning, he's been a dynamo," says M. Ricordi.

"I know him," Boito adds, "the Maestro is always like that on the eve of his premières."

I approach Verdi and ask him if he is content.

"Yes, yes, very content," he replies with a smile. The orchestra is admirable. Delna sings with great verve and gaiety. Grandjean has such a pretty voice, Maurel is perfect. If it's not a success, it will be my fault, definitely my fault. . . ."

JULES HURET

NOTES

1. Cf. *Carteggio Verdi-Boito*, cit., p. 435.
2. Cf. *Carteggio Verdi-Boito*, cit., p. 444.
3. After the fire at the second Salle Favart in 1887, the Opéra-Comique was housed at the Théâtre Lyrique in Place du Châtelet (see introduction to N. XXXI).
4. Léon Carvalho (Port-Louis, Mauritius, 1825 – Paris 1897), husband of the soprano Carolyne Carvalho, made his début as a baritone. In 1856 he became Director of the Théâtre Lyrique, which under his management quickly acquired great prestige. The Lyrique made its name by specializing in avant-garde opera: to make known the young French composers (Massenet made his name there as an opera composer), and to revive foreign masterpieces in French translation: most of Mozart's operas, Weber's masterpieces, early Wagner (*Rienzi* and *Der fliegende Holländer*) but also Verdi (*Rigoletto* in 1863–4, *La traviata* in 1864, *Macbeth* in 1865, *Un ballo in maschera* in 1869, *Aida* in 1878). Having left the Théâtre Lyrique, Carvalho became resident producer at the Opéra and in 1876 succeeded Du Locle as Director of the Opéra-Comique. After the fire of 1887 he was initially condemned, as being responsible for the disaster, to six months' imprisonment and fined 200 francs, but was acquitted on appeal. In 1891 he returned as Director of the Opéra-Comique – a post he held to his death.
5. Marie Delna, stage-name of Marie Ledan (Paris 1875–1932), was very young at this time, and had in the January of the preceding year created in France the role of Charlotte in Massenet's *Werther* (there had been a German version the year before in Vienna). She took part in the first performance of the *Pezzi sacri* (Paris, 7 April 1898).
6. Louise-Léonie Grandjean (Paris 1870–1934) had just been engaged by the Opéra-Comique; she too took part in the première of the *Pezzi sacri*.
7. Jules Danbé (Caen 1840 – Vichy 1905), violinist and conductor; in 1871 he founded the Concerts Danbé, which he conducted until 1876; in 1877 he was appointed conductor at the Opéra-Comique, where he remained till 1898, conducting 82 premières (including Massenet's

Manon and *Werther*). From 1899 to his death he was conductor at the Théâtre Lyrique.

8. See above, note 4.

9. Verdi is mistaken here, or perhaps the journalist misunderstood him. *Macbeth* was never performed at the Théâtre Italien; indeed Verdi, despite the entreaties he received from Paris, always tried to prevent it from being given there, for the very reason that the composer never received royalties for operas staged in this theatre, at least during Calzado's management (against whom Verdi lost a court case). *Macbeth* was none the less on the verge of being performed at the Théâtre Italien in December 1858, with the soprano Giulia Grisi (then in distinct vocal decline), and the Graziani brothers, Francesco and Lodovico, as baritone and tenor respectively. In October of that year, the chorus rehearsals had already begun; but several weeks later, the Escudiers' *France Musicale* (XXI, 47: 21 November 1858, p. 395) reported:

> Verdi's *Macbeth* – rehearsals for which were, as already announced, under way – will not be performed next winter. The decision has been taken, and we thank the Directors of the Théâtre Italien for recognizing that an opera of such calibre requires soloists other than Signora Grisi and the Graziani brothers.

10. With several new passages, the revision of others and the addition of a new finale (to replace the death of Macbeth on stage) and a *divertissement*, the new version of the opera had been performed at the Lyrique in a French translation on 21 April 1865; Verdi had not travelled to Paris to stage it, but confined himself to informing Léon Escudier of his own intentions by letter.

11. Between the end of March and the beginning of May; see NN. XXV and XXVI.

12. In fact, Verdi had already been able to appreciate Maurel's artistic and vocal quality during the rehearsals of the new version of *Simon Boccanegra*, performed at La Scala on 24 February 1881; the composer had decided to entrust the difficult role to the young French baritone, having heard him in *Ernani*, again at La Scala. At the beginning of 1886 he had received contradictory information on Maurel's vocal form, and he wanted to make sure by travelling personally to Paris. But this was not the only reason for the journey: there was business to attend to, and above all he wished to revisit the city he loved so dearly (see N. XXVI and the relevant notes).

13. *I masnadieri*, of course, excepted, which was premièred in London in 1847, with Verdi himself as producer.

14. Verdi forgets here that, having been to St Petersburg in the autumn of 1862 to stage the première of *La forza del destino*, he travelled to Madrid in the following January to produce the same opera at the Teatro Real, where the Frenchman Bagier was impresario.

15. See the following chapter for Verdi's views on the position of the conductor.
16. Verdi refers very probably to the second tale of the first day of *Il Pecorone*, a collection of tales written between 1378 and approximately 1385 by Ser Giovanni, perhaps a Florentine (little or nothing is known of him), and not published till the sixteenth century. This tale is considered to be one of the possible sources for the episode of the laundry basket in *The Merry Wives of Windsor* (see "Una fonte italiana del Falstaff di Shakespeare" in *Verdi e il "Falstaff"*, Numero speciale, cit., pp. 4–6, where most of Ser Giovanni's tale is quoted); the episode also recurs in the "fourth tale" of the "second night" of the *Tredici piacevolissime notti* of Giovanni Francesco Straparola da Caravaggio. In the tale from *Il Pecorone*, however, the hero is not "a mere village braggart" but a young man from a rich family, Bucciolo, who had gone to Bologna to finish his studies at the university; and the Ford of the situation is none other than his tutor . . . Presuming that Huret's account is accurate, Verdi clearly exaggerates when he traces Boito's libretto right back to an ancient Italian source. It is possible that Boito had had before him the tales by Ser Giovanni and Straparola, but there can be no doubt that the libretto of his *Falstaff* derives directly from Shakespeare. Verdi himself, as soon as he had received the "sketch", had written to the poet on 6 July 1889:

> *Wonderful! Wonderful! Before reading your sketch, I wanted to re-read* The Merry Wives, Henry IV, *parts 1 and 2, and* Henry V; *and I can only repeat* wonderful, *because no one could have done better than what you have done* (autograph: Istituto di studi verdiani, Parma).

(See also introduction to N. XXXV.) As for the possible sources of Shakespeare's *Merry Wives*, Gabriele Baldini writes in his invaluable *Manualetto Shakespeariano* (Einaudi, Turin 1964, pp. 369–72):

> No direct sources are known for the *Merry Wives*. As far as we know, even though he put to good use a great variety of themes, Shakespeare must have provided the plot himself [. . .]. There is no dearth of analogies between the plot of the *Merry Wives* and recurrent themes encountered in short-story writing, particularly in Italy. Bollough [. . .], for example, refers to these incidents in Boccaccio (*Decameron*, VII,2; VII,1; VII,7; and IX,1) which all, in varying ways, repeat the theme of the disgraced lover, subjected to humiliating trials and the inconvenience of escaping a jealous husband in pursuit. But these examples merely serve to confirm how widely certain themes were spread; and these very themes vouch for the infinite possibilities of variation to which they lend themselves. Closer to the *Merry Wives* is the situation in a tale by Ser Giovanni Fiorentino (*Il Pecorone* I,2) – and one should bear in mind that Shakespeare, only a

few years previously, had taken from this collection the plot for his *Merchant of Venice* [. . .]. An almost identical theme [. . .] was also to be found in a tale by Straparola (*Piacevoli Notti*, IV,4). Straparola was in circulation in Italian from 1550–1553 and in French from 1560–1563, and it is not unlikely that Shakespeare browsed through the volume [. . .].

XXXIX

AN INTERVIEW WITH VERDI

1894

H.F.G.: "Une entrevue avec M. Verdi", in *Journal des Débats*, Paris, 5 April 1894.

THIS INTERVIEW IS of interest because it reveals Verdi's opinion (partially described in the preceding interview) on the arrangement of the orchestra in opera, and on the position of the conductor, which evidently in France, or at least at the Opéra-Comique, was the traditional one of the first half of the nineteenth century, with the conductor placed behind the prompter's box and the orchestra at his back. For many years Verdi had tried to change this arrangement, at least from the time of *Simon Boccanegra*, which he had produced at the San Carlo in Naples in November 1858. Eleven years later he tried to introduce a new way of arranging the strings at La Scala, at the première of his new version of *La forza del destino*. On 23 July 1869 he wrote to Florimo:

I do not know whether we shall be able to agree about giving La forza del destino *in Naples [. . .]. Without mentioning the company, which is not suitable, I would like your theatre (I'm speaking to the Artist, not to the Neapolitan in you) to adopt several modifications, which with modern scores have become indispensable, regarding the manner of production, the chorus and perhaps the orchestra itself. How can you, "just to mention one point", still put up with divided violas and divided cellos? How can you in that way achieve any* bow-attack, nuance, accent, *etc. etc? Besides which, you thus sacrifice the full sound of stringed instruments en masse. This is a remnant of the past, when violas and cellos played in unison with the double-basses. Accursed customs! And talking of customs, I must tell you of one. When I went to Vienna[1] and saw all the double-basses massed together in the very middle of the pit, I (who had been* accustomed *to seeing them sprinkled here and there), I gave a great gesture of surprise and a little smile, which meant:* "these foolish Germans etc . . ." *But when I went down into the orchestra pit and found myself sitting opposite these double-basses, and heard the powerful* attack, the

accuracy, the cleanness of tone, the pianos, the fortes *etc* . . .
I realized that I was the fool, *and laughed no more. From this you will*
understand how I think the violas and cellos, which combine so often in
modern operas, should be arranged. They will have laughed loudly here,
when I had those instruments placed together in Simon Boccanegra!! *So*
much the worse for those who laugh! And so much the worse for them, if
they haven't followed my advice.[2]

On the eve of *Aida*, Verdi confirmed his ideas on the arrangement
of the orchestra in a letter to Ricordi, dated 10 July 1871:

[. . .] *the arrangement of the instruments of the orchestra is much more*
important than is usually believed, for the instrumental colouring, *the*
sonority and effect. – These small improvements will open the way to
other innovations, that one day will certainly come. One of these will be
the removal of the audience boxes from the stage, thus enabling the curtain
to reach the footlights. Another would be to make the orchestra invisible. *This is not my idea, but Wagner's, and it is excellent. It's*
extraordinary that we should still tolerate seeing miserable tails and white
ties *between us, and, for example, Egyptians, Assyrians or Druids etc.*
etc., and furthermore see the entire orchestra "which is part of an
imaginary world", almost in the middle of the stalls, among the hissing or
applauding crowd, not to mention the unseemliness of seeing the tops of
harps and the necks of double-basses as well as the conductor waving his
arms about like a windmill.[3]

And at the time of *Falstaff*, in other words a few months before this
interview, Verdi wrote to Mascheroni on 8 December 1893:

For the orchestra, which is part of an ideal poetic world etc. etc., to play in
the middle of an applauding or hissing audience, is the most ridiculous
thing in the world. The enormous advantages of an invisible orchestra
would more than compensate for the inevitable lack of power and sonority,
or the nasal, childish sound due to its playing, as it were, with mutes.
[. . .] *And I do not believe that your sounding box beneath the orchestra*
will make any difference. Whether it's there or not, the sonority will
remain the same. I also believe that the orchestra, as it is, is well placed
and laid out (and I don't say this because I was guilty of this arrangement
for Aida) but because the instruments blend well, and the strings surround
and enclose the wind instruments in the middle, especially the brass. This
would not be the case, if you placed all the double-basses in a single row

*close to the stage: the brass would be too exposed and would, so to speak,
echo off the walls of the theatre. If you leave the double-basses where they
have been till now, you avoid the problem of their necks sticking out!*
[. . .][4]

Equally interesting and surprising(!) is the aged Maestro's opinion on
the composers of the so-called "young school". In an unsigned
article, entitled *Verdi in France*, a Milanese arts magazine with an
affiliated theatrical agency, *La Lanterna*[5] – very sympathetic to the
verismo school and the interests of the Sonzogno publishing house –
quarrelled with Verdi over his assertions, reported in the *Journal des
Débats*. As we read these assertions, we would be entitled to doubt
Verdi's sincerity, now that we are familiar with his interview with
Ehrlich (see N. XXXIII) and his letter to Giulio Ricordi about
L'amico Fritz (see N. XXXIII, note 10). But one can also understand
the composer's irritation when confronted with persistent news-
items in the press, that attribute to him words he never uttered and
opinions and sayings he never expressed (like his alleged exclamation, having examined the score of *Cavalleria rusticana*: "Now I can
die content!" or something similar (see N. XXXV, note 16, and
N. XLV). The one indispensable mode of defence for Verdi, in the
face of so much rumour, was henceforth to claim ignorance of all
young Italian composers and their works . . .

An interview with Verdi

Like the majority of our colleagues, we saw M. Verdi yesterday at
the Opéra-Comique. But the eager crowd of artists and all the
theatre staff hardly gave us an opportunity of approaching the
famous composer. Today we were at the Grand-Hôtel[6] at eleven
o'clock. After the customary compliments, we sat down next to the
great artist and questioned him immediately on the interpreters of his
opera:

"Upon my word," he said, "I do not yet have any fixed opinions.
Till now I have only heard the ladies, two of whom, I must admit,
are perfect and have what I consider to be essential – the right voices
for their roles. Mlle Delna's beautiful voice in particular has given me
infinite pleasure. She is still very young, I believe?"

"Nineteen, my dear Maestro."

"Extraordinary . . . Today I shall hear the gentlemen," the

Maestro continued. "Tomorrow the orchestra. Boito has complained about the lack of sonority in the orchestral playing. In my
opinion the arrangement of French orchestras is unsound, and it
would be desirable in this respect if the French followed the example
of Italian orchestras. In the first place, the conductor does not stand
immediately behind the prompter's box, but in front of his orchestra
and near the front row of the audience. He is thus in a position to
survey his players, who in Italy are often more undisciplined than
here. In front of the conductor are grouped those instruments which
form the harmony – flutes, clarinets, oboes – which we call the
concerto. Behind them are arrayed the horns, trumpets and trombones; and behind them, forming a circle to enclose the other
instruments, come the first violins, violas, cellos and double-basses.
In this way, the brass never drown the quieter instruments and one
achieves a better, and at the same time, clearer ensemble. I must,
however, say that whenever I have had occasion to hear the orchestra
of the Opéra-Comique, I have been satisfied by the fine quality of its
playing and its delicate and polished performances of the operas in
the repertoire."

And discussing once again the position of the conductor in Italian
theatres, Verdi said: "It is true that this arrangement will hardly
delight the singers, but they are supposed to know their roles, are
they not? The rehearsals are designed to give them plenty of time to
work at their roles, and it is up to them to listen to the orchestra."

We simply could not miss this golden opportunity of asking Verdi
his opinion on several artistic matters of great interest.

"How, my dear Maestro, can you explain why the young Italian
composers have been able to escape the influence of Wagner, whereas
in every other country every artist feels the effect of the Bayreuth
Maestro's system and style. It is, in fact, remarkable that Mascagni
and Leo Cavallo [sic], whose operas are now performed everywhere,
have retained a very Italian form in their compositions, quite independent of Wagnerian theory."

"You will be amazed," Verdi replied. "You will not believe my
words or else you will doubt my sincerity: I do not know the music
of either of these young composers. I have never seen them face to
face and I have never heard their operas. The reason for this . . .
indifference can be explained. When *Cavalleria* achieved the great
success you know of, I was credited with having said the most extraordinary things. I knew nothing about the opera, and it was reported
in a great many newspapers that I was delighted that Italy now

possessed another composer, etc. etc. I never said anything of the sort. It was the same with M. Leo Cavallo's [sic] early successes. Hence my indifference to the music of these composers."

"A propos Wagner, my dear Maestro, may I ask you why *Die Walküre* failed recently in Milan?"

"To begin with," our famous interlocutor replied immediately, "the performance was far from perfect, although Mme Adiny sang the Valkyrie's savage cries with wonderful verve. And then the large audience found the opera frankly boring. After a week they had had enough."[7]

At that moment the servant entered with the coffee. We withdrew, thanking the Maestro for the charming welcome he had given us.[8]

H. F. G.

NOTES

1. At the beginning of April 1843 to conduct the first foreign performance of *Nabucco*.
2. Autograph: Biblioteca del Conservatorio "San Pietro a Majella", Naples.
3. Autograph: Archivio della Casa Ricordi, Milan.
4. Autograph: Houghton Library, Harvard University, Cambridge, Mass.
5. See n. 9–10 (XVI) of 23 April 1894, pp. 1–2.
6. Verdi had reluctantly decided not to stay at the old Hôtel de Bade, to which he was devoted but which, he was informed, had seen better days. He had, moreover, objected to the very prospect of going to Paris to stage *Falstaff*; on 12 March 1894 he wrote to Giulio Ricordi:

   And now to Paris!! . . . *you say in your telegram! Alas, alas! But amen! But what would I do there? More bad than good. And then . . . to face a long and tiring journey at the age of nearly 81!* [. . .] *Besides, I no longer know anyone in Paris, and I would be as lost as in a desert. And then you all say I can no longer stay in my old hotel, where I felt so at home, and I would need to stay at the Grand Hotel, which I dislike!* (Autograph: Archivio della Casa Ricordi, Milan.)

   When he read in an article by Folchetto in the *Tribuna* that they were hoping to see him again in the "legendary little apartment in the Hôtel de Bade", he wrote once more to Ricordi on March 25:

   Ah!!! *I am pleased to hear this, for it means that this* hôtel *is not so dilapidated as you yourself told me! You will be in Paris before me – please do me a great favour and send me accurate information. And if the hotel is at all habitable, reserve for me at once my usual apartment, I believe it is Number 1 just off the stairs on the first floor. In any case, the hotel reception will see that I have stayed there many times, for months and months.* (Autograph: Archivio della Casa Ricordi, Milan.)

7. *Die Walküre* had been staged at La Scala for the first time on 26 December 1893, in Italian; there were fourteen performances. It is not known whether Verdi attended one of the last performances during his stay in Milan between mid–February and May 5; it is more certain that he went to a performance of Puccini's *Manon Lescaut*, new to Milan, on February 7. About the Milan *Die Walküre*, however, he received the following information from Boito in a letter dated 31 December 1893:

> *The Milanese press has hurled abuse at Mascheroni, as though on a rabid dog, calling him responsible for the infinite tedium the opera caused. That is unfair. The prime cause for the opera's unpopularity must be sought in the opera itself and Wagner's system of composition. Another cause is the vastness of the stage, which makes the drama seem wretchedly small. Then there is the insipid action which moves more slowly than a passenger train stopping at every station, and the interminable sequence of duets during which the stage stays miserably empty and the characters stupidly motionless. All this is not calculated to please. The ride of the Valkyries and their entreaty, two scenes that impressed me so much in Turin, left me cold at La Scala. This is easily explained: in our huge theatre, you would need not nine but about thirty Valkyries to produce the effect made at Turin.* (Carteggio Verdi–Boito, cit., p. 221.)

Three days earlier, on December 28, Verdi had received another report from Giulio Ricordi:

> Die Walküre *was inexpressibly tedious, as I predicted! I also predicted that the famous Wagnerians would get it wrong. Orchestrally and vocally the performance was magnificent!! – contrary to what has been said. But three and a half hours of such great heaviness is impossible to swallow!* (Autograph: Villa Verdi, Sant'Agata.)

8. A few days later, on April 14, a music critic of the *Journal des Débats*, while discussing performances at the Opéra, commented on Verdi's statements about Mascagni and Leoncavallo:

> [. . .] the performance of *Salammbô* [by Reyer, to a libretto by Du Locle], in honour of Verdi, would surely have been postponed on account of Rose Caron's taking on more than she could manage, if Signora Bosman, always ready to sacrifice herself, had not taken over the role in the second act and saved the honour of the Opéra. Rose Caron, that incomparable Salammbô, certainly would have wanted to finish the performance, since the Directors of the Opéra did after all suggest to the Italian composer that she and Saléza should sing the parts of Desdemona and Otello in his *Iago*, which will eventually be performed in Paris! Now, it is Verdi's habit to refer to no one and to judge everything for himself: he knows full well what he wants, what

he desires, what he feels to be necessary for the performance of his own operas. And the most ingratiating of speeches, the finest articles in the world will not convince him that he's satisfied when he is not. In addition, he knows full well what music might interest him or give him some pleasure – as for other pieces of music, no matter how great an interest they have aroused, he will not bother to go and hear them, neither will he bother to read them. Seven or eight years ago, the last time he visited Paris, he only wanted to hear *Sigurd*; and this time, the first wish that he expressed was that *Salammbô* should be performed for him – something that should flatter all French composers. But if you ask him about the young Italian composers, who are filling the entire world with the clamour of their rising fame, if you ask him about Pietro Mascagni and Leoncavallo – he has never heard of them, he has never met them and he has never heard their operas. It is almost as if, for him, *Cavalleria rusticana*, which is performed throughout Italy, and *I Rantzau* and *L'amico Fritz* did not exist. *Pagliacci* and *I Medici*, which have recently enthralled the Emperor of Germany, have passed Verdi by, without him even noticing them. Was there ever such a snub? And when his opinion is asked on either of these composers, he not only affirms, but he explains his "complete indifference" towards them, his absolute ignorance of the alleged masterpieces. He recalls that he had to deny vociferously all the eulogies about *Cavalleria rusticana*, which the press attributed to him on several occasions. To create the greatest sensation possible, they claimed that Verdi had not been able to rest until *Cavalleria* had been performed, and that having read, studied and analysed – what a task! – the score of the young Leghorn composer, he had written to him: "Now I can die content!" These words have often been attributed to Méhul, referring to his pupil Hérold; the composer of *Joseph*, near to death, had wished to be kept informed, minute by minute, about the performance of *La clochette*, and hearing the news of its eventual success, he had turned his head, saying: "Now I can die: I bequeath a composer to France." A heart-rending story which the facts cruelly belie, as Méhul had died twelve hours too soon, i.e. on the very morning of Hérold's début as a composer at the Opéra-Comique. It was truly a brilliant idea to re-publish this story à propos Mascagni, but they reckoned without the composer of *Aida*, who has never loved *réclame*, either for himself or others, and who immediately set about denying this charming tale. So we do not yet know, and probably never will know his opinion of these beautiful masterpieces. They will perhaps have vanished, like several other French operas, before Verdi has even noticed their existence. He is a wise man, who does not waste his time criticizing and listening to trivia.

XL

A VISIT TO VERDI

1894

DESZÖ SZOMORY: "Látogatás Verdinél", in *Magvar Hírlap*, Budapest, 26 April 1894 (reprinted in P. P. VÁRNAI: "Verdi Magyarországon" ("Verdi in Hungary"), in *Verdi*, Bolletino dell'Istituto di studi verdiani, Parma, n. 7, pp. 261–2; English translation, pp. 304–5).

DESZÖ SZOMORY (Budapest 1869–1944), author and journalist, pupil of the Budapest Conservatoire. From 1890 to 1906 he lived in Paris, where he made his literary début in 1895 with a volume of stories, and where, as a correspondent on literature and the arts, he wrote articles for several Hungarian newspapers, especially the *Magyar Hírlap*. It was in the French capital that he visited Verdi, a short time after the first performance of *Falstaff* at the Opéra-Comique.

A visit to Verdi

Ah, at last, Tobia Gorio [sic],[1] or if you prefer, Arrigo Boito, appears on the estradée of the Grand-Hôtel, and smiling wanly through his glasses, lets me know everything has been arranged. You understand what I'm referring to . . . Giuseppe Verdi is receiving.

Tobia Gorio follows me. He, too, is an interesting person, but above all modest. He has written an opera, in any case knows music; and yet is content with the laurels of librettist, and is completely at Verdi's service. As we climb the stairs, I speak with feigned enthusiasm about his *Mefistofele* and Tobia-Boito nods humbly, as though for him the opera were nothing but a nightmare.

The door opens at last and in the room at the Grand-Hôtel, dear to Dénes Pázmándy,[2] I catch sight of an old gentleman with little eyes. Next to him, looking like an old bird, Donna Verdi. A lovely and charming couple, who have aged together in the world of music.

"Ah, Falstaff! Falstaff!" I begin, and the answer is unexpected, for the old gentleman with the little eyes, imitating my voice, exclaims: "Ah! Falstaff! Falstaff!"

Then he says in French (since up until then we had spoken no language):

"*For you all it's easy!* It's easy to listen to a performance! But to rehearse it, to get an opera on to its feet, that's difficult. Or rather," Verdi adds hastily, "in Paris that was easy, too. Maurel, for whom Falstaff was actually written, proved this time, as well, as he already had in Milan, that he is a magnificent singer."

"And in Berlin," I add. And Verdi replies, in a low whisper: "You're wrong, M. Maurel did not sing Falstaff in Berlin."

"I'm not wrong at all," I thought to myself. I know perfectly well that Maurel, the singer–politician, didn't go to Berlin saying: I won't sing here until the Germans hand back Alsace-Lorraine. But I hoped Verdi would talk about it. But he remained silent, like a musical rest. And I delivered the judgement:

"Politics are bad for music."

Then Arrigo Boito, or rather Tobia Gorio, started talking about the weather, praising the beauty of the horse chestnuts in the Tuileries, which are already flaunting their little white hoods of flowers. Donna Verdi praises Paris, then Verdi also refers to this subject.

"I went to the Grand-Opéra," he says. "A magnificent production. They were doing *Thaïs*. . . ."[3]

"Did you like it, sir?"

"Oh, yes. Massenet's an excellent composer."

"And Ambroise Thomas, whose *Mignon* is just now reaching its hundredth performance, and who in Paris is considered a mediocre composer?"[4]

Verdi laughs:

"Mediocrity and a hundred performances! That's a contradiction in terms. And besides, composers shouldn't be criticized lightly. For example, you see, *I've had some trouble because of Gounod.* They claim I made a remark criticizing *Roméo et Juliette*. But it's not true. I only expressed, and continue to express, the opinion that, believing the Shakespeare play to be much fuller of pathos, if I wrote an opera on it (as was once my intention) *I would not have ended with a duet, as Gounod did.*"[5]

"They say, sir, that when you return home, you will be writing a new opera . . . perhaps for Mme Delna! . . ."

"Oh, yes," Verdi replies with a smile, "I'm very fond of Mme

Delna, she's a very great artist; in *Falstaff*, together with Maurel, much of the success is due to her. *I'd be even fonder of her if I were twenty years younger, indeed I would write an opera for her!*"

Then he starts laughing:

"You're young, you can do it . . ."

This magnificent display of good will is accompanied by the gift of an autographed portrait. Amidst the expressions of gratitude and farewell, I ask if *Falstaff might be put on in the Hungarian capital.*

Verdi, perhaps out of politeness, answers:

"Probably . . . In any case, it depends on my publisher, Ricordi, he's the one who usually settles with the theatre directors."[6]

"Oh! If you would only come to Budapest, too! It's closer to Rome than Paris."

So Verdi replies:

"No, no, this I cannot do. I'm not travelling any more, *this trip to Paris is the last.*"

Then turning to his wife:

"We're not going to travel any more, are we?"

Ah! What a wonderful, adorable couple!

DESZÖ SZOMORY

NOTES

1. Tobia Gorrio, anagram of Arrigo Boito, which he used as a pseudonym to sign what he considered to be minor works (e.g. the libretto of *La gioconda* for Ponchielli).
2. Dénes Pázmándy senior (1771–1854), Hungarian landowner of noble family, a politician who espoused the cause of liberal reform. Dénes Pázmándy junior (1816–1856), his son, was a politician and representative in the Hungarian Diet, of which he became President for some time. It is not clear to which of them the journalist refers.
3. It had been performed for the first time on March 16 of that year at the Opéra.
4. Not the *hundredth* but the *thousandth* performance was about to be reached (on 13 May 1894) at the Opéra-Comique, where *Mignon* had been premièred on 17 November 1866. Verdi and Thomas admired one another and enjoyed each other's friendship. On April 15, the Italian composer attended a concert at the Paris Conservatoire, of which the almost 80-year-old Thomas was at that time Director. An account of the meeting between the two composers can be read in the *Gazzetta Musicale di Milano*:

Thomas was waiting for Verdi at the foot of the grand staircase; it is well known that the two illustrious composers are old friends. Thomas offered his arm to Signora Verdi, Verdi offered his to Signora Anna Erba, and Arrigo Boito his to Signora Giuditta Ricordi. [. . .] As soon as Verdi and Thomas appeared at the balustrade of their box, the packed audience broke out in great applause, rising to their feet and joining together in this imposing, rare and perhaps unique demonstration. It was most moving to see Thomas and Verdi holding each other by the hand, standing in the centre of the box; there is a marked resemblance between the two composers, even though Thomas' expression is rather suffering as a result of a long nervous disease, while Verdi's preserves all its manly vigour. [. . .] After the concert, Thomas invited Verdi and his entourage to join him in his apartment [. . .]. (XLIX, 16: 22 April 1894, pp. 251–2.)

5. See Destranges' interview in N. XXXII.
6. *Falstaff* was performed in Budapest (as a rule, one of the first capitals to welcome new Verdi works) many years later: on 12 May 1927, in Hungarian.

XLI

A VISIT TO VERDI

1894

JULES MASSENET: ["Visite à Verdi"], in *Le Gaulois du Dimanche*, Paris, 1, 17 (special Verdi edition): 9–10 October 1897.

THIS VERDI EDITION of the *Gaulois du Dimanche*, published on the occasion of the Italian composer's 84th birthday, contains a "homage to Verdi" by French musicians – Ernest Reyer, Théodore Dubois, Camille Saint-Saëns, Victorien Joncières, Camille Erlanger, Rose Caron, Desirée Artôt and others. Amongst these was Jules Massenet, who recalls a visit made, according to him, in January 1896, during a journey to Milan to supervise the rehearsals of *Manon* and *Werther* – both of which had in fact already been performed two years previously, at the Teatro Carcano[1] and the Teatro Lirico[2] respectively, and then again at La Scala in the winter of 1895. Years later, as he recalled the same visit in his memoirs, published in the same year as his death,[3] the French composer assigned it to the time he travelled to Italy for the rehearsals of his *La Navarraise* at La Scala, which was performed there on 6 February 1896. . . . Clearly Massenet's memory was rather weak, since there exists a letter from Boito to Verdi, dated December 2, and assignable with certainty on the grounds of its contents to 1894, in which the poet wrote: *"I saw gentle old Massenet who spoke of his visit to the Palazzo Doria."*[4]

The composer of *Manon*'s presence in Milan during that period is also confirmed by a news-item in the *Gazzetta Musicale di Milano* of 25 November 1894 (n. 47, p. 740):

> As we announced, Maestro Giulio Massenet has arrived in Milan to attend the rehearsals of *Werther*; last Thursday he was at the [Lirico] theatre for a performance of *Manon*, and since the audience knew of his presence, there was a lively demonstration, which obliged him to appear several times on the stage.[5]

That "last Thursday" was November 22; Massenet's visit to Verdi, therefore, must have taken place between the 19th and 21st of the same month (not before, since Verdi had left Genoa for a short trip to Sant'Agata).

[A visit to Verdi]

It was at the beginning of January 1896 [sic], almost yesterday it seems, so quickly do the years pass for composers. My wife and I were travelling through our beautiful Provence, as is our custom each winter, to pay homage to the sun which holds court there . . . thinking as little as possible about music, when a telegram from our dear friend Sonzogno[6] arrives in the midst of our tranquillity: without delay we were to take the road for Milan and attend to that coquette *Manon* and that dreamer *Werther*, who are up to their old tricks again as far away as Piedmont! Those two characters have strewn my life with disquiet and anxiety.

Milan? After all, why not? We would travel by easy stages, off the beaten track. On this adorable coast road from Nice to Genoa, gleaming landscapes, sun, and sparkling seas murmuring at the foot of cliffs can still be enjoyed. But let there be no mistake – at the end of the plain, music will await us! But we shall never arrive. One always says that . . . yet I have travelled before on this florid road, by carriage with friends, to visit the Académie de France in Rome and the Medici villa, and we did eventually arrive. This time too there was a suitable destination. Genoa! A stop of several hours.

Quickly, where does Verdi live? The Palazzo Doria, I'm told, and I run there. On the first floor, to the right, there is a door with the simplest of visiting cards:

VERDI

Here! And I ring, most moved at finding myself in the presence of this vigorous and incomparable Maestro, whom I respect as much as I admire.

There can be no doubt that the Genoese nobility of former days lived in sumptuous surroundings, and that these Dorias must have been very well off. Many artists of my acquaintance, including composers too, could fit a whole apartment into one of these vast Palace rooms.

Having crossed an immense ante-chamber and then a drawing-room, whose windows gave on to a broad terrace, I found myself in the illustrious Maestro's study.

Verdi was writing at a little table; he rose and approached with great warmth. I told him that I would only feel at ease in Italy, after I had paid him my respects.

"Then it's a passport you require? Do you prefer *lettres de grande naturalisation?*"

. . . And for half an hour he chatted with charming affability, asking for news about French opera and showing a sympathetic interest in the works of our young composers.

Then, opening one of the tall windows of the drawing-room, he drew me towards the terrace, from where one looked out on to the marvellous harbour of Genoa. An unforgettable spectacle!

But my most vivid recollection of this enchanting vision is Verdi himself and his demeanour. I shall always see him bare-headed and upright beneath the scorching sun, showing me the iridescent town and the golden sea beneath us, with a gesture as proud as his genius and as simple as his beautiful artist's soul.

. . . It was almost an evocation of one of the great doges of the past, stretching over Genoa his powerful and beneficent hand.

In *Mes souvenirs* (pp. 208–9) the account of this visit is virtually identical; in the final pages, however, Massenet adds the following detail:

Leaving Verdi, I was constrained to tell him that "now I had visited him, I was in Italy! . . ."

As I went to fetch the case that I had left in a dark corner of the large ante-chamber with its tall gilt armchairs, in the style of eighteenth-century Italian taste, I told him that it contained manuscripts, which never left my side during my travels. Verdi suddenly seized my luggage and declared that he too acted in exactly the same way, never wishing to separate himself from the composition he was working on. If only my case had contained his music instead of mine! The Maestro accompanied me across the gardens of his stately home to my carriage.

JULES MASSENET

NOTES

1. *Manon* had been performed at the Teatro Carcano on 19 October 1893, at the Teatro Lirico Internazionale in November 1894, and finally at La Scala on 13 January 1895.
2. *Werther* had been given at the Teatro Lirico Internazionale on 1 December 1894 and then at La Scala on 20 March 1895.
3. J. MASSENET: *Mes souvenirs, 1848–1912*, P. Lafitte, Paris 1912.
4. *Carteggio Verdi-Boito*, cit., p. 234; on p. 459 there is an account of the visit described in *Mes souvenirs*.
5. In the next issue (n. 48: 2 December 1894, p. 757) the *Gazzetta Musicale di Milano* reported:

   The first performance of Massenet's *Werther* is advertised for this evening. [. . .] The composer has attended the final rehearsals, but will be present at the first performance only, since he must be in Paris on Monday to resume teaching at the Conservatoire.

6. Edoardo Sonzogno (Milan 1836–1920), publisher, founder of the daily paper *Il Secolo*. He started out as a music publisher in 1874, entrusting the management of the paper to Amintore Galli. His success coincided with the importation of the most celebrated foreign operettas, then with the operas of some French composers, including Bizet and Massenet himself, and finally with the four famous competitions for an opera in one act, the second of which was won by Mascagni's *Cavalleria rusticana*. The nineties marked the zenith of Sonzogno's career as publisher and impresario; in 1894 he acquired the old Teatro della Canobbiana and opened there the Teatro Lirico Internazionale, and he managed La Scala during the 1894–95 season, which he opened with Reyer's *Sigurd*.

XLII

A PERSONAL RECOLLECTION

1895

ARNALDO BONAVENTURA: "Un ricordo personale", in *Scena Illustrata*, Florence, XXXVI, 22, n. 271 (Verdi edition): 15 November 1900.

THIS ARTICLE DESCRIBES a visit to Verdi on 5 July 1895 in Montecatini. Arnaldo Bonaventura (Leghorn 1862 – Florence 1952) was one of the leading Italian musicologists in the first half of the twentieth century; he was librarian of the department of music at the Biblioteca Nazionale Centrale in Florence, then Professor of music history as well as librarian and assistant director of the Florence Conservatoire, and finally vice-president of the Association of Italian Musicologists. He wrote numerous historical publications, manuals, profiles and scientific articles, including a critical biography of Verdi,[1] which was reprinted in French[2] in a new edition, with numerous changes and additions. He gave greater details of his visit to Verdi many years later in the chapter "Giuseppe Verdi", dated May 1945, of his final book *Ricordi e ritratti (fra quelli che ho conosciuto)*, Quaderni dell'Accademia Chigiana, XXV, Sienna 1950 (pp. 11–15). We shall have to refer to these in order to understand better the article published in *Scena Illustrata*. He recalls, for example, the reason for that visit:

[. . .] It happened that on one day of the year of grace 1895, without so much as a reason or the excuse of an anniversary or some other occasion, I wrote an *Ode to Verdi* in the metre (but alas not the manner) of Carducci's ode to Victor Hugo. The Ode was recited in public by a celebrated actress of the time, Maria Rosa Guidantoni who, on 17 March 1890 and subsequent evenings during the first performances of *Cavalleria rusticana*, screamed from the wings "Hanno ammazzato compare Turiddu", the closing words of Mascagni's opera. [. . .] The Ode was then published in a newspaper, and several offprints were made, one of which (Oh, the impudence of youth!) I intrepidly sent to the following address: "To Maestro Giuseppe Verdi – Palazzo Doria – Genoa."

This Ode, recited on 12 January 1895 in Pisa and printed there in the same year by Nistri, was discussed in those days by the *Gazzetta Musicale di Milano*, which informed its readers that the poem, divided into three sections, "comprises about one hundred rhythmic, most delightful and spontaneous lines, which review all Verdi's works from *Nabucco* to *Falstaff*".[3] Bonaventura continues in his *Memoirs*:

> Two days later I received from Verdi a note written in his own hand, in which he expressed his thanks and referred to my verses as being "much too fine for their subject!" Always *so humble amid such fame*! I leave you to imagine my joy and my desire to take advantage of his words, to meet Giuseppe Verdi face to face. And so it was that, when summer had arrived, I travelled to what was then called Bagni di Montecatini [. . .], where I knew that the Maestro habitually took the waters[4] and where I hoped to find the means of approaching him. [. . .] My first thought had been to consult my friend Professor Carlo Fedeli,[5] a doctor and friend of Verdi, in the belief that he, being something of a musicologist, might introduce me to the Maestro. But Fedeli procrastinated. He reminded me that Verdi was somewhat unsociable and difficult to approach [. . .] and finally advised me to send him, at about three o'clock, when his afternoon siesta was usually over, my visiting card with a request to receive me [. . .]. I followed his advice.

The conclusion of this reminiscence of 1945 is quoted after the article from the *Scena Illustrata* (page 284).

A personal recollection

When at Montecatini (five years have since passed) I had the joy of conversing for more than an hour with Verdi, I took care not to report our conversation in the press, for that would have shown a lack of respect on my part towards the Maestro and reduced for me the impact of our conversation by transforming it into an *interview*.

Such dangers are now past. Today there can no longer be any question of narrating an interview, which would in any case lack the chief attraction of interviews, namely actuality. Today one can simply relate a most affectionate personal reminiscence, which I offer most willingly to the special edition that the *Scena illustrata* intends dedicating to our immortal Maestro.

Having arrived at Montecatini in the early hours of July 5, I first encountered the Maestro at the Regina, then at the Tettuccio baths – but I confess I did not have the courage to introduce myself in such impromptu fashion. It is true that Verdi had recently honoured me, by writing a courteous and wonderful note that I treasure as one of my dearest possessions – indeed I was relying on this to provide me with an introduction to the Maestro – but I was not known to him and I repeat that I lacked the courage to confront him directly. I therefore contented myself with observing him and walking past him several times, but always at a certain distance, so as not to appear intrusive.

Finally, at about three o'clock, I decided to present myself at the hotel; I handed my visiting-card to the servant, requesting him to pass it to the Maestro, and ask if I might be received. Need I explain the commotion I felt while waiting in the ante-chamber for the servant to return? I seemed to hear the Maestro reply that he was unable to receive me or, to sweeten the pill, that he was resting. A few seconds later, however, the servant returned and uttered the longed-for word: enter!

I entered with pounding heart and found myself face to face with the Maestro who, as if to give the lie to those who describe him as ill-tempered and surly, had suddenly risen from his armchair and came to meet me, smiling and politely holding out his hand.

The conversation soon became animated, but I shall only relate those aspects which have some bearing on art.

Having succeeded in the difficult task of getting the Maestro to talk about music, we approached the subject in a roundabout way by discussing Greek music. When I asked the Maestro his opinion of the recent discovery and reconstruction of the famous *Hymn to Apollo*,[6] he seemed rather sceptical.

Even supposing, he said astutely, that one could translate the ancient symbols into modern musical notation, and that the notes of those melodies could be exactly determined, what would we know of the length of the notes and the rhythm? And are not changes of note length and rhythm sufficient to change the character of the melody, and transform both its shape and meaning? The history of music, such as we understand it, the Maestro added, is merely the history of the modern period, beginning, one could almost say, with the great Palestrina.

From a discussion of history it was easy to pass on to a consideration of aesthetics, the Maestro's opinions on which I most eagerly awaited.

One should not be reactionary, he said; one should, on the contrary, move forward with the times (and he has achieved this, I thought). However, it is wrong simply to disregard the past, ignore the importance of tradition and deliberately do the precise opposite of what has been done heretofore, simply to be modern at all costs. The most serious fault of modern music is the tendency to over-elaborate. Certainly one should explore new avenues, but not at the cost of substituting artificiality and mannerism for the spontaneity of true inspiration. In art (oh wise and blessed words!) simplicity is everything. When the form is intricate, contorted, difficult – communication will inevitably fail, and the aim of art is precisely this: communication. And not only in music, but in all visual arts and poetry. Dante, whatever people might say, is not obscure; and those passages of his poem which to us appear obscure, were certainly not in his time. Moreover, when we read Dante (and Verdi reads him continually), the very depths of our soul are affected, and the aim of art has thus been attained.

The Maestro now digressed and spoke of literature, and here too I immediately appreciated the depth of his learning; above all he spoke of the three giants, Homer, Dante and Shakspeare [sic]. He quoted from memory entire scenes from Shakspeare with wonderful accuracy. At that moment I thought that the Maestro's genius still dwelt among the spirits created by the English tragedian, and that he would turn again to Shakspeare, should he once more wish – to the great fortune of Italy and art – to reveal his might. Who knows? . . . We then returned to aesthetics.

Art and systems of art, the Maestro reiterated, are opposites; and those artists act wrongly who sacrifice imagination and invention to a preconceived system. It is for this reason that the influence of the great and titanic Wagner has been harmful. Let us sincerely follow our impulses and inclinations, without becoming the slaves of a system. There is no doubt that our art has for some time now enjoyed a certain revival; and we, confident of the merit of our young composers and in the future of music, can predict success, if they do not insist on substituting new for old conventions,[7] but endeavour to remain on the right path without indulging in over-elaboration . . .

Of these and other matters, not relevant to this article, the Maestro

spoke on that unforgettable day; and I take delight in informing
readers of this special Verdi edition, as I take delight in telling my
sons, that I knew him, conversed with him and shook his hand.

ARNALDO BONAVENTURA

The account of the same visit in the slim volume of *Memoirs*
published in 1950 adds nothing substantially new to that published in
the *Scena Illustrata*; it does, however, have the not inconsiderable
merit of reproducing in inverted commas some of Verdi's words,
which Bonaventura scrupulously recorded on a sheet of paper "the
very evening" of his meeting. The voice of Verdi reaches us via these
phrases half a century later with great authenticity.

It is easier to imagine than to describe my feelings when I saw myself
before him, when rising straight from his armchair he came to greet
me with outstretched hand, saying, "But it is I who must thank you,
come, make yourself at home," when shaking the hand that had
penned so many immortal pages, when staring into those deep-set
eyes that lit up his austere yet gentle and expressive face framed by
white hair and flowing beard, when sitting down beside him, when
hearing his voice . . . Giuseppe Verdi talked with me for more than
half an hour in his room. And the variety of subjects we discussed!
First of all, of course, Verdi once again spoke most politely of my
poem – which led us on to literature, about which he appeared to me
most knowledgeable, making acute observations about Homer,
Dante and Shakespeare. He told me he read Dante continually. Then
(mirabile dictu) we began to talk about music, which amazed me,
because I knew Verdi always avoided mentioning it. We did not, of
course, discuss living composers, but rather the history of music
and, above all, aesthetics. Giuseppe Verdi began by saying (and that
very evening I jotted down on a sheet of paper some of his ideas and
phrases) that "simplicity in art is everything", that "spontaneity and
inspiration are crucial", that when "form is intricate, contorted and
difficult, communication fails, and communication is the aim of art".
He then added: "Art and systems of art are opposites. The great
Wagner left much evil in his wake." And again: "The same occurs in
literature, painting and sculpture. One feels compelled to do the
opposite of whatever went before." Then, beginning to discuss

history, he said: "Music as we understand it begins with Palestrina: prior to that we neither know nor can know what it was." I naturally made some silent reservations on this point, as I did on what he then said about Greek music: "Research into the art of Greek music is pointless: though the notes might be deciphered, we do not know the note-length, and a change of note-length and rhythm is enough to change the character of a melody." He then returned to the general question of new trends in music: "It is wrong to disregard the entire past and deliberately proceed in the opposite direction: yet one must always move with the times. In poetry, no one could today write like Dante – but that is no reason to cram our rich and beautiful language with neologisms and latinisms. And one must above all be clear. Dante is not obscure: many things that to us seem obscure, were not so in his time. Moreover, when we read Dante, he communicates directly – and that is the crucial consideration." Finally he added: "We must not create a new conventionalism in the opera house. Today, a remarkable revival is abroad in music that augurs well; but the young composers must remain on the right path and not err from it – otherwise they will indulge in over-elaboration."

These were the chief thoughts that Verdi confided to me on that memorable day; and the phrases between inverted commas are the very words he uttered, which I recorded scrupulously on the sheet of paper I have just called to mind. The conversation, which was both animated and affable, continued for a long time; I finally rose, shook the Maestro by the hand and left his apartment moved and inspired. I saw him for a few moments later, at the "Rinfresco" baths, and in the evening sat near him at the round table (hotels in those days did not have separate tables, and all the guests used to dine at the same large table which, if not exactly round, was elliptical or shaped like a horse-shoe, which made for greater harmony and easier conversation). I was thus able to converse with him again and with the others who were gathered around him, namely Signora Giuseppina Verdi, Teresa Stolz, Giuseppina Pasqua[8] with her husband Giacomelli, Maestro Mugnone, Professor Grocco and, if I remember correctly, the violinist Frederico Consolo. I also saw Verdi the next morning, but did not talk with him. And on that morning, just to say that in one respect I too had acted like Giuseppe Verdi, I drank what he drank: two glasses of water at the "Regina" and four at the "Tettuccio".

FLORENCE, MAY 1945   ARNALDO BONAVENTURA

NOTES

1. *La figura e l'arte di Giuseppe Verdi*, R. Giusti, Leghorn 1919.
2. *Verdi*, Libr. Alcan, in *Les Maîtres de la Musique*, Paris 1923 (reprinted 1930). This is practically an adaptation of the preceding work (which has an advantage over the French edition, in that it supplies a substantial bibliography, which for many years was the best of its kind).
3. *Gazzetta Musicale di Milano*, L, 9: 3 March 1895, p. 145.
4. It was from the summer of 1882 that Verdi, together with Giuseppina, periodically went to Montecatini to take the waters. That first journey is documented by a letter, without date but probably written in the first half of June 1882, to Teresa Stolz:

> *So the decision has been taken! We shall go to purify ourselves, as Peppina says. I honestly start to laugh, when I think of this poetic cure. The decision to travel by night seems best, and it's an excellent idea to meet us at Parma for dinner, followed by a game of briscola – as long as you are not frightened of losing a pair of napoleons, like last time!* (Autograph: Biblioteca Estense, Modena.)

5. Probably the son of Fedele Fedeli, Professor at the University of Pisa, who died in March 1888 and was in his time Director of the Montecatini baths; he was succeeded by Pietro Grocco.
6. This is a reference to one of the two Delphic hymns, inscribed on marble slabs, that covered the walls of the Athenian Treasury, and which were discovered in 1893 during excavations at Delphi. Annotated by Heinrich Weil and transcribed into modern notation by Theodor Reinach, they were published in 1894 in the *Bulletin de Correspondence Hellénique*. Edited by Maestro Lorenzo Parodi, they were performed for the first time in Italy at Genoa; this concert had been announced by the *Gazzetta Musicale di Milano* (XLIX, 26: 1 July 1894, p. 408), which quoted a news-item from the Genoese daily *Il Caffaro*:

> We read in *Il Caffaro*: "The Greek hymn that has been baptized *Hymn to Apollo* is soon to be performed at Genoa, edited and conducted by Maestro Lorenzo Parodi. [. . .] The *Hymn to Apollo*, performed for the first time at Athens, then Paris, London, Brussels etc., is at present the greatest attraction at all the music festivals abroad."

The problem of transcribing ancient Greek music was at that time the subject of lively debate in the *Gazzetta Musicale di Milano* (see the August editions on pp. 445, 486–7, 503–4, 518 and 540–1) in which Oscar Chilesotti, Tancredi Mantovani and Lorenzo Parodi took part. Verdi, a regular reader of Ricordi's paper, must therefore have been well informed about the important discovery and the questions it raised.

Some of his observations can be read in a book of Verdi memoirs by Italo Pizzi (see N. XLIX).

7. Many years previously, in a letter to Arrivabene of 27 April 1872, Verdi had written:

> [. . .] *It has now become fashionable to scream and not listen to cabalettas. This is as wrong as the fashion which once wanted nothing but cabalettas. They object loudly to conventionalism but only abandon one to embrace another! Oh, the great fools!!* (*Verdi intimo*, cit., p. 144.)

8. Giuseppina Pasqua (Perugia 1855 – Bologna 1930); one of the most distinguished mezzos of the end of the nineteenth century, she was chosen by Verdi for the role of Mistress Quickly in the première of *Falstaff* at La Scala in 1893.

XLIII

A VISIT TO THE 84-YEAR-OLD VERDI

1897

HEINRICH EHRLICH: "Beim 84jährigen Verdi", in *Deutsche Revue*, Stuttgart, XXII, vol. 2: 1897, pp. 325–8.

WE HAVE ALREADY met the name of Ehrlich when he interviewed Verdi during April 1892 in Genoa (see N. XXXIII). This new interview (more correctly an interview of Ehrlich by Verdi) took place in Milan on 24 February 1897. Verdi had arrived two days earlier with Giuseppina whose declining health seemed to improve a little in that period. The chief purpose of the journey to Milan, where the composer would stay till March 16, was to keep an eye on the construction of the future Casa di Riposo per Musicisti beyond the Magenta gate.[1] But there was other work in store for him during those days in Milan: the soprano Rose Caron, the Desdemona in the French *Otello* at the Opéra, wished him to rehearse her in the same role, in anticipation of the scheduled April performances of *Otello* at the Opéra with Tamagno, in Italian. The composer did not, apparently, relish this task, fearing that he would tire himself, having only just recovered from an "incident", caused by a heart disease from which he had been suffering for several years – a secret known only to very few close friends and jealously guarded by them. It had occurred at the beginning of January. Gatti writes:

> One morning Strepponi, entering her husband's bedroom before he rose, sees him lying motionless and convulsed; she calls him, but Verdi fails to utter a word. He makes a sign that he wishes to write, and on a small sheet of paper he scribbles with difficulty: *coffee* – asking for a sip of his favourite beverage, which he drinks very strong and in great quantities. Thus assisted, he recovered and was shortly himself again. It was not the first attack of that sort; on another occasion, relatives found him semi-conscious on his bed. The incident was hushed up, since the Maestro cannot abide any leaks of his own private affairs.[2]

He recovered so rapidly, that a month and half later Ehrlich, who knew and suspected nothing, found him "almost rejuvenated", his head held upright like a soldier, robust as a "60-year-old". The incident, however, caused him temporarily to break off work on his last composition, the *Stabat Mater*, which he had been about to orchestrate. As for Caron's wish to rehearse the role of Desdemona in Italian, that would bring more fatigue, which the composer now attempts to avoid. On February 20 he writes to Giulio Ricordi:

It is now five o'clock; as I haven't received a second telegram, I take it that Caron will stop in Milan, where I shall arrive the day after tomorrow, Monday, at 12.50. I imagine that she will wish to rehearse the role of Desdemona in Italian! A pity that I am a little poorly and hoarse, with almost no voice to explain myself. In addition, I cannot remember the music of Otello *and my fingers are now too stiff to accompany . . . Finally, the doctor tells me not to tire myself, and tells me with such insistence that he frightens me — Warn Caron of all my ailments!* [3]

The next day, on the eve of his departure, he writes again to Ricordi:

So Caron is staying! . . . to rehearse the part in Italian, I imagine. I admire this zeal and feeling for Art, but I very much regret that my state of health will not permit me to explain what I want, to make observations and accompany her well on the harpsichord. One could easily find a repetiteur, but then I couldn't and wouldn't make observations with a third person present. We'll see! [4]

Ehrlich's interview with Verdi deals chiefly with the new conductors and new problems of interpretation, problems, however, that Verdi had always debated from the very start of his career (see N. 4 à propos *Macbeth*) and which had become of crucial importance to him at the time of *Don Carlos*, *La forza del destino* and *Aida* — the period when Angelo Mariani established his reputation and Franco Faccio began to make a name for himself — when it was proposed to introduce changes into Italian orchestras, the role of the conductor, style of performance and production, and above all to ensure that the composer's intentions, score-markings and the integrity of the work of art were respected. It was about this that he wrote to Giulio Ricordi on 5 February 1871:

[. . .] *Ah, these conductors are a veritable scourge! The operas of today require both musical and dramatic direction. There was a time when a prima donna and a tenor together with a cavatina, a Rondo and a Duet etc. etc. could sustain an opera (if you could call it such); today this is not the case. Modern operas, whether good or bad, have quite different aims! You, who run a music magazine, should concern yourself with this subject, which is of the utmost importance. Preach the absolute need we have for talented operatic conductors; demonstrate that success can never be won without an intelligent interpretation; and castigate those asses who are massacring our operas, asses, moreover, who are impertinent to boot. Do you know that a conductor at Naples dared to write on a Mayerbeer [sic] score (L'Africaine, I think) something to this effect:* "Omit this aria — it is awful and appallingly written. How could such a Maestro have composed such a monstrosity?" — *Have you understood me?* [5]

Ricordi accepted Verdi's exhortation and prepared an article which he submitted to the composer for his approval. Verdi replied on 11 April 1871:

[. . .] *I've read your article on the orchestra, which I enclose. There are, I think, several things to cavil at: firstly on the artistic intentions and instrumental effects of our composers, that you quote; and secondly on our conductors and* the way they over-interpret at every perform- ance . . . *This is a principle that leads straight to what is false and contrived. It is the path that led music to the false and contrived at the end of the last century and the beginning of this, when singers took the liberty of creating (as the French say) their own parts, thus producing every kind of chaos and absurdity. No: I want one creator only, and I am satisfied when what is written is performed simply and accurately; the trouble is, one never performs what is written! — I often read in the newspapers of* effects undreamt-of by the composer; *but for my own part, I have never found these effects. I understand that all you say refers to Mariani. We are all agreed on his worth. However, we are concerned here not with individuals, however great they might be, but with Art. I cannot allow singers or conductors the right to create, for that is a principle which leads, as I said earlier, to catastrophe . . . Do you want an example? You once praised an effect that Mariani drew from the orchestra in the overture to* La forza del destino, *having the brass enter* fortissimo *in G. Well, I disapprove of this effect. I had meant the brass, played* mezza voce, *to express — or rather they could only express — the religious chant of the friar. Mariani's* fortissimo *completely changes its character, and that passage becomes a war-like fanfare, which has nothing to do with the theme of the drama, whose war-like moments are entirely episodic. Here we are again on the path to what is false and contrived.*[6]

Above all, then, respect for the score and the composer's intentions. It is, however, Verdi's view that the conductor must supervise and direct, as the *mente unica*, the whole performance of an opera; apart from his indispensable musical gifts, therefore, the conductor must display an energetic will, inflexible character and an ability to control large forces. But for Verdi this does not diminish the importance of the role of the singer in the dramatic and musical performance: on the contrary, the conductor's task is if anything to exalt the role of the singer, to display its importance within the structure of the music drama. It was with this in mind that he wrote to Piroli from Milan on 28 June 1887:

[. . .] *A most intelligent and serious person has spoken openly to me about Mascheroni's qualities and defects: "Having risen very rapidly and with little experience to the post of conductor, it went a little to his head, and he thinks too much of himself." "He neglects to rehearse with the singers – the so-called harpsichord rehearsals – and prefers to concentrate on the orchestra." This is a most serious fault!! The opera will not be well performed, if the singers have not been well rehearsed. The orchestral players have their music before them, in general they know the music better than the singers, and they have the conductor in their midst to guide them etc. etc. The singer is left to his own resources, he is preoccupied with the stage, his movements, his voice, and in addition the three or four thousand eyes fixed upon him. The skilled and experienced conductor must therefore, above all, concern himself with rehearsing the singers. Publishers and composers sometimes accuse him of neglect or indifference, and then Ricordi entrusts him with D. Carlos. Another grave error – grave indeed – is his lack of authority over both orchestra and chorus, which results in lack of discipline. – [. . .]*[7]

At the time of Verdi's second meeting with Ehrlich, the conductor had assumed an essential role in German-speaking countries. This was the time of the great virtuosi, Richter, von Schuch, Mottl, Weingartner, Levi, Nikisch, Mahler – all "creative" interpreters who infused each performance with their own unique personality. And in Italy, after the death of Faccio in 1890, a new generation of conductors was emerging, including Luigi Mancinelli, Giuseppe Martucci,

Cleofonte Campanini, Vittorio Maria Vanzo, Leopoldo Mugnone and Edoardo Mascheroni. Towering above them during these very years by virtue of his legendary performances of orchestral concerts and operas at Turin's Regio, was the young Arturo Toscanini from Parma, destined shortly, i.e. in little more than a year, to take over the reins of La Scala, Milan. The authority and pre-eminence of the conductor perhaps exceeded what Verdi had in mind and led to *the false and contrived*; alarmed by Giulio Ricordi's critical review of Toscanini's *Falstaff* at La Scala[8] – a review not devoid of prejudice against the young conductor – Verdi wrote to the publisher on 18 March 1899:

I have read your forceful and beautiful article (Falstaff). *If things are as you say, it would be better to return to the modest conductors of the past . . . (and yet there were names like* Rolla, Festa, De Giovanni *etc.). When I began to shock the musical world with my sins, we had to contend with the scourge of the prima donna's rondo, now we must contend with the tyranny of our conductors! Bad, bad! But the former is preferable!!* – [9]

In Ehrlich's interview, there is also a brief mention of Richard Strauss, the new standard-bearer of German music, already famous beyond the Alps for the tremendous success of his tone-poems: *Don Juan* (1889), *Tod und Verklärung* (1890), *Till Eulenspiegels lustige Streiche* (1895), *Also sprach Zarathustra* (1896). Strauss had only recently made his début as an opera composer with *Guntram* (first performance at Weimar on 10 May 1894). And it was by presenting him a copy of the score of *Guntram* that Strauss had paid homage to Verdi two years previously, after a performance of *Falstaff*, which he had heard in Berlin, had sent him into raptures. With the score he sent the following letter, dated Munich, 18 January 1895:

Sir!
From my own experience I know very well how irritating dedications can be; nevertheless, I venture to entreat you, the true master of Italian opera, to accept a copy of my first work in this genre, Guntram, *as a token of my sincere admiration. I can find no words to describe the impression made on me by the extraordinary beauty of* Falstaff, *and being otherwise unable to convey to you my gratitude for this rekindling of your genius, I beg you at least to accept this score. Should one day the occasion ever present itself, I should be most happy to converse with you about the divine art of music,*

Verdi at the rehearsals of *Falstaff* at La Scala (1893)

Verdi and Boito (summer 1892, Perego garden)

Below: Caricature from the *Guerin Meschino*, inspired by the photograph reproduced above, with the title: "The new pose of the young Italian school of music"

Verdi and
Boito
(summer
1892, Perego
garden)

Below left:
Arturo
Toscanini
Below right:
Jules
Massenet

Pietro Mascagni at the time of *Silvano* and *Guglielmo Ratcliff*

Verdi at Montecatini: Teresa Stolz is seated on his right
(photograph by Pietro Tempestini, *c.* 1898)

At Montecatini. From left to right: Giulio Ricordi, Leopoldo
Mugnone, Teresa Stolz and Giuseppina Pasqua

Giovanni Tebaldini

Above: Verdi at Sant'Agata in 1900. From left to right seated: his adopted daughter, Maria Carrara, his sister-in-law Barberina Strepponi, and Giuditta Ricordi, wife of Giulio. Standing, from left to right: Teresa Stolz, the lawyer Umberto Campanari, and the publisher Giulio Ricordi

Right: Verdi in the study of his apartment at the Hotel Milan, Via Manzoni

Verdi in 1899

and thus be stimulated to find new inspiration for my compositions – a day that my friend and protector Hans von Bülow never lived to see, either because of his own fault or fate.[10]

The name of Strauss conjured up in the old Italian composer's mind a very different image than would have been the case, had he listened to his music; on January 23 he asked Giulio Ricordi for information:

I would be grateful if you could give me information about a composer from Munich, who has written an opera, Guntram. He is called Richard Strauss – tell me, if you can, if he is the composer of the Waltzes.[11]

Ricordi replied three days later, without letting slip the opportunity of showing off by expressing an opinion that certainly baffled Verdi:

Richard Strauss has no connection with the Strausses, the waltz-kings, of Vienna. He is a conductor and a composer – much esteemed in Germany, but to my mind a puffed-up braggart – [12]

On 27 January 1895 from Genoa, Verdi sent his letter of thanks to the Bavarian composer, which is still perhaps unpublished in Italy:

Dear Sir,
A few days ago I received your work which you kindly sent me and which has had such success. Today I am leaving for Milan, where I shall stay for some weeks, and I have had no time to read your score. A cursory glance, however, shows me that this Guntram of yours was composed by a most expert hand. A pity that I do not know your language, not in order to judge (since that is beyond me, and I dare not in any case) but to admire better your opera and rejoice with you. I thank you for your great kindness and remain your esteemed G. Verdi.[13]

A visit to the 84-year-old Verdi

I had last seen Verdi in 1892; he was then 79 and working vigorously at his lyric comedy *Falstaff*, which though it has few "theatrical effects" and can be criticized on several counts, is none the less a remarkable work of art, which will certainly gain universal recognition. While I was returning this year from the Riviera, I proposed paying my respects to the great old Italian composer, and wrote that I wished to visit him in Genoa, where he usually spends the winter. At Genoa station I was told that the grandissimo[14] had left two days ago for Milan . . . where I too was bound.

On February 24 at half-past eight, I sent a note to Verdi at the Hôtel de Milan, requesting that he name a time when I might visit him. The conveyor of this message had strict instructions to hand the porter the note, and not disturb the Maestro's sleep.

How mistaken I was! Within ten minutes came a card from Verdi, written in his own hand: *Tout de suite* (at once). I hurried to the hotel. The sound of piano-playing came from the Maestro's room, and when I entered there he was, sitting in his town clothes at the piano; he rose and greeted me vivaciously. Not only had his features not changed in the five years since I had seen him, he almost seemed younger and resembled his portrait of 1889. He held his head erect, like a soldier, and his upright bearing suggested more a 60-year-old than one who was born in the year 1813! To begin with he spoke conspicuously slowly, but soon he was talking in a livelier manner. He asked where I had travelled from, joked about Monte Carlo, where he had once gambled away 25 francs,[15] and enquired about the society there; then he switched immediately to the new school of German conductors (*nouvelle école des chefs d'orchestre allemands*) and wished to hear about those, who were now considered the most important. I mentioned Weingärtner [sic],[16] Nikisch,[17] Mottl;[18] he asked about Hermann Levi,[19] whom he esteems greatly, and heard with regret that constant poor health had virtually forced this most important conductor to retire. He then said:

"Could you tell me the chief qualities which distinguish these conductors from others?"

"These gentlemen," I replied, "are orchestra virtuosi, highly-gifted, with a thorough musical education; the instrument they play is the orchestra, and they have developed its technique to an extent hitherto unknown and impose their individual interpretations on a great variety of works. They are the precise opposite of conductors of former generations, whose overriding concern was to play everything most accurately and scrupulously in time. This endeavour led with rare exceptions to mechanical routine. Operas and symphonies were sung and performed correctly; the most popular singers were allowed to take liberties with the tempi, but the conductor resisted these temptations. Today the opposite applies. The young conductors, who all follow Richard Wagner's example and teachings, do not hesitate to change the tempo of an aria or any piece of music, according to how they see fit, if it is a question of obtaining new effects. The first to do this was von Bülow, whose all-embracing knowledge and incomparable memory won him successs even in the boldest of enterprises; Weingärtner [sic], Nikisch and Mottl, all gifted with genius, now followed suit. They make the most intensive and detailed study of operas and orchestral works, and are able to throw into bold relief, in the most masterly fashion, beautiful and interesting moments which had till then gone unnoticed, and thus obtain remarkable effects. No one can deny that they have brought about significant progress in orchestral technique, the rendering of timbre and in developing the dramatic moment; yet during their performances of orchestral works the audience will often attend more to the orchestra's virtuosity and the conductor's individuality than the sequence of ideas in the work itself."

"You are absolutely right; that was my experience, too, when I heard Beethoven's first symphony some time ago in the Concerts de la Société du Conservatoire de Paris. The symphony is not yet true Beethoven, only occasionally do you recognize his mark (*la griffe*). But the performance was so wonderful, the violin passages were played with such flawless virtuosity, everything sounded so beautiful, that sometimes you only seemed to hear the sound and not the composition itself – and it occurred to me that the essence (*valeur intègre*) of the work of art was more (*plutôt*) obscured than emphasized. Moreover, what you were just telling me about performances of German conductors and their arbitrary treatment of tempi – that is beginning to spread rapidly in Italy too; it is almost comic to observe how many of our young conductors endeavour to change the tempo every ten bars or introduce completely new nuances in every insignificant aria and orchestral piece. The audience, it is true, do not always bite (*le public n'y mord pas toujours*), there have already been many displays of hissing; but this style is spreading. Many orchestral works of the new school of composers are being performed in Germany – has this movement achieved anything of significance?"

"Richard Strauss is certainly the most important, a highly gifted and able man. For the rest, the new school displays as much ineffectualness as the classical movement, except that the ineffectual composers of that movement were only very boring (*embêtants*) whereas the new Romantics are repulsive (*répugnants*). The former produce insignificant and insipid phrases, the latter a profusion of every imaginable and unimaginable discordant nonsense, in order to appear original. Nor is this type of romanticism peculiar to music alone, it is prevalent in all the arts: in painting you have *plein air* or symbolism, in literature *verismo*[20] or mysticism. Dear old Ferrari★ had this to say to me ten years ago about verismo:[21] '*Caro*[22] Ehrlick [sic], this striving for truth is a great lie, because it presents isolated psychological problems as the norm.' It is impossible to pass any definitive judgement on the present movement – for as well as the grotesque and the topsy-turvy, it has produced much that is wonderful and beautiful. But I am certain that Menzel,[23] the greatest of them, and other truly great artists such as Böcklin,[24] Klinger,[25] Thoma,[26] and Uhde[27] shake their heads when they see many paintings that are described as belonging to their school, just as Richard Wagner must shake his head at some of the modern German cacophonies. But it is, as I have said, a phenomenon of the age."

"You are right, *c'est le courant*; and the trend will last for a long time yet, twenty to twenty-five years. We shall not see the end of it."

As I took my leave, he asked: "How do you plan to spend the day?"

"I cannot decide between the Certosa di Pavia and Luini's frescoes in Saronno."†

"No problem there!" Verdi exclaimed. "Paintings like Luini's can be seen everywhere in galleries; the Certosa is unique."

He accompanied me to the stairs; his steps were firm and confident, almost elastic like those of a robust fifty-year-old. And the manager of the Hôtel Cavour, where I was staying, assured me with sparkling eyes: "When Verdi walks through the streets with his hat cocked over his right eye, he looks like a widower in search of a wife. But he also lives like no one else in Italy."

And that is true. In winter the Maestro rises at dawn, in summer at five o'clock. In winter, which he spends in Genoa at the Palazzo Doria, he gets down to work (he is at present composing an oratorio, but is silent on the matter and does not wish to be questioned), in summer, which he spends on his estate at Sant'Agata, he visits the sheepfolds and stud-farm, on which he lavishes his care and of which he is justly proud, for they are considered to be the best for miles around. He socializes little. In Genoa he is quite inaccessible to foreigners and strangers of all ranks; his admirers, both gentlemen

★ Paolo Ferrari, who died in 1889, was the most popular playwright of his time in Italy. His exact words were: "Questo verismo é una gran bugia."

† Saronno is about an hour's journey from Milan.

and ladies, have told me the strangest things about his fear of making new acquaintances. For example, in Genoa he sometimes enjoys going to the nearby railway station *buffet* for a sandwich or to gaze at passers-by. But if any of the staff addressed him by name, he would never return.

He does not wish to hear about politics, although his name was once a secret watchword: *Viva Verdi* stood for Viva Vittorio Emmanuele *Re d'Italia*. But there is no one in Italy more loved and honoured by all the parties.

HEINRICH EHRLICH

1. The *Gazzetta Musicale di Milano* (LII, 11: 18 March 1897, p. 152) wrote:

   Giuseppe Verdi and his wife, after a lengthy sojourn in our midst, left last Tuesday for Genoa. The illustrious Maestro discussed with the architect Boito [Camillo] the resumption of work on the building in Piazzale Michelangelo: it is hoped that by the coming November all the masonry work will be completed. We were delighted to find Giuseppe and Giuseppina Verdi in the best of health [. . .].

2. C. GATTI: *Verdi. L'esordio. Le opere e i giorni. La fine*, Alpes, Milan 1931, vol. II, pp. 471–2.
3. Autograph: Archivio della Casa Ricordi, Milan.
4. Autograph: Archivio della Casa Ricordi, Milan.
5. Autograph: Archivio della Casa Ricordi, Milan.
6. Autograph: Archivio della Casa Ricordi, Milan.
7. Autograph: Biblioteca Nazionale dei Lincei, Rome.
8. An unsigned article, but almost certainly by Giulio Ricordi, as the letter from Verdi confirms, which appeared in the *Gazzetta Musicale di Milano* (LIV, 11: 16 March 1899), and which is described as "a curious document difficult to assess" by Andrea Della Corte, when he quotes several passages from it in his *Toscanini visto da un critico*, [new edit.], ILTE, Turin 1958, pp. 80–81:

   We shall not make an issue of hurried tempi or slow tempi, since metronome markings are only authoritative up to a certain point! [. . .] It could be true, therefore, though we doubt it, that the tempi adopted by Maestro Toscanini corresponded mathematically to the composer's own markings. But the result (and of course this is only our own impression) was that this *Falstaff* did not achieve the overall effect that was so genial and charming, when the opera was produced by Verdi himself. The impression we received was precisely that of a (if the word is permitted) metallic performance, as if the pages of the score were of rolled steel and the conductor's baton a well-whetted blade, which sheared Verdi's entire score into thin, identical, immaculate smooth slices! It was, in short, the inexorable pendulum of the Spanish Inquisition [. . .] which conducted the music of *Falstaff* for the whole evening with a baton of steel. [. . .] Just as discipline must not become tyranny, so accuracy must not become rigidity! [. . .]

9. Autograph: Archivio della Casa Ricordi, Milan.
10. A. Luzio: *Carteggi verdiani*, cit., IV, p. 35.
11. Autograph: Archivio della Casa Ricordi, Milan.
12. Autograph: Villa Verdi, Sant'Agata.
13. Autograph: Dr Franz Strauss, Villa Strauss, Garmisch-Partenkirchen. A facsimile of the autograph was published for the first time in *Dramaturgische Blätter*, Munich, 1939, n. 1, pp. 30–31.
14. Italian in the original.
15. This had occurred in March 1878, during a tour with Giuseppina and Maria Carrara. Verdi himself had told Clara Maffei of the incident in a letter dated March 19 of that year:

> *Did you know that I went to Monte-Carlo? I gambled and lost! I lost, because I wanted to lose to increase even further my disgust for this ghastly thing called* gambling . . . *But I lost very little: twenty gold napoleons, and Peppina lost five* . . . *The views and climate are enchanting.* (Autograph: Biblioteca Nazionale Braidense, Milan.)

On the same day he wrote to Arrivabene (see *Verdi intimo*, cit., p. 210), Piroli (see A. Luzio: *Carteggi verdiani*, cit., III, p. 135) and his first ·Amneris, Maria Waldmann:

> *Last week I was with Peppina and our niece at Monte Carlo! A Paradise and an Inferno in one! Nothing more horrible to me than those gambling halls – a veritable hall of the damned! And nothing more beautiful than that resort and that climate.* (Autograph: Biblioteca del Conservatorio G. B. Martini, Bologna.)

16. Felix Weingartner (Zara 1863 – Winterthur 1942), composer, musicologist, and above all conductor, one of the greatest of his age, "wholly devoted to the task of giving quintessential and intimate renderings of works of art" (Dreyer on Weingartner in the *Enciclopedia dello Spettacolo*). Having studied the piano with Liszt in Weimar, he began his career as a conductor in 1884 at Königsberg. In those years he conducted in Berlin at the Königliche Oper, of which he was appointed Director in 1891, and where he scored a success with *Falstaff* on 6 March 1894. He then decided to write an essay on the masterpiece of

Verdi's old age, which was published in the *Signale für die musikalische Welt* of 8 October 1913, pp. 1451–4: "Verdi, der Begründer der modernen Spieloper".

17. Arthur Nikisch (Lébény Szent Miklos 1855 – Leipzig 1922) had at first started a career as violinist: as a stand-in violinist he had played in Vienna under Wagner's direction, then in 1875 as second violinist under Verdi in *Aida*. The meeting with Verdi "turned out to be most valuable for him. He himself always spoke of the great impression the rehearsals for *Aida* made on him [. . .]. He never forgot them and noted down in great detail the tempi, accents and nuances prescribed by Verdi. Nikisch was thereafter considered a truly Verdian conductor of *Aida*." (A. DELLA CORTE: *L'interpretazione musicale e gli interpreti*, Unione Tipografico-Editrice Torinese, Turin 1951.) He made his mark as conductor in 1880 at the Leipzig Gewandhaus, where Liszt described him as "the elect among the elect". Dreyer describes him thus in the *Enciclopedia dello Spettacolo*: "His conducting was based on creative gesture rather than the metronome." He was the first conductor for whom critics began to use such descriptions as "magnetic", "bewitching", "mysterious". In those years he was conducting the Berlin Philharmonic, and he succeeded Hans von Bülow as their permanent conductor.

18. Felix Mottl (Unter St Veit, Vienna 1856 – Munich 1911), a fellow-student of Nikisch, he was one of the great Wagnerian conductors. He made his début in 1872 in Vienna, conducting the concerts of the Wagnerverein, which had been founded by young Wagnerians; in 1876 Wagner summoned him to Bayreuth with Hans Richter, Arthur Seidl and H. Zumpe. From 1886 to 1907 he conducted at the Bayreuth Festival. In those years he was also active at the Karlsruhe Hofoper, where he was appointed principal conductor in 1880, and Generalmusikdirektor in 1893.

19. Hermann Levi (Giessen 1839 – Munich 1900), a close friend of Brahms, he only slowly accepted Wagner, without ever attaining the fanaticism of the Leipzig composer's most fervent supporters. He first made his name at Karlsruhe, where he conducted from 1863–1872; he then moved as Generalmusikdirektor to Munich, where in 1878 he conducted the entire *Ring*. Having heard him conduct *Tristan* in Munich in 1881, Wagner entrusted to him the première of *Parsifal* (Bayreuth, 28 July 1882), and he remained its sole conductor (except in 1888 when Mottl took his place) until 1894. He retired from conducting in 1896.

20. Italian in the original.

21. Italian in the original.

22. Italian in the original.

23. Adolf Menzel (Breslau 1815 – Berlin 1905), painter, draughtsman and engraver; famous for his woodcuts.

24. Arnold Böcklin (Basle 1827 – San Domenico di Fiesole 1901), the

famous Swiss–German artist; he lived for a long time in Italy and became an exponent of a new movement in romantic painting, that was inspired by Classicism.

25. Max Klinger (Leipzig 1857 – Grossjena 1920), engraver, sculptor and painter; he partly absorbed Böcklin's teaching, and was one of the most important exponents of German Neoclassicism.

26. Hans Thoma (Bernau 1839 – Karlsruhe 1924), one of the most popular German painters of his time, he was an engraver who painted allegorical and symbolic scenes.

27. Fritz von Uhde (Wokenburg, Saxony 1848 – Munich 1911), a painter who was converted to *plein air* painting.

XLIV

VERDI AT TURIN
VERDI VISITED BY TOSCANINI

1884–1898

GIUSEPPE DEPANIS: ("Verdi a Torino – Una visita di Toscanini a Verdi"), in
*I Concerti Popolari ed il Teatro Regio di Torino. Quindici anni di vita musicale.
Appunti – Ricordi*, Società Tipografico-Editrice Nazionale, Turin, 1914–15,
2 vols; v. vol. II, chapter XVII, pp. 234–40.

GIUSEPPE DEPANIS (Turin 1853–1942), journalist and arts critic was
the son of Giovanni Depanis, an amateur musician and then impresario who, called upon to run the Teatro Regio at Turin and the
Istituzione dei Concerti Popolari, succeeded within very few years in
making Turin one of the foremost cities of Italian musical life, where
Lohengrin was revived in 1876 (after its failure at La Scala three years
earlier), where Massenet's *Il re di Lahore*, Goldmark's *La regina di
Saba* and Catalani's first opera *Elda* all had their Italian première, and
where *Carmen* was finally successful in 1881. In 1886, as impresario
of the Carignano, he arranged Toscanini's début there, on the
conductor's return from his first appearance in Rio de Janeiro.

Giuseppe Depanis, a prominent figure in the musical life of Turin,
collaborated closely with his father, organized the music festivals of
the Turin Exhibitions of 1884, 1898 and 1911 and formed close
friendships with the most important musicians of the era, particularly Catalani and Toscanini. He was, above all, a disciple of
Wagner, and one of the first subscribers to the Bayreuth Festival,
which he attended regularly; he organized tours of Wagner operas
around Italy and published several works on the operas. His two
volumes on the Concerti Popolari and the Teatro Regio constitute a
most precious source of information concerning the musical life of
the second half of the nineteenth century; they still represent a model
of musical historiography which stands out clearly among the rather
modest Italian publications of the time on the history of institutions
and musical events. Even today these works can be read with
undiminished interest.

Verdi's presence at a concert given by the Turin orchestra, conducted by Franco Faccio in June 1884, encouraged Depanis to recall

not only this episode but also his meeting with Verdi in 1898 at Genoa, where he and Toscanini had travelled to arrange the performance of the three *Pezzi sacri*★, which Toscanini was to conduct at the Turin Exhibition of 1898 and which had been premièred very recently in Paris.[1] To Depanis' request for a meeting at the Palazzo Doria with Toscanini and Venturi, the chorus-master, Verdi made the following reply from Genoa on April 18:

Please excuse my brief reply, but I am tired and not in the best of health. Maestri Toscanini and Venturi may come here whenever they like. After midday I am always at home. – A chorus of 200 voices seems excessive. Such large numbers always produce too fat and inflated a tone and a sound that is, so to speak, profane. There's no need for it here; even if you divide the chorus in two, you would require at the very most 120 voices, plus a few exra basses. We can discuss this better when we meet. Thank you for everything [. . .][2]

The meeting must therefore have taken place after April 18 but before the 26th of the same month, when Verdi travelled to Milan to remain there till the end of May. The three *Pezzi sacri* were performed in Turin on 26 May 1898 in the Salone dei Concerti dell'Esposizione, and repeated on May 28 and 30.

Whenever he was questioned about his dealings with the great composer, Toscanini always spoke of this meeting with Verdi in Genoa for the *Pezzi sacri*, alluding especially to a remark made to him by Verdi about the rendering of an unmarked "allargando", which we students at the Milan Conservatoire at the end of the 1950s often heard from Antonino Votto, Professor of Conducting and Toscanini's faithful collaborator, who had heard the story several times from Toscanini himself. Alceo Toni, in conversation with Toscanini, writes:

Naturally, we discussed a variety of topics during our conversations which were by now held in a spirit of mutual artistic trust, and thus it was that he came to tell me of his first visit to Verdi. Toscanini, always thoughtful when dealing with matters of art, which he approached with a reverence that might be termed priestly, was to conduct for the first time [. . .] the *Pezzi sacri* by

★ *Stabat Mater, Laudi alla Vergine Maria* and *Te Deum*. In accordance with Verdi's wishes, the *Ave Maria* was omitted from both the Paris and the Turin concerts [translator's note].

the Busseto composer; and he asked Verdi himself for advice on how to interpret his own music. Verdi sat him down at the piano. Toscanini, having reached a certain passage, yielded to the temptation – not without misgiving, he told me, but instinctively as he had always done in studying the work – of playing a short *allargando*, not marked in his score.

"Good, good," Verdi interrupted him, "that's how it should be played."

Toscanini, half puzzled and half delighted, gazed at him without speaking.

"Exactly like that. And do you know why I didn't write in the *allargando* that you, quite correctly, just played? Who knows how and how often certain interpreters would have then exaggerated the marking?" [3]

Della Corte gives an almost analogous version of this episode in his monograph on Toscanini. [4] The latter's first real encounter with Verdi took place in 1887 during rehearsals for *Otello*; in that year Toscanini had been engaged as second cellist in the La Scala orchestra. And connected with this encounter is an episode related here by Filippo Sacchi:

[. . .] Toscanini offered his services and in fact played as second cellist on that memorable evening which witnessed the astonishing new triumph of the grand old man of opera. Faccio conducted but Verdi assiduously attended the rehearsals. Despite his veneration for the Maestro, the young Toscanini did not always agree with him on matters of interpretation in that performance. He confided this some years ago to a friend: "I sometimes imagine that in my dotage I too will, without wishing to be careless, sometimes miss the mark, a bit like Verdi during the rehearsals of *Otello*. For example, I was not at all convinced by some of the double-bass passages. But Verdi said nothing."
And it is well-known how, during one of these rehearsals, Toscanini was criticized personally by Verdi. The full version runs like this. After the end of the first act, the grand old man was seen making his way through the stalls towards the orchestra. Toscanini, who was the cellist nearest the auditorium, had remained motionless, spellbound at the sight of the approaching composer; suddenly, the cellist sharing his desk nudged him with his elbows and said: "Look, everyone's standing up."

Toscanini then rose too. Verdi turned to none other than Toscanini and said that he had played too softly in the quartet, and that next time he must play louder. He would have liked to reply that he had played softly, because his part was marked *pianissimo*, but said nothing. The truth was that the first cellist, Magrini, had played too loudly. Magrini was a magnificent cellist, but being slightly pushing by nature and accustomed to hearing his powerful touch praised, had been unable to restrain himself from playing for mere effect, and Faccio, who never felt up to arguing, let things be.[5]

The passage that earned Toscanini Verdi's criticism was the solo for four muted cellos that ushers in the final duet of the first act of *Otello*, "Già nella notte densa", in which the melody is given to the first cello. When we were told this episode by Antonino Votto (who naturally had it from Toscanini himself) he added that in those years the first cellist, in order to accentuate the sonority of his own playing, avoided using the mute as much as possible when it was required; and when compelled to use it by the sharp command of a strict conductor, who would not tolerate suggestions from an instrumentalist, however expert he might be, he resorted to the trick of setting the mute precariously in position, in such a way that at the slightest vibration from the string on which it barely rested, it would fall to the ground. . . . A trick which Toscanini wished to expose and eradicate when, as chief conductor of La Scala in 1898, he found himself confronted by Magrini, "still a fine player but still accustomed to exaggerate [. . .] and since Toscanini did not permit him these excesses, Magrini left after two years".[6]

[*Verdi at Turin – Verdi visited by Toscanini*]

[. . .] There was however no lack of happy episodes, among the happiest of which was the presence of Giuseppe Verdi at the sixth concert given by the Turin orchestra on 22 June 1884. No one had got wind of the visit. Franco Faccio, who was on the best of terms with Verdi, was not even aware that he had arrived in Turin. The Maestro bought two tickets at the box-office and he and his wife quietly took their places. At first he passed unnoticed, although the portrait of him that stood out above the orchestra threatened to expose his incognito. Then someone pointed out the sprightly old man with the greyish beard and energetic appearance, and Faccio promptly recognized him. The orchestra would have liked to pay him homage by including the overture to *I vespri siciliani* in the programme, but Faccio advised against it: "he would take flight at once and never pardon me", and waited till after the concert to pay him his respects. That was sufficient for the audience, now aware of the distinguished guest, to burst into applause from which Verdi and his lady expressing their thanks, hastily escaped, escorted by Faccio, through the orchestra's dressing-room, into the gallery.

[. . .] Verdi, however, then displayed such an interest in the concert which he had attended on June 22, that he wished to study the score of Liszt's *Mazeppa*[7] at leisure in the Albergo Trombetta, where he was staying; and because he had to leave for Montecatini and would therefore miss the next concert on the 29th, he was invited to a rehearsal and was welcomed and fêted by the players.[8]

It was then that I had the honour of approaching Verdi and was struck by his affability and simplicity of manner – not what legend had led me to believe. To win his favour, you merely had to refrain from discussing his own music; as soon as some unwise individual thought it his duty to touch on that theme, Verdi's face would darken, he would reply monosyllabically, seek to change the subject, and if he failed, would then ignore his interlocutor. A certain festival official, who had substituted Franco Faccio's *Cantata Inaugurale* for the overture of *La favorita*, learnt this to his own cost. At a firework display on the River Po he happened to meet our little party, consisting of Verdi, his wife, Faccio, Count Villanova, my father and me, and expressed a wish to be introduced to the Maestro. Suddenly, after the conventional compliments, he astounded us all by asking Verdi point-blank: "Well then, Maestro, what beautiful piece are you working on at present?" Verdi, thunderstruck by this unexpected blow, frowned, shot his victim a disdainful glance, restrained himself and, without so much as a reply, continued describing the misfortune he had experienced during an excursion to Soperga on the Agudio railway which had just opened. With half the journey over, the train had remained stationary for an hour in a tunnel because of damage to the wire cable. And he now described, with a tinge of affectionate humour, the fears of the female passengers, including those of his wife, who protested against the mockery and denied the charge.

I have mentioned the firework displays on the Po [. . .] arranged by the Festival Committee. [. . .] Faccio was a firework fan. At the sight of every catherine wheel, every rocket and every explosion, he shouted, stamped his feet like a little boy, clapped his hands, and his enthusiasm was so infectious that he finally managed to persuade Giuseppe Verdi and his wife to attend a display. For a while the Maestro, wishing to amuse himself at Faccio's expense, affected a cold indifference. "What? You mean to say that was all? A few fire-crackers and rockets, a great din for no good reason. It wasn't worth the bother. They did better at the Busseto village festival!" Faccio, now in quite a state, made every effort to convince Verdi that he had merely seen the preliminaries which were, he had to admit, not unimpressive, but nothing compared to what he would see later: whistling bombs – precisely like the ones they needed in the theatre – bombs with seven bangs, bombs with seven colours, enchanting, wondrous. . . . Verdi smiled and hesitated. Suddenly, accompanied by a deep roar, a ball of fire soars into the sky, bursts, scatters in all directions smaller bombs, which in turn burst into a myriad of green, white, gold, blue and violet stars. The waters of the Po reflect the countless lights raining from the sky, and the beaches, balconies and house-roofs teem with momentarily illumined heads, which plunge the very next instant back into darkness. Verdi utters an exclamation of wonder. Faccio replies with a cry of gratitude, since he had ended up by immersing himself in the firework display and deluding himself that he had contributed to its success. Verdi and his wife returned to subsequent displays, and Faccio regarded this as his most cherished triumph.

I next saw Giuseppe Verdi between trains at Turin station in 1893, when he was returning from a performance of *Falstaff* in Paris;[9] and once again I found in him a courtesy which was all the more exquisite for being spontaneous. It was always said that he disdained official demonstrations and shunned everything that smacked of pomp, but enjoyed displays of affection in which the soul of the people spoke. And indeed no artist was more genuinely popular than he, no one was more intimately at one with his race and no one represented better than he, in good fortune or bad, the national idea. In 1848, "Viva Verdi" was a symbol of liberty and a watchword that incited revolution; in 1887 and 1893, with *Otello* and *Falstaff*, he broke his long silence, and in what were for us sad times raised once more our depressed spirits and boosted the prestige of Italy abroad. The Italian people, conscious of this, recognized in Verdi not only the composer of Manrico, Violetta and Rigoletto, but the patriarch, the guardian deity of the fatherland, and felt attracted to him by a fascination that was at once admiration and gratitude. Indeed, as soon as Verdi's presence at Turin station was discovered, all sorts of people rushed towards him from all directions: skilled workers, unskilled workers, white collar workers, porters, carabinieri – all who were able to leave their work for a moment rushed towards the Paris train, crowded round the wagon-lit where the Maestro was about to sit down, and doffed their hats in reverence, while travellers appeared at the windows of stationary trains and enquired about the cause of the unusual throng, and once they had been informed, they too doffed their hats and gazed emotionally at the grand old man, who was talking with us. When the train began to move, a mighty cheer burst from the crowd, which till then had remained silent, and the men waved their hats and the women waved their handkerchiefs in an irresistible impulse of affection. Standing upright at the window, Giuseppe Verdi waved back, visibly moved. Ah, that was not the popularity of which many men foolishly boast, a popularity which feeds off curiosity and leaves no trace; that was the strong, indestructible popularity fashioned by love.

My final meeting with the Maestro was in Genoa at the Palazzo Doria in April 1898. Arturo Toscanini, Venturi (the chorus-master)[10] and I had come to discuss details with the Maestro for the performance of the three *Pezzi sacri*, his last work, which Toscanini was to conduct at the Turin Exhibition to celebrate the fiftieth anniversary of the Constitution. Verdi received us in his bedroom, whose walls were adorned with sketches, drawings and caricatures – French for the most part, I thought – which portrayed him in a variety of ways, one of which, executed at the time of *I vespri*, depicted him wearing a huge top hat. Toscanini sat down at the piano, and the Maestro and the young conductor were not long in understanding each other. Verdi was amazed at Toscanini's quickness of perception. For my part I was astonished at the 85-year-old who rediscovered his old energy at the piano. His voice was veiled at first but grew clear and imperious, his eyes sparkled, no detail of the performance escaped him. He explained his own intentions with brief, precise, vivid phrases, which said much more than a long commentary. One phrase in particular remained in my memory and made us all smile, the Maestro included. Towards the end of the choral *Te Deum*, a single soprano voice suddenly cries out for mercy. This solo of very few bars in a piece that is essentially choral arouses a certain surprise. To enhance its effect Verdi recommended that the singer be placed as far away as possible, hidden from the audience, almost as a voice from beyond, a voice of awe and supplication. "It is the voice of humanity in fear of hell," he said to explain the idea more graphically, stressing in the French manner the ü of *umanità* and *paura*, as our forefathers used to in Piedmont. [. . .]

As we took our leave we expressed on behalf of the town council and the committee their keen desire to see him once again in their midst at the first performance of the *Pezzi sacri*, and I reminded him of the Exhibition of 1884. For a moment or two he was lost in thought, he then expressed his thanks, praised the city of Turin but replied that his doctors had forbidden him to expose himself to any emotion. "I am old, gentlemen, old," he repeated and smiled wearily as he spoke. And thus it was that my final vision of Giuseppe Verdi resembled that of another great man, Richard Wagner: the vision of a fighter who, conscious of having performed his own duty and sure of immortality, longs for ultimate peace.

GIUSEPPE DEPANIS

NOTES

1. On 7 April 1898 under the baton of Paul Taffanel, for the Société des Concerts of the Paris Conservatoire.
2. Autograph: Collezione Giulio Benelli, Turin; facsimile in G. DEPANIS: *I Concerti Popolari* [. . .], cit., opposite page 236.
3. A. TONI: "Lettera e spirito", in *Musica d'Oggi*, Milan, new series, 1, 10: December 1958, p. 608.
4. A. DELLA CORTE: *Toscanini visto da un critico*, ILTE, Turin 1958, pp. 70–71:

> [Verdi] had commented thus on the *Te Deum*: "The whole piece must be performed in the same tempo, as indicated by the metronome," and he added that "in certain passages the tempo may be broadened or quickened to provide the necessary expression and colour, as long as the conductor returns to the original tempo." Easier said than done. The meticulous and uncertain Toscanini wished to consult the composer, especially about a passage he felt he rendered well with a *ritardando*. [. . .] He hoped that Verdi himself would play them [*I Pezzi sacri*]. He could thus have checked his interpretation at the authentic source. But the aged Maestro did not wish to tire himself. It was up to Toscanini to perform them. Hesitantly, he began the *Te Deum*; then, growing bolder, he played it with the elasticity he felt to be right. When he had finished, Verdi did not wait for the young man to ask him his opinion. "Bravo, that's how I conceived it," he exclaimed and, pleased, gave Toscanini a

friendly pat on the shoulder. With rising spirits, the artist ventured to ask: "Maestro, why did you not write it in?" Verdi replied: "For fear that it would be played too slowly."

5. F. SACCHI: *Toscanini. Un secolo di musica*, Longanesi, Milan 1960, pp. 71–72. For the same episode see also A. DELLA CORTE, *op. cit.*, pp. 26–27.

6. F. SACCHI, *op. cit.*, p. 72.

7. Besides Liszt's *Mazeppa*, which closed the programme, the concert of June 22 included Rossini's *Semiramide* overture, the overture to Goldmark's *Sakuntala*, a *Minuetto* for strings by Bolzoni, Meyerbeer's overture to the tragedy *Struensee*, Chabrier's rhapsody *España* and Schubert's *Moments musicaux* for strings (cf. G. DEPANIS, *op. cit.*, p. 280).

8. The programme for the concert of June 29, also conducted by Faccio, included the overture to Weber's *Der Freischütz*, the first movement of Beethoven's String Quartet in C minor, op. 18, no 4, Faccio's overture to the tragedy *Maria Antonietta*, *Notte Primaverile* by Burgmein (pseudonym of Giulio Ricordi), the overture to Wagner's *Der fliegende Holländer* and the "Coronation March" from Meyerbeer's *Le prophète* (cf. G. DEPANIS, *op. cit.*, p. 281).

9. It was not in 1893 but 1894 (cf., however, NN XXXVIII and XXXIX), that Verdi was passing through Turin on April 4 en route from Genoa to Paris (see an article by Depanis, "Verdi di passaggio a Torino", published in the *Gazzetta Piemontese*, then reprinted in the *Gazzetta Musicale di Milano* n. 14, 8 April 1894, pp. 209–10) and then again around April 26, returning from Paris to Milan.

10. Aristide Venturi, born at Finale Emilia in 1859, became chorus-master at La Scala in 1894, a post that he held for more than twenty years.

XLV

VERDI
(PERSONAL REMINISCENCES)

1895–1900

PIETRO MASCAGNI: "Verdi (ricordi personali)", in *La Lettura*, Milan, XXX, 1: January 1931, pp. 4–8.

ACCORDING TO MASCAGNI'S own assertion, his first meeting with Verdi was arranged by Giulio Ricordi. Mascagni does not specify the month or the year but merely gives a vague indication of the date: "after *Cavalleria*". This first meeting can perhaps be placed a little earlier than the composition of *Iris* (1896–98), the opera which the composer from Leghorn, having proved himself in the Concorso Sonzogno with *Cavalleria rusticana*, had undertaken to write for the publisher Ricordi. The meeting probably took place at the time of the first performance of *Guglielmo Ratcliff*, his fourth opera, produced at La Scala on 16 February 1895, and based on Heine's verse tragedy of the same name, in the translation made years previously by Andrea Maffei, the poet and translator so close to Verdi between 1845–47, the years of *Macbeth* and *I masnadieri*.[1] The very name of Maffei could have roused Verdi's curiosity about Mascagni's new opera, all the more so as he found himself in Milan at the precise time of the première of *Ratcliff*. Verdi had arrived in the Lombard capital on 28 January 1895 and departed on about March 7.[2] This coincidence of dates can also help to explain the passage in Mascagni's narrative about his "naïve ambition" to stay at the Hôtel de Milan "in the very apartment where Verdi was wont to stay", and his readiness, however, "to move out as soon as the Maestro's arrival was announced". Mascagni had touched upon this "weakness" of his in a previous article recalling a visit to Verdi, published in 1913 in the *Scena Illustrata*'s special edition on Verdi:[3]

> Several years ago I was in Milan, occupying the apartment at the *Hôtel Milan* that was called *l'appartamento di Verdi*. What do you expect? I longed to live for a while in the surroundings where *he*

lived for a good part of the year; I felt at home in that spacious drawing-room, adorned with his splendid portrait in oil (by Pagliano, I think), gazing down from high on the wall, gazing with those eyes that always brimmed with life; and I was supremely happy to sit in front of the writing-desk, where *he* had so often rested his hand; and it was blissful to fall asleep in the bed, where he had so often lain . . . What dreams! What visions! . . . Maybe it was a weakness . . . but I find no fault in that. Just as the weakness I once had for ties was pardoned me, so too this weakness will be pardoned. . . . But hotels do have the notable advantage of allowing one to live and sleep where a great genius has lived and slept.

Several years ago, then, I was occupying *l'appartamento di Verdi*. One morning at about 3 a.m. I heard a knock at the door: it was Signor Giuseppe (Cavaliere) Spatz, the genial proprietor of the hotel, ever blond, ever young, who resembled the son of his son-in-law, who had already made him a grandfather . . . (It's a little complicated, but there are extenuating circumstances; Signor Spatz's son-in-law is our friend Giordano, the remarkable composer of *André Chénier*.)

"What is it?" I asked, still sleepy.

"It's that . . ." he replied, embarrassed and hesitant.

"I have it!" I exclaimed with a sudden flash of lucidity, simply unimaginable at that early hour. "I have it: Verdi's arriving!"

. . . I gathered together my things and moved into another suite, while the multitude of servants and porters removed from the *appartamento di Verdi* the final traces of my brief residence, cleaning, tidying, sweeping . . . [. . .]

In this same article Mascagni recalls a visit to Verdi with his wife and children in April 1900, at a time when he was in Milan "to conduct the orchestral concerts at La Scala". It was not in 1900, as Mascagni asserts, but in 1898 that he conducted five symphony concerts at La Scala: between March 27 and April 24 (in 1900 it was Toscanini's turn to conduct), on the eve of those riots, provoked by a huge and unforeseen increase in the price of bread, that during the course of the winter had already shaken whole regions of Italy, and which exploded in Milan from May 7–9 and were bloodily suppressed by General Bava-Beccaris' guns, which killed at least 400 men and earned the general the Croce di Grande Ufficiale from King Umberto. In that year Verdi had travelled to Milan on April 26 to remain there till mid-May.[4] The article from the *Scena Illustrata* evokes in particular, and somewhat sentimentally, an intimate scene between Verdi and Mascagni's children. It is consequently of no interest, except for this brief passage which speaks of music (and confirms that the earlier meeting took place in 1895):

> Verdi wished to know which one of my children played the violin; we spoke of the Liceo Rossini,[5] and we spoke of all the Italian Institutes of Music. Recalling the Parma Conservatoire, Verdi paused for a moment and then exclaimed:
> "What a fine orchestra they had at Parma!"
> And without the slightest delay he recalled the names of all those great players who once made that Conservatoire famous. And we then spoke of orchestras, virtually continuing the conversation that I had been honoured to have with Verdi in 1895 and from which I had learnt the extent of his knowledge about all European orchestras. We also spoke of the concerts I was at that time conducting at La Scala; Verdi showed great interest in my opinion of the symphonies of Svendsen and Tchaikowsky;[6] indeed, at one point he interrupted me to say, almost speaking to himself:
> "Who *when I was young* could have supposed that those fellows would have been able to compose music!"
> When we took our leave, he wanted to accompany us to the door [. . .].

And here finally is the article that appeared in *La Lettura*, or at least that part of it concerning conversations with Verdi.

Verdi (*personal reminiscences*)

[. . .] I owe to the immortal Verdi some of the acutest pleasures of my life. I first made his acquaintance after *Cavalleria*, and I am still grateful to Giulio Ricordi for the emotion I felt at having been introduced to the Maestro.

In Milan I used to stay in the Hôtel de Milan, in the very apartment which Verdi was wont to occupy – a naïve ambition that brought comfort to my spirit. It goes without saying that I quickly moved out into a nearby room as soon as the Maestro's arrival was announced. Verdi was aware of this and forgave me.

One day Giulio Ricordi entered my room and said: "Come, I wish to introduce you to Verdi."

Trembling I followed him. Verdi! . . . You must understand what it meant for a composer to be introduced to Verdi. As soon as he saw me, he shook my hand most warmly. He was not, as a rule, expansive, but rather a man of few words. His eyes made a profound impression. One did not see them immediately, they were so deeply set between his thick eyebrows, but you *felt* them at once: penetrating, bright, enquiring. They were the sort of eyes that read everything in our hearts, even those things we wished to keep secret. He spoke slowly, pensively, savouring his words. He never talked randomly or sententiously or over-excitedly. When he spoke, he weighed his words like gold.

What attracted one towards him and banished any uneasiness was his smile. He did not smile at everyone; but when he smiled . . . it was as though one were borne aloft and carried towards him. The proximity of our rooms led to other encounters and also to a certain intimacy of an artistic nature. Whenever he knew I was in Milan, he summoned me and was pleased to discuss matters of art. He once confessed to me that the Parisian orchestras seemed to be more resonant than Italian ones, and this he attributed to the quality of the stringed instruments, all of which had been made at the same workshop and therefore possessed exactly the same sound. I boldly disagreed that the instruments of the great Italian violin-makers could not be compared with those of even the most perfect modern makers. In order to modify my stance, I immediately remarked that it certainly was not possible to form a complete orchestra of musicians all playing signed instruments: and one could attribute the weaker sonority of the ensemble to the different total quality of each instrument. The Maestro made no reply, but I had the impression that he still stuck to his own opinion.

Another time he asked with a smile whether the critics treated me well. I was covered with confusion and could not immediately find the words to reply to this unexpected question. But he understood perfectly what I did not say, and still smiling exclaimed: "Ah, my dear Mascagni, to be esteemed and loved you need to grow old!" And nor was this an aphorism – he was simply reminiscing.

One day he seemed even more confidential and affectionate, and wished to know which subjects I had in mind for future operas; without giving me time to reply, he told me that he knew I was considering *King Lear*. "If that is true," he continued, "I can tell you that I possess a vast amount of material on that monumental subject, which I would be delighted to give you to make a heavy task lighter."[7]

I was seized with acute emotion, finding myself before that great man who was confiding to me such portentous things with sublime simplicity. The lump in my throat prevented me from speaking, but with a great effort and trembling voice I managed to stammer a question that came from my heart: "Maestro, why have you not composed *King Lear?* . . ."

Verdi closed his eyes for several seconds, perhaps to remember, perhaps to forget. Softly and slowly he then replied: "The scene when Lear is alone on the heath terrified me!"

I sprang to my feet with wide-open eyes, and I must have looked very pale. He, the colossus of music-drama, had felt fear . . . and I . . . and I . . .

Never in my life did I again speak of *King Lear.*

I never heard Verdi speak of himself or his own art. He spoke willingly of art in general — and as he spoke the vast extent and depth of his knowledge of art emerged. And still he studied, continually.

One day I noticed a volume of Bach open on the music-rest. Verdi saw me, approached and said: "There's someone you must study. And I'm delighted that you perform him in your concerts at the Pesaro Conservatoire."

It was true. The Maestro even followed my concerts.

After the first performances of *Cavalleria rusticana*, a legend grew up which was believed both in Italy and abroad. It was said that Verdi, having read my opera, exclaimed: "Now I can die content!" Verdi never uttered these words, which were certainly invented by the fertile imagination of some enthusiast, who was imperfectly acquainted with an affectionate episode. And to put the record straight, I wish to recall that episode, even at the cost of appearing immodest. Besides, no one has ever sung my modesty. Not even I.

It was told me by Giulio Ricordi, *el Giuli*, as Verdi used to call him.

One evening at Sant'Agata, Boito, Ricordi, Gallignani[8] and Tebaldini[9] were guests of Verdi. At a certain hour — which was always the same, for Verdi was orderly and precise in all he did — he rose to go to his room. He was going to bed. The others remained in the drawing-room, talking and playing cards. At Sant'Agata the Maestro had a piano in his bedroom — indeed that was the piano he regarded as his own. Those who have visited Sant'Agata remember it well, along the wall (next to the little door which led to the store-room) where in splendid simplicity he used to compose. *Fuge magna*, as Horace said.

A little time had passed and Verdi should by now have retired to rest, when the guests suddenly heard some chords. Was the Maestro composing? What divine inspiration had come to visit him in that moment? . . . With genuine awe, Ricordi and Boito very slowly approached his bedroom and eavesdropped. A few bars sufficed for them to understand that he was at the piano, reading the score of *Cavalleria rusticana* which Giulio Ricordi had sent him at his own request.

"The next morning," it is Giulio Ricordi speaking, "I found the Maestro sitting as usual in the grounds of his villa beneath the great trees in the silence of that verdure, which only for him possessed such divine and fruitful eloquence. We exchanged a few words; then, re-entering his bedroom and pointing to the score of *Cavalleria*, he said:

"But it's not true that the tradition of Italian melody is dead!"

This was the way Verdi praised my opera; and no praise, no homage could ever have been more dear to me. [. . .]

One day Verdi, knowing that I was in Milan, wished to see my small children. He took them in his arms and kissed them. My wife and I witnessed this moving scene with a swelling heart and eyes bathed in sweetest tears. [. . .]

PIETRO MASCAGNI

NOTES

1. See N. III (including note 6) and N. XI, p. 68.
2. Cf. *Carteggio Verdi–Boito*, cit., p. 462.
3. P. MASCAGNI: "Una visita a Verdi" in *Scena Illustrata*, Florence, XLIX, 21: 1 November 1913, p.14.
4. Cf. *Carteggio Verdi–Boito*, cit., pp. 490–92.
5. The G. Rossini Conservatoire in Pesaro, of which Mascagni was Direc-tor from 1895 (the year of *Ratcliff* and his first meeting with Verdi) to 1902.
6. Among the pieces conducted by Mascagni at the concert of 27 March 1898 was the Symphony in D Major, op. 4 (1867) by Johan Svendsen (Oslo 1840 – Copenhagen 1911) which he repeated at the final concert on April 24. In the third concert of April 12 Mascagni included in his programme the Symphony in B minor, op. 74 (1893), the *Pathétique*, by Tchaikowsky.

7. From 1843, or perhaps earlier, Verdi had thought of composing an opera on Shakespeare's play, as we learn from his letter of 6 June 1843 to the President of La Fenice, Count Alvise Mocenigo:

> *I shall inform you at the earliest possible moment of the title of my opera, which will also depend on the singers at my disposal. If, for example, I had an artist of similar stature to Ronconi, I would choose either* King Lear *or* Il corsaro [. . .] (autograph: Archivio del Teatro La Fenice, Venice).

He considered the project again in 1848, and a little later he gave Cammarono the task of fashioning a libretto from the scenario that he himself had prepared (cf. *I Copialettere di G. Verdi*, cit., pp. 478–82). When Cammarono died in the summer of 1852, Verdi did not abandon the project but asked Antonio Somma, the librettist of *Un ballo in maschera*, to draw up the libretto (cf. A. Pascolato: " 'Re Lear' e 'Un ballo in maschera' ", *Lettere di Giuseppe Verdi ad Antonio Somma*, S. Lapi, Città di Castello 1902; reprinted *ibid.* 1913). It seems that *Re Lear* was finally abandoned in the years between *La forza del destino* and *Don Carlos*. For further information on the subject, see A. Luzio: "Il 'Re Lear' di Verdi" in *Carteggi verdiani*, cit., II, pp. 58–79; L. K. Gerhartz: "Il 'Re Lear' di Antonio Somma ed il modello melodrammatico dell'opera verdiana. Principi per uno definizione del libretto verdiano", in *Atti del I Congresso internazionale di studi verdiani*, cit., pp. 110–15; *id.*: *Die Auseinandersetzungen des jungen Giuseppe Verdi mit dem literarischen Drama*, Merseburger, Berlin 1968, pp. 282–95; V. Godefroy: *The Dramatic Genius of Verdi*, vol. 2, Gollancz, London 1977, in the chapter "King Lear, the Opera that never was", pp. 325–48.

8. Giuseppe Gallignani (Faenza 1851 – Milan 1923), composer and teacher, he was maestro di cappella at Milan Cathedral from 1884–1891, the year in which, on the recommendation of Verdi and Boito, he succeeded Boito as Director of the Parma Conservatoire (cf. M. Conati: "Arrigo Boito direttore onorario del Conservatorio di Parma", in *Parma, Conservatorio di Musica. Studi e Ricerche* edited by G. Piamonte and G. N. Vetro, Battei, Parma 1973, pp. 109–69). In 1897 he was appointed Director of the Milan Conservatoire, which, after Verdi's death, he wished to be named after the great composer. Dismissed from his post for alleged administrative irregularities, he committed suicide.

9. For Giovanni Tebaldini, see the final chapter of this anthology.

XLVI

A MEETING WITH VERDI AT MONTECATINI

1898

Z.: "Una lettera di Giuseppe Verdi", in *Nuova Antologia*, Rome, XLI,
16 July 1906, pp. 320–24.

MONALDI,[1] Paladini[2] and others[3] have given accounts of Verdi's stay at Montecatini, where he regularly used to take the waters. But their writings – with the exception of Bonaventura (see N. XLII) – even when not swollen with tiresome rhetoric, are usually of precious little interest. The account of a meeting at Montecatini in July 1898, contained in this article which appeared in the *Nuova Antologia*, at least has the merit of brevity and is, apart from a few errors, some of gross proportions, reasonably reliable.

But the chief merit of the article and the real reason for its inclusion in this anthology is Verdi's unpublished letter to the singer Barbieri Nini, concerning the interpretation of *Il corsaro*, a letter of great interest which, strangely, seems until now to have escaped the attention of Verdi scholars and biographers, and thus forms a pair with another Verdi letter, also concerning *Il corsaro*, published by Jacopo Zennari in 1923 in the Bologna periodical *La Cultura Musicale*,[4] and which also for a long time escaped the attention of scholars. (This is hardly surprising, if one bears in mind, for example, the period in which the letter to Barbieri Nini was published – a period in which Verdi's operas suffered an eclipse in the musical life of Italy. The esteem shown for the composer's last works almost seemed in those years to imply a rejection of the "popular" operas;[5] and if sporadic performances of *Rigoletto*, *Il trovatore* and *La traviata* were still graciously tolerated in some large theatres,[6] it is easy to imagine that *Il corsaro* and similar works were rarely spoken of, if at all. . . .).

The letter to Barbieri Nini – which the anonymous author of the article (from Romagna? . . . Jacopo Zennari? . . .) quotes without indicating the whereabouts of the autograph, which as far as we know has been lost – concerns, as we have said, *Il corsaro*. This was the opera – libretto by Piave, based on Byron's eponymous poem –

which Verdi originally contemplated composing for London.[7] But in December of the same year the composer, who had undertaken to provide the publisher Francesco Lucca not only with an opera for London but also a new opera to be performed in one of Italy's principal theatres by a first-rate company at the 1848 Carnival Season,[8] informed Lumley, the London impresario:

Last year I had chosen Il corsaro *as the subject, but when the libretto was finished, I found it cold and lacking in dramatic effect, so that I changed my mind and resolved, although this doubled my expenses, to have another libretto written, Schiller's* I masnadieri.[9]

None the less, in the summer of 1846 Verdi, convalescing from a serious illness,[10] had already begun composing *Il corsaro*, starting with the final act, as we learn from a letter, dated August 27, to Piave who, when informed about the choice of a different subject for London had requested the return of his libretto:

But what is all this? You've either gone mad or are going mad?! You ask me to return Il corsaro? . . . Il corsaro, *which I have so cherished, which causes me such concern and which you yourself versified with greater care than usual . . . Return it to you? . . . and you don't even tell me for where or for whom? . . . It is true that* Il corsaro *had been fixed for London, but although the London venture has come to nothing, I must still write the opera for Lucca. And almost without noticing it, I was gradually composing this* Corsaro, *for which I've sketched some of the things I like best – the prison duet and the final trio. . . . And you wish me to return it? . . . To the hospital with you, and get your brain seen to – You beseech me in the name of friendship to save you from a serious commitment. Well, listen to me. Had you been any other man, I would not even have bothered to reply: I would, in other words, have refused the poet, . . . but I cannot refuse my friend this request to return the libretto, my friend* Francesco Maria Piave, *who lavished more than fraternal care on me at the time of my illness – something which I shall never forget. But be warned, if it were not to help you out of a quandary, your asking such a sacrifice of me would amount to impertinence. Do, then, as you think fit, and if you want* Il corsaro *I shall surrender it – on condition that you fashion me another libretto with the same love as you lavished on this one. . . .*[11]

Piave clearly did not insist that the libretto of *Il corsaro* be returned to him; but we should have heard no more of this opera, had it not been a question of honouring the contract of October 1845, which bound Verdi to that "most intolerable and vulgar Signor Lucca",[12] who persistently and with very little tact insisted that Verdi compose the opera for 1848. Finally he got his opera, *Il corsaro*; but all further relations with Lucca were broken off by the indignant Verdi, who did not even bother – and this was almost unprecedented throughout his entire career – to supervise the staging. Having obtained *Il corsaro*, Lucca had it performed at Trieste, where it was premièred on the evening of 25 October 1848 with a cast who had already performed in other Verdi premières: Barbieri Nini (*I due Foscari*, *Macbeth*), the tenor Gaetano Fraschini (*Alzira*) and the baritone Achille de Bassini (*I due Foscari*). There now follows the letter to Barbieri Nini printed in the *Nuova Antologia* article,[13] which at least seems to make it clear – contrary to the assertions of some biographers – that *Il corsaro*, although reluctantly completed and delivered to Lucca, was not in fact disowned by Verdi.

Paris, October 6 1848

Dear Signora Barbieri,
I believe that Il corsaro, *performed by you, Fraschini and Bassini will go well, especially as, with the exception of the principal singers, it is not a work that demands great artists.*

You ask for some advice about your pieces. Well, the cavatina is easy to perform: it must be sung simply, and this you can do. Sing the adagio softly and with breadth. And do not take the cabaletta too quickly either but only quicken the tempo at the final flourish. I think this cavatina will be most effective. See to it that the finale[14] is well staged. The first agitato, if not well staged, could cause laughter. Let the adagio be broadly declaimed and the stretta not too quick.

The first section of the duet with the bass[15] should be declaimed, sostenuto; think more about the words than the notes. Sing the cabaletta briskly but not too fast.

The bass has the first phrase – let him declaim it at the top of his voice; but you will sing softly throughout (remember your mezza voce in Macbeth*).[16] You know better than I that anger is not always expressed by shouting, but sometimes with a stifled voice – and so it should be here. So, sing the entire final section sotto voce, with the exception of the last four notes; wait until the bass has almost left the stage, until you break out into a cry, which should be accompanied by a terrifying gesture, as though foretelling the crime you are about to commit.*

As for the duet with the tenor, I can recommend both the drama and the music; this is certainly the least bad number of the entire opera. When you come on stage, do so slowly; and deliver the recitative sotto voce and slowly. The first section should be moderato, and try to express the words with all your soul. The beginning of the adagio should be sung equally slowly and sotto voce; then from the words "ah! fuggiamo", let your voice expand and sing the rest with passion. Then, when you make your exit, do so hastily, and when you return pale and shocked, take each step virtually as the music indicates, until the moment when you can no longer stand on your feet. The following words should be uttered on the ground: "già . . . l'opra è finita, per destarsi egli stava". Sing them, without paying too much attention to the tempo or the notes, but with a stifled and scarcely audible voice. The cabaletta should be slow and sung with all your passion. The drama of this entire duet is, as you can see, stupendous.

In the final trio do not forget that you have killed a man, and let your remorse be evident in all the words you sing, even when you are consoling Medora. The C major passage in ¾ should be sung assai moderato and with passion. The final passage should be largo, as in the trio from I Lombardi. Be sure to keep together. If everyone sings with extreme passion, I am certain it will be a success. A final warning: the opera should be divided into two acts only: the first act should close at the end of the finale, the second with the trio.[17] The whole opera will thus gain in brevity and interest.

You paint a sad picture of Italian theatres, but French theatres are certainly no better.[18] The new Director of the Italiens has dismissed all the singers who received a high wage, has merely kept on those who sing virtually for nothing and has engaged new artists, who receive only token wages. The Opéra, likewise, has retained its old singers, cutting their wages, without exception, by two-thirds, and does not aim to engage new artists for lack of argent. All of us − artists and non-artists − have made great sacrifices and suffered great casualties, and . . . are no better off than before.*

Please drop me a line after the first performance of Il corsaro.

> Your friend and admirer
> G. Verdi

A leap of 50 years, from 1848 to 1898, and we are at Montecatini, at the round table of the Locanda Maggiore, where Verdi usually dined with the other guests:

* The final words are written above an illegible line that has been crossed out by pen-strokes.

[A meeting with Verdi at Montecatini]

[. . .] At Bagni di Montecatini, in the *Locanda Maggiore* – the oldest of all the inns which honourably parades its name along with other similar establishments that have arisen in such number in this little village, whose houses and population have increased to such an extent that they now constitute by law a separate borough from the old village – you will be shown with a kind of religious reverence, a well-situated apartment of a few rooms, which bears the name of Verdi.

The same is true in Milan in the large hotel which is named after the city itself.

For many years Verdi used to spend several weeks taking the waters at Montecatini, and during the winter[19] he would reside at the Hôtel de Milan. It was said, and he believed it, that those waters had played a part in keeping him fresh and strong in his old age.

During the many years that I took the waters at Montecatini, it was never my good fortune to meet the spa's most illustrious and popular guest, but finally I arranged to be there at the same time, and was introduced to him by my friends Professor Pietro Grocco[20] and Antonio Mordini,[21] who were both on intimate terms with the composer.

He was not at all exuberant; stern-faced, a man of few words, averse to crowds and noise, he kept very much to himself. Dressed in black with a soft, broad-brimmed hat, he went in the mornings to drink the waters at the *Regina* and *Savi* more often than at the *Tettuccio* springs, which are the most abundant and most frequented; and he sipped them slowly. In the afternoon he would walk as far as the *Rinfresco* springs. Whenever he realized that he was the object of too many inquisitive eyes, he moved or went away.

He would spend almost the entire day in his apartment; he lunched in his room, but usually came down to dine, sharing the communal meal at the head of the round table, a place which everyone reserved for him reverently. In the evenings he would retire early, and before going to bed would amuse himself for an hour or more with a game of *tressette*, *briscola* or *pitocchetto*, his favourite game which can also be played by four hands and immediately put him in a good mood. He prided himself on his skill at these games.

At the end of August 1898[22] I too found myself sitting near him at this round table, with Grocco, Mordini, Teresa Stoltz [sic], the once famous singer and his constant companion, and Giuseppina Pasqua, the definitive Aida.[23] I do not recall how we began to discuss music, or rather opera – a subject that the great composer usually avoided, but that day was a veritable exception.

"Franchetti has great learning," he was saying; "but Puccini is more inventive and theatrical. Franchetti, you see, refused *Tosca*,[24] from which Puccini will compose a great opera – whereas Franchetti has fallen for that *Monsieur de Pourceaugnac*,[25] which even God would find impossible to turn into a decent opera."

Here he paused, and Mordini continued: "There are other contemporary composers whose operas are applauded . . ."; and since the Maestro remained silent, I ventured to say, turning to Mordini: "Yes, but none has yet written a great opera." "And what do you understand by a great opera?" – "I wouldn't know! . . . *Nabucco*, for example." "Ah, I had forgotten," he replied with apparent satisfaction. *Nabucco*, after two or three moderate successes,[26] had marked the beginning of his glorious career.

Verdi was in good form that day. We tried to prolong the conversation: Mordini told him that he and his contemporaries had enjoyed identifying themselves with *Ernani* – a lover, conspirator and outlaw. The Maestro then seemed to dwell willingly on his Egyptian memories of *Aida*. "I no longer compose," he said at a certain point, "but I sometimes read ancient music. And not only Palestrina; there are many other Italian composers worthy of study including," he said politely turning to me, "Corelli from Romagna."
[. . .]

                                                                      Z.

NOTES

1. G. MONALDI: *Verdi nella vita e nell'arte*, cit., pp. 24–35 and *passim*; *I miei ricordi musicali*, Ausonia, Rome 1921, see chapter "A Montecatini". *Conversazioni verdiane*, pp. 87–97; *Verdi aneddotico*, Vecchioni, L'Aquila 1926, *passim*.

2. C. PALADINI: "La musica ai Bagni di Montecatini", in *Gazzetta Musicale di Milano*,LI, 33 and 34: 13 and 20 August 1896, pp. 549–53 and 570; *Verdi in Valdinievole*, ibid., LIV, 36: 7 September 1899, pp. 437–48; "Il romito di S.'Agata", in *Rassegna Nazionale*, Florence-Milan, XXIII, 2: 16 February 1901, pp. 529–61.

3. R.M.: "Verdi a Montecatini", in *Scena Illustrata*, Florence, XXXVI, 271: 15 November 1900; E. FRATI: *Edenia (Montecatini e i suoi Bagni)*, Razzolini, Florence 1911, pp. 279–92; C. GUSTINELLI: "Verdi a Monte-

catini", in *Nicia*, October 1932; A. Mordini: "Musica e patriottismo", in *Rassegno Nazionale*, Florence–Milan, XXIII, 2: 16 February 1901, pp. 562–3; etc. etc. See also Pietro Tempestini's valuable photographs, published with Paladini's two articles, mentioned in the preceding note.

4. J. Zennari, *art cit.*, letter of 27 August 1846 to Piave, autograph at the Biblioteca Concordiana di Rovigo; reprinted by M.Conati: "Una lettera sconosciuta di Verdi a Francesco Maria Piave", in *L'Opera*, Milan, II, 5: October–December 1966, pp. 83–86, with facsimile of the autograph. Barblan is therefore wrong to write in his essay on *Il corsaro* (in *I Lunedí della Fenice. Conferenze Musicali (1970–71)*, Venice 1972, p. 104) that this letter was hitherto unpublished, as it had in fact been published twice in specialized journals.

5. Several years ago Massimo Mila wrote:

> In those years people distinguished within Verdi's oeuvre two separate types of art: popular art and superior art, Art with a capital A. And while audiences throughout the world continued to show particular affection for *Rigoletto*, *Il trovatore* and *La traviata* and were gradually approaching the more difficult and mellow art of *Otello* and *Falstaff*, the new cultural highbrows in Italy were more and more tempted to share the contempt for these masterpieces of Verdi's youth that prevailed in German and French musical circles. The over-refined ears of D'Annunzio's Italy could not but be offended by the brutality of such linear and astringent masterpieces as *Rigoletto* and *Il trovatore* [. . .] Educated Italians of today do not like to be reminded of this repudiation of Verdi's most popular works. When it is discussed, someone always feigns amazement: Verdi? But whoever doubted his greatness? It would not be difficult to glean from the literature and essays of the first decade of this century a fine crop of evidence; indeed, it would be worthwhile if someone set about this task of restoring historical truth. (M. Mila: "L'unità stilistica nell'opera di Verdi", in *Nuova Rivista Musicale Italiana*, Rome, II, 1 January–February 1968, pp. 63–64.)

6. The Teatro Comunale at Bologna, for example, records between 1895 and October 1912 (excepting of course *Otello* and *Falstaff*) only two performances of *La traviata* and of *Rigoletto* in 1901 (to commemorate no doubt the death of Verdi on January 27 of that year), and one performance of *Aida* in 1908. At Trieste, a Verdian city par excellence, there was only one performance of *Il trovatore* (in 1906) between 1902 and October 1911. Parma's Teatro Regio registers from January 1904 to January 1912 an eight-year silence of Verdi's music, interrupted only in 1907 by one performance of *Rigoletto* and one of *Aida*. At La Scala between 1894 and 1901, excepting revivals of *Otello* and *Falstaff*, there were in all three performances of *Rigoletto* and one of *Don Carlos* . . . And it was only due to Toscanini's obstinate will that *Il trovatore* was

included in the programme for 1901–02, and *Luisa Miller* in that for the subsequent season. And the examples could continue. . . .

7. On 24 February 1846 Verdi wrote a sharp reply to Lucca, who was suggesting a different subject for London:

> [. . .] *It's* Il corsaro *or nothing. Your reasons have only served to make the subject more attractive to me.* (Autograph: Archivio della Casa Ricordi, Milan.)

In 1843 he had already considered *Il corsaro* as a subject for the new opera to be peformed at Venice (see N. XLV, note 7).

8. Verdi's letter of contract to Lucca of 16 October 1845 (*I Copialettere di G. Verdi*, cit., p. 16) which was renewed on 2 August 1847 (*ibid.*, p. 42).

9. Letter of 4 December 1846 (*I Copialettere di G. Verdi*, cit., p. 33).

10. Cf. N. XI, note 13.

11. Autograph: Biblioteca dell'Accademia dei Concordi, Rovigo (see also note 4).

12. Verdi informs Giuseppina Appiani on 22 September 1847:

> *Signor Lucca springs something on me every day; last Sunday he sent me a thousand francs! . . . What does he wish? . . . To buy me? . . . Imbecile?!!*
> (*I Copialettere di G. Verdi*, cit., p. 461.)

13. As transcribed, of course, by the anonymous columnist of the *Nuova Antologia*.

14. He refers to the Act II finale.

15. The character of Seid is sung by a baritone, which in those days was still termed bass.

16. Cf. N. IV, including note 4.

17. i.e., by merging the original acts 1 and 2 into a single act (ending with the second finale) and changing act 3 into act 2.

18. As a consequence of the political situation after the February Revolution, which had deposed King Louis-Philippe and spread insurrection throughout Europe. Paris was in a greater state of commotion than ever before: in June, following the closure of the *ateliers nationaux*, instituted by Blanc to guarantee work for the workers, the Socialists had revolted and had then been bloodily crushed (about 10,000 dead) by Eugène Cavaignac, the Minister of War. In those days the Constitution of the Second Republic was being prepared, of which Louis Napoleon, the future Napoleon III, was elected President in December.

19. This is not accurate. Verdi's usual residence in the winter season was, to the very last, the Palazzo Doria in Genoa. The Hôtel de Milan was his customary residence during his occasional visits to Milan, which increased considerably in his final years.

20. Verdi's doctor who attended the composer till his death.

21. Antonio Mordini (Barga 1819 – Montecatini 1902); a politician, he took

part in the Florentine uprisings of 1847 and was a member of the Comitato Nazionale Italiano di Londra (1850). Having broken with Mazzini, he took part in the Second War of Independence and was elected Deputy to the first Italian parliament. Minister of Public Works (1867–9), Prefect of Naples (1872–6), Deputy until 1895 and then Senator, he moved ever closer to the right, towards the most conservative wing of the liberal ranks.

22. This will have been the end of July, the month in which Verdi usually took the waters at Montecatini. That year the composer definitely left Milan for Montecatini on July 11 and left the spa on the evening of August 1 (cf. *Carteggio Verdi–Boito*, cit., pp. 493 and 267).

23. The "definitive" Quickly in *Falstaff* rather! (see N. XLII, note 8). It is well-known that the "definitive" Aida was none other than Teresa Stolz.

24. Cf. M. MORINI: "La Tosca all'anagrafe della storia", in *La Scala, Rivista dell'opera*, Milan, n. 160: March 1963, pp. 12–18.

25. *Il Signore di Pourceaugnac*, to a libretto by Ferdinando Fontana (after Molière) had been staged at La Scala on 10 April 1897.

26. On the contrary! After its triumphant success at La Scala, *Nabucco* never met any obstacles and was always warmly received.

XLVII

A MEETING WITH VERDI

1898 – 1899

FELIX PHILIPPI: "Begegnung mit Verdi. Ein Auftakt für die Jahrhundert-feier", in *Berliner Tageblatt*, n. 350: 13 July 1913.

AS THE CENTENARY of Verdi's birth approached, the journalist of the *Berliner Tageblatt* (whose biographical details have eluded us) recalls a meeting in Milan with the composer two years before his death. "At that time he [Verdi] was already in his 86th year": the meeting therefore took place in the months between 1898–1899, more precisely between the first days of December 1898 and the beginning of February 1899, a period which Verdi spent in Milan.

A meeting with Verdi

I am at present busy with a work for which I have the highest hopes. It will, I hope, enthuse the audience, delight the theatre-directors, intoxicate the artists, transport the critics, gladden my loyal publisher and also make me happy. It will probably, therefore, at the very second performance meet stubborn resistance from the holders of free tickets. As I was busy working, I was disturbed by a most unpleasant noise. I investigated the cause and discovered in the music room of the hotel a female of fabulous flat-chestedness, clearly an eye-witness of the much lamented death of King Rameses the Second. This moss-covered ruin was extorting from the piano, in a hostile manner devoid of any emotion, Liszt's *Rigoletto Phantasy*, – a piece of pianistic clownishness, with which only the most awful piano-thumpers of the wildest American West dare to assail their public. And since this physical wreck was playing the show-piece despicably badly and, as Hans von Bülow once said, was surmounting the easiest passages with the greatest of difficulty, I took the most obvious course of action to escape the horror – flight. But no matter how far I fled, the wonderful melody of the quartet which a bungler had distorted, pursued me everywhere, remained my faithful companion as I resumed work and followed me out on to the green meadows and across the cool woods. And as I mused and dreamed in the shade of an ancient, broad-branched fir-tree covered with cones, with the ardent, passionate music from *Rigoletto* humming continuously in my ears, a memory awoke within me, fond memories of one of the most interesting hours of my life, which is hardly devoid of remarkable encounters.

On the numerous journeys I used to make in Italy and on the Riviera, I always stayed in Milan. The beautiful, distinguished, noble town always detained me for a few days, I was always refreshed by its magnificent buildings, beautiful art treasures, colourful street life and delightful inhabitants. From the cathedral roof I would always look out into the Lombard plain as far as the Apennines, I was always drawn to the Brera to feast my eyes on Bramante's frescoes, the Titians and Tintorettos, the Mantegnas and the Correggios and Raphael's wonderful *Marriage of the Virgin*; I always strolled through the Vittorio Emanuele arcade, drank Tuscan wine at Biffi's and imagined that it tasted excellent. And I always – getting on for thirty times – stayed in the Via Manzoni at the delightful Hôtel de Milan, where I always admired the greatest attraction of the entire town: the head waiter. This kind and corpulent man, who looked like an invitation to a Lucullan banquet, sported what were indisputably the most impressive side-whiskers I had ever seen, which in most remarkable fashion defied both the years and the turmoil, without ever losing their intense black colour. Far be it from me, however, to blacken[1] this adornment – I suspect that its fortunate owner had already seen to that. Once you had won his trust by a handsome tip, he was easy to talk to: he gossiped with a southerner's liveliness. During one of these hour-long chats, I suddenly heard above me the soft and timid notes of a piano. A few bars from the *Rigoletto* quartet floated down and then merged into a pure Italian melody, unknown to me.[2] When I asked my loquacious friend, since when the hotel had tolerated such a cacophony at such an early hour in the morning – it was scarcely seven o'clock – he replied with a smile that an exception was made with the gentleman who lived over the restaurant, and he added proudly that the gentleman was Verdi. . . .

Yes, my dear Luigi or Antonio – unfortunately I have forgotten your name – from this moment on I no longer regarded you as Milan's greatest attraction. But I do not wish to be ungrateful. At my wish you immediately fetched the hotel-proprietor, Signor Spatz, who was well-known to me and whom I requested to arrange an introduction to the Maestro. He replied that all would be arranged within a quarter of an hour, that Verdi was an unusually kind and courteous man, who turned no one away who knocked on his welcoming door, that he occupied rooms one to five, and that his neighbour who lodged in rooms six to ten was also a most famous man, called Mascagni.[3] After a moment or two I was shown into Verdi's study, a very tall room, looking out on to the noisy Via Manzoni. It was tastefully furnished in the good old-fashioned style of Italian hotels. I hardly had the time to glance at the opened piano with sheets of music, covered in notes, lying on its rest. Above the piano hung a life-size oil-painting of the artist. The old Maestro entered in a solemn black jacket, despite the early hour. At that time he was already in his 86th year. He was small,[4] but not bent. His hair was still thick and, like his beard, grey but not yet white. And from his face, in which time had scrawled a thousand wrinkles and lines, gleamed a pair of eyes of wonderful warmth and compelling kindness; his whole being breathed such perfect serenity and such refreshing gentleness, and the first words he addressed me in good French were imbued with such genuine kindness and profound humanity, that all my trepidation which had threatened to overwhelm me, vanished at once, as on the occasion of my first meeting with Wagner. I had thought I was to meet an awe-inspiring, world famous celebrity and found instead a lovable person. After a few polite personal enquiries, the conversation turned at once to music and with the utmost honesty I laid bare my feelings and expressed my most fervent admiration. I told him that, as a young lad, I had been able to play from memory the scores of Il trovatore, La traviata, Rigoletto and Un ballo in maschera, and that I adored his wonderful Aida and exquisite Falstaff. He listened to me with a smile, but without the blasé condescension typical of many great men; he smiled at me, because it gave him pleasure. He was then silent for a moment, during which a question seemed to hover on his lips. I thought I could recognize the question and was not mistaken. (Here I follow the notes in my diary.)

"You are German and therefore, of course, a follower of the Bayreuth master?"

"I am more than a follower," I replied, "for as long as I can remember I have been one of Wagner's most ardent and passionate admirers; I believe I am one of his oldest and most loyal vassals."

"You do well to honour your Maestro. He is one of the greatest geniuses. He has made people happy and presented them with treasurers of immeasurable and immortal worth. You will understand that I, as an Italian, do not yet understand everything. That is due to our ignorance of German legend, the strangeness of Wagner's subject-matter, its prevailing mysticism and the pagan world with its gods and Norns, its giants and dwarfs. But I'm still young," the 86-year-old smiled with genuine childlike goodness, "I never cease exploring Wagner's sublime world of ideas. I owe him an enormous amount – hours of most wonderful exaltation."

And those words were spoken by a man, whose works had conquered the entire world in an unparalleled triumphant march, by this king, whose rule in the realm of sound knows no bounds – and they were spoken with such fervent, ungrudging warmth, with such profound modesty, that I instinctively clasped both his hands and held them for a long time in mine. And when I asked him which of Wagner's works stood nearest to his heart, suggesting that it might be the operas from his early period, *Rienzi* or *Der fliegende Holländer*, Verdi replied:

"The work which always arouses my greatest admiration is *Tristan*. This gigantic structure fills me time and time again with astonishment and awe, and I still cannot quite comprehend that it was conceived and written by a human being. I consider the second act, in its wealth of musical invention, its tenderness and sensuality of musical expression and its inspired orchestration, to be one of the finest creations that has ever issued from a human mind. This second act is wonderful," and utterly immersed in his thoughts, he kept repeating: "Wonderful . . . quite wonderful!"[5]

We then spoke of the musical scene in Germany, and he showed himself to be very well informed. He praised the stability of our great municipal and court theatres and lamented the ineradicable institution of the Italian *Stagione*,[6] with its random collection of staff and monstrous system of stars. On the other hand, he spoke enthusiastically of the Italian conservatoires, where the teaching was beyond praise. I replied that Germany too possessed colleges of music that were run in exemplary fashion, and that I, for example, in my youth – in the sixties – had been taught in a private conservatoire by Hans von Bülow and Karl Tausig. Bülow's name was well-known to Verdi, and he made keen enquiries about the events which caused Bülow and Wagner to break off relations with one another. He then expressed great regret at knowing Germany and the world so little; of the large cities he only knew Vienna and Cologne, Paris and London. He loved his fatherland best of all, he loved his native soil.

He explained how he had acquired his estate at Agata [sic], near his birthplace Busseto outside Parma, and had set up there a model farm. He spent the cold winters alternately in Genoa and Milan. He had just lost his second wife, the once famous singer Giuseppina Strepponi, with whom he had spent 50 years of most happy marriage. He was communicative without being garrulous, spoke frankly without gossiping. He treated me as a familiar. And all that he said was uttered with such agreeable and unforced modesty. When I think back to this beautiful, uplifting hour, that chance had bestowed on me, my heart is moved. For never in my life have I met a man of such serene, or rather, such transfigured appearance. Successes and triumphs, you will say, have ennobled his soul. I have known other geniuses, whom the wave of fortune has raised as high but who have shown no "transfiguration" and not even gratitude. Verdi was a genius with the soul of a child. The chasteness of his thoughts, the purity of his feelings, his charm, his forbearance, his artistic and human morality were wonderfully moving. His whole being resembled one of those beautiful tunes he sang, one of his sweet and tender melodies devoid of discord, resembled a still, unruffled mountain lake, from whose clear depths golden treasures gleam. [. . .]

FELIX PHILIPI

NOTES

1. A play on words: *anschwärzen* has two meanings: to blacken, to darken; and, in the figurative sense, to denigrate.
2. This episode recalls another, told by Monaldi, that occurred during one of his meetings with Verdi at the Hôtel de Milan on the morning of 10 February 1893, i.e. the day after the première of *Falstaff* at La Scala. It is not without authenticity, if only for Verdi's harsh phrase about the audience's triumphant reception the evening before, which in turn is reminiscent of the episode contained in a letter to Arrivabene on 29 January 1884:

> *As for my impassibility, I can tell you that even this time I was not much moved. I know what was meant by that, shall I say, fine reception I received. It was not for* Don Carlos [the new four-act version had been performed at La Scala] *or for the composer of the operas written before. That applause meant:* "You who are still of this world, work yourself once more to death if need be, but thrill us once more . . ." *Forwards, Pagliaccio, and long live glory! (Verdi intimo, cit., p. 305.)*

But here is the episode narrated by Monaldi:

I shall also narrate an episode that I have never wished to reveal, but which, now that I am confiding my memories to the public, I feel the need to publish. The next morning at about eleven o'clock I went to the Hôtel de Milan, which teemed with people wishing to see the Maestro. But on that morning he had left strict orders: no one was to be received! Despite this I climbed the stairs up to the first floor and having rung for Verdi's trusty servant, I asked him to announce me. As he had known me for some time he consented, returned after a few minutes and ushered me into the drawing-room, where the piano stood. I had been there for several moments when Verdi entered. His expression, which was usually both serene and austere, had changed. He forced a smile and said: "You too have come for the customary congratulations . . . haven't you?" "My congratulations," I replied frankly, "are of small account, compared with those of yesterday's audience." "Yes, yes," he exclaimed in rather a high voice, "in fact I thought the audience were saying: 'Come on, Pagliaccio! You can still make us laugh! . . .'" Having said these words, the muscles of his mouth contracted strangely. I confess that I was taken aback and did not know how to reply. And I knew very well that Verdi was unable to indulge in small talk. After a minute's silence Verdi, understanding my embarrassment, looked at me with his customary benevolence and said: "Do you know what I thought of last night? Well, I thought of a romance written by Donizetti for *Lucrezia Borgia* that I once heard and which is now sung no more." "A romance for tenor?" I asked. – "No, for soprano. Oh! a wonderful melodic opening it had . . . I shall play it you." – And he moved to the piano, opened the lid, placed his hands on the keyboard, and with the sweetest half-voice, that I'd never heard, he hummed the first bars of the romance. Then all of a sudden he nervously closed the piano and said: "It would be interesting to track it down! . . . Isn't it beautiful?" – "But I've hardly heard it . . ." I said, hoping to hear it again, but Verdi dismissed me, saying: "Excuse me, I must return to the bedroom – Giuseppina is none too well." Now that I was outside I made every effort to remember the theme I had just heard, but it was impossible. I have also made every kind of research, but neither old scores nor the memories of those still living have revealed information about the romance. And yet Verdi could not have improvised it . . . A mystery . . . (G. MONALDI: *I miei ricordi musicali*, cit., pp. 131–3.)

3. Cf. N. XLV.
4. Cf. N. XIV, note 6.
5. Monaldi offers us further evidence of the octogenarian Verdi's admiration for Wagner - though his assertions should always be accepted with some caution:

"Wagner," Verdi told me one day, "is a great musical genius. Like Paganini he came on the scene in difficult circumstances. He was reduced to copying music, having composed *Tannhäuser*! He suffered terrible disappointments. For example, having presented *Der fliegende Holländer* to the Commission of the Paris Academy of Music, the opera was turned down, and he was asked instead if he wished to sell the libretto! [cf. introduction to N. VII]. Wagner deserves to be ranked among the greatest. His music, however far removed from our way of feeling, is genuine music, full of life, blood and nerves – music, therefore, that has a right to live. He seems to experience patriotism in art to an exceptional degree. He has carried his fanaticism to the point of writing music to a pre-established programme. But this system harms him . . . The harm, however, has not come from him, but from his imitators! . . . (G. MONALDI: *Verdi nella vita e nell'arte*, cit., pp. 179–80.)

6. Italian in the original. See also N. XXII, note 1.

XLVIII

PERSONAL REMINISCENCES OF VERDI

1898–1900

ADOLPH KOHUT: "Persönliche Erinnerungen an Verdi", in *Der Merker*, Vienna, IV, n. 20: October 1913 (Second October issue), pp. 776–80, and n. 21: November 1913 (First November issue), pp. 810–4.

ADOLPH KOHUT (Mindszent 1847 – Berlin 1917), of Hungarian descent, was a graduate in philosophy at Jena and a music critic, who contributed to daily newspapers in Breslau, Düsseldorf, Berlin and Vienna. He published about twenty books on music including monographs on Weber, Friedrich Wieck, Meyerbeer, Joachim, Rossini, Auber, Wagner, Liszt, Schiller in music etc. He married the singer Elisabeth Mannstein. From his long article (an evocation of Verdi through his letters and some anecdotes), which was written to commemorate the centenary of the composer's birth and appeared in two instalments, we quote only those parts that refer to a visit he made to Sant'Agata after the death of Giuseppina Verdi, presumably, therefore, between May 1898 and November 1900.

Personal reminiscences of Verdi

The centenary of Verdi's birth has aroused interest not only in Italy but the entire civilized world; for Verdi is a true master of theatrical art, whose popularity is not restricted to his own country. The realm of melody is boundless.

It will therefore be permitted if I too make a small contribution towards the Verdi celebrations, by recording my personal reminiscences of the Maestro. The composer of *Rigoletto, Ernani, Il trovatore, La traviata, Aida, Falstaff, Otello, Un ballo in maschera, I vespri siciliani* and other immortal operas was, in life, I mean in conversation and society, a serious, taciturn gentleman, inclined to melancholy. But when he was in a small circle of intimate friends and admirers, and the conversation became more stimulating, and particularly – though this occurred seldom – in front of a *fiasco*[1] of good French or Italian wine – he would suddenly grow eloquent, witty, humorous and scintillating. [. . .]

Like many of Verdi's admirers throughout the world, I too made a pilgrimage many years ago to his Sant'Agata estate near his home town Busseto, where he used to spend the summer in the final decades of his life. I had been provided with letters of recommendation from some close friends of the Maestro and had the good fortune of being received by him many times. Even though he was immensely busy and productive to a ripe old age and resented any disturbance, he enjoyed the occasional visit. He was certainly not averse to a stimulating conversation with foreigners. Much has already been written about the Maestro's haven, and I therefore consider another description to be superfluous. [. . .]

Verdi used to recount with pleasure that he was one of those composers who had been forsaken by God – dismissed, that is, by Conservatoire directors as ungifted or unreliable. When, as a boy, he went to Milan to sit the entrance exam for the Conservatoire, which was directed by Francesco Basili [. . .], he was turned down with the comment that he possessed absolutely no musical ability and would do better to say farewell to music.[2]

Although Giuseppe Verdi was an intuitive artist who, obeying his creative genius and inner impulse, wrote his works with facility and almost as a physical necessity, he was well aware of the problems of his art. A journalist once asked him how the musical thought presented itself to him, when he was composing one of his operas, whether he first of all thought of the principal theme and then arranged the accompaniment by studying the best combination of instruments . . . flutes or violins and so on. Verdi gave a vehement reply: "No, no, no! The thought presents itself whole, especially the feeling whether flute or violin be the suitable accompaniment. The difficulty is always writing it down fast enough to express the musical thought in its entirety, precisely as it came into my mind."[3] [. . .]

As a composer who thought and wrote in the spirit of his own nation, he was little impressed by those composers whose music was an eclectic kaleidoscope of different colours and who took their themes from Italian, German and French music. As patriot and composer, he wanted to be nothing but Italian. He thus had a particular predilection for those Italian singers who, as he told me, remained true to the ancient Italian art of bel canto. He was also of the opinion that Italian singers, because of the climate or centuries of tradition, were made for the art of bel canto, whereas the philosophical and ever brooding German singers, who were more concerned with power than beauty of tone, were more suited to German song, as Gluck and Wagner understood it, than Italian cantilena.[4]

Verdi always showed a keen interest in nature, but always felt uncomfortable in large and noisy gatherings. He loved solitude, and direct contact with mother nature always refreshed and restored him. He was happiest in his oft mentioned country estate at Sant'Agata. And he was more than a little proud that by his indefatigable zeal, diligence, skill and understanding, he had contributed more than a little to the cultivation of the somewhat barren soil of his estate. With a satisfied air he would point out the orchards he had planted, the charming parks he had designed and the dams he had had built against the flooding of the River Po. Just as he never exhibited bad taste in his music, he always called upon his sense of good taste and his refined feeling for what was beautiful and harmonious in the practical arts of gardening and architecture.

"When my thoughts torment me too much," he told me once, "when I am tired of working or oppressed with worry, I always feel the need to seek refuge in this park and commune with the invisible and mysterious spirits who hover busily about me. I listen to their softly whispered tales and observations. My heart expands, and to my surprise I often rediscover here my intellectual and physical vigour. Now, of course, that I have lost my beloved wife, who was not only an affectionate mistress of the house but also my companion, who shared with me both joy and pain, and possessed such a marvellously sensitive feeling for my creative activity, I do not always feel at ease in this solitude. And those spirits, that I have just mentioned, now appear more seldom and it seems as if evening were falling both in and around me, as if life were about to fade with its charms and delights, its hopes and desires, its aims and ideals."

Verdi was a great animal-lover,[5] and, like Richard Wagner, spoke out repeatedly against cruelty to animals. Nor did he agree with vivisection, especially as he thought that the doctors, as they dissected, often went beyond what was permissible and exhibited some animals at their autopsies with a certain sadistic pleasure. He was equally fond of flowers. His study, that was crammed full of books and music, was resplendent with cacti and palm-leaves, which had been dedicated to him by his numerous female admirers and friends.

He, who usually accepted such presents reluctantly, was always delighted by such gifts. And while he never wore a medal ribbon in his buttonhole, he often wore a flower.

[. . .]   ADOLPH KOHUT

NOTES

1. Italian in the original.
2. This is not exactly true. The opinion of the examination committee of the Milan Conservatoire as to the young Verdi's potential in composition was substantially positive, as one can read from Basily's report of 2 July 1832 to the President of the Conservatoire, Count Sormani:

> *I am in absolute agreement with the assistant examiner Signor Piantanida, Professor of counterpoint, when he says that if he* [Verdi] *applies himself attentively and patiently to the study of the rules of counterpoint, he will be able to control the imagination that he clearly possesses, and therefore succeed well enough in the art of composition.*

The adverse criticism came from the piano professor, Angeleri, who

> *found that the said Verdi would need to alter the position of his hands, which, as he had reached the age of eighteen, would be difficult.*

It was Angeleri, therefore, who was responsible for Verdi's failure. And it should be added that, though Verdi was entering as a *paying* pupil, he was a foreigner, and the Milan Conservatoire, which at that time was run as a boarding-school, was suffering from a dearth of accommodation. On this subject, see also G. BARBLAN: "Rimpianto per un mancato allievo", in *Annuario 1963–64* of the Conservatorio di Musica Giuseppe Verdi, Milan 1963, pp. 171–85, with a facsimile of Basily's report.
3. Here Kohut quotes a statement collected by Quintino Sella (see *I Copialettere di G. Verdi*, cit., p. 599). Cf. chapter XXV.
4. Italian in the original.
5. Cf. N. XX, p. 132.

XLIX

UNPUBLISHED VERDI MEMOIRS

1891–1900

ITALO PIZZI: *Ricordi verdiani inediti*, Roux e Viarengo, Turin, 1901, *passim.*

ITALO PIZZI (Fornovo 1849 – Turin 1920) was a distinguished orientalist. A university fellow in Sanskrit, as well as in Persian and Arabian literature and language, he translated into Italian verse the epic Persian poem, Firdausī's *The Book of Kings*, an anthology of Persian poetry, the epic German poem *Die Nibelungenlied*, and also published grammars and manuals of oriental literature and languages.[1] He met Verdi, as he himself recounts, in July 1883 at the Laurentian library in Florence, of which he was at that time Assistant Librarian, and had occasion to pay him frequent visits up to September 1900, enjoying numerous conversations with him, which he then collected in his slim volume of *Ricordi verdiani*: "I wrote them infrequently, but I can vouch for their accuracy and authenticity." The volume is, moreover, enriched by several letters from Verdi (of no great interest) and some anecdotes recounted to him "either by eye-witnesses or by the very people who featured in the anecdotes" – particularly Giovanni Barezzi, son of Antonio. We quote here (not always in the order given by the author) the greater part of those conversations that took place in the space of about a decade, during Pizzi's visits to Sant'Agata at the end of summer or the beginning of autumn.[2] (The dates of the meetings, indicated from time to time by the author, are: summer 1891, 9 August 1892, 26 August 1893, summer 1894, 10 September 1895, 7 September 1896, 10 September 1897, 20 September 1898, 24 September 1899, 12 September 1900.)

Unpublished Verdi Memoirs

[. . .]
    And so I, a native of the same province of Parma, who have had the fortune and honour of knowing the great Maestro personally and have corresponded with him without interruption for almost twenty

years, discussing at length matters of literature, art, public life and
current affairs on most of the occasions I have had the honour of
being with him – I have decided to collect within these pages the
majority of my conversations with him, since I feel that some are
intrinsically important, while others, although of little account, serve
to reveal the man. [. . .] Certain opinions, that I shall record just as
I heard him utter them, will perhaps appear fresh and unexpected,
since the Maestro's great reticence in expressing an opinion on
anything and anybody is well known. But since I, as he said, never
abused his confidence, he perhaps considered it possible to tell me
things that he would not have told others. A part of what I write
might be contradicted by others, who have heard the Maestro
express different opinions on the same subjects – but what can never
be contradicted is the veracity of what I report: face-to-face conversations with the Maestro.

It has been stated at length, and often read, that Verdi was ill-
tempered and often almost ill-mannered in conversation. On certain
occasions this could, and indeed must have been true, when, for
example, he was working feverishly at his operas [. . .].

As for my own experience, I can say that only very rarely have I
met a person as polite and affable as he – on every occasion that
I visited him in all the many years of our acquaintance, or rather
friendship, he always, without exception, treated me with the
utmost gentleness and kindness. [. . .]

I have always found his conversation affable, gentle, affectionate,
friendly, often even shy and almost naïve and childlike, in the way he
would hesitate to assert his own opinions and ask questions of
others. I have thus been able to understand how he was an arch-
enemy of artificial, empty, insipid conversation that bristled with
bombast and exaggeration, which precisely for this reason signified
nothing; he takes pleasure, on the other hand, in calling a spade a
spade, and expressing his thoughts with the utmost sincerity. [. . .]
I can still remember with what a strange voice of disgust and
irritation, and with what contortions he replied to one of those
guides in the Laurentian library at Florence, who, with the most
stilted and fulsome phrases, had requested him to sign his own name
in the visitors album. [. . .]

Although I have never been a truly intimate friend, I have
observed that he would never break out into strange, eccentric or
bizarre phrases or behave in an unusual or irregular way – his

behaviour has always been correct and dignified, his speech truthful, precise, aptly chosen and unexaggerated. [. . .]

I first met him personally in 1883. I had previously seen him several times at Parma on market-days, for as an expert agricultural-ist he loved to trade in cattle, for which the Parma market is particularly renowned. This was many years ago. He later fre-quented the Cremona market. I had also seen him in 1872 at the Parma opera house, where *Aida* was being given – the best perform-ance of it, he said, that he had ever seen [. . .].

On Saturday 14 July 1883, a day memorable for its terrific heat, I and my office companions were in the Laurentian library in Florence passing away the afternoon hours drowsily and torpidly. An official guide – one Battaglia – entered, accompanying a handsome gentle-man, already advanced in age but still nimble and robust, followed by two ladies. This was the Maestro, returning from Montecatini, and he had with him Signora Strepponi, his wife, and Signora Teresina Stolz, the celebrated singer. Verdi studied with great atten-tion the precious things that were kept in that famous library, of which I was then Assistant Librarian: the illuminated pages on display, Petrarch, Cellini and Alfieri autographs, the second century Virgil, the Tacitus that had been discovered in Westphalia, the Paulus Orosius. He enquired about many things, including the celebrated Foligno edition of the *Divine Comedy* – all with the assistance of the library usher, while I, sitting in a corner of the great hall, was watching him with curiosity, since his face seemed far from unfamiliar. Indeed, having read the evening before in a Florentine newspaper, that he and two ladies had been at Montecatini a few days previously, I suddenly suspected, partly because of this circumstance and partly because I had already seen him several times and his face was so well-known from a thousand portraits, that this was, in fact, the Maestro. I questioned the guide, but he knew nothing. Then someone thought of asking the stranger to sign the visitors album, and the guide Battaglia (I still seem to see him!) approached him with comic courtesy and said: "If, sir, you would do us the honour of inscribing your esteemed name! . . ." These words were uttered with such awkwardness that Verdi, with those contor-tions I mentioned earlier, replied in a voice that was anything but harmonious and musical. But then he controlled himself and, taking the pen that was offered him, wrote his name in the album. I was now certain of who he was, and delighted by the fortuitous meeting,

I showed the Maestro the most precious exhibits that the library possessed, those that are usually kept jealously under lock and key and are shown to but a few: the Codex Amiatinus, that celebrated manuscript of the sixth century, the Syriac Gospels, also of the sixth century, the magnificent illuminated anthem books of Florence Cathedral, the illuminated Missal of the school of Ghirlandaio à propos which, when I told him that a similar missal had been sold a few years previously, he said with obvious bitterness: "In Italy they sell everything!"

Verdi admired these and many other treasures in the library, and he admired them with warm enthusiasm and a real feeling for art. He told me that he had once seen at the Cava dei Tirreni, among the friars, a most sumptuously illumined breviary of the Madonna, and he added with sparkling eyes: "Oh, if only I could have taken it away from the friar who showed it me!" – But he did not only admire, he also displayed an erudition that gives the lie to what has been or still is said of him – namely, that apart from music he knew very little. [. . .] I was astonished when, showing him a most rare edition of the works of Aristotle in Greek, produced in Venice and embellished with the most beautiful illumined miniatures of animals, he said: "I know no Greek, but this must be Aristotle's *The History of Animals.*" And it was true. And so he knew that Artistotle had written about natural history, a fact that is perhaps not known to all those students in Italy's schools who, with such a useless expenditure of time and money, learn Greek badly. Discussing the Laurentian Library, he asked if that was the library whose manuscripts one occasionally saw exhibited – a rare piece of knowledge, most rare in a composer and not even common in scholars who are highly thought of. Every time, moreover, that I met him, I was able to confirm that his knowledge of literature and art was out of the ordinary. Of the arts in general he seemed to possess sufficient learning to be able to discuss them with authority.

Having seen those treasures of the library worthy of being seen, Verdi took his leave, not without asking me for my visiting card which I handed to him solicitously. From then on I saw him every year, in August or September, until September 1900 which was, alas, the last time; I often visited his villa at Sant'Agata near Busseto and was always welcomed with the greatest affability.

[. . .] One day (I do not quite recall which year) when we had started to discuss Shakespeare, I asked him if he believed in the authenticity of the dramatist's works, which was at that time in doubt. He had no doubt whatever, and touching on many details of the controversy, he showed himself to be very well informed. He also had the very highest opinion of Shakespeare. When one reads Shakespeare's works, he said, with their sharp thoughts and profound observations that spring up so suddenly, one has to cry out: "But that could well be true! But it is true! It is like that!" – Shakespeare, according to him, analyses the human mind so acutely and penetrates it so profoundly, that the words he puts into his characters' mouths are essentially human, essentially true, as they should be. He remarked that Victor Hugo inflated his characters too much and, by exaggerating them, robs them of truth; that Schiller, too good, too naïve and too idealistic, fails to penetrate as much as Shakespeare into the human mind, and for this reason does not analyse it so profoundly. Many of his characters are thus idealized and unreal. Just such a character – one of the most lovable and attractive – is the Marquis of Posa in *Don Carlo*. This character (and these were Verdi's words) is a veritable anachronism, who finds himself professing humanitarian ideals in the most modern sense of the word – and that at the time of Philip the Second!*

"If Philip," he said, "had encountered such a character, he would have crushed him – instead of warning him, as Schiller makes him do: *Beware of my Inquisitor!*"

[. . .] He was so convinced of the incongruity of this character, that he wanted to omit it.

He told me: "Although I have set this character to music, I am quite aware of how he holds up the drama, and I had already intended cutting him entirely, when my friends (he did not say who) discouraged me, and I retained him."

I remember his words, just as he said them. [. . .]

He added that Philip, although a tyrant, appeared to be one from conviction – for he had led a most austere life. He said that he had visited the plain, bare room in the Escurial, where the King used to sleep on a wretched little bed.[3]

The Maestro had the greatest regard for Zola, precisely because he searched the human heart so deeply. He considered him worthy to be ranked alongside Shakespeare, and he read his novels avidly. He spoke with undisguised disgust of *La Terre*, on account of the filth (he used this word) that it contained; *L'Assommoir* pleased him

* It is well known that Schiller was criticized from several quarters on this character's idealism, to which he replied in the *Deutscher Merkur* of 1788. [Author's note]

greatly, but he had a particular admiration for *La Débâcle* with its subtle psychological analysis. This novel of Zola had only recently appeared, and perhaps Verdi spoke in this way, because the impression it had made was so fresh. Whatever – on 9 August 1892, having recently returned from Montecatini, Verdi said to me:

"All the officers at Montecatini are enthusing about it. Moltke, in *La Débâcle*, cuts a very fine figure and poor Napoleon III a wretched one! But everything is true!"

Returning now to the subject of trifling, petty-minded criticism, I remember very well how Verdi, while respecting the learning of German critics, found fault with certain of their methods of over-meticulous criticism and certain of their bizarre systems, and how, raising and waving his hands, he said:

"Oh! The Germans! The Germans! For every flea's leg or fly's leg they write a volume of three hundred pages!"

[. . .] When, I do not recall the year, our best literary critics were writing again and again, ad nauseam, about *gl'irrevocati dí* in the famous chorus from *Adelchi* [tragedy in verse by Alessandro Manzoni], Verdi, recalling with me this strange fact, exclaimed:

"Before those reviews, I understood something of the *irrevocati dí*. That line gave me a distant, uncertain, undefined idea of Emengarda's grief, as she mused on her past, and that idea accorded well with my own feelings. But now they've tried to explain those words too clearly, I understand absolutely nothing!"

[. . .]

Only very rarely did I speak of living authors with Verdi who, as is well-known, was always reluctant to discuss his contemporaries. But of some living writers, apart from Zola, he spoke to me not infrequently. He held Michele Lessona in high esteem.[4] He praised him as a scholar, a man of letters and even more for his special ability to write in such a way that everyone could understand him. Thus everyone read him. He also spoke very highly of Carducci but expressed great doubt as to whether the school of poetry, that he had begun so gloriously, would flourish.

One day he told me that he was reading Professor Angelo Mosso's *La Fatica*, which impressed him greatly. He was at that time working on *Falstaff*, and because it was I who asked him if *Falstaff* would soon be finished, he replied: "I work on it every day but not for long. Since reading Mosso's book, I no longer work so much. Too much work enfeebles our brain, and our blood is not as strong as peasant blood."

Laughingly, he told me something strange (on 7 September 1896), about a celebrated professor of psychiatry and his theory, according to which every man of genius is necessarily mad or half-mad.[5] Verdi disagreed with this doctrine and asserted repeatedly that Manzoni, a man of genius and great brilliance, was anything but strange or eccentric or mad, but was instead perfectly balanced. On the same occasion we also spoke of the calligraphy of famous men, from which one can, or should be able to deduce innate insanity, according to the theory that the same celebrated professor had recently discussed in a work that was certainly of great value. Verdi observed that one's style of hand writing depends to a large extent on the school of hand writing that prevailed at this or that time, and added that while in the past one was taught to write with vertical strokes of the pen, one was now taught to write in the English manner with slanting strokes. He distrusted the doctrine of calligraphy. When I then observed that another foreign professor taught the same doctrine and complained that he had been comprehensively plagiarized, the Maestro laughed and said:

"That man needs to be given a fifteen week, or rather fifteen month diet of bread and water – which would most certainly cure him."

But although he has a wide knowledge not only of Italian, but also classical and modern literature (in translation, apart from French and Latin writers), he has always exhibited, if not an undisguised aversion, at least a strong dislike for that Nordic literature which is utterly Nordic and has no connection with classical or even modern Italian literature. I refer to all that literature which concerns the ancient heroic traditions of old German paganism, from which source Wagner drew many subjects for his dramas [. . .]. Indeed, à propos Sigurdh, the main hero of the *Edda* and the subject of an opera by a talented modern German composer,[6] Verdi exclaimed one day, horrified by the cruel characters of almost all the Germanic heroes:

"Oh! Sigurdh and all those other heroes – how horrible!"

That he had never liked the *Nibelungenlied* is evident from the following letter which he wrote me when I sent him my translation of it:

Busseto Sant'Agata, 24 October 1889.

Dear Professor Pizzi,

Thank you for the two elegant volumes of the Niebelunghi [sic] *which you so kindly sent to my wife and me.*

Although I do not much care for the poem (at least in the abridged version that I read in Cantú's History), I hope that by re-reading it in your translation, I shall like it better. [. . .]

And we talked of music, which the Maestro had always seemed somewhat loath to do [. . .]. Lessona had said to me one day that, provided one resisted the temptation of drawing him into a discussion on music, he gradually fell into the trap. For my part, I never broached the subject first – and then proved that Lessona was right, because the Maestro, without provocation and of his own accord, began to talk of music. [. . .]

One day he summarized for me the life of Meyerbeer – a friend of long standing – and praised the kind, rare quality of his soul and mind. "But he was a great banker," he added, "and made money. He also set great store by praise and took infinite pains to obtain it. He subscribed to numerous journals, and if one was about to go bankrupt, he either gave his own help or became a shareholder on the board. He was thus assured of that journal's praise. Journalists on suitable occasions would often beg financial assistance from him."

Verdi then gave his opinion of Meyerbeer's operas. In *Robert le diable* he particularly admired the successful blend of the fantastic with the true, and meant by "true" the same as he meant previously, when applying the word to Shakespeare. Perhaps the character of Bertram induced him to say this, for in *Robert* he is the most Shakespearian character with his diabolical iniquity tempered by a hint of passionate tenderness. In *Le prophète* he acknowledged the unusual dramatic power, greater perhaps than in *Robert* and *Les Huguenots*, particularly in the fourth act at the marvellously dramatic moment when the mother of John of Leyden, who has been made King and prophet, is forced by her son's magnetic power to deny him. But he added that the whole opera possessed a wearisome heaviness, for which reason it is not the Meyerbeer opera he enjoys or understands most. He said of *Les Huguenots*:

"Some say that the libretto is badly written. But what do I care! The libretto is true theatre. And the final act, too, which in the opera house is always either misunderstood or cut, because the work is too long, is also true theatre. The third and fourth acts are stupendous."[7]

[. . .] I asked him what he thought of Meyerbeer's refusal to comply with the King of Prussia's request, that he should compose operas to the tragedies of Aeschylus, the *Eumenides* in particular. Verdi replied:

"I believe that Meyerbeer did exactly right, for in Aeschylus one is never sure whether characters are men or gods. The only true character in Aeschylus is Clytemnestra." [. . .]

On the question of Wagner and his music, which has given rise to so many lively and tempestuous arguments, this is what I could discover of Verdi's thoughts: like all discerning people, he approved the Wagnerian principle of adapting the music to the drama, but he did not approve the method, because Wagner, and his imitators to an even greater extent, often deliberately overstepped the limits. Verdi rightly admitted that the music must accord with the spirit and particular character of the nation, where the composer was born and for which he composed, but he could not and did not approve of Italians who, like so many wretched modern composers, wished at all costs to compose German music. [. . .]

One day in 1892 (it was Tuesday August 9), speaking with me very affably and happily in his elegant drawing-room at Sant'Agata, Verdi suddenly said to me in a mischievous way:

"Well then! This year and last year you've heard some fine music in Turin! *Die Walküre* and *Die Meistersinger!*"[8]

Then, a little more seriously, he added these words, which I noted down verbatim that very day when I arrived home:

"That music is fine in a German environment. Here in Italy, no. But in Germany it's fine. The curtain is hardly up, the lights go down and you are left in the dark like quails. In that darkness, in that stale air, your mind is so benumbed that that sort of music is fine. I have heard *Lohengrin* in Vienna[9] and I also dozed off in that torpor. Even the Germans dozed!"

Our conversation then continued in this manner. I added:

"And in Turin, at the performance of *Tannhäuser*, no small number were dozing, and they only woke when there was a hint or snatch of Italian melody, and they said . . ."

And Verdi interrupted, saying:

"Ah, I see! – And that was all, I imagine?"

I then said jokingly:

"Elisabeth's enormously long prayer, for example, in *Tannhäuser*, sung over endlessly drawn out chords, is so extremely pleasing that one cannot understand how our Lord, in front of whose cross Elisabeth kneels and prays, did not swing a leg and give her a boot."

"To shut her up once and for all!" said Verdi, with an animated smile.

Neither did he approve the German custom of absolute silence in the opera house, and even less that ecstatic silence which, it is said, Wagner imposed on his audience; what pleased him most, he said (as long as a certain moderation was observed, and trivial, indiscreet interruptions banished), was when all the audience, carried away by a single emotion, participated in the action that unfolded before their eyes, and followed it trembling, quivering and weeping. [. . .]

I then reminded him of that cry of enthusiasm which, in the Parma opera house, in April 1872, at the first performance there of *Aida*, greeted the famous phrase:

Rivedrai le foreste imbalsamate

[. . .] I remember, because I was in the theatre that evening, how the entire audience erupted in an almost wild cry, entreating the Maestro to take a bow on stage and asking for the phrase to be repeated. In Germany this would have been an unforgettable scandal. But how can one control – and here Verdi agreed with me – the enthusiasm, I would almost say the delirium, that at certain powerful phrases, at certain melodies that touch and shake every fibre of the soul, takes possession of an entire audience? The Maestro, with undisguised pleasure, then told me that he remembered that evening very well, and smiled with great contentment.

Nonetheless, the behaviour of the Parma opera house did not please him greatly; two years previously, in September 1890, I mentioned to him that the audience at Parma was often impossible to please and frequently even criticized (occasionally somewhat harshly) artists of merit. He replied:

"Ah, politics rule at the Parma opera house. There is too much politics. But that is now the case everywhere."

At the Busseto theatre, at the very same time, there were performances of *Luisa Miller* which, as I told him then, I very much wished to hear. He replied:

"You will enjoy it more at Busseto, for they are less fastidious in provincial theatres, and the *donnina* there is excellent."

I don't recall the name of the singer whom Verdi, to describe the soprano, called *donnina*[10] – a term, incidentally, which is current in Parma, and I believe elsewhere. [. . .]

Verdi spoke to me very rarely about his own operas, particularly the early ones; but he more often mentioned *Don Carlo*, *Aida* and *Falstaff*, revealing several curious details not devoid of interest.

[. . .] On 10 September 1895 I went, as usual, to Sant'Agata. On that day he was in the best of humour, affable as always and very jovial. I too was in good humour, and so the conversation was very varied and long, beginning, I don't well remember why or how, with a discussion of certain ancient musical instruments which sold at exorbitant prices and were collected by some people, like Krauss in Florence. I then reminded him of a concert, given in Krauss's house, of oriental music played on oriental instruments at the fourth Orientalists' Congress at Florence in September 1878 which I attended. He then asked me:

"And both the performance of the oriental music and the manner in which the instruments were played were supposed to have been authentic?"

I replied that I did not know, and asked him if he had seen the Greek Hymn to Apollo that had been recently discovered and performed with voice and instruments, after the notes had been arranged to accord with our system of notation. He replied:

"Yes, I saw it, but understood nothing." [11]

And then, somewhat more seriously:

"I do not understand," he added, "the pride of certain mediocre minds who do their utmost to unearth novelties, even useless trifles, just to give themselves the air of great discoverers. Each summer I go to Montecatini, I always find a gentleman there, who has taken it into his head to re-establish and recreate ancient Hebrew music."

"But what does he wish to achieve?" I asked, "since we have no idea of either the music or Hebrew pronunciation, as the vowels that indicate how the text of the Bible should be pronounced were added much later in the sixth century of the Christian era, whereas the most ancient Hebraic writings date from many centuries before the birth of Christ and simply cannot, therefore, reveal the correct pronunciation."

And Verdi replied:

"That gentleman wishes to re-establish Hebrew music by studying tradition, believing that in those chants that accompany the reading of the Bible in synagogues must lie the origin of ancient Hebrew song of two thousand years ago. What an extraordinary notion! Consider, for example, Rossini's aria *di tanti palpiti*: if we hear the aria in different theatres, in different concerts, sung by different singers, we shall find that it is never performed in exactly the same way. And yet Rossini belongs to our own century. Consider the *Te Deum*, attributed to Saint Ambrose. If we go to different churches, we hear it sung in a multitude of different ways. How then, if even quite recent songs can change so easily, can we hope to conjecture, by studying the modern way of singing in synagogues, the form of ancient Hebraic music of thousands of years ago? And with our scanty and nebulous knowledge of Greek music, how can we, for example, recreate a chorus by Aeschylus? Ask ten musicians to interpret a single line of verse that has been set to music, when neither the rhythm nor length of notes have been marked, and you will find that the ten musicians give you ten wildly different interpretations. I do not believe it possible to recreate or reconstruct ancient music – neither Hebraic, Grecian or any other."

[. . .] Having heard this wise conclusion about ancient music, that some scholars would like to recreate, I suddenly said to him:

"On the subject of antiquities and the discovery of antiquities, Maestro, guess what I heard at Pieve★ last night about your *Aida*. You will never have heard such rubbish."

And Verdi, curiously attentive, asked:

"And what was said?"

"They said," I replied, "that you must have consulted many parchments to compose the music of *Aida*!"

"Parchments for *Aida*?" he asked with an almost disdainful smile. "Who could say such a thing?"

And he continued:

"À propos *Aida*, hear what happened to me. When I was composing the opera, I read in an article by Fétis, an authority on musical matters, that an Egyptian flute was preserved in a Florentine museum. You can imagine, if this were true, the importance it could have for me. The flute could have been reconstructed, changed from its own key, say D, to one that would have suited my purposes, and I'd have written some special music that would have contributed greatly to local colour for the opera. With this in mind I sped to Florence. I requested the Director of the museum to admit me an hour before the general public, to avoid any inquisitive visitors and study the famous Egyptian flute in my own good time. The Director handed it to me, I examined it carefully, and guess what it was!"

"I have no idea," I replied.

"A peasant's whistle with five holes! I let it be and did nothing."[12]

After a brief silence he continued with a smile:

"In a similar way, I was told that at Nîmes, I forget whether in the

---

★ Pieve Ottoville, a small wealthy town in the Province of Parma, six miles from the composer's villa at Sant'Agata. [Author's note]

museum or elsewhere, that there were Roman trumpets to be seen! But I paid no attention, for I no longer believed in such discoveries."
[. . .]

When the newspapers (with those of Milan to the fore), announced that Verdi was composing *Falstaff*, the excitement, as everyone knows, was enormous, and it was natural for me, a very great admirer, to ask the Maestro about the new opera when I visited him in the summer of 1891. He then told me that, alarmed by Mosso's book, he was only working on it a little each day, and added:

"I am not writing an opera buffa but depicting a character. My Falstaff is not merely the character of Shakespeare's *The Merry Wives of Windsor*, where he is just a buffoon and made fun of by the women, but rather the Falstaff who has appeared in Henry IV, parts 1 and 2. And Boito has written the libretto with this in mind."

In the summer of the following year (August 9), when I asked him about *Falstaff*, he replied:

"The opera is finished, but I am having great difficulty in finding singers. There are many characters in *Falstaff* and not one is secondary."

"But everyone," I remarked, "will be anxious to have the honour of singing in the first performance of *Falstaff*."

"Yes," he replied, "but they all want the main roles, even though every role is of equal importance. None of Shakespeare's characters are secondary. All of them are of equal importance, even those who only have a few words to say. They all have their own individuality, their own very distinctive characteristics.
[. . .]

And so I was not able to hear *Falstaff* on that occasion [at La Scala]. On my arrival at Sant'Agata (26 August of the same year, 1893), I naturally first enquired about *Falstaff*, as I wished to congratulate the Maestro on its resounding success. I told him that I had tried to play the opera on the piano, although I was a most inept pianist, but had failed to understand it properly, and that I still found many things difficult, even very difficult to grasp. He replied rather affectionately:

"Oh, it's impossible to form an idea of *Falstaff* on the piano! You need to hear it! I have orchestrated it very lightly. Certain pianissimo passages cannot be performed on the piano. The effect is nil. Besides, everything springs from the ensemble, and that cannot be obtained on the piano because the opera, in the piano reduction, has been butchered. Great singers are not required for *Falstaff*, but artists with good intentions. That is why I'm pleased with the performances at Brescia, because the singers work as a team – they are not prima donnas but ordinary mortals; they are *de bons enfants*.[13] I have read many articles on *Falstaff* in various newspapers, but of all the music critics I prefer Cora, Egidio Cora of Turin, because he has no ultramontane ideas and because he states what is good and bad about the Italian and German schools, and does not wish Italians – like certain other critics – to compose music like ultramontanes. There's no denying it: art must have a national character, science, no. Italians are Italians, and music for Italians must be Italian. We differ from the Germans, differ even more from the French (and he stressed these words) and from the Russians, and we have a different way of feeling." [. . .]

I asked him if, after *Falstaff*, he would continue composing, and he replied very thoughtfully:

"Oh no, no! At my age one can compose no more, and I shall compose no more."

"But," I pointed out, "the papers say you will."

"Oh," he replied, "take no notice of the press who report such rubbish! They have but one aim, to be read and to sell as many copies as possible."

[. . .]

In the spring of 1894, a university Congress was held by students at Turin, attended by scores of Italian and foreign students; for this event a hymn was written in goliard Latin. It was decided to have the hymn set to music, and Professor Salvatore Cognetti De Martiis, being aware that I knew Verdi personally [. . .], asked me to approach him. I was quite sure that the Maestro would refuse, but unable to deny a friend and colleague and the students a legitimate favour, I wrote [. . .]. Verdi replied immediately:

> Genoa, 5 February 1894
>
> Dear Prof. Pizzi,
> I have never been able, or rather, I have never known how to write occasional compositions, *not even when I was young*.
>   Now, when I'm over eighty, my pen . . . and the curtain falls!
>   I beg you to convey my apologies to the students. [. . .]
>
> G. Verdi.

When in the summer I saw him again at his villa, I offered him my apologies, saying that, although I had never imagined that he would

grant the request, the least I could do was to write as I did. To which
he replied:

"Do not give it a thought. Every day I receive such requests.
A few weeks ago, for example, I was sent from Loreto a painting of
the Madonna, surrounded by a multitude of little pictures in which
the principal events of her life were depicted, and every picture
contained a little verse. And I was to set all these little verses to
music. As if I could do that!"[14]

[. . .]

Still on the subject of the press and its relative unreliability, I
remember how in 1899 one of the most authoritative papers reported
that the Maestro was writing his *memoirs*. Visiting him at Sant'Agata
in the autumn of the same year (September 24) I asked him about this
and he replied at once:

"Let the press say what they like, but be sure to believe *none* of
it!"[15]

"But they keep insisting that it's true!"

"Believe nothing! I am so tired of seeing my name in the papers,
I've no wish to contribute to this continual game."

I then respectfully observed that this book, if he did write it,
would be of great importance for the history of art. And he, slightly
angered, replied:

"What I have achieved is of little consequence. And then I don't
approve of this writing about one's own life!" And I added: "None
the less, I hope that one day we shall see something." And he replied
very curtly: "Rest assured, that you shall see nothing."

[. . .] I never spoke to him of politics, which never interested me
– and which Verdi loathed.[16] [. . .]

One day in September 1896 we somehow started to talk about
India, and he, amongst other things said:

"Here you have a great and ancient people who have now fallen
prey to the English. But the English will be sorry! A people might
suffer tyranny, oppression, maltreatment – and the English are sons
of bitches. Then comes the moment, when national sentiment,
which no one can withstand, reawakens. That's how we treated the
Austrians. Alas, we are now in Africa in the role of tyrant –
inopportunely, and we shall pay for it. It is said that we are going
there to bring those people our own civilization. A fine civilization
we have, with all its unhappiness. Those people will not know what
to make of it, and in many respects they are much more civilized
than we!"

I then told him that I had heard from a dear pupil of mine –
the much lamented Vittorio Verdelli of Parma, captain of the
bersaglieres who died valiantly in action at Abba Garima and had
often been in Africa – that those Abyssinians, whom we call
barbaric, possess excellent mental and physical attributes [. . .], can
speak with clarity, confidence and dignity both to their chiefs and us,
and have a very clear concept of true justice. At this point the
Maestro suddenly interrupted: .

"And their justice is not the law with which we content ourselves
in lieu of justice!"

[. . .]

On that day the Maestro seemed to have it in for doctors, whom
he always abused. He did not greatly like women being cared for and
examined by doctors, and said:

"Since our universities are overrun with so many women students,
who then graduate in literature, philosophy, mathematics – which
does not please me at all – it would be better if they studied medicine,
so that they could look after women. It is natural for a woman to
confide more willingly in another woman rather than a male doctor,
to whom she will never dare to reveal everything. A degree in
medicine is therefore the only one I approve of for women."

[. . .]   .

And other indications suggested to me that Verdi, perhaps because
of his mild hypochondria, feared death. Professor Gaetano Zini of
Parma once told me that he had found himself travelling in the same
carriage as Verdi from Borgo[17] to Parma, in those happy days before
one used to travel by train. After a few preliminary exchanges and
the kind of conversation travellers are wont to have, when obliged to
spend long, slow hours together, Zini (he told me) congratulated
Verdi on the fame he had won thus far in his career, and the
composer replied gloomily: "Yes, yes, all that is fine! But I work so
much and then I shall have to die!" – In August 1889, I went with my
wife and Carlo, then a little boy, to visit Verdi at Sant'Agata. As
always he welcomed us very politely, but he was not in a good mood
and complained of a headache. After a short silence one of us said to
him that he must feel comfortable in such a beautiful villa, and he
suddenly said: "Yes, to escape the tedium of town-life and feel a little
at ease, one must either seek refuge in this solitude or commit
suicide!" – [. . .]

On 12 September 1900 I found him very depressed. My regular coachman had told me that the day before he had refused to receive a foreign visitor, excusing himself that he had not felt well. I then feared that I would not be received; nonetheless I tried and was admitted. At that moment (it was midday precisely) a terrible storm was raging beyond Sant'Agata. The wind whistled in the many tall poplars that surround the Maestro's villa and the rain lashed down cold and almost icy. This was partly the reason, I thought, why on that particular day he was more melancholy and sad. He gave me a kind welcome, smiled a little and said:

"I apologize, Pizzi, if I cannot welcome you as I used, but I do not feel well today, not at all well!" – And after a pause: "I no longer talk or read or compose or play!" I tried to cheer him up and blamed the time of year for his depression, and he replied: "It is not the time of year, it is all my years that depress me."

Our conversation was brief and left me, alas, with a feeling of disquiet.

[. . .]

As I took my leave, he contined to complain about his state of health. "My legs no longer carry me!" he said, and indeed, as he accompanied me to the door, he leant heavily on my hand and moved with difficulty, taking exceedingly short steps. I said to him: "Don't lose heart, Maestro! Your doctor, Battistini, told me a few hours ago in Busseto that you have a most robust constitution." Verdi replied rather peevishly: "I know, I know – if I hadn't, I wouldn't have reached the age of 87. But those 87 years are weighing me down!"

And so I left him and drove from the villa with the fear that I would never seen him again. Alas, I never did.

ITALO PIZZI

NOTES

1. Cf. G. BATTISTINI: "Italo Pizzi e Busseto", in *Aurea Parma*, XLVI, 3: 1962, pp. 148–56; F. BOTTI: "Verdi e Italo Pizzi", in *Gazzetta di Parma*, 22 January 1951 (reissued in *Nuove spigolature verdiane*, Battei, Parma 1971, pp. 22–23).
2. These conversations were for the most part collected by Pizzi in his subsequent book on Verdi: *Per il I° centenario della nascita di Giuseppe Verdi. Memorie – aneddoti – conversazioni*, Lattes, Turin 1913.
3. Verdi was in Spain between February and March 1863 to stage *La forza*

del destino (February 21) at Madrid's Teatro Reale. He took the
opportunity of visiting the Escurial, and on March 22 he wrote to
Arrivabene from Paris:

> The Escurial *(pardon the blasphemy) does not please me. It is a mass of
> marbles, and although it contains some most sumptuous and beautiful things
> (including an amazingly beautiful* fresco *by Luca Giordano), there is a
> general lack of good taste. It is austere and terrible, like the ferocious
> sovereign who constructed it.* (*Verdi intimo,* cit., p. 24.)

4. Michele Lessona (Venaria Reale, Turin 1823 – Turin 1894); he gradu-
   ated in medicine and surgery and began a career in medicine. After
   several journeys in Europe and the Middle East, he returned to Italy in
   1849 and decided to devote his time to teaching and natural history
   research: first at Asti, then at the University of Turin, then in Genoa,
   Bologna and finally once more in Turin, where he taught zoology and
   comparative anatomy. He became Rector of the university and in 1892
   was appointed Senator. He wrote works of a scientific nature, literary
   criticism and short stories; he is known chiefly for his work as a
   popularizer and for two books in particular: *Conversazioni scientifiche*
   (Milan, 1869–74, 4 volumes) and *Volere è potere* (Barbèra, Florence 1869
   – reprinted numerous times). Compiled on the pattern of Smiles' *Self-
   Help*, *Volere è potere* gathers together numerous biographies of contemporary Italians, illustrious names from the sciences, arts and indus-
   try who, born in poverty and brought up in hardship, were able to
   conquer adversity through their own will. Chapter IX (pp. 287–307) is
   devoted to the youth and rise of Verdi and contains information from
   an interview with the composer, which took place in September 1868 at
   Tabiano (see Verdi's letter to Arrivabene of 7 March 1874 in *Verdi
   intimo*, cit., p. 174). Lessona's biography of Verdi concludes with the
   following words:

> [Verdi] adores the spectacle of the sea as he does the spectacle of all
> nature's beauty; but when he wishes to compose, he prefers a with-
> drawn room; he works at the same speed throughout the day, but on
> rainy, cloudy days he feels listless – which makes him think that he
> would have accomplished little of worth, if he had had to live for
> long in England or France. When it rains, he reads all day with the
> same passion as in his youth. He will often re-read some passages
> from the Bible, and after Dante he enjoys Ariosto, whose descrip-
> tions, particularly of storms and battles, never cease to arouse his
> admiration. Because he is a great admirer of Ariosto, he does not
> deem it necessary to dislike Tasso. He is familiar with the works of
> our great authors and those of the best foreign writers. He has a fine
> understanding of painting, loves Guido Reni and the Bologna school,
> but above all Correggio, in whom he finds something of Raphael's

gracefulness and Michelangelo's strength. As for the ancient music of our composers, he has the very highest praise for the *Messa di Papa Marcello* of Palestrina, who restored a simple and noble approach to composition, in the teeth of manneristic, fugal writing. He is an ardent admirer of Pergolesi. Renowned and praised throughout the world for his genius, Verdi endears himself to those who know him personally by the noble and dignified simplicity of his manners, his courtesy, sound judgement, his delightful conversation and his exquisite manners. His companion in life is worthy of him in every way, and he appreciates her greatly. He is at the height of his powers, and uses them nobly; his vigorous appearance reveals the happiness and serenity of a man, who has been able to assert his will. [. . .]

5. A clear allusion to Cesare Lombroso (Verona 1835 – Turin 1909), the famous criminologist, well-known for the theory that genius, like delinquency, is caused by epileptiform phenomena and psychic distortions. Exactly two and a half years before this conversation with Verdi, Lombroso had published an article: "Il fenomeno psicologico di Verdi", (*Gazzetta Musicale di Milano*, XLVIII, 10: 5 March 1893, pp. 159–60 – subsequently published in numerous foreign reviews), in which, consistent with his own theory, he attempted to deny that Verdi was a genius, while at the same time acknowledging his very great artistic merit.

6. Allusion to *Sigurd* by Ernest Reyer (see XXV, note 10) who was, however, French.

7. About libretti in general, Pizzi obtained from Verdi a statement which he was to quote in his second book on the composer, *Per il I° centenario della nascita di Giuseppe Verdi*, cit., pp. 190–91:

His opinion about opera libretti is strange and utterly characteristic, though shared, one might say, by other Italian composers, Bellini excepted. He said that the libretto ought and could only be a fabric, an ordinary scenario almost, upon which or around which the composer should display the mastery of his art. An opinion that is certainly erroneous, unless he made it lightheartedly and without reflexion, as is often the case with people who assert things which they will then promptly deny on another occasion.

Verdi's opinion is certainly proving to be the only valid and correct one – and not merely with regard to his own libretti. . . . Cf. the exemplary essay by F. FLORA: "Il libretto" [of *Un ballo in maschera*], in *Verdi*, Bollettino dell'Istituto di studi verdiani, n. 1, 1960, pp. 44–72; as well as the excellent contribution, one of the best to appear in recent years on Verdi's dramaturgy, by M. LAVAGETTO: *Quei piú modesti romanzi*, Garzanti, Milan 1979.

8. *Die Walküre* had been performed at Turin's Teatro Regio on

22 December 1891, conducted by Vittorio Maria Vanzo. *Die Meister-singer* had not yet been performed at the time of Pizzi's conversation with Verdi: the first night was on 26 December 1892, under the baton of Alessandro Pomé.

9. Perhaps he meant to say *Tannhäuser*, which was being performed in Vienna, when Verdi was there to conduct his *Requiem* and *Aida* (cf. N. XV, including note 10).

10. Her name was Luisa Negroni. *Luisa Miller* had been performed at Busseto on 23 August 1890.

11. Cf. N. XLII, including note 6.

12. See also N. XI, note 12: Verdi's letter of 8 February 1878 to Arrivabene on the same subject.

13. *Falstaff* had been performed at Brescia's Teatro Grande on 12 August 1893, with Mascheroni conducting, as at La Scala, and with the same cast (Emma Zilli, Adelina Stehle, Edoardo Garbin, Antonio Pini-Corsi, Vittorio Arimondi, etc), except for a new protagonist, Arturo Pessina, instead of Maurel, and with a new Quickly. On September 2 Verdi wrote to Ricordi:

> *I have always believed and still believe that* Falstaff *is the easiest of operas to stage, and that with a little instruction everyone, or almost everyone can perform it. The proof is that, despite the dearth of talent, we have found two presentable* Falstaffs *in addition to the first. And there are dozens who could give a good account of Ford (though not like Pini) and many who could sing the Wives.* (Autograph: Archivio della Casa Ricordi, Milan.)

14. This very probably refers to the *Litanie lauretane* and the proposal, made to him personally at Sant'Agata by Caterina Pigorini Beri. The journal-ist had written about this visit and proposal in a rather frivolous article that had appeared in the *Fanfulla della Domenica* of Rome on 2 April 1893: *Giuseppe Verdi e le litanie lauretane*, in which, however, she does not quote the composer's reply. She mentions the subject again in the special edition of the review *Natura ed Arte* that was published in 1901 on the death of Verdi (see N. XXI, note 1) and finally in the article *Verdi intimo* that appeared in *Nuova Antologia* on 16 October 1913.

15. A few days later, on 3 October 1899, Verdi made the following reply to Onorato Roux, who had asked for confirmation of the statement:

> *I have never thought of writing my memoirs and never shall. God forbid! – Thank you for your good wishes.* (*I Copialettere di G. Verdi*, cit., p. 403, note.)

16. In his next book, *Per il I° centenario della nascita di Giuseppe Verdi*, cit., p. 198, Pizzi added the following information:

> A close friend of his, Canon Giovanni Avanzi, parish priest at

Vidalenzo, the last village in the district of Parma towards the Piacenza border, in whose graveyard Verdi's parents are buried, maintained that Verdi's feelings were frankly republican. He added, however, that he was a theoretical republican, and held the House of Savoy in high esteem.

17. Borgo San Donnino, now Fidenza.

L

VERDI MEMOIRS

1897–1900

GIOVANNI TEBALDINI: "Ricordi verdiani", in *Rassegna Dorica*, Rome, XI,
n. 1: 25 January 1940, pp. 4–8; n. 3: 25 March 1940, pp. 49–55; n. 4:
25 April 1940, pp. 73–79; n. 5: 25 May 1940, pp. 93–99; n. 6: 25 June 1940,
pp. 118–23. (Excerpts also published by same author in: "Ricordi", in
Il Resto del Carlino, Bologna, 23 January 1941; "Ricordi personali", in
La Stampa, Turin, 26 January 1941; "Incontro a lui – Flectamus genua!", in
Verdiana, review cit., Milan, n. 6: January 1951, pp. 19–22).

GIOVANNI TEBALDINI (Brescia 1864 – San Benedetto del Tronto
1952) was a musicologist and composer; having studied in his native
town and later in Milan under Bazzini, Ponchielli and Amelli
(1883–85), he finished his studies in Germany at Bayreuth and
Munich and then at Ratisbon under Haberl and Haller. In 1889 he
was appointed assistant maestro di cappella at Saint Mark's in
Venice, in 1894 he became maestro di cappella at the Santo in Padua,
where he re-arranged the musical archives. In 1897 he was appointed
Director of the Parma Conservatoire, which he left in 1902 to
become maestro di cappella at Loreto's Santa Casa, where he
remained until his retirement in 1924. In that year he was given the
chair of Palestrina studies at the Naples Conservatoire. Apart from
composing sacred and symphonic music and small vocal works, he
made arrangements of much Renaissance music and published many
musicological works, mainly on sacred music, the musical archives
at Padua and Loreto, the history of the organ, as well as monographs
on Felipe Pedréll, Gaspare Spontini, Ildebrando Pizzetti. He met
Verdi personally in October 1897, but had corresponded with him
during the previous two and half years. The story of his dealings
with the aged composer is told in these *Verdi Memoirs*, from which
we quote the principal passages.

Verdi memoirs

[. . .] The weather was foul in Milan during that January of 1884. Ice and mist everywhere. On one of the many terrible evenings, when sleet whirled in front of your eyes before whipping into your face, and horse-drawn trams with ringing bells crawled forwards and gas jets burned dim and low, a closed carriage halted in Corso V[ittorio] E[manuele] in front of the Teatro Milanese. I happened to find myself close by. I saw Arrigo Boito descend hastily from the left side and move round to the right to open the carriage door from which, unobserved, Verdi stepped; with Boito he then entered the popular theatre to attend the notorious . . . *Minestron* – the humorous parody of *Il trovatore* by Edoardo Ferravilla. I was present at that merry evening, which at times became downright noisy, especially when the audience, knowing that the Maestro was hiding at the back of a first-tier box to the left of the stage, cheered enthusiastically and turned laughingly in the direction of Verdi's box.

Count Luna was played by Ferravilla, Manrico by Giraud, Leonora by Emma Ivon, Ferrando by Sbodio and Azucena by Giovannelli.

The success of the singing-actors of the Teatro Milanese on that and many other evenings was indescribable. Thirteen years later at Sant'Agata I saw on the Maestro's writing desk two grotesque statuettes of Ferravilla and Giraud in their garish *Minestron* cloaks.

[. . .]

Venice. Spring 1893. Every Sunday afternoon at the hospitable Casa Fortuny on the Grand Canal near San Gregorio, a select group of Italian and foreign personalities used to gather for lively discussions on art or play good music.

[. . .] Some of the guests were regular visitors to the Munich and Bayreuth opera houses, I too perhaps could be classed among them. As a consequence we moved in the purest of Wagnerian circles.

[. . .]

News arrived, almost unexpectedly, of the great success at La Scala of *Falstaff* by that 80-year-old magician Verdi; and the Italians especially, even though Wagnerians, rejoiced.

Among the guests on that Sunday were D. Henry Thode of Heidelberg University and his wife Frau Thode von Bülow, the daughter of Cosima Wagner, who usually lived at Villa Cargnacco in

Gardone Riviera on Lake Garda – now Vittoriale d'Annunziano, the
home of d'Annunzio.

Frau Thode appeared delighted with the news that was on everyone's lips, but expressed neither amazement nor surprise since, as she
proclaimed aloud: "My grandfather (Franz Liszt) repeatedly
expressed his faith in Verdi's genius."
[. . .]
Meanwhile in my daily seclusion, even though surrounded by the
golden nimbus of the Basilica which welcomed me every day, I
continually asked myself if I would ever have occasion to kiss the
hand that had penned the score of the merry comedy which I had
heard. [. . .]
A year after the appearance of *Falstaff*, on 21 June 1894, I received
this letter, marked *confidential*:

> *Would it be possible to discover any information about*
> 1   Popular Venetian Songs and Dances 1400–1600;
> 2   *Ditto*   Greek   *ditto*   *ditto*
> *Do you think you could find these either in the Biblioteca Marciana or*
> *elsewhere? You would be doing a great favour to M. Verdi, who would*
> *appreciate some notion of the above.*
>
> > Yours Sincerely,
> > Giulio Ricordi

From a manuscript in the Museo Bessarione della Marciana and
from Bourgault-Ducodray's writings on Greco-Byzantine music I
assembled an assortment of works which seemed to meet the
requirements of the request, and I sent everything to Giulio Ricordi.[1]
A few months later *Otello* was performed at the Paris Opéra with
the addition of the *Dances*, composed on themes that I had collected
and sent to the illustrious publisher.[2] [. . .]
In 1895, with the Santo's centenary celebrations just a few weeks
away, I was given charge of the Cappella Musicale of Padua's
Basilica Antoniana. I had undertaken to write an illustrated history of
the archives which house, amongst other things, the major works of
P. Vallotti and Giuseppe Tartini.[3] Its publication interested those
critics, musicians and musicologists who were in a position to
appreciate its importance. The Paduan, Arrigo Boito, was one of the
first to send me kind words of encouragement and approbation. His
brother Camillo, architect to the famous Basilica, urged me to send
Verdi a complimentary copy of the volume.

Uncertain at first, I finally followed the distinguished professor's advice, and sent the volume to Genoa with a simple note, expressing my respect and apologies for my boldness. A few weeks later I received this letter which only now – after forty-four years – do I publish for the first time.

Genoa, 18 February 1896

Dear Maestro Tebaldini,

Please accept my apologies for not having spoken to you about your book which you so kindly sent me. I was in Milan for quite some time and was so busy that I did not have a moment to read your excellent illustrated history – which I find very useful, both for its critical and historical sections: always calm, impartial and profound.

You write at length of P. Vallotti, whom I also admire and to whom I owe a debt of gratitude, since in my youth I composed several studies on his themes; and on page 45 I see quoted a Te Deum *by P. Vallotti!*

This truly surprised me, as I have long been searching for a musical setting of this Canticle and have failed to find examples either in Palestrina or his contemporaries. I have little interest in other Te Deums, *written for certain occasions at the end of the last or the beginning of this century. But it would please me greatly to see this* Te Deum *by Vallotti . . . whatever its quality. I would therefore ask you, if it is at all possible, to make me a copy of it, at my expense of course, and send it to me here at Genoa. Should this not be possible, then let us speak no more of it, and please pardon my bold request.[5]*

I thank you meanwhile for your kindness and remain

Yours very sincerely, G. Verdi

I had to reply, in spite of myself, that the Presidenza of the Santo had always been reluctant to make copies of music possessed by the archives, as had been the case with Tartini. And for this reason I begged the Maestro to apply to the Presidenza who, *for him*, would perhaps make an exception.

And here is his second letter[6] in which he expounds a veritable exegesis of the *Ambrosian Hymn*.

Genoa, 1 March 1896

Dear Maestro Tebaldini,

I find most commendable the regulation which forbids music held in the Arca's archives to be copied – far be it from me to seek to break this regulation.

I know some ancient Te Deums and have heard a few modern ones, and leaving aside the musical quality, I am not convinced by the way in which this canticle has been interpreted. It is usually sung on great, solemn, noisy feast-days, or on the occasion of victories or coronations etc. The opening words are therefore suitable: Heaven and Earth cry aloud . . . . "Sanctus Sanctus Deus Sabaoth"; but towards the middle there is a change of colour and expression. . . . Tu ad liberandum . . . it is Christ, born of the Virgin Mary, who opens the Regnum coelorum to man. Man believes in the Judex venturus . . . and invokes him . . . Salvum fac . . . and ends in a prayer: Dignare in die isto . . . moving, gloomy and sad to the point of terror! None of this has anything to do with victories and coronations. It was for this reason that I wished to see whether Vallotti, who had at his disposal an orchestra and fairly rich harmonies, had found this colour and expression or understood the work differently from many of his predecessors.

I am beginning to believe that this wish of mine will never be fulfilled, unless you with your great erudition and scholarship should chance to find some Te Deum, composed according to my, perhaps wrong, ideas. Should you find such a work, I beg you to forward it.

I return with warmest thanks the volume you kindly sent me. These Te Deums by Anerio and others are, of course, well constructed – but they do not enlighten me, nor do they remove my doubts.

Please forgive me, dear Maestro Tebaldini, for inconveniencing you and believe me

Yours very sincerely, G. Verdi

Verdi's opinions and criteria for interpreting the text of the *Ambrosian Hymn*, which he expounded with such perspicacity in the above letter, are, I notice, corroborated by the development of the melodic phrase on which the hymn is based. And I wrote to the Maestro about this, deploring the fact that a scarcely commendable restriction – that other countries do without – should hinder one from studying and making generally known the works of our foremost composers.

Verdi replied immediately:

Genoa, 20 March 1896

Dear Maestro Tebaldini,
For lack of time I'm merely dropping you a line to thank you for your good wishes and to tell you that you have misinterpreted my words (or perhaps I have explained myself badly) on the prohibition concerning the

archives of the Cappella del Santo. On the contrary, I wish that the truly worthwhile works of our great composers were made available, but that the originals be jealously preserved in the archives. But I shall talk to you of this when things are less hectic.

I have just received the Te Deum *which you so kindly sent me. I shall look over it and return it as soon as possible.*

Thank you for everything, and believe me

Yours very sincerely, G. Verdi

The Presidenza of the Arca del Santo, at the special request of Camillo Boito, decided to satisfy the Maestro's wishes and sent him Vallotti's *Te Deums*. The Maestro informed me of this.

Genoa, 1 May 1896

Dear Maestro Tebaldini,

You will know that Vallotti's Te Deums *have been sent me in the name of the Presidenza of the Cappella del Santo, through the intervention of Comm. Boito.*

I have read through the Te Deums *and returned them yesterday, with thanks, to the Presidenza.*

I know that I owe this favour to you, dear Maestro, and I am truly grateful – also for the other Te Deum *by Tinel that you sent me and which I return today by post.*

The work is very well constructed but it did not provide me with what I was looking for.

Please excuse the briefness of this discussion – I'm leaving tomorrow or the day after for the country, and have many papers to put in order.

Thank you once again, and believe me

Yours very sincerely, G. Verdi

It is interesting at this point to know Verdi's opinion when he had read P. Vallotti's *Te Deums*. He told me shortly afterwards: absolutely negative! (See page 6 of the Preface to my Saint Anthony volume.)[7]

[. . .]

Having corresponded with the Maestro, it was only right for me to seek an opportunity of meeting him. I had harboured this wish for many years – since the first dreams of my youth!

On one bright sunny morning in the spring of 1897 I was in Genoa. I happened to be walking in the Galleria Mazzini, where in those days the main post-office was to be found. At one of the windows I noticed Verdi: alone and unobserved, he was attending to some everyday business. Behind him others awaited their turn. I saw him move away. I gave a start, followed him for a few paces, considered introducing myself, but my courage then failed me. Should I approach him in the street? Unbecoming, I thought. I followed him at a little distance. As I left the Galleria, I saw him enter Zerega, the chemist's (I discovered later that this was a favourite haunt), which faced the Teatro Carlo Felice. I halted on the pavement opposite and waited. After a short while he left the chemist's, climbed into a small open carriage which moved along Via Roma and headed for Piazza Fontane Marose and Via Balbi. I imagined he was returning to his abode at the Palazzo Doria, beyond the Principe station to the Marittima, and I too headed in that direction with a beating heart.

"Go on up," said the concierge. Anxiously I climbed the wide staircase; at the door of his apartment I rang the bell and asked to be announced, but the servant replied that it was not possible. It would have been easy for me to remind the inflexible servant of my connections with the Maestro, but I was reluctant to do so. I did not insist but merely requested that my visiting card be handed to the Maestro. Impossible! The pitiless servant would not accept it. Did I really resemble a beggar or an adventurer?

I returned to the concierge who, being more gentle, reasonable and polite, assured me that he himself would hand my respectful card to the Maestro. And that is what happened.

Four or five days later at the Albergo Santa Chiara in Rome, on my way from Padua, I received a note from the Maestro: ". . . and I am sorry that when you were in Genoa you did not honour me by climbing the stairs of the Doria, since I would gladly have shaken an artist's hand" etc. (it is not for me to repeat what he said).

I replied immediately: "You are mistaken, Maestro! Your servant took fright and refused to announce me."

Ah, even now I see before me "that proud-looking man" with his scowling countenance, that relentless Giuseppe, with whom I later became firm friends and laughed about the Genoa episode!

[. . .]

I spent the summer of the same year, 1897, for the third time, at Munich, Ratisbon, Bayreuth and Nuremberg.

I was enthralled by the great moments of Palestrina's *Missa Papae Marcelli*, Beethoven's Ninth Symphony, Wagner's *Tristan*, *Siegfried* and *Parsifal*, but all these great works did not succeed in silencing my secret ambition to meet the man who had created the last act of *Otello*. I had occasion to write to him again. It is not for me to quote in full the text of his letter, dated 12 October 1897. Others will do this, perhaps, if they consider it worthwhile, when I shall no longer have cause to blush or turn pale. I would simply emphasize the final sentence, which affected me so decisively: "I hope that when you next pass through Genoa, you will not flee like last time but honour me with your visit. I shake you by the hand."

Thus in his kindness and at the height of his fame spoke the great Maestro, whom legend considers ill-tempered, gruff, unsociable and inaccessible, to the 33-year-old Maestro of the Cappella del Santo of Padua.

Encouraged by these clear signs of good-will and kindness, I cabled him that, having very soon to travel from Bologna to Milan, I would take the liberty of visiting him at Sant'Agata. He replied, likewise by cable, and advised me to alight at Fiorenzuola and enquire after a certain coachman who would have appropriate further instructions.

[. . .]

And there I was before the walls of his villa; there I was before the gate. The carriage moved forward, as if by force of habit. I was met by the inflexible servant from Genoa. He looked at me, recognized me and smiled. I said to him: "Yes, it was I who called at the Palazzo Doria six months ago." "But what do you expect," he replied, "so many people come and often they do not know how to behave. Enter."

And he led me into the first room – the billiard room.

"I shall inform the Maestro of your arrival."

[. . .]

All of a sudden I heard what seemed to be a light and hurried shuffling across the soft carpet. The Maestro!

His long white hair fell characteristically over his brow and he wore his habitual jacket of black velvet and a black, fluttering neck-tie. He came towards me in a friendly and confidential manner. It pleased him greatly to make my acquaintance – especially, he added, after the incident at Genoa.

My first gesture was to bow my head spontaneously and kiss his cold white hand; I thanked him for providing me with the opportunity of repeating to him personally my respects – a dream I had cherished for many years. He did not allow me to continue. "Come, come," he said, and led me without further ado across two or three *boudoirs* into the spacious ground-floor room with its yellow damask drapery.

It was mid-October,[8] but the Franklin stove was already lit. He motioned me to sit down first, to his left. Our conversation, in that first hour of intense joy, touched on a variety of subjects.

Without mentioning the reasons behind his request, he spoke to me again of Vallotti's *Te Deums*, which had been sent him from Padua; he discussed the personality of Benedetto Marcello who, he observed, was several decades older than Vallotti; and he drew clear analogies between the creator of the *Fifty Psalms* and . . . Johann Sebastian Bach! I took advantage of that to draw his attention to the strange similarity between the first subject of Marcello's *1st Psalm* "Beato l'uom" with the subject of Bach's first fugue from *The Well-tempered Clavier* – both of which are identical. "What is their source?" we both asked.

At a certain moment – perhaps without intending to – he changed the subject, and mentioned how concerned he was about the health of his wife, the much revered Giuseppina Strepponi, who was seriously ill.[9] Knowing nothing of this, I apologized for arriving at Sant'Agata at such a sad hour. But he reassured me in a friendly voice, insisted that I stayed and asked me many questions about the Cappella del Santo of Padua – how it was constituted, how it was thriving and what works were in its repertoire. I told him that Palestrina – as at Saint Mark's, Venice, six years previously – had returned to the repertoire with the *Missa Aeterna Christi munera, Sine nomine, Papae Marcelli* and several 5 and 6 part offertories and motets – and this delighted him because, in his opinion, the composer from Palestrina remained the cornerstone of Italian music, above all because of the vocal quality of his music. And he would often insist upon the need to *sing* and *let sing*.

[. . .]

During my occasional summer trips to Sant'Agata, the main topic of conversation was – as every reader can imagine – music. However, knowing of my Wagnerian sympathies (and perhaps for this very reason), he never spoke to me of Wagner. But he mentioned Bellini several times, drawing attention to the instrumentation of his operas and hinting at how he himself would have approached certain passages.

He spoke to me of several contemporary composers. In this connection, however, I prefer to remain silent in order to avoid the common danger of hearing myself misinterpreted and of having to read distorted accounts of the discreet opinions that the Maestro had expressed to me alone. I merely call to mind the statement, that he had not wished to hear a note of Boito's *Nerone*, for fear that any observations he made might be to the disadvantage of the composer who was already late with the work. [. . .]

During the first weeks of 1899 at the Parma Conservatoire, which was now run as a boarding school, unexpected reforms were introduced which had been prepared by my predecessor Maestro Gallignani and which failed to convince the Presidenza, which had been accustomed till then to conduct its affairs according to its own administrative criteria – which were highly dubious, in that they militated against a broader vision of studies. This resulted in immediate resignations. And so I remained alone, with a year and several months practical experience to my credit. I was President, Governor, Director all in one, obliged to bear the burden of systems designed by my predecessors and not endorsed by me.

And so I drew up a type of programme which would, however, have required from the Ministry of Education, the repayment into our account of monies that had been spent. I travelled to Genoa to disclose the programme to the Maestro.

And so I finally entered the grand apartment of the Palazzo Doria. The very long room where Verdi received me is the one which looks out on to the arterial road which runs westward along the Riviera towards Pegli, Savona and San Remo.

The apartment, which is divided into three, immediately caught my attention. At the far end the bedroom, in the middle the reception room, and in the part which looks out on to the great terrace the study with the grand piano. [. . .]

As I waited for the Maestro I looked about me. On pieces of furniture, on *consoles*, on ebony *étagères* inlaid with ivory, on the little pinnacles of several tiny shelves I could see pocket watches of different ages, sizes and quality arranged or hung – from the copper alarm-clock (commonly called a *warming-pan*) to the brass or silver repeater, from the so-called chain cylinder watch to the gold remontoir – all beautifully displayed. And on the walls there were masterful paintings, materials and damask arranged in an ordered artistic disorder.

But now he approached majestically and hastily from the far end of the drawing-room. He invited me to sit down opposite him, and from my armchair I gazed towards the large glass window, through which I could see the façade of the Stazione Marittima and all the bustle of the port and wharves.

I explained to him the reason for my visit, which he both understood and appreciated – he assured me that he would recommend to Minister Baccelli the demands which I had drawn up and already presented.

[. . .]

In the meantime our conversation – not unexpectedly – turned to music. He spoke about his admiration for Puccini's theatrical instinct; about Giordano, pausing to recall how he himself had once considered composing *Fedora*.[10] And he also spoke of Alberto Franchetti, to whom he felt particularly well disposed, after *Colombo*.[11]

In the summer of that year I saw the Maestro fairly often. He was fond of coffee and during the day would frequently call for his servant to bring some. He offered me a cup once, twice, three times. I would always decline. "But why?" he asked, after several polite refusals.

"I don't take coffee, because it upsets me and prevents me from working and sleeping."

"Well, well," he remarked; "when I was as young as you, I drank coffee to help me work."

"Oh Maestro," I replied, "in that case you must be right, for you have created so much while I, in comparison, have achieved nothing!"

On another occasion, when Teresa Stolz, Arrigo Boito and Giulio Ricordi were present, he asked the habitual question: "Shall we have a coffee?"

The distinguished guests accepted, I declined. "Tebaldini is nervous!" Boito remarked. To which Verdi, turning to Teresa Stolz, said: "You and I, I think, no longer suffer from that illness?!"

After celebrating the 60th anniversary of the première of *Oberto conte di San Bonifacio* at the Parma Conservatoire, on a grey, gloomy and almost wintry morning, the Maestro received me in Milan, as usual in the Hotel Spatz. But I arrived late.

"What has happened?" he asked. "Why are there no trams this morning in the streets of Milan?"

"The tram drivers are on strike," I remarked, "and so everyone has to walk to their destination, even if it means arriving late, as happened to me."

"And it really inconveniences you walking through Milan? If you had been here during my young days, when public transport consisted solely of three stage-coaches, one at Santa Margherita, one at Cordusio and the other at San Babila, what would you have done?"

And he continued: "Few people boarded these primitive, lumbering carriages, where the postillions sat perched on top in gaudy uniforms, with coloured feathers in their top-hats and silver bandoleers and tassles on shoulder and chest. No one wished to avail themselves of such a novelty! And so when they tried to introduce the first public carriages, the enterprise sadly failed!"

[. . .]

I had several times considered bringing the Parma Conservatoire Orchestra to Busseto, to pay homage to Giuseppe Verdi in the theatre that bears his name. [. . .]

Having reached an agreement with the Mayor of Busseto, a charity concert was organized for the evening of 28 October 1900. [. . .] Ildebrando Pizzetti later recounted the details of that event – a feast for arts and hearts – in an article for the *Gazzetta Musicale di Milano*.[12]

"[. . .] We made our way towards Sant'Agata in small groups, talking about the Maestro. Everyone expressed the ardent hope of catching a glimpse of him, since many of us, young as we were, had never seen him before.

"We entered the silent garden with its rather sad and gloomy aura.

"Our Director, the Prefect, the Mayor of Busseto and the Mayor of Parma were already with the Maestro. With a few others I stood behind the villa, troubled by an indefinable feeling of anxiety.

"After some time a door opened, the visitors appeared and behind them . . . Verdi. . . .

"The Maestro entered majestically with marvellous simplicity of movement. I cannot describe what I felt in that moment. I felt I ought to cry, to shout a hymn of admiration with all my strength . . . and I doffed my hat, as if obeying some higher power, as if entering a church.

"If I lived to be a hundred, I should never forget the impression made on me by those few moments, when he was there, a few paces from me, serene and grave, with white hair and beard – a biblical figure, an apparition. . . .

"A little later, on the other side of the villa, he exchanged a few friendly words with his companions. It never occurred to me, however, to wish to hear him speak.[13] I had seen him, and in that brief moment when he had appeared before my eyes, my soul had been overwhelmed by so many emotions that there was no room for any more. [. . .]

"[. . .] and even today I remember that moving moment when Giuseppe Verdi walked down the hall steps towards the garden facing the front of the villa, greeted us as we departed in our carriages towards the villa gate, which gives on to the little bridge that crosses the Ongina, and saw himself unexpectedly surrounded by several students. He put his arms about one of them, who was about to kiss his hand, and turning towards us exclaimed with a smile: 'Art places its hopes in you.'"

[. . .]

On the 12th of the same month [November] I went once more to Sant'Agata to thank the Maestro for the kind welcome he had extended to those same students and us during our trip to Busseto. He was exceedingly good-natured and exuberant that day, which was to be the last time I visited him.

The sky was bleak, leaden, almost hazy. The Maestro wished me to stay for luncheon; he spoke of many things and recalled, with that most lucid mind of his, far-distant events and occasions of interest in his glorious and luminous life as an artist. He then enquired about the students at the Conservatoire, asked me if there were any students for whose future I entertained high hopes. I mentioned the name of Ildebrando Pizzetti.

"High hopes?"

"I'm certain of it!"

"Well then, tell him to hold his head high and set himself ever higher goals, and above all remember to be Italian."

[. . .]

Although the day was bitterly cold, the Maestro, as nimble and forthright as ever, wished after lunch to go out into the garden in his black velvet jacket and without a hat. His fine, sculptural head – as in Gemito's bronze – with silver hair falling on to his wide forehead, occasionally still struck a leonine pose.

Some peasants wielding axes were felling a huge magnolia tree, whose ancient foliage now covered a large part of the villa's left face. Verdi sat down not far from the group of peasants, as if to survey the work.

"That magnolia tree," he told me, "was planted with my own hands when I first came to Sant'Agata. And now that it gets in the way and gives off too great a scent, I am having it removed!" And a little later, while some attacked it with axes and others pulled it with ropes, the tree fell to the ground. I don't know why, but at that moment I felt a pang in my heart. The old felled tree seemed to symbolize impending fate! I had sensed the truth. [. . .] A month later the great man was no more.[14]

GIOVANNI TEBALDINI

NOTES

1. As a letter from Ricordi to Verdi tells us, Tebaldini actually sent a *pavaniglia* of 1597, taken from a *Raccolta di varii balli fatti in occorenza di nozze* that had been composed by Fabritio Caroso da Sermoneta and published by him in Rome in 1630.
2. Quite the contrary! Verdi did not use these themes, as we learn from the composer's letter to Ricordi of 10 July 1894, in which he has this to say of the material sent him by Tebaldini:

    How dismal that music is which Tebaldini sent you! Even in those days there must have been something better. What I need is something from a later age. Keep searching! But all these scholars know no more than I. But what need is there for scholars?! It is not worth the trouble. In the meantime, send me a beautiful Furlana [. . .]. (Autograph: Archivio della Casa Ricordi, Milan, which also preserves the music sent by Tebaldini.)

3. G. TEBALDINI: *L'Archivio musicale della Cappella Antoniana di Padova*, Padua 1895.
4. Francesco Antonio Vallotti (Vercelli 1697 – Padua 1780), organist, composer and theorician, he was maestro di cappella at the Santo in Padua. He was praised by Tartini as the greatest organist of his day, and had dealings with Padre Martini.
5. The same day Verdi wrote to Boito:

    Eureka! I've found a Te Deum! No mistake! The composer is P. Vallotti whom I value greatly, as you know. I have written to Tebaldini, asking him to make me a copy. I tell you all this, so that you remember that it was on 14 February 1896 that you saw my Te Deum, in case I was accused . . . But no, no, there's no danger of that, because I shall not publish it. (*Carteggio Verdi-Boito*, p. 243.)

    Verdi had first considered composing a *Te Deum* at the beginning of the previous year. On January 31 the composer had written from Milan to Gallignani:

    Before leaving Genoa the other day, I could not find the little book of Plain Song with the settings of the Te Deum and other hymns, that our excellent friend the priest sent me. I shall find it when I am less busy; but in the meantime I do not have here the two settings of the Te Deum! . . . *If it is not asking too much, I would request the eminent priest to transcribe them for me on a small sheet of paper.* (I Copialettere di G. Verdi, note to page 411.)

Three months later, on April 21, he wrote to Mascheroni:

You say that you were surprised to see some manuscript paper on my desk! . . . Perhaps it is true! I wanted to compose a Te Deum!! *A thanksgiving, not for me, but for the public who have had to hear other works of mine over the years and are now released!!* (Autograph: The Houghton Library, Harvard University, Cambridge, Mass.)

6. The facsimile was published by Tebaldini in his article "Giuseppe Verdi nella musica sacra", in *Nuova Antologia*, Rome, XLVIII, vol. 251: 16 October 1913, pp. 566–9. The text of the facsimile is quoted here.
7. Soon afterwards, through Arrigo Boito, Tebaldini tried to send Verdi other *Te Deums*; the composer, however, replied to Boito on 11 June 1896:

Give my warm thanks to Tebaldini for his kind efforts with the Te Deum. *But what is now done is done. I could not now alter my ideas on the interpretation of this poem, even if a perusal of the* Te Deums *by Purcell and Vittoria should prove to me that I got it all wrong.* (Autograph: Istituto di studi verdiani, Parma.)

8. On October 16 Boito went to Sant'Agata and remained there for several days (cf. *Carteggio Verdi–Boito*, pp. 251–2 and 480). Since Tebaldini makes no mention of Boito's presence during this first visit of his to Sant'Agata, it is possible that it took place during the first fortnight of October, certainly before the 16th.
9. Giuseppina's health was in rapid decline. On September 9 Verdi had written to Giulio Ricordi:

Peppina gets up for a few hours; her cough and catarrh have improved, but she is extremely weak. She doesn't eat, and says she cannot?! It's distressing and we are at our wits' end. (Autograph: Archivio della Casa Ricordi, Milan.)

And on the 22nd of the same month:

There's been a slight improvement in Peppina's health. Her cough and catarrh have improved. She has been up for several hours a day but is still not eating. Her extreme weakness robs her of almost all desire of speaking or listening. (Autograph: Archivio della Casa Ricordi.)

On October 14 Giuseppina found the strength to visit her sister Barberina in Cremona. On November 11 she went down with severe pneumonia. Three days later, in the late afternoon, she died (cf. *Carteggio Verdi-Boito*, p. 480).

10. It had been performed at Milan's Teatro Lirico on 17 November 1898. Umberto Giordano had married Olga Spatz, daughter of the proprietor of the Hôtel de Milan, on 18 November 1896. During their honeymoon at Nervi, the young couple decided to visit the old composer. On December 1 Giordano gave a vivid description of that visit to his father:

Dear Father, the other day Olga and I were at Genoa and, in an attempt to be received by Verdi, we brought our visiting cards and asked the concierge when we might be received. The concierge returned and said "At once!" Nothing was like what I had imagined. The Palazzo is the famous Palazzo Doria, which has a wonderful courtyard; but beneath an arcade there are several small doorways which open on to stone (not even marble!) staircases, and hung on these doors are brass plaques which bear the names of various companies. To my great surprise the concierge led us through one of these little doorways where there is, among the many residences, a small staircase hardly lit by the sun. On the first floor we found ourselves opposite an ordinary door, bearing a small white sign: G. Verdi. To one side of the door there hung a gas-torch for the evenings (without even a shade!) . . . There was no electric bell. We pulled the cord, the servant opened the door and led us through an antechamber and into the drawing-room. Nothing special or luxurious was to be seen . . . nothing to reveal that a composer resided here except a small clay statue of Falstaff. Nothing else! A door soon opened and Verdi entered, still young and fresh. He paid us many compliments and then sat down to converse. He enquired about Nervi and its climate. After a while his wife entered, an old lady with a pink complexion and an auburn wig; she is short, plump and seems scarcely able to sustain herself on her legs. He was most affectionate with his wife, went to meet her, helped her to sit down and stayed near her. Having discussed the pleasant warmth of the drawing-room, she wished us to experience the warmth of her own room. We left the drawing-room and passed through Verdi's bedroom. What a shrine! It was like entering a church. Here too, there was nothing special to be seen: a grand piano, manuscript paper on the music-stand that showed he was working, many books in various little book-cases without glass fronts, a large writing desk and his bed. His wife's room was a beautiful lady's bedroom, hung with photographs of Verdi at several different ages, one of Manzoni and one of Princess Elena. And that is all I saw! No portraits of artists, no crowns, not a single sign of greatness. I was dumbfounded. Do you understand? And we, when we have written a single opera, consider we have to keep a carriage and horses and live in a palace. You see the modesty of the great? Superfluous to say that they were both delightful. We never spoke of music. He accompanied us to the door – and yet they say he is uncivil! Lies! He is only uncivil to those bores who wish to show off by mentioning his name . . .

(D. Cellamare: *Umberto Giordano. La vita e le opere*, Garzanti, Milan 1949, pp. 62–64; new edit.: Palombi, Rome 1967, pp. 91–92.)

Some years later Giordano recalled to Amintore Galli a conversation he had had with Verdi a few weeks before the latter's death:

The idea of making an opera out of *Madame Sans-Gêne* was suggested to Giordano by Verdi in January 1901, shortly before the grand old man of Busseto departed from this earth which he had blessed with his songs. [. . .] As if struck by a prophetic idea, Verdi asked Giordano: "Why don't you tackle *Madame Sans-Gêne?*" "And what about Napoleon, Maestro?" Giordano observed. And Verdi, with the intuition of a genius, replied: "I could not imagine Napoleon coming to the footlights to sing a romance with his hand across his heart. Certainly not. But a Napoleon who uttered dramatic recitative would be perfectly fitting, even in an opera." (A. Galli – G. Macchi – G. C. Paribeni: *Umberto Giordano nell' Arte e nella Vita. Note biografiche ed estetiche*, Sonzogno, Milan 1915, p. 66.)

Giordano later recalled to Cellamare (*op. cit.*, pp. 106–9) other conversations he had had with Verdi:

I had the good fortune to visit him often. It would have been better if I had taken notes of what the Maestro told me during the visits; but some things I can recall merely be exerting my memory. He once asked me, point-blank: "Giordano, what is your method of composition?" I replied: "Maestro, I cannot possibly speak to you of my method – but pray give me some advice." "Good," he replied, "I shall tell you immediately: never correct what you wrote on the previous day – you will not like it any more and you will mistakenly destroy all that you have done. Compose the first act, without pausing, without corrections; when you have done this, put the sheets of music to one side and start the second act. Proceed with the second act in exactly the same way, and then continue with the third and fourth acts. Then rest. When you have recovered your strength, revise and correct everything; you can be sure that this is the only way of avoiding error." Another time he recommended me to work every day, at any work to hand – without such daily exercise the hand . . . grows stiff. He then gave me other advice: "Never read newspaper reviews after a première and never pay homage to journalists with your visiting-card." We then talked about the dearth of good singers, about which he had this to say: "It is not nature who deprives us of our voices (all canaries sing, for example), but the fact that we lack good singing teachers." During my many conversations with him, I never heard him praise either singers or conductors – except Patti, for whom he had a special admiration and whom he considered the greatest of Violettas. On another occasion, before going to a concert, I mentioned that Saint-Saëns' Third Symphony for orchestra, organ and piano was to be performed. He did not know it. For a moment he was pensive, then said: "What is that piano doing in the company of those two giants, the orchestra and the organ?" I also recall another piece of advice: "When writing music, do not concern yourself with other composers, least of all foreign ones, and do not seek to imitate them; write as you feel, without fear, and be sincere. It is sincerity alone, and not bad faith that counts in art." I recall that Verdi greatly admired Alberto Franchetti, whom he knew to be a close friend of mine; he often enquired after him and asked several times to be introduced, which I did most willingly. [. . .]

11. The committee for the celebration of the 400th anniversary of the discovery of America had invited Verdi to compose a new opera for the occasion; he declined and in all probability suggested Franchetti as being the most worthy of the young Italian composers.

12. Signed with the initials I.P., the article appeared on 8 November 1900, n. 45, pp. 583–5. Pizzetti was later to recall several times his only meeting with Verdi; e.g. in "Giuseppe Verdi" in *Marzocco*, Florence, XVIII, 41: 12 October 1913, pp. 1–2, reprinted later in his collection of essays *Musicisti contemporanei*, Treves, Milan 1914, pp. 3–36; "La grandezza di Verdi", in *La Lettura*, Milan, XLI, 1 January 1941, pp. 26–34, reprinted in *La musica italiana dell'Ottocento*, Edizioni Palatine di R. Pezzani, Turin 1947, pp. 243–78; "Come ho visto Verdi", in *Il Resto del Carlino*, Bologna, 9 April 1963, pp. 106–7; later in *Verdi*, Bollettino dell'Istituto di studi verdiani, n. 7, pp. XIV–XVI (facsimile of the manuscript text), and finally, in shortened form, in *Carteggio Verdi–Boito*, pp. 509–10.

13. Years later Pizzetti wrote in his article "La grandezza di Verdi":

> I should be able to recall his voice, since he addressed several words to my companions who were only a few feet away from me – it is therefore possible that I heard him, and I probably did. But I regret to say that I of all people, whose ear should be sharper than his eye, remember nothing at all of Verdi's voice, although I can picture his expression and figure, as if I had seen him yesterday or a week ago.

14. About twenty days after Tebaldini's final visit, on 4 December 1900 to be exact, Verdi left Sant'Agata in the company of Maria Carrara for Milan. "The distinguished Maestro is in excellent health," according to the *Gazzetta Musicale di Milano* of December 6. On the 22nd the composer wrote to his sister-in-law Barberina Strepponi:

> *Thank you for your letter – it cheers me that you are well. As for me, it is the*

*same old story; I am not ill, but with every day that passes my strength
declines and my life draws nearer to its close. That is only natural: I am 87.
Excuse the brevity of this letter, but even writing wearies me, as you know.
Goodbye, and keep a place in your heart for me, as I do for you.* (Facsimile
of the autograph in A. MARTINELLI: *Verdi: Raggi e penombre*, Studio
Editoriale Genovese, Genoa 1926.)

In the seclusion of the warm Hôtel di Milan, Verdi spent Christmas in
the company of Boito and a few close friends. Cesare Pascarella (see
Gazzetta Musicale di Milano of 3 January 1901) joined them to celebrate
"the first evening of the 20th century". Meanwhile, the La Scala season,
conducted entirely by Toscanini, had opened with Puccini's *La Bohème*
and was to continue with *Tristan und Isolde*. January 17 saw the
première of Mascagni's *Le maschere*, which received simultaneous
performances at Rome – conducted by the composer – Venice, Genoa,
Verona and Turin. On January 18 Verdi wrote again to his sister-in-law
Barberina (this is perhaps his very last letter):

*I have not been out for almost two weeks now, because I am afraid of the
cold!! I am reasonably well, as I have been for some time, but I repeat that I
am afraid of the cold. Today, however, is beautiful, but I am glued to my
chair and do not move. You do well to stay indoors [?], but I'm sorry that
your room is so* [an illegible word follows]. *Let's hope that we have a
succession of beautiful days like today and thus be free from the cold. I write
little because writing tires me; but you who have a steady hand, write to me.
I know that Maria tells you my news – she is well and sends her love. I shake
you warmly by the hand.* (Facsimile of the autograph, as above.)

The catastrophe occurred three days later, on January 21. At nine
o'clock in the morning, the family doctor, Dr Caporali, had made his
usual visit, and finding the Maestro in good health had agreed to let him
go out later in his carriage. At about half-past ten Verdi prepared to
rise:

He was getting dressed, seated on the edge of the bed and helped, as
usual, by his loyal housekeeper. The latter noticed that the old man's
trembling hand was threading the buttons of his waistcoat into the
wrong button-holes, and respectfully drew his attention to the fact.
"What's a button here or there," the Maestro replied, amazed at the
remark; he could utter no further word, however, and fell back on to
his bed in a swoon.
   [. . .]

At the cries of the housekeeper, Signora Maria Carrara-Verdi, who
had accompanied him to Milan, ran from the adjacent room with the
hotel doctor. This latter and Dr Caporali, who had been summoned

in haste, administered first aid to the sick man who showed clear signs of having suffered a right-sided hemiplegia. (G. BRAGAGNOLO – E. BETTAZZI, *op. cit.*, p. 326.)

Summoned from Florence by telegram, Professor Grocco, who for several years had tended Verdi during the latter's visits to Montecatini, also arrived. But all hope was now vain. On the 22nd Boito was already informing Bellaigue: *Ce que vous lisez sur les journaux n'est que trop vrai. Le Maître se meurt.* (Autograph: Museo Teatrale alla Scala, Milan.)

On the morning of the 24th the end seemed imminent; extreme unction was administered to the now unconscious Maestro. A slight improvement during the course of that day seemed to raise the hopes of those present, but the doctors were not deceived. There follows Giuseppe Giacosa's description of the Maestro's final hours, as it appeared in the *Corriere della Sera* of 27–28 January 1901:

All yesterday the Maestro remained in a state of peaceful sleep – not dissimilar, it seemed, to his condition on previous days. There was nothing to suggest to those present that he was approaching death. And yet the pupils of his eyes no longer reacted in the slightest way to the light, the back of his throat, when tickled with a feather moistened with glycerine, no longer contracted, and his hand, which on previous days had often been raised to his face or engaged in puerile attempts to button his shirt or throw back the blankets, had lain inert since the morning.

On previous days the Maestro was wont to lie with one arm placed across his chest. Since then, the doctors had tried several times to lift the arm away to prevent it from pressing on those poor muscles which, already greatly weakened, aided his breathing. But whether by an act of will or by mere habit he would immediately move his arm back into the same spot. Yesterday Grocco tried one last time and placed it by the composer's side, and the dying Maestro no longer had the strength to move it. But it was only the doctors who, from these external signs, observed his physical decline. His face remained flushed thoughout the day, the rhythm of his breathing did not appear to alter and he uttered no sound that resembled a death-rattle.

His pulse fluctuated between 150 and 180, his temperature remained feverish, above 39 degrees.

Towards midnight his face grew pale and suddenly appeared emaciated, a hissing note indicated that his breathing was obstructed – and gradually it grew shorter and more laboured and was very soon reduced to a mere gurgling. Dr Grocco, Dr Caporali, Dr Odescalchi and Dr Bertarelli were present, and the glances they exchanged seemed to announce the imminent struggle. Who had alerted all the relations and friends who were snatching a few hours sleep in various rooms of the hotel? Suddenly they were all assembled around the bed.

Every ten or twelve breaths were followed by a pause, and the pauses gradually became longer and more frequent. And then the rhythm resumed. Towards one o'clock all seemed finished. For several interminable seconds he neither moved nor gasped. But life returned. Then another longer pause; Grocco was already rising to his feet to certify his death, when Verdi's chest rose once more and he resumed his laboured breathing. All exchanged terrified glances. It seemed that death had been conquered.

In fact, an hour of more peaceful sleep ensued, and those surrounding his bed dispersed once again into their nearby rooms. At half-past two, hurried footsteps in the corridor and frantic calls suddenly gathered everyone together in the hallowed room. Long pauses followed short breaths. At 2.45, after an interminable painful wait for another breath of life, the weeping Grocco bent over the motionless face and kissed his forehead. Thus was his death announced.

BIBLIOGRAPHY

LIST OF SOURCES
AND WORKS CONSULTED

BIBLIOGRAPHY

LIST OF SOURCES
AND WORKS CONSULTED

Anonymous

"Giuseppe Verdi", in *Il Fuggilozio*, III, nn. 1, 6, 9: January, February and March 1857, pp. 13–16, 92–96, 139–44.

Ralph: "Une soirée chez Verdi", in *L'Art Musical*, Paris, VII, 8: 22 February 1866, pp. 92–93.

"Ritratto di Verdi disegnato da una penna americana", in *Il Trovatore*, Milan, XVIII, 33: 17 August 1871.

"Verdi in Wien", in *Neue Freie Presse*, Vienna, n. 3874: 9 June 1875 (republished in *Signale für die musikalische Welt*, Leipzig XXXIII, 30: June 1875, pp. 465–7); extracts in WALKER 1951, pp. 51–52).

"A visit by Verdi to the Vienna Conservatoire", in *Wiener Fremdenblatt*, Vienna, 23 June 1875 (republished in *Gazzetta Musicale di Milano*, XXX, supl. n. 27: 4 July 1875, p. 5).

["Interviews with Mathilde Marchesi"], in *Neue Freie Presse*, Vienna, 27 June 1875 (republished in *Verdi aus der Nähe. Ein Lebensbild in Dokumenten*, compiled and translated by F. WALLNER-BASTÉ, Manesse Verlag, Zürich 1979, pp. 291–3).

["Verdi on singing"], in *Signale für die musikalische Welt*, Leipzig, XXXIII, 33: July 1875, p. 521 (republished in WALKER 1951, pp. 54–55).

["Verdi e i drammi di Grillparzer"], in *Gazzetta Musicale di Milano*, XXX, n. 27: 4 July 1875, p. 6.

["A visit by Marie Wieck to Verdi"], in *Allgemeine deutsche Musikzeitung*, Kassel, V, March, 1878 (republished in *Gazzetta Musicale de Milano*, XXXIII, 12: 24 March 1878, p. 109, and in *Svensk Musiktidning*, Stockholm, XXI, 9; 1 May 1901, p. 67).

"L'Arte del leggere", in *Gazzetta Musicale di Milano*, XL, 20: 17 May 1885, pp. 176–7 (republished from *Corriere della Sera*).

"Una futura nuova opera del Verdi. *Falstaff*", in *Il Teatro Illustrato*, Milan, X, 120: December 1890, p. 189.

"Una fonte italiana del 'Falstaff' di Shakespeare" in *Verdi e il "Falstaff"* 1893 (1913), pp. 4–6.

"Verdi fotografato", in q.v., *Verdi e il "Falstaff"* 1893 (1913), pp. 15–16.

H.F.G.: "Une entrevue avec M. Verdi", in *Journal des Débats*, Paris, 5 April 1894.

[Article from Paris], in *Gazzetta Musicale di Milano*, XLIX, 16: 22 April 1894, pp. 251–2.

[Interview with Verdi in *Journal des Débats*], in *La Lanterna*, Milan, XVI, 9–10: 23 April 1894, pp. 1–2.

["L'Inno ad Apollo"], in *Il Caffaro*, Genoa, June 1894 (republished in *Gazzetta Musicale di Milano*, XLIX, 26: 1 July 1894, p. 408).

R.M.: "Verdi a Montecatini", in *Scena Illustrata*, Florence, XXXVI, 271: 15 November 1900.

"Il racconto di un astante", in *Il Corriere della Sera*, Milan, XXVI, 27: 27–28 January 1901 (republished in C. GATTI: *Verdi*, Alpes, Milan 1931, vol. II, pp. 519–20).

Z.: "Una lettera di Giuseppe Verdi", in *Nuova Antologia*, Rome, XLI, 16 July 1906, pp. 320–24.

Edipi: "Come conobbi il Maestro", in *Scena Illustrata*, Florence, XLIX, 21: 1 November 1913, p. 36.

"Uno dei rari giudizi critici del Maestro", in *Verdiana*, Milan, n. 9, April 1951, pp. 10–11.

Joint Authors

"Verdi e l''Otello'", Special Edition of the *Illustrazione Italiana*, compiled by Ugo Pesci and Ed. Ximenes, Treves, Milan (February 1887; reprinted 1913).

"*Otello*" [. . .] *Giudizi della stampa italiana e straniera* compiled by Ugo Pesci and Ed: Ximines, Ricordi, Milan [1887]. Special supplement for the Rossini Commemoration of the Teatro alla Scala, *Gazzetta Musicale de Milano*, XLVII, 16: 17 April 1892.

"Verdi e il 'Falstaff'", Special Edition of the *Illustrazione Italiana*, Treves, Milan [February 1893; reprinted 1913].

"Hommage à Verdi", *Le Gaulois du Dimanche*, Paris, I, 17: 9–10 October 1897.

Lissone a Giuseppe Verdi, Monza, August 1913.

Nel primo centenario di Giuseppe Verdi. 1813–1913, Special Illustrated Edition, compiled by L. Grabinski-Broglio, C. Vanbianchi, G. Adami, Milan 1913.

Per il cinquantesimo anniversario della morte di Giuseppe Verdi, Teatro di San Carlo, Naples 1950.

Verdi e Roma, compiled by Adriano Belli e Ceccarius, Teatro dell'Opera di Roma, 1951.

Enciclopedia dello Spettacolo, 9 vols, Le Maschere, Rome 1954–62.

Centocinquantesimo anniversario della nascita di Giuseppe Verdi, Parma, Teatro Regio, 1963.

Atti del I Congresso internazionale di studi verdiani: Venice Isola di San Giorgio Maggiore, Fondazione Cini, 31 July –2 August 1966, Istituto di studi verdiani, Parma 1969.

Atti del III Congesso internazionale di studi verdiani: Milan, Piccola Scala, 12–17 June 1972, Istituto di studi verdiani, Parma 1974.

ABBIATI, Franco: *Giuseppe Verdi*, 4 vols., Ricordi, Milan 1959.

(ALBERTI, Annibale): *Verdi intimo. (Carteggio di Giuseppe Verdi con il conte Opprandino Arrivabene 1861–1886)* compiled and annotated by Annibale ALBERTI, Mondadori [Milan] 1931.

BALDINI, Gabriele: *Manualetto Shakespeariano*, Einaudi Turin 1964, *id.: Le acque rosse del Potomac*, Rizzoli, Milan 1967.

BARBIERA, Raffaello: *Ideali e caratteri dell'Ottocento*, Treves, Milan 1926 (reprinted: Garzanti, Milan 1940).

BARBLAN, Guglielmo: "Rimpianti per un mancato allievo", in *Annuario 1963–64* del Conservatorio di Musica Giuseppe Verdi, Milan 1963, pp. 171–85.

—— "La lunga quarantema de 'Il Corsaro'", in *I Lunedí della Fenice, Conferenze Musicali. 1970–1971*", Teatro la Fenice, Venice 1972, pp. 101–29.

BARIDON, S.: *Marc Monnier e l'Italia*, Paravia, 1942.

BARILLI, Bruno: *Il paese del melodramma*, Carabba, Lanciano (1930) (new edition, edited by Enrico Falqui: Vallecchi, Florence 1963).

BASSO, Maurizio: *Giuseppe Verdi: La sua vita, le sue opere, la sua morte. Storia popolare*, G. Corsi & C., Milan 1901.

BASTIANELLI, Giannotto: *Pietro Mascagni*, Ricciardi, Naples 1910.

BATTISTINI, Giovanni: "Italo Pizzi e Busseto", in *Aurea Parma*, XLVI, 3: 1962, pp. 148–56.

BERLIOZ, Hector: *Correspondance inédite (1819–1868)*, edited by D. Bernard, Paris 1876.

BLAZE DE BURY, Henri: "Le directeur de l'Opéra chez Verdi", in *Revue des Deux Mondes*, Paris, 15 November 1879, pp. 460–65.

BOCCA, Giuseppe: "Verdi e la caricatura", in *Rivista Musicale Italiana*, Turin, VIII, 2: 1901, pp. 326–59.

BONAVENTURA, Arnaldo: "Un ricordo personale", in *Scena Illustrata*, Florence, XXXVI, 22, no. 271: 15 November 1900.

—— *La Figura e l'arte di Giuseppe Verdi*, R. Giusti, Leghorn 1919.

—— "Verdi", coll. *Les Maîtres de la Musique*, Alcan, Paris 1923 (reprinted 1930).

—— *Ricordi e ritratti (fra quelli che ho conosciuto)*, Quaderni dell'Accademia Chigiana, XXV, Sienna 1950.

BOTTI, Ferruccio: "Verdi, Carducci e Annie Vivanti", in *L'Avvenire d'Italia*, Bologna, 28 January 1951 (reprinted by the author in *Spigolature d'Archivio: Spigolature Verdiane*, third series, Battei, Parma 1963, p. 17).

—— "Verdi e Italo Pizzi", in *Gazzetta di Parma*, 22 January 1951 (reprinted by the author in *Spigolature d'Archivio: Nuove Spigolature Verdiane*, fifth series, Battei, Parma 1971, pp. 22–23.

BRAGAGNOLO, Giovanni – BETTAZZI, Enrico: *La vita di Giuseppe Verdi narrata al popolo*, G. Ricordi, Milan 1905 (reprinted 1913).

BUDDEN, Julian: *The Operas of Verdi*, vols 1, 2 and 3, Cassell, London.

CAMETTI, Alberto: *Il teatro di Tordinona poi di Apollo*, 2 vols, Tivoli 1918.

CAMESASCA, Ettore: "L'opera completa di Boldini", coll. *Classici dell'arte* n. 36, Rizzoli, Milan 1970.

CAPONI, Jacopo: "Verdi à Paris", in *Le Figaro*, Paris, 17 April 1886.

—— See POUGIN 1881.

CARRARA VERDI, Gabriella: "Preliminari di 'Aida'", in *Biblioteca 70*, Busseto, II, 1971, pp. 9–21.

—— "Le lettere di Rossini a Verdi", *ibid.*, III, 1973, pp. 9–16.

Carteggio Verdi–Boito, see (MEDICI–CONATI) 1978.

Carteggi verdiani, see LUZIO 1935–47.

CAVALLI, Hercules: *Biografías artísticas contemporaneas de los célebres José Verdi maestro de música y Antonio Canova escultor*, published by J. M. Ducazcal, Madrid 1867, see pp. 7–45.

—— "Giuseppe Verdi. Nuovi particolari inediti ed interessanti" in *Il Pensiero di Nizza*, 29, 30 and 31 December 1876 and 4 January 1877.

CELLAMARE, Daniele: *Un cinquantesimo glorioso: Mascagni e la "Cavalleria" visti da Cerignola*, Palombi, Rome 1941.

—— *Umberto Giordano, La vita e le opere*, Garzanti, Milan 1949 (new edit.: Palombi, Rome 1967).

CENCETTI, Giuseppe: "Il maestro Verdi e l'impresario Iacovacci", in *Omnibus*, Naples, March 1959 (reissued in *Teatri Arti e Letteratura*, Bologna, XXXVII, vol. 71, n. 1788: 7 April 1859, pp. 25–26.

(CESARI, Gaetano – LUZIO, Alessandro): *I Copialettere di Giuseppe Verdi*, Milan 1913.

CHECCHI, Eugenio (Tom): "Il nuovo Jago di Verdi", in *Fanfulla*, Rome, 15–16 March 1887.

—— *Giuseppe Verdi. Il genio e le opere*, Barbera, Florence 1887 (revised edit.: *ibid.* 1901, reprinted 1913; 3rd edit. with addition of last chapter: *ibid.* 1926).

CIAVARELLA, Angelo: "Un piccolo cimelio manzoniano: Manzoni presenta Verdi a Giusti", in *Aurea Parma*, XXV, 4: October–December 1951, pp. 208–16.

CLARETIE, Jules: "Une répétition de 'Don Carlos' – Verdi", in *Le Figaro*, Paris, XIV, 94: 17 February 1867, pp. 1–2 (reprinted in *Gazetta Musicale di Milano*, XXII, 8: 24 February 1867, pp. 57–60; in *Scena Illustrata*, Florence, XXXVI, 271: 15 November 1900, p. 4; in BASSO, Maurizio: *Giuseppe Verdi*, [. . .] *Storia Popolare*, G. Corsi, Milan, 1901, pp. 110–15; in *Les Annales politiques et littéraires*, Paris, XXXI, 1581: 12 October 1931, p. 316; in *Musica d'Oggi*, Milan, XVII, 1: January 1935, pp. 12–14; in *Per il cinquantesimo anniversario della morte di Giuseppe Verdi*, Teatro di San Carlo, Naples 1950, pp. 81–85).

CONATI, Marcello: "Una lettera sconosciuta di Verdi a Franceso Maria Piave", in *L'Opera*, Milan, II, 5: October–December 1966, pp. 83–86.

—— "L' 'Oberto, conte di San Bonfacio' in due recensioni straniere poco note e in una lettera inedita di Verdi", in *Atti 1966*, pp. 67–92.

—— "Cronologia delle prime rappresentazioni di 'Aida' dal 1871 al 1881, in

Genesi dell' "Aida", edited by Saleh Abdoun, Istituto di studi verdiani, Parma 1971, pp. 156–77.

—— "Mascagni, Leoncavallo, Puccini & C. in Germania. Contributo per un'indagine sull' 'opera verista' nei teatri di lingua tedesca" (1890–1895), in *Discoteca Alta Fedeltà*, Milan, XVII, 162: August 1972, pp. 18–25.

—— "Arrigo Boito direttore onorario del Conservatorio di Parma (con oltre 70 documenti inediti), in *Parma, Conservatorio di Musica, Studi e Ricerche*, edited by Guido Piamonte and Gaspare Nello Vetro, Battei, Parma 1973, pp. 109–69.

—— "Bibliografia verdiana. Aspetti, problemi, criteri per la sistemazione della letteratura verdiana" in *Atti 1972*, pp. 456–63.

—— *Canti popolari della Val d'Enza e della Val Cedra* edited by the Comunità delle Valli dei Cavalieri, Parma 1976, with disc enclosed.

—— "Saggio di critiche e cronache verdiane dalla *Allgemeine musikalische Zeitung* di Lipsia" (1840–48), in *Il melodramma italiano dell'Ottocento*, Studi e ricerche per Massimo Mila edited by Giorgio Pestelli, Einaudi, Turin 1977, pp. 13–43.

—— "Formazione e affermazione di Gomes nel panorama dell'opera italiana. Appunti e considerazioni", in *Antonio Carlos Gomes: Carteggi italiani*, edited by Gaspare Nello Vetro, Nuove Edizioni, Milan 1977, pp. 33–77.

—— "Il 'popolare' in Verdi, e Verdi nel 'popolare'. Appunti e considerazioni", in *Atti della IX Sessione musicologica italo-polacca dedicata alla musica del tardo Romanticismo: Varsavia 4–5 Ottobre 1977*, soon to be published.

—— "Aspetti della messinscena del 'Macbeth' di Verdi", in *Verdi's Macbeth: A Sourcebook*, edited by David Rosen, Norton, New York 1984 (for a more detailed discussion, see "Il melodramma romantico in Italia", *Atti del Convegno Internazionale di Studio organizzato dalla Fondazione G. Cini* September 1977, Venice, in course of publication).

—— See (MEDICI–CONATI) 1978.

I copialettere di Giuseppe Verdi, see (CESARI–LUZIO) 1913.

DE ANGELIS, Alberto: *La musica a Roma nel secolo XIX*, 2 edit., G. Bardi, Rome 1944.

DELLA CORTE, Andrea: *L'interpretazione musicale e gli interpreti*, Unione Tipografico-Editrice Torinese, Turin 1951.

—— *Toscanini visto da un critico*, ILTE, Turin 1958.

—— *La critica musicale e i critici*, Unione Tipografico-Editrice Torinese, Turin 1961.

DEMALDÈ, Giuseppe: "Cenni biografici del Maestro Verdi", edited by M. J. Matz in *Verdi Newsletter*, n. 1: May 1976, n. 2: December 1976, n. 3: June 1977.

DEPANIS, Giuseppe: "Verdi di passaggio a Torino", in *Gazzetta Piemontese*, April 1894 (reissued in *Gazzetta Musicale di Milano*, XLIX, 14: 8 April 1894, pp. 209–10).

—— *I Concerti Popolari e il Teatro Regi di Torino, Quindici anni di vita musicale. Appunti – Ricordi*, 2 vols., S.T.E.N., Turin 1914–15.

DESTRANGES, Étienne: "Une visite à Verdi", in *Le Monde Artiste,* Paris, April 1890 (reprinted by the author in *Consonnances et Dissonnances. Etudes musicales,* Fischbacher, Paris 1906, pp. 465–8; reissued in *Carteggio Verdi–Boito,* pp. 395–8).

—— *L'Évolution Musicale Chez Verdi: Aida – Othello – Falstaff,* Fischbacher, Paris 1895.

DUPRÉ, Giovanni: *Ricordi autobiografici,* Le Monnier, Florence 1878; new edit., "Pensieri sull'arte e Ricordi autobiografici", *ibid.* 1880 (cf. "Giovanni Dupré e Giuseppe Verdi", in *Gazzetta Musicale di Milano,* XXXIV, 34: 24 August 1879, pp. 293–5).

DUPREZ, Gilbert: *Souvenirs d'un chanteur,* Calmann-Lévy, Paris 1880.

EHRLICH, Heinrich: "Verdi's Othello", in *Die Gegenwart,* Berlin, vol. XXXI, n. 8: 19 February 1887, pp. 124–5.

—— "Die Entwicklung der dramatischen Musik in Italien", in *Nord und Süd,* Breslau, vol. XLII, n. 126, 1887, pp. 409–20.

—— "Giuseppe Verdi", in *Nord und Süd,* Breslau, vol. 51, n. 152: November 1889, pp. 197–220.

—— "Verdi über Mascagni", in *Berliner Tageblatt,* XXI, 208: 25 April 1892 (extracts in *Signale für die musikalische Welt,* Leipzig, L, 34: May 1892, p. 536; in WALLNER-BASTÉ, pp. 313–15).

—— "Beim 84 jährigen Verdi" in *Deutsche Revue,* Stuttgart, XXII, vol. 2, 1897, pp. 325–8.

ESCUDIER, Léon: "L'Orchestre de l'Opéra", in *L'Art Musical,* Paris, III, 30: 23 July 1863, pp. 271–2.

ESCUDIER, [Marie?]: "Une visite à Verdi – Un ténor en plein vent", in *La France Musicale,* Paris, VIII, 21: 25 May 1845, p. 164 (reissued in *Il Pirata,* Milan, X, 100: 6 June 1845, pp. 405–6, in *Iberia Musical y Literaria,* Madrid, IV, 1845; reissued in *Il Vaglio,* Venice, X, 32: August 1845, pp. 254–5; reprinted in CONATI, M., see *Atti 1972,* pp. 553–4).

FÉTIS, François-Joseph: "Verdi", in *Revue et Gazzette Musicale de Paris,* XVII, n. 35: 13 September 1850, pp. 308–10; n. 39: 29 September 1850, pp. 322–5 (reissued in *Biographie universelle des musiciens et Bibliographie générale de la musique,* 2 edit., 9 vols, F. Didot, Paris 1878–84).

FORTIS, Leone: "Il vecchio maestro", in *Gazzetta Musicale di Milano,* XLV, 49: 7 December 1890, pp. 773–5.

FRESNAY, Paul: "Verdi à Paris", in *Voltaire,* Paris, 28 March 1886.

FRATI, Emidio: *Edenia (Montecatini e i suoi Bagni),* Razzolini, Florence 1911.

GALLI, Amintore – MACCHI, Gustavo – PARIBENI, Giulio Cesare: *Umberto Giordano nell'Arte e nella Vita. Note biografiche ed estetiche,* Sonzogno, Milan 1915.

GARA, Eugenio: "Peripezie di un librettista di Verdi", in *1941: Anno Verdiano Chiusura della manifestazione,* Teatro Regio, Ass. Turistica Pro Parma, Parma 1941, pp. 21–27.

(GARIBALDI, Luigi Agostino): *Giuseppe Verdi nelle lettere di Emanuele Muzio ad Antonio Barezzi* edited by Luigi Agostino Garibaldi, F.lli Treves, Milan 1931.

GATTI, Carlo: *Verdi. L'esordio. Le opere e i giorni'. La fine,* 2 vols., Alpes, Milan 1931 (2nd edit. in one vol.: Mondadori, [Milan] 1951; 3rd edit.: *ibid.,* 1953).

—— *Verdi nelle immagini,* Garzanti, Milan 1941.

GEIGER, Benno: "Erlebnisse mit Giuseppe Verdi", in *Deutsche Revue,* Stuttgart, XXIV, 1902, pp. 71–80 (reissued in ZOFF, Otto: *Die grossen Komponisten gesehen von ihren Zeitgenossen,* Scherz Bern 1952, pp. 25 ff.; extracts in NETTL, Paul: *The Book of Musical Documents,* New York 1948, pp. 302–3).

—— *Memorie di un veneziano,* Vallecchi, Florence 1958.

GERHARTZ, Leo Karl: "Il Re Lear di Antonio Somma e il modello melo-drammatico dell'opera verdiana. Principi per una definizione del libretto verdiano", in *Atti 1966,* pp. 110–15.

—— *Die Auseinandersetzungen des jungen Giuseppe Verdi mit dem literarischen Drama,* Merseburger, Berlin 1968.

GHISLANZONI, Antonio: "La casa di Verdi a Sant'Agata" in *Gazzetta Musicale di Milano,* XV, 30: 26 July 1868, pp. 242–6 (reissued in *Il Trovatore,* 26 July 1868, pp. 1–3: 26 July 1868, pp. 1–3; in *La Lombardia,* Milan, X, July 1868; in *L'Universo Illustrato,* Milan, July 1868; reprinted by the author in *Reminiscenze artistiche. Scritti piacevoli,* Brigola, Milan, 2nd edit., 1870, pp. 25–49; with the addition of a note in *Libro Serio,* Milan 1879, pp. 151–68; reissued in POUGIN 1881, pp. 123–6; in POUGIN 1886, pp. 288–93; in *Verdi Intimo,* cit., pp. 49–51; in *L'Illustrazione Popolare,* Milan, XXIV, 7: 13 February 1887, p. 104; *ibid.,* XXX 6: 5 February 1893, p. 86; in BRAGAGNOLO, Giovanni – BETTAZZI, Enrico: *La vita di Giuseppe Verdi narrata al popolo,* Ricordi, Milan 1905, pp. 252–4).

GIACOSA, Giuseppe: "Verdi in villa (Note)", in *Gazzetta Musicale di Milano,* XLIV, special suppl. to n. 48: 27 November 1889, pp. 774–5 (reissued in *L'Illustrazione Popolare,* Milan, XXVI, 50: 15 December 1889, pp. 790–91; in q.v.: *Verdi e il "Falstaff"* 1893 (1913), pp. 17–18; in *L'Illustrazione Popolare,* Milan, LXIV, 45: 9 October 1913, pp. 705–7; in ROVERSI, Anna: *Gli artisti di ieri: Storia della vita di Giuseppe Verdi,* Bologna 1939, pp. 25–9; in CENZATO, Giovanni: *Itinerari verdiani,* 2nd edit., Ceschina, Milan 1955, pp. 55–57; in *Carteggio Verdi–Boito,* pp. 326–8; with variants and new notes in *Verdi e il "Falstaff",* special edition of *Vita Moderna,* II, 7: 12 February 1893, pp. 50–52).

—— "La morte di Giuseppe Verdi", in *Corriere della Sera,* Milan, XXVI, 27: 27–28 January 1901.

GODEFROY, Vincent: *The Dramatic Genius of Verdi,* 2 vols, Gollancz, London 1975–77.

GRADENWITZ, Peter: *Musik zwischen Orient und Okzident. Eine Kulturges-chichte der Wechselbeziehungen,* Heinrichshofen, Wilhelmshaven–Hamburg 1977.

GUCKEISEN, August: "Vierundfünfzigstes Niederrheinisches Musikfest unter Leitung von Dr Ferd. Hiller. Gefeiert in Köln am 20., 21. und 22 Mai", in *Kölnische Zeitung,* 21, 22 and 23 May 1877.

GÜNTHER, Ursula: "La genèse de 'Don Carlos', opéra en cinq actes . . .", in *Revue de Musicologie*, Paris, LVIII, 1, 1972, pp. 16–64; LX, 1–2, 1974, pp. 87–158.

—— "Zur Entstehung von Verdis 'Aida'" in *Studi Musicali*, Rome, II, 1, 1973, pp. 15–71.

GUSTINELLI, Carmelo: "Verdi a Montecatini", in *Nicia*, October 1932.

HALLIDAY-ANTONA, Annetta: "An Afternoon with Verdi", in *The Musician*, Boston, X, 9 September 1905, pp. 350–51.

HANSLICK, Eduard: *Die moderne Oper*, 9 vols., Berlin 1875–1900.

—— "Verdi's 'Falstaff'", in *Neue Freie Presse*, Vienna, April 1893 (reissued in *Musical Courier*, New York, XXVI, 21, no. 690: 24 May 1893, p. 8; extracts in *Signale für die musikalische Welt*, Leipzig, LI, 31: May 1893, p. 492).

—— *Aus meinem Leben*, 2 vols, Berlin 1894.

HOPKINSON, Cecil: *A Bibliography of the Works of Giuseppe Verdi*, 2 vols, Broude Brothers, New York 1973–78.

HURET, Jules: "Deux interviews – Giuseppe Verdi", in *Le Figaro*, Paris, 5 April 1894.

—— "Une répétition de 'Falstaff'", in *Le Figaro*, Paris, 18 April 1894.

JULLIEN, Adolphe: "Verdi en face des divers opéras", in *Journal des Débats*, Paris, 14 April 1894.

KLOIBER, Rudolf: *Handbuch der Oper*, new edit., DTV–Bärenreiter, Kassel 1973.

KOHUT, Adolf: "Persönliche Erinnerungen an Verdi", in *Der Merker*, Vienna, IV, 1913, n. 20: Zweites Oktoberheft, pp. 776–80; n. 21: Erstes Novemberheft, pp. 810–14.

KÜMMEL, Werner Friedrich: "Vincenzo Bellini nello specchio dell' *Allgemeine musikalische Zeitung* di Lipsia, 1827–1836", in *Nuova Rivista Musicale Italiani*, Rome, VII, 2: April–June 1973, pp. 185–205.

LAUZIÈRES-THÉMINES, A. de: "Verdi" in *Le Figaro*, Paris, XXV, 284: 11 October 1879 (reissued in *Signale für die musikalishe Welt*, Leipzig, XXXVII, 56: October 1879, pp. 881–4).

—— "Verdi à l'Opéra", in *Le Figaro*, Paris, 17 September 1887.

LAVAGETTO, Mario: *Quei più modesti romanzi*, Garzanti, Milan 1979.

—— *Un caso di censura: il "Rigoletto"*, Edizioni il Formichiere, Milan 1979.

[LICHTENTHAL, Peter?]: "Frühlingsoper in Italien. (Fortsetzung). Grossherzogtum Toscana", in *Allgemeine musikalische Zeitung*, Leipzig, XXXIX, 39: 24 September 1845, pp. 667–8 (reissued in CONATI, M., see *Atti 1972*, pp. 555–7).

LOMBROSO, Cesare: "Il fenomeno psicologico di Verdi", in *Gazzetta Musicale di Milano*, XLVIII, 10: 5 March 1893, pp. 159–60.

LESSONA, Michele: *Volere è potere*, Barbera, Florence 1869 (numerous reprints).

LOSCHELDER, Josef: "Rossinis Bild und Zerrbild in der *Allgemeinen musikalischen Zeitung* Leipzig", in *Bollettino del Centro Rossiniano di studi*, Pesaro 1973, n. 1, pp. 23–42, and n. 2, pp. 23–42.

Luzio, Alessandro: *Profili biografici e Bozzetti storici*, new edit., 2 vols, Cogliati, Milan 1927.

—— *Carteggi verdiani*, vols I and II, R. Accademia d'Italia, Rome 1935; vols III and IV, Accademia Nazionale dei Lincei, Rome 1947.

—— "Verdi e Pascarella", in *Il Corriere della Sera*, Milan, 10 July 1940, p. 3.

—— See (CESARI–LUZIO) 1913.

MARCHESI, Gustavo: "Verdi, merli e cucú: Cronache bussetane fra il 1819 e il 1839", Quaderno n. 1 di *Biblioteca 70*, Busseto 1979.

MARCHI, Virginio: "Un'invocazione dell''Aida'", in *Aurea Parma* XLIV, 2: April–June 1960, pp. 100–104.

MARESCOTTI, Ercole Arturo: "Una visita a Verdi", in *Il Teatro Illustrato*, Milan, VII, 76: April 1887, p. 58.

—— "Una visita a Verdi", in *Il Palcoscenico*, Milan, IV, 38: 22 October 1900, p. 5 (reissued in *L'Aurora Italiana*, II, suppl. to n. 4, 1901, pp. 5–6; in *Lissone a Giuseppe Verdi*, Monza, August 1913, p. 2).

MARIANI, Gaetano: *Storia della Scapigliatura*, S. Sciascia, Caltanissetta-Roma, 2nd edit., 1971.

MARTIN, George: "Lettere inedite; Contributo alla storia della 'Forza del destino'" in *Verdi*, Bollettino dell'Istituto di Studi verdiani, Parma, n. 5, pp. 1088–1102.

MARTINELLI, Aldo: *Verdi: Raggi e penombre*, Studio Editoriale Genovese, Genoa 1926.

MASCAGNI, Pietro: "Una visita a Verdi", in *Scena Illustrata*, Florence XLIX, 21: 1 November 1913, p. 14.

—— "Verdi (ricordi personali)", in *La Lettura*, Milan, XXX, 1: January 1931, pp. 4–8.

MASSENET, Jules: [Visite à Verdi], in *Le Gaulois du Dimanche*, Paris, I, 17: 9–10 October 1897.

—— *Mes souvenirs*. 1848–1912, P. Lafitte, Paris 1912.

MASTRIGLI, Leopoldo: *Gli uomini illustri nella musica da Guido Arezzo fino ai contemporanei. Cenni storico-biografici* . . . , Paravia, Turin 1883.

MATZ, Charles: "Blanche Roosevelt", in *Opera News*, New York, XXVII, 20: 23 March 1963, pp. 26–28.

MATZ, Mary Jane: "Le 'radici' dell'albero genealogico verdiano", in *Verdi*, Bollettino dell'Istituto di studi verdiani, n. 7, pp. 790–844.

MAUREL, Victor: "À propos de la mise en scène du drame lyrique 'Othello'", Bocca, Rome 1888 (reprinted by the author in *Dix ans de carrière*, Dupont, Paris 1897; anastatic reprint: Arno Press, New York 1977).

—— "À propos de 'Falstaff'", in *Revue de Paris*, I, 8: 15 May 1894, pp. 211–24 (reprinted by the author in *Dix ans de Carrière*, cit.).

(MEDICI, Mario – CONATI, Marcello): *Carteggio Verdi–Boito*, edited by Mario Medici and Marcello Conati, with the collaboration of Marisa Casti, Istituto di studi verdiani, Parma 1978.

MILA, Massimo: *Giuseppe Verdi*, Laterza, Bari 1958.

——— "Verdi e Hanslick", in *La Rassegna Musicale*, Rome, XXI, 3: July 1951, pp. 221–4 (reprinted by the author in *Giuseppe Verdi*, cit.).

——— "L'Unità stilistica nell'opera di Verdi", in *Nuova Rivista Musicale Italiana*, Rome, II, 1: January–February 1968, pp. 62–75.

——— "Fétis e Verdi, ovvero Gli infortuni della critica", in *Atti 1972*, pp. 313–21.

——— *La giovinezza di Verdi*, Eri, Turin 1974.

MINGARDI, Corrado: "Verdi e Berlioz [. . .]", in *Biblioteca 70*, Busseto, I, 1970, pp. 45–49.

MONALDI, Gino: "Verdi e le sue opere", in *Gazzetta d'Italia*, Florence 1877.

——— "Un colloquio con Verdi", in *Il Popolo Romano*, Rome, n. 45: 15 February 1887.

——— *Verdi (1839–1898)*, Bocca, Turin 1899 (reprinted 1913, 1943, 1951).

——— *Verdi nella vita e nell'arte (Conversazioni verdiane)*, Ricordi, Milan 1913.

——— *I miei ricordi Musicali*, Ausonia, Rome 1921.

——— *Verdi aneddotico*, Vecchioni, L'Aquila 1926.

MONNIER, Marc: "Giuseppe Verdi", in *Bibliothèque Universelle de Genève*, IV series, vol. XXXII, June 1856, pp. 209–24 (cf. "Il Maestro Verdi", in *Gazzetta dei Teatri*, Milan, XIX, 44: 15 August 1856, p. 176).

MONTEFIORE, Tommaso (Rastignac): "Roma a Verdi", in *La Tribuna*, Rome, 17 April 1893; "Ancora del 'Falstaff'", *ibid.*, 19 April 1893.

MORDINI, Arturo: "Musica e patriottismo", in *La Rassegna Nazionale*, Florence–Milan, XXIII, 2: 16 February 1901, pp. 562–3.

MORINI, Mario: "La Tosca all'anagrafe della storia", in *La Scala, Rivista dell'opera*, Milan, n. 160. March 1963, pp. 12–18.

NARDI, Piero: *Vita di Arrigo Boito*, Mondadori, Milan 1942.

NETTL, Paul: *The Book of Musical Documents*, New York 1948.

NOSEDA, Aldo (il Misovulgo): ["La nuova opera di Verdi"], in *Il Corriere della Sera*, Milan, 27 November 1890.

OJETTI, Ugo (Tantalo): "Giuseppe Verdi e Cesare Pascarella", in *Il Corriere della Sera*, Milan 1924 (reprinted Mondadori, Milan 1942).

OSBORNE, Charles: *The Complete Operas of Verdi. A Critical Guide*, Gollancz, London 1969 (Italian translation by Giampero Tintori: Mursia, Milan 1975).

PALADINI, Carlo: "La musica ai Bagni di Montecatini", in *Gazzetta Musicale di Milano*, LI, 33 and 34: 13 and 20 August 1896, pp. 549–53 and 570.

——— "Verdi in Valdinievole", *ibid.*, LIV, 36: 7 September 1899, pp. 437–48.

——— "Il romito di S. Agata", in *La Rassegna Nazionale*, Florence–Milan, XXIII, 2: 16 February 1901, pp. 529–61.

(PASCOLATO, Alessandro): *"Re Lear" e "Un ballo in maschera". Lettere di Giuseppe Verdi ad Antonio Somma*, published by Alessandro Pascolato, S. Lapi, Citta di Castello 1902 (reprinted 1913).

PERINELLO, Carlo: "Giuseppe Verdi", *Harmonie*, Berlin 1900.

PESCI, UGO: "Le prove dell' 'Otello'", in q.v., *Verdi e l'Otello 1887* (1913), pp. 39–40.

PETROBELLI, Pierluigi: "Osservazioni sul processo compositivo in Verdi", in *Acta Musicologica*, Basle, vol. XLIII, no. III–IV: July–December 1971, pp. 125–42.

PHILIPPI, Felix: "Begegnung mit Verdi. Ein Auftakt für die Jahrhundertfeier", in *Berliner Tageblatt*, n. 350: 13 July 1913.

PIGORINI BERI, Caterina: "Una visita a Giuseppe Verdi", in *L'Illustrazione Italiana*, Milan, VIII, 44: 30 October 1881, p. 279.

—— "Giuseppe Verdi e le litanie lauretane", in *Fanfulla della Domenica*, Rome, XV, 14: 2 April 1893.

—— "Verdi intimo", in *Natura ed Arte*, Milan, X, 15 February 1901, pp. 19–26.

—— "Verdi intimo", in *Nuova Antologia*, Rome, 16 October 1913, pp. 543–60.

—— "Un giorno a Sant'Agata", in *Falstaff*, rivista illustrata per i Festeggiamenti Verdiani, Busseto, n. 9–10: 25 December 1913, p. 2.

PIZZETTI, Ildebrando (I.P.); "L'orchestra del Conservatorio di Parma e Busseto", in *Gazzetta Musicale di Milano*, LV, 45: 8 November 1900, pp. 583–5.

—— "Giuseppe Verdi", in *Il Marzocco*, Florence, XVIII, 41: 12 October 1913, pp. 1–2 (reprinted by the author in *Musicisti contemporanei*, Treves, Milan 1914, pp. 3–36).

—— "La grandezza di Verdi", in *La Lettura*, Milan, XLI, 1: January 1941, pp. 26–34 (reprinted by the author in *La musica italiana dell'Ottocento*, Edizioni Palatine di R. Pezzani, Turin 1947).

—— "Come ho visto Verdi", in *Il Resto del Carlino*, Bologna, 9 April 1963 (reissued in *Aurea Parma*, XLVII, 1–2: January–August 1963, pp. 106–7; in *Verdi*, Bollettino dell'Istituto di studi verdiani, n. 7, pp. XIV–XVI; extracts in *Carteggio Verdi–Boito*, pp. 509–10).

PIZZI, Italo; *Ricordi verdiani inediti*, Roux e Viarengo, Turin 1901.

—— *Per il I° centenario della nascita di Giuseppe Verdi. Memorie – aneddoti – conversazioni*, Lattes, Turin 1913.

POUGIN, Arthur: *Giuseppe Verdi. Vita aneddotica, con note e aggiunte di Folchetto* [Jacopo Caponi], Ricordi, Milan 1881.

—— *Verdi. Histoire anecdotique de sa vie et de ses oeuvres*, Calmann Lévy, Paris 1886.

RADICIOTTI, Giuseppe: *Gioacchino Rossini. Vita documentata. Opera ed influenza sull'arte*, 3 vols, Tivoli 1927–29.

REGLI, Francesco: *Dizionario biografico dei piú celebri Poeti ed Artisti Melodrammatici . . . che fioririono in Italia dal 1800 al 1860*, E. Dalmazzo, Turin 1860.

RESASCO, Ferdinando: *Verdi a Genova* (including: DE AMICIS, Giuseppe: "Pensando a Verdi", D'ALBERTIS, Enrico Alberto: "L'ultima fotografia di Verdi"), Pagano, Genoa 1901.

RICORDI, Giulio: "Un'opera nuova di Giuseppe Verdi", in *Gazzetta Musicale di Milano*, XLV, 48: 30 November 1890, p. 757.

ROOSEVELT, Blanche: *Verdi, Milan and "Othello"*, Ward & Downey, London 1887.

SACCHI, Filippo: *Toscanini. Un secolo di musica*, Longanesi, Milan 1960.

SAINT-SAËNS, Camille: article in *Voltaire*, Paris, 19 October 1979 (reissued in *Gazzetta Musicale di Milano*, XXXIV, 43: 26 October 1879, p. 367).

—— Letter to the "Pungolo" of Milan, 7 November 1879 (reissued in *Gazzetta musicale di Milano*, XXXIV, 45: 9 November 1879, pp. 383–4).

SANTLEY, Charles: *Student and Singer: Reminiscences*, London 1892.

SARTORI, Claudio: "Giuseppe Verdi", in *La Musica: Enciclopedia storica*, under the direction of G. M. Gatti, edited by A. Basso, Unione Tipografico-Editrice Torinese, vol. IV (1966), pp. 729–63.

SCHMIDL, Carlo: *Dizionario universale dei Musicisti*, 2 vols, Sonzogno, Milan 1926–28; supplement, *ibid.*, 1938.

SCHÖNBERG, Arnold: *Style and Idea*, London 1950, trans. into Italian by M. G. Moretti and L. Pestalozza: Rusconi e Paolazzi, Milan 1960.

SCUDO, Paolo: "Revue Musicale", in *La Revue des Deux Mondes*, Paris, 1 July 1855, pp. 217–27 (includes the "I vespri siciliani" review).

[SIVELLI, Stefano]: "L'origine d'un motivo dell''Aida'" in *L'Italia*, Milan, 14 January 1941, p. 3 (reissued in *La Giovane Montagna*, Parma, XLII, 1: 15 January 1941; in *Aurea Parma*; April–June 1960; see MARCHI, V., 1960).

SPITZER, Leo: *Marcel Proust e altri saggi di letteratura francese*, Einaudi, Turin 1959: see chapter: "L'etimologia di un 'cris de Paris'", first published in *Palatina*, Parma, n. 3, 1957.

SZOMORY, Deszö: "Látogatás Verdinél" (A visit to Verdi), in *Magyar Hírlap*, 26 April 1894 (reissued in VÁRNAI, Péter Pál: "Verdi in Ungheria", in *Verdi*, Bollettino dell'Istituto di studi verdiani, Parma, n. 7, pp. 261–2).

TEBALDINI, Giovanni: "Giuseppe Verdi nella musica sacra", in *Nuova Antologia*, Rome, 16 October 1913, pp. 561–73.

—— "Ricordi verdiani", in *Rassegna Dorica*, Rome, XI, nn. 1 and 3, 4, 5, 6: January and March–June 1940.

—— "Ricordi personali", in *Il Resto del Carlino*, Bologna, 23 January 1941; and in *La Stampa*, Turin, 26 January 1941.

—— "Incontro a lui – Flectamus genua!", in *Verdiana*, Milan, n. 6: January 1951, pp. 19–22.

TONI, Alceo: "Lettere e spirito", in *Musica d'Oggi*, Milan, new series, I, 10: December 1958, pp. 607–9.

VÁRNA, Péter Pál: "Verdi in Ungheria", in *Verdi*, Bollettino dell'Istituto di studi verdiani, Parma, n. 5: pp. 988–1030; n. 7: pp. 287–332; n. 8: pp. 1083–1130.

VENTURI, Franco: "L'Italia fuori d'Italia", in *Storia d'Italia*, vol. 3, Einaudi, Turin 1973, pp. 987–1481.

VERDI, Giuseppe: letter to the *Europe Artiste*, Paris, reissued in *Gazzetta dei Teatri*, Milan, XVIII, 15: 21 March 1855, p. 57.

—— letter to Richard Strauss, in *Dramaturgische Blätter*, Munich, 1939, n. 1, pp. 30–32.

Verdi intimo . . ., see (ALBERTI) 1931.

(VETRO, Gaspare Nello): *Antonio Carlos Gomes: Carteggi italiani*, compiled and annotated by Gaspare Nello Vetro, Nuove Edizioni, Milan 1977.

[VIVANTI, Annie]: "Verdi's 'Falstaff'. A Visit to the Composer", in *the Daily Graphic*, London, 14 January 1893.

—— "Giosuè Carducci", in *Nuova Antologia*, Rome, 1 August 1906.

WALKER, Frank: "Verdi a Vienna", in *Giuseppe Verdi*, Scritti [. . .], Sienna 1951, pp. 49–60.

—— *The Man Verdi*, J. M. Dent, London, and Knopf, New York, 1962 (Italian translation by F. Medioli Cavara: U. Mursia & C., Milan 1964).

(WALLNER-BASTÉ, Franz): *Verdi aus der Nähe. Ein Lebensbild in Dokumenten*, compiled and translated by Franz Wallner-Basté, Manesse Verlag, Zurich 1979.

WEINGARTNER, Felix: "Verdi, der Begründer der modernen Spieloper", in *Signale für die musikalische Welt*, Berlin, LXXI, 41: 8 October 1913, pp. 1451–4.

WINTERFELD, A. von: "Unterhaltungen in Verdis Tuskulum", in *Deutsche Revue*, Stuttgart, XII, 1887, pp. 327–32 (reprinted as "Persönliche Erinnerungen an Verdi", in *Neue Musik-Zeitung*, Stuttgart–Leipzig, XXII, 5, 1901, pp. 57–58).

ZAVADINI, Guido: *Donizetti. Vita – Musiche – Epistolario*, Istituto Italiano d'Arti Grafiche, Bergamo 1948.

ZENNARI, Jacopo: "Una lettera inedita di Giuseppe Verdi", in *La Cultura Musicale*, Bologna, II, 2: 1923, pp. 83–86.

INDEX

INDEX

Figures in **bold** indicate authorship; superior figures refer to notes.